A History of 945

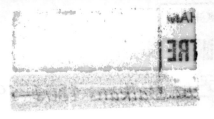

A History of the Balkans
1804–1945

Stevan K. Pavlowitch

LONGMAN
London and New York

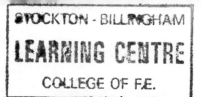
Addison Wesley Longman Limited
Edinburgh Gate,
Harlow, Essex CM20 2JE, United Kingdom
and Associated Companies throughout the world.

Published in the United States of America by Addison Wesley Longman, New York.

First published 1999

ISBN 0–582–04585–1 CSD
ISBN 0–582–04584–3 PPR

Visit Addison Wesley Longman on the world wide web at http://www.awl-he.com

British Library Cataloguing in Publication Data

A catalogue entry for this title is available from the British Library

Library of Congress Cataloging-in-Publication Data

Pavlowitch, Stevan K.
 A history of the Balkans, 1804–1945 / Stevan K. Pavlowitch.
  p. cm.
 Includes bibliographical references and index.
 ISBN 0–582–04585–1 (hardcover). — ISBN 0–582–04584–3 (pbk.)
 1. Balkan Peninsula—History—19th century. 2. Balkan Peninsula—History—20th century. I. Title.
 DR43.P34 1999
 949.6—dc21   98–46175
                                                  CIP

Set by 35 in 10/12pt Bembo
Produced by Addison Wesley Longman Singapore (Pte) Ltd.,
Printed in Singapore

Contents

List of maps

CHAPTER I

Introduction

The geography and its impact on the history. Byzantium, the medieval monarchies, the Ottoman conquest and the Habsburg reconquest. The transition of the eighteenth century.

FROM THE ROMAN TO THE OTTOMAN EMPIRE

The Balkan peninsula is characterized both by geographical unity and a unity imposed by history. The word 'Balkanization' is often used to mean fragmentation and turbulence, but historians of the peninsula[1] have pointed out that its history is no more turbulent than that of any other part of Europe before the First World War. Fragmentation and turbulence are, in any case, the result of its make-up, its place on the map, and the struggle for its control.

The Turkish word *balkan* means 'wooded mountains'. Unlike the Iberian and Italian peninsulas, the Balkan peninsula is defined by the mountainous mass itself. The Dinaric mountains run from the Alps of Slovenia down the Adriatic coast to Albania, then turn inland as the Pindus range into central Greece, allowing only the most narrow of coasts to the west. The Carpathian chain forms a reverse 'S' that begins north of Romania, goes south to divide the plains of Moldavia and Wallachia from the uplands of Transylvania, before turning southwest to cross the Danube at the Iron Gates, then east through Bulgaria as the Balkan range proper. Finally, the ancient Macedonian and Thracian land mass thrusts fingers into northern Greece.

The discontinuous structure of these mountains has discouraged integration from within, but has formed no barrier to penetration. Connected valleys, plateaux and basins have provided access. They have fostered particularities and connexions, conquests and exchanges. The most important passageways have been the Danube and the Belgrade–Salonika road – forming between them a

---

1 Such as Dimitrije Djordjević and Stephen Fischer-Galati, *The Balkan Revolutionary Tradition*, New York: Columbia University Press, 1981, xi; or John R. Lampe and Marvin R. Jackson, *Balkan Economic History, 1559–1950: From Imperial Borderlands to Developing Nations*, Bloomington: Indiana University Press, 1982, 3.

huge T-shaped interchange. While the great river has been a link to central Europe and to Russia, a vital road runs through depressions in the ancient land mass from the Danubian plains, by way of the Morava and Vardar valleys, to the Aegean.

The lasting influences came from the open north or from the south by the Eurasian link, and followed the north–south routes. The Romans conquered most of the Balkans, but did not settle except along the Adriatic coast and the Danube. By the beginning of the sixth century, there were two mainly urban linguistic areas – Roman north and west, Greek south and east. The Romanized zone comprised a coastal Adriatic and a Danubian bloc, separated by a more lightly Romanized mountainous interior, with a mixed zone fading into the Hellenized south.

The South Slavs, who had come from north of the Carpathians in the wake of the migrations originating from the central Asian steppes, then crossed the Danube. They swept over the Balkans from the Alps to the Peloponnese, completely modifying the ethnic structure of the peninsula as they settled. The natives – Hellenized, Romanized or otherwise – withdrew to mountain, coastal and island retreats, or were absorbed by the newcomers, who were themselves assimilated the further they penetrated into Greek lands.

Eventually a broad middle belt from the Adriatic to the Black Sea was Slavicized. The general name Slovene stuck to frontier populations where there was a distinct contrast with non-Slavs. Old names of leading tribes spread to those who had settled from the western plains to the Adriatic – Croat – and to those along the southern tributaries of the Danube and in the depressions – Serb. Germanic, Slav and Greek populations applied the name Vlach (variants such as Welsh and Walloon were used elsewhere), which may have come from a Romanized Celtic group, to the Romanized in their midst, but also to others who had a similar way of life.

A first effort at Christianization had been interrupted by the invasions. The further conversion of the Slavs by the overlapping influences of the papacy and of Byzantium led to the Latin variant prevailing in the west, with Greek forms in their vernacular adaptation spread well beyond the Hellenic cultural sphere by Byzantine missionaries.

The confusion resulting from the onslaught of new populations, followed by changes in the west, enabled South Slav feudal organizations to emerge in the interstices between the Byzantine Roman Empire in the east and the successive claimants to the Roman inheritance in the west. Originating from beyond the Sea of Azov, the Bulgars were encamped on both sides of the Danube by the ninth century. They were assimilated by the local Slavs, but not before they had given them their name and an organization, and welcomed Christian missionaries. The peak of their realm came when their ruler Simeon assumed the title of *tsar* (Caesar), as he tried to take Constantinople in 925. The Bulgarian Empire subsequently raised tribute from territories that ranged, at one time or another, from the Danube to the northern Greek lands and to the Adriatic.

To the north, as the Magyars or Hungarians settled in the Pannonian plains and adopted Christianity, feudalism was carried out under Germanic rule in the Slovene lands, but a native development emerging out of Slav tribal structures enabled a Croatian realm to dominate the roads from the northern Adriatic to the plains. The crown that King Tomislav secured from the pope in 925 (at the same time as Simeon become tsar) came into the possession of the king of Hungary in 1102. This was when Hungary also first acquired control of Transylvania, an upland territory within the arc of the Carpathians with a mixed but probably basically Romanized population, which retained, like Croatia, an autonomous position.

It was only under her first Hungarian king that Croatia extended over her full 'historic' range, but this did not obliterate what came to be called her 'tri-unity' – the nucleus of inner Croatia with its institutions, the plains of Slavonia subjected to Hungarian influence earlier and more intensively, and the Dalmatian coast whose towns struggled to uphold their autonomy. Embryonic political structures also formed in the southern Dinaric uplands in the ninth century. Venice and Hungary were obstacles which diverted the Serbian rulers' ambitions from the Adriatic and the plains, to the nominally Byzantine lands of the Morava–Vardar corridor. As the Empire started on its long decline, the Serbian realm moved on to the greatest political development attained by the Balkan Slavs in the Middle Ages.

It exploited the fascination of the west with Byzantium and the Holy Land which had hardened the differences between Rome and Constantinople. When the Fourth Crusade carved up the empire and plundered its capital, the Nemanjić rulers played off Latin against Greek, and Greek against Greek. They expanded at the expense of Bulgars and Byzantines, took the title of *kralj* (Carolus), obtained a royal crown from the pope in 1217, and ecclesiastical independence from the exiled patriarch in Nicaea. When King Dušan had himself crowned emperor of Serbs and Greeks in 1346 at Skopje, his dominions stretched from the Save and the Danube to the Adriatic and the Gulf of Corinth. At the time of his death ten years later, he appeared on the brink of achieving his twin ambitions of setting himself up in the 'Emperor's City' (as the Slavs called Constantinople), and of leading Europe's defence against the Turks as the pope's 'captain'.

Modelled on Byzantium though it was, medieval Bulgarian and Serbian civilization was not turned exclusively to the east. Rulers had looked to both centres of Christendom until they realized the potent force of integration provided by the Byzantine concept in its local adaptation, and obtained autocephalous (independent) patriarchates in exchange for their support of the Church of Constantinople, but they were also strongly influenced by their links with the west. Between the twelfth and the fifteenth century the whole peninsula was a bridge between east and west.

Heresies had flourished as long as Christianity had been dependent on distant centres, and they continued to do so in areas of late development of an institutionalized church and in remoter mountains, but also where east and

3

west overlapped, and along major routes of communication. They challenged authority, prevented the stabilization of the Bulgarian monarchy, and sank roots in the feudal class of Bosnia as it initiated an autonomous development in the twelfth century under the loose suzerainty of Hungary. Hungary was also involved in the struggle for supremacy over the gradually Slavicized trading cities of Dalmatia. Only the richest of these, Ragusa – better known nowadays by its Slav name of Dubrovnik – survived by scheming among the powers, to develop into an intermediary between Italy and the Balkans.

Areas of Romanized populations remained here and there, but essentially in present-day Romania, in the lower Danubian plains and over the Carpathians. Invasions and migrations had passed through on their way to the south, but not stopped in the plains where the first native polities appeared in the thirteenth century – the Romance-speaking, Slav-writing and Eastern Christian 'Valachiae' of Moldavia and Wallachia. Other pre-Slav populations had been pushed back into mountains, notably in Albania, a region many had raided and attempted to control from Italy and from the Balkans, and eventually included in Dušan's empire.

Even he had done no more than impose a personal ascendancy on the feudatories of an empire which disintegrated on his death. The end of Serbian power created a vacuum in the Balkans. Hungary and Venice from the north, and more so the Ottoman Turks from the south, hastened to fill it. Freed from the overbearing shadow of Serbia, Bosnia managed a period of glory under King Tvrtko. Related to the Nemanjić dynasty, whose heir he wanted to appear, he expanded into Serbian lands, but also to Croatia, along the coast, with the title of king of Serbia, Bosnia, Croatia and Dalmatia, yet his rule remained poised between his Catholic Hungarian suzerain and his heretical vassals. After Tvrtko's death in 1391, his realm in turn slid down the path of feudal anarchy, caught between Turks and Hungarians. The strength of her heresy had put Bosnia beyond the pale of Catholic Europe's sympathies.

Since setting foot in Europe in 1357, the Ottomans had obtained the fealty of Dušan's magnates in Macedonia, of the fragmented Bulgarian monarchy, and even of the shadow that was the Byzantine emperor himself. The battle of Kosovo in 1389, in which the ruler of Serbia, allied to King Tvrtko of Bosnia, was defeated, did not seal the fate of the Balkans, but it was regarded as portentous because of the efforts to form a Christian alliance that had preceded it, and because of the slaughter it produced.

Pushed north against Hungary, the remains of the Serbian realm survived until 1459. In 1463 it was the turn of Bosnia to fall. Feudal society gradually dissolved, eliminated by battle and repression, included for a time in the new Ottoman order, taking refuge in mountain principalities, on the coast, or across the rivers in Hungary where feudal anarchy was rampant. By paying tribute and trading with everyone, only Ragusa was left in peace to turn into a fifteenth-century Switzerland where Balkan potentates kept their money and took refuge. The Hungarian-Croatian realm broke up as the Turkish threat grew near. In 1493 a big offensive went right up to Styria and back through the heart of Croatia, whose nobility overcame its rivalries at the battle of Krbava, only to be defeated in another great massacre. Most of the surviving nobles from the exposed southern regions left, and Croatia with its very name also moved north.

When Charlemagne's renewed Holy Roman Empire had set up its 'Eastern March', Austria acquired the rôle, on the flank of Germany, of defender against dangers from the east. The 'march' fell to the Habsburgs, whose head was first elected emperor in 1273. They had already gathered into their family domains the feudal entities inhabited by the Slovenes, and their influence expanded in the lands of the Hungarian crown. When in 1526 the Turks routed the Hungarians at Mohács, where their heirless king met his death, the Habsburg takeover of what remained of his dominions was given sanction with the election of Ferdinand of Habsburg as king of Hungary, and then as king of Croatia.

Having entered the Balkans as mercenaries for the rival Christian rulers, the Ottoman Turks had slowly moved north between the fall of Gallipoli in 1357 and the battle of Mohács, by making the most of the peninsula's crumbling feudal order and of its religious disunity. The conquest of the Greek lands was completed only after the fall in 1453 of Constantinople (Istanbul in Turkish, but usually called in Europe by its old Greek name until the twentieth century) and the death in action of the last emperor. Both the city and the emperor remained powerful symbols to the very end. By the beginning of the sixteenth century, with the defeat of Venetian naval power, the Turks had secured the sea approaches to their conquests, and had gone on to obtain the land approaches by crossing the Danube and defeating Hungary.

The medieval Balkan realms had extended over widely fluctuating territory. Their centres had shifted; they had overlapped. As they had grown, their rulers had assumed royal titles and then, in the case of Bulgaria and Serbia, the imperial title to set themselves up as successors to Byzantium, which although culturally Greek remained imperially Roman to the end. They had increasing links with one another and with the west. Their populations were no more ethnically homogeneous than their titles. Rulers were not interested in ethnicity, because they had higher aims.

It was in this changing world that the Ottomans arrived. Their advance into Europe affected the whole of the peninsula. Even what remained outside their pale served as buffer zones into which they directed their raids, and from which their neighbours defended themselves. Turkish rule spread across the Balkans as part of what Traian Stoianovich has generically called the European Hundred Years' War.[2]

The war to which we allude was not simply the war between France and England but the complex strife of Catholic against Catholic, Christian against Muslim, Orthodox against Catholic, Hussite against Imperial and Catholic,

2 Traian Stoianovich, *Balkan Worlds: The First and Last Europe*, Armonk, NY, & London: M.E. Sharpe, 1994, 154.

Taborite against Utraquist, Poland and Lithuania against the Teutonic Order, Ottoman against the kingdom of Hungary and the fragments of the empire of Byzantium and of Stephen Dušan, Muscovite against Tatar and Novgorodian, Venice and Milan against Genoa, Tamerlane against Bayezid, Denmark against the Hanse, one feudal lord against another, peasant against lord.

OTTOMAN AND HABSBURG RULE

Balkan society was a field of strife where nobles were trying to turn into a closed estate in alliance with foreign merchants, at the expense of native middle elements and peasants. The Turkish advance was motivated initially by the push of others. From the rocky uplands of Anatolia, the Turks were lured to the better lands of the Balkans. They had military superiority and they found support, with which they imposed the order and the unity that central monarchies came to impose in the west.

They did so gradually. The first period of the conquest was characterized by accommodation. The Ottomans themselves wanted to be considered as having taken up the inheritance of the Eastern Roman Empire, and Islam tolerated Jews and Christians. During its last throes, Byzantium had viewed itself as doomed, whether it fell to Latins or to Turks. To be rescued by the Latins meant loss of Orthodoxy, a danger which did not exist if the Turks took over, and most Greeks at any rate seem to have preferred the latter. On the eve of the fall of Constantinople, a desperate emperor had been ready to accede to the union of the churches under the pope. This was formally achieved in Florence in 1453, but was rejected at home, not to mention by the Orthodox elsewhere.

The emperor's rule was by then no more than a shadowy symbol. The patriarch, however, remained religious head of many Christians already under Ottoman rule, while the Slav rulers of the Balkans were anxious to be in full communion with the Mother Church even if they did not want their bishops to be dependent on Constantinople. The holy Empire remained an ideal.

The Orthodox Church had been the commonwealth of the faithful of the Christian Roman Empire seen as the inhabited world (*oikoumene*). The emperor represented God on Earth, yet his authority was bound by law, by the tradition of the Church, and by public opinion. With a Graeco-Roman tradition of governance and a cultured lay political class, there was no need for a monolithic church organization. The head of the hierarchy was the bishop of the ecumenical capital, hence his dignity as ecumenical patriarch. The Eastern Church was never 'clerical' as in the west, where after the collapse of the Roman Empire the clergy in ordinary parlance became 'the Church', and one which was well organized to keep up civilization and defend itself.

Ottoman sovereignty was the right of the sultan to exploit and defend all sources of wealth, and to maintain harmony between social estates and religious-ethnic groups or 'millets' (now the modern Turkish word for 'nation'). The first estate was that of the officeholders, the Ottomans; they shared in the revenues of the imperial possessions in return for service.

An important function of that tenurial system was to supply cavalry. The *sipahi* landlord was originally an officer who provided a number of men in proportion to the size of his *timar* holding. He had no claim to the land, but received an income from it and a few days of peasant labour. He collected the prescribed tithe of the farmers' harvest to maintain the horsemen he had to bring to the summer campaign, and he collected on behalf of the sultan the head tax due by non-Muslims in lieu of military service. For the peasants, the system was less oppressive and offered greater security than previously. As timar agriculture provided the agricultural surpluses to feed a large military establishment, so urban guild manufacture supplied its equipment.

The Turkish conquerors preferred to live in towns and to use fertile lowlands as estates. In so far as they did settle, it was in plains and river basins of the eastern and central Balkans, and in towns. The Ottoman period did, however, witness migrations on a scale unprecedented since the arrival of the Slavs. People moved out of the way of armies, and were resettled for strategic or political reasons.

Part of the population went north with the remnants of the Serbian realm, out of Macedonia, and subsequently beyond the Save and Danube, as refugees were welcomed by Hungarians and Habsburgs to till and defend the border area. The Turks too, in order to restore the economy and man the defences of their recent acquisitions, attracted settlers with privileges. There were frequent local migrations to avoid retribution for outbreaks, or the *devshirme* conscription of Christian boys brought up for slave service in the sultan's administration and in his élite 'new army' of janissaries.

The original Turkish onslaught had disrupted settlement in the grain-growing lowlands, the rural population often fleeing to higher and safer ground, where Slavs mingled with Vlachs, Slavicized them and adopted their pastoral ways. Many also migrated to Dalmatia where they pushed back Romanic speech. Mountains became refuges in times of danger and population reserves at other times. People were not subjected to effective control and preserved, or reverted to, a semi-nomadic way of life, with its subsistence agriculture, pastoral economy and communal organization. Each successive wave of migrants in and out of the uplands freshened historical memories and carried further the process of mixing together Slav ethnic groups and dialects, consolidating ethnic culture at grass-roots level and developing local communities as a source of identity.

At the same time, on the periphery of the empire and just beyond, among the populations spilling or pushed over borders into the Venetian maritime fringe and into the Hungarian and Habsburg border plains, there developed more complex social structures as intermediaries between the Balkan world and the rest of Europe. Further east, the weakening of the Slav realms and of Byzantium had enabled the Romanian principalities to strengthen themselves. When the Ottoman Empire eventually extended its control over them, it was on the basis of treaties concluded between 1392 and 1413 which made their rulers the sultan's allies, vassals and tributaries.

7

The Ottoman Empire needed them as buffers contributing money and supplies. No Turks settled in Wallachia and Moldavia, whose political existence was never questioned. As the only Orthodox rulers left in the Balkans, their princes (locally known by the title of *domn*), elected by the landed *boier* nobility, saw themselves as continuing the Byzantine tradition. In contrast to the rest of the peninsula, the culture of their lands was one linked to the princely courts, the nobility and the Church hierarchy. Summed up by the Romanian historian Nicolae Iorga as 'Byzantium after Byzantium',[3] it was a post-Byzantine culture that faced both the Turkish empire and Europe.

The Ottoman Empire was the largest Muslim state. Its ruler was in theory the head of all Muslims everywhere since the caliphate had been taken up by the sultan in the sixteenth century, but he also had a Christian majority in his European dominions. The Ottoman Turks belonged to the mainstream Sunni branch of Islam, and followed the Hannafite interpretation of Koranic law, the most widespread and the most liberal. Islam in the Balkans remained a frontier religion, in touch with Christian beliefs and heresies, with many converts and crypto-Christians. It also had a heterodox stream in the Bektashi sect favoured by many of the devshirme converts – a Shia offshoot that had numerous points of contact with Christianity.

Christians and Jews were treated as autonomous millets, allowed to retain their laws and customs, but subjected to restrictions. Their heads, confirmed by the sultan, were part of the official hierarchy of the empire and a useful channel for implementing government decisions. The Jews expelled from Spain had found refuge in the cities of the Ottoman Empire. The patriarchate of Constantinople was strengthened by the conquerors to prevent their Christian subjects from being tempted to unite with a papacy associated with the struggle against the Ottomans. The Turks did not understand the canonical niceties of autocephaly, and considered all Orthodox as part of the 'Roman' (Byzantine) millet. The local hierarchies resentfully accepted the protection of the patriarch of Constantinople.

Its unity enabled the Eastern Church in the Ottoman Empire to be a preserver in more ways than one. Since its senior prelates were Greek, Hellenic culture endured. At a lower level, ethnic individuality was preserved with kinship associations. The Christians of the Balkans were protected from the confusion that tormented Europe during the Wars of Religion. They withstood the onslaught of uniatism on the fringes, as Catholic powers expanding over Orthodox populations used the 1453 terms, under which the supremacy of the pope was accepted in exchange for the maintenance of eastern practices.

Orthodox unity also protected from Islamization, not that assimilation was actively pursued. The Ottoman government in fact contributed to the survival of various ethnic groups through the non-ethnic character of its élite. The officeholders were Muslims, but that was merely a qualification for service,

3 Nicolas Iorga, *Byzance après Byzance*, Paris: Balland, 1992 (originally published in Bucharest, 1935).

which explains the high rate of conversion among seekers of privilege and position. Political allegiance to the Ottoman order was required, but religious loyalty and ethnic identity were confined to different groups.

The archbishopric of Ohrid was the first Orthodox organization to be included in the Ottoman system. The Turks extended it as they advanced north, until they got into Hungary. Then, in order to give some satisfaction to the Serbs who had taken a large part in the war on both sides, and to ensure that they should remain under a spiritual authority which he could control, in 1537 the sultan restored the Serbian patriarchate of Peć. It had its largest jurisdiction ever, from northern Macedonia and eastern Bulgaria, across Serbia, Montenegro, Bosnia and Herzegovina, to the Orthodox settlements in Habsburg and Venetian territory.

When the Ottoman framework was imposed on the Balkan lands, it was at its strongest under Suleiman the Magnificent (1520–66). A century later, Ottoman might had been checked by the Habsburg emperors consolidating their power at the expense of the feudal aristocracies of their newly acquired dominions. The Turks were forced back to the Danube and the Carpathians, and Venice again controlled the sea approaches.

Ottoman domination had isolated most of the Balkans from the rest of Europe, and the Orthodox world from the rest of Christendom. Greek Orthodoxy was already anti-western as a result of the disruption of its world by the Crusades and the stranglehold of Italian merchants. Such feelings had been reinforced by the way in which Catholic Europe had sought to impose papal supremacy as the price for military help against the Ottomans, and, for Slavs and Romanians, by the uniatism that went with the reconquest.

The Orthodox had to adapt to being second-class inhabitants of a Muslim-ruled empire. Their bishops or hierarchs had also become ethnarchs, or leaders of ethnic communities, involved in administration and politics, for which the Byzantine tradition had not equipped them. Prelates were servants of the sultan, whom they had to placate. They were expected to pay subsidies; debts accrued which had to be recouped from the faithful.

The Ottomans rarely took the Orthodox Church seriously as a potential danger. Fanatics roused a Muslim rabble now and then, and there was haphazard persecution, but in general the authorities did not object to the practice of Christianity so long as Christians remembered their inferior status. Its very weakness as an organization ensured the survival of the Orthodox Church. It was kept alive by the fact that most Christians clung to their faith. It learnt to endure humiliations passively.

Religion was characterized by a deep sense of identity. To become a Muslim was to become an Ottoman – a 'Turk' in general parlance. Otherwise, the Balkan Turks were not all that different from their Christian subjects. From the end of the fifteenth century, the majority was made up of converts, and native elements were constantly absorbed. Bulgaria, Albania and Bosnia were particularly affected by the spread of Islam. Turks had begun to settle in eastern Bulgaria before the conquest, and there had been heresy in the mountains of eastern Thrace, but conversion did not really start there until the seventeenth century.

The feudal lords of Albania were small and independent. The Ottomans came to terms with them with the offer of timars, but it was more difficult to subdue them. In a land that had been a battlefield between west and east, they had 'led an amphibious life between Catholicism and Orthodoxy'.[4] Large-scale Islamization began after Skanderbeg's revolt in alliance with Venice had been put down in 1468, along with an exodus of Catholics to southern Italy. By the eighteenth century, some two-thirds of the population are estimated to have been Muslim, and the Catholics had further declined after reprisals for siding with the Austrians. Many had become Orthodox, and many more had converted to Islam. Most of the conversions occurred in the central lowlands where there had been religious oscillations and where Turkish rule was more efficient.

Catholics remained in the north; most Orthodox were in the south. With the decline of the archbishopric of Ohrid to which their dioceses belonged, and with the reprisals that followed the wars of the eighteenth century, the Orthodox, too, felt the pressure to convert and Bektashism spread more than anywhere else. The migration of Muslim Albanians to Kosovo, Macedonia, Thessaly, the Peloponnese and even the Greek islands, contributed to the Islamization and the Albanianization of Slav and Greek regions. In so far as the nobility converted, it became part of the Ottoman caste, locally as well as by serving throughout the empire.

In Bosnia and Herzegovina, Muslims reached a peak of 75 per cent of the population by the end of the sixteenth century, before declining to under 50 per cent by 1800. The Orthodox may not have exceeded 10 per cent of the population originally. Continued immigration may have brought them up to 40 per cent by the early nineteenth. On the other hand, the Catholic population, which had made substantial progress on the eve of the conquest, fell continuously through emigration and conversion until the early nineteenth century, when it was under 10 per cent.[5]

Islamization occurred most in central Bosnia where the authority of the 'Bosnian Church' had been strong, and in the districts that had been a bone of contention between two of the three contending Christian faiths. The nobility retained its rôle as part of the Ottoman caste, enhanced by the importance of Bosnia as a frontier province, later attracting Ottoman refugees from the lost territories. Power was held by a Muslim military class, Slav or Slavicized.

The declining military strength of the Ottomans had allowed another imperial dynastic power, that of the Habsburgs, to encroach upon the Balkans and influence the peninsula directly or indirectly. By the end of the seventeenth century, the Turkish threat had been repelled, most of the lands of the Hungarian crown reconquered, the vassal principality of Transylvania incorporated and more South Slavs brought into their lands.

4 Stavro Skendi, *The Albanian National Awakening, 1878–1912*, Princeton, NJ: Princeton University Press, 1967, 5.
5 Stoianovich, 145–146.

Those of the Adriatic and Alpine fringes had been most affected by European developments since the sixteenth century. At a time when Venice was past her prime and the west had not yet begun seriously to enter the Levant trade, the oligarchic city-republic of Dubrovnik was better placed than ever to act as intermediary between the developing manufactures of Europe and the sources and markets in the Ottoman east. It participated in the Renaissance, its position between Italy and the Balkans gave its inhabitants the feeling of a distinct identity and made them aware of similarities with all South Slavs.

The reduction of the local estates was easily accomplished by the Habsburgs in the Alpine duchies where the Slovenes lived, but these already partly Germanized lands were never cut off from the rest of Europe. In what remained of Croatia in the seventeenth century, reducing the power of local institutions was more of a problem. The nobility, while appreciating the protection offered by the Habsburgs against the Turkish danger, also nurtured that offered to their privileges by the identity of their medieval realm. The imperial authorities organized the defences by attracting frontiersmen whom the Ottoman authorities had previously settled on their side. All sorts of refugees and renegades were resettled on crown lands granted to farm communally, with religious freedom and no feudal obligations, in return for military service.

The failure of the last Turkish thrust into central Europe with the lifting of the siege of Vienna in 1683 definitely turned the tide. The Austrians, with many South Slav soldiers, marched into Serbia, where they met with support. The Treaty of Karlowitz (today's Sremski Karlovci in Serbia) in 1699 formally returned most of Hungary with Croatia to the emperor. When the Austrians withdrew, the élite of Serbs went with them. As war resumed in 1718–39 and in 1787–92, the Austrians penetrated deeper into the peninsula, with appeals to the population, and each time when they withdrew, there was more emigration.

Southern Hungary had been practically depopulated. In order to keep the intractable Magyar nobles out of this strategic region, the emperor resettled it with foreigners. Most of the landed estates in the recovered territories were granted to foreign nobles. After the Peace of Karlowitz, Leopold I had invited the immigration of Serbian refugees on the border by issuing a charter to the Orthodox 'nation'. This gave them the right to their own metropolitanate in the Hungarian dominions as an offshoot of the patriarchate of Peć.

This was the Habsburg version of a millet, dependent entirely on the protection of the court of Vienna against the pressures of the Hungarian-Croatian institutions and of the Catholic Church. The possibility had also been mentioned of an Orthodox *voyvod* or military leader: the Hungarian diet would not have it, but the territorial name of Vojvodina stuck. Military reasons helped the Serbs to implement what had been granted, for the Austrian generals needed them.

Each new war or raid across a highly permeable frontier set large numbers of people in motion, planting Serb settlements in the heart of Croatia and Hungary. Although the majority of settlers in the institutionalized Military

Frontier (*Militärgrenze* or *Vojna Krajina*, the same Slav word as in Ukraine) were Orthodox Serbs, the solidarity between Catholic and Orthodox was long characteristic of that farmer-soldier society which was both a bulwark against Turkish encroachments and an instrument of Habsburg ascendancy.

Manoeuvring between Croatian and Hungarian nobles, Charles VI put the Pragmatic Sanction to the diet of Croatia in 1712 before submitting the delicate question of succession through females to the reluctant estates of Hungary. The Croats voted for it, but stressed again their realm's special status. The Austrian monarchy's centralizing policy in the eighteenth century was first and foremost financial and military. Failing to bring the Hungarian nobility under effective control, it had to defend and tax the newly acquired lands by other means.

The colonization of the borderlands was meant to defend the southeastern territories, but also to spread skilled labour and increase taxable wealth. From its sixteenth-century beginnings in Croatia, the Military Frontier was extended to Vojvodina and to Transylvania, placing the eventually tolerated Orthodox Romanians under the jurisdiction of the Serb metropolitanate. More generally the Habsburg reforms improved the position of peasants and extended the benefits of education, increasing the number of educated South Slavs and Romanians.

At the end of the seventeenth century, the Habsburgs sought the support of Balkan Christians against the Turks with promises of privileges, presenting themselves as liberators. Each of the several bishops, boiers, tribal leaders and brigand chiefs who cast his lot with Austria was out for opportunities for his own sake and mobilized variable popular support. The wars waged on Ottoman territory opened opportunities to the opponents of any order. The variety of hajduks (from the Magyar *hajdu*, plural *hajduk*) and klephts (from the Greek *klephtes*) were atavistic rebels harking back to some confusedly perceived older forms.

By the eighteenth century, the Balkans had a floating population of soldiers, deserters, bandits – men who had lost land, home or kin as Ottoman rule retreated or retaliated. There were tame bands which cooperated with authorities, there were wild bands opposed to authorities, and they were often interchangeable. They could be used by the enemies of the Porte (the sultan's government) for creating diversions in times of war, for they also often drove peasants into the arms of the enemy, turning jacquerie into rebellion.

Conspiracies and revolts for ridding the Balkans of the Infidel were engineered by outside forces, took place in areas remote from Turkish control and occurred in times of war. Montenegro's topography had prevented the Turks from ever imposing effective rule. She led the way in a constant struggle against neighbouring Ottoman commanders or Muslim grandees, developing a feeling of unity under her native bishop and cultivating her image as the only Serb land that had never lost its freedom. Popular support otherwise reflected no more than local discontent with specific abuses.

Peter the Great's 1711 appeal to the Balkan Christians had been calculated to achieve the same aims as Emperor Leopold's 1690 declaration. It, too, wanted to exploit what was believed to be massive expectations by the Christians of an anti-Turkish crusade. As Russia went to war again with Turkey, on her own or in alliance with other powers, she showed no greater comprehension of the mood of the Balkan leaders and their followers. In the Greek lands, Ottoman troops were actually welcomed in reaction to the enmity aroused by the Venetians' attempt to convert the Orthodox. By 1774 the Peace of Kuchuk-Kainardji (Kainarzha in present-day Bulgaria) had, nevertheless, given Russia's diplomats at the Porte the right to 'make representations' in favour of Orthodox Christians.

The Hellenized hierarchy of Ohrid, like that of Peć, had agitated against the Turks, and even looked to Rome for support. This led the sultan to abolish them both in 1767 and formally turn them over to Constantinople. The Orthodox Church had had its rights gradually whittled down. It had been sucked into the general atmosphere of corruption and intrigue and forced to seek the protection of foreign powers, usually the sultan's enemies. If these were Catholic, it was seen as even more disloyal, especially within the ranks of the Church itself. Looking to Orthodox Russia seemed more natural. Russia's rulers had taken over the imperial title and considered Moscow to have become the Third Rome, but they had not inherited the Graeco-Roman tradition of government along with Christianity. They viewed the bishops as their servants, and offered churchmen in the Balkans a perversion of the Byzantine ideal of an Orthodox empire.

Uncertain of the loyalty of their Christian subjects, the Turks in the eighteenth century did encourage Islamization in sensitive areas. This was done through the resettlement of Ottomans returning from the lost territories, but even more so through the expansion of Muslim Albanians into the surrounding plains and valleys that had been largely abandoned by Serbs and Greeks. There had been no great Greek emigration on a par with the Serbian, but repression had prompted extensive movements from the coasts and from northern rural areas where many had sided with the enemy.

By the end of the seventeenth century, the population of the Balkans is estimated to have become ethnically or linguistically Turkish in proportions ranging from a maximum of over a third in the east to under a tenth in the west. The Slav character of the western territories and the Romance character of the trans-Danubian eastern territories had been affirmed. The Hellenism of the southern maritime zone was not challenged until the Albanian incursions. The southern and eastern inland regions, however, had become a conglomerate – Hellenic, Slav, Romance, Turkish, Albanian – of people of ambivalent identity with a floating consciousness.[6]

6 Stoianovich, 133. He surmises that up to 10 per cent of the population south of the Danube may have been Vlachs at the end of the seventeenth century (128).

In religious terms the Counter-Reformation, tied to the Habsburgs, had got the better of the Protestantism that had spread to the Slovenes through German nobles and burghers. In the meanwhile, vernacular religious literature had provided the basis from which a Slovenian ethnic identity could develop in the absence of any institutional framework. The Germanic element helped the Counter-Reformation elsewhere, as the Habsburgs welcomed and settled Catholic colonists from German and other imperial lands to the reconquered provinces. They were used as a lever against the Magyar nobles, many of whom were Protestant, and to repopulate devastated areas.

Elsewhere it was the Orthodox whom the Habsburgs used. Serbs were valuable allies in the struggle against the Croatian nobility. When the Military Frontier was extended, Serbs along with Croat frontiersmen played a similar part against the Hungarian nobility to that played by Romanians in Transylvania. The Habsburgs thus obtained a loyal military which held the southeastern frontier. The Austrians also at times occupied, administered and even formally took over Ottoman territories, notably parts of Serbia and Wallachia between 1714 and 1739.

The relatively favourable situation of much of the Ottoman Balkans once again deteriorated after the Turks had crossed into Hungary. Armies went through and hibernated. The need to fight technically more advanced opponents obliged the Ottomans to rely more on firearms and on urban-based infantry, who were salaried even if recruited from among slaves. The janissaries had no obligations to the population, and by the seventeenth century they also supplemented their salaries by taking over the guilds. Not unlike other European monarchs in the early modern era, the sultans, in an effort to create a large standing army and to feed their capital city, had to extend their powers for taxing agricultural production. They needed taxes in money rather than kind to pay for troops and artillery. The two economic institutions that had stood behind the army – the timar system of nominally temporary tenure on state lands for service, and the restrictive guild system of artisan manufacture – were no longer sufficient.

THE TRANSITION OF THE EIGHTEENTH CENTURY

The traditional Ottoman social structure fell apart at the end of the eighteenth century. The devshirme had declined along with slave service and labour. Patrons imposed themselves on the peasantry as second or effective landlords, promoting sharecropping arrangements that strove to satisfy the needs of towns, employing armed retainers and enforcing more arduous forms of tenancy. This form of property went by the Turkish word *chiftlik*, meaning originally the land that a *chift* or team of oxen could plough in a day.

Chiftliks were concentrated in the core Balkan provinces, the most secure and the best endowed for grain, cotton and tobacco. They were the property of Muslim lords and other notables who had the means of defending them from the disorders that were becoming the rule in the Balkan countryside as established order collapsed. They drove the peasantry into near serfdom. Although the Porte in fact came to accept this usurpation, it was not formalized. As the original name implies, most chiftliks were not large – usually a village of ten to twenty families. Only a handful of estates in eastern Macedonia and western Bulgaria extended to hundreds of hectares and villages.

The predominant rural pattern in the lowlands remained that of smallholders. Kinship, households, villages, village federations and clans were sources of support, of protection and of labour. Such communities dealt with the official tax farmers who had been introduced since the Porte could no longer count on the sipahis, and who came to demand several times the prescribed harvest tithe. Diminishing central government control, the inability to enforce economic regulations, and the rudimentary character of a fiscal system where only Christians paid direct tax, all contributed to increased hardships.

Many lowland peasants left and dispersed into upland hamlets that were more difficult to reach. Organized around an even more closely structured extended family, they supported themselves by raising livestock, subjected to lower taxes and easier to hide. Disorders in the lowlands, the limited numbers that uplands could support and emigration caused a sharp decline in the overall population of the Balkans – but with a parallel growth of the urban population – from its sixteenth-century peak of around eight million to less than three by the mid-eighteenth century.[7]

The new land régime went along with greater local autonomy on the peripheries and with the development of Christian, mainly Greek, urban groups. The absence of a Christian landowning nobility enabled traders to rise by a multiplicity of rôles. In the eighteenth century, through trade and credit, some of these notables even came to have control if not possession of land. Various systems of farming and tenancy had in fact become hereditary for Christian communities, families and even individuals, notably in fringe areas further from the central chiftlik core and from Constantinople. Rural notables were producers, but also tax collectors within the community, traders in agricultural products, shopkeepers, importers and moneylenders. For the rank-and-file peasants, they provided credit and protection in exchange for services, especially in the Greek lands, where this relationship turned into hereditary rent and labour services.

Longer-distance migration towards Wallachia and Hungary had been another response to the turmoil. Thus a growing number of Slavs joined Greeks in a commercial network on the periphery of the Ottoman economy. Their new location provided the base for a more secure existence – often urban – and for trade with the Ottoman Balkans. These movements broadened the increasing flow of Balkan trade away from Constantinople and towards central Europe. The Ottoman Empire relied ever more on imported manufactures as domestic production could no longer meet state and urban demands. Thus merchant activity outside Ottoman regulations, even outside Ottoman territory, became

7 Lampe and Jackson, 38.

more important than had ever been intended in original Ottoman Islamic conceptions and ethics.

As European traders feared hostilities and disorders on the overland routes, it was essentially Greek traders, but also Jews and other natives, who set up an urban network through the Balkans. With the exception of southern Greece, it radiated towards central Europe. Most of the commerce on both sides of the border was in the hands of native Balkan merchants. The Habsburg Monarchy had not made much use of the growing trade with the Ottoman Empire to dominate the borderlands, let alone to penetrate the Balkans economically.

The Greek-speaking population of Constantinople had preserved its merchant groups. Remnants of the Byzantine aristocracy had also grouped in Thrace and in the capital itself under the umbrella of the patriarchate. Adapting to the new circumstances as the conquest stabilized and taking advantage of the removal of Italian traders, they made the most of opportunities, became bankers to the Porte and advisers to the patriarchate. These were the Phanariots (called after the Phanar area of the capital where the patriarch resided) around whose original nucleus gathered new recruits. Whatever the reality of their genealogical claims and of their ethnic origins, they were in effect an Orthodox aristocracy, the apex of the Greek world in the Ottoman Empire. Their location, their cultural background and the openings offered by the Porte allowed them to develop.

Nowhere were the Phanariots more successful than in the Principalities, where the declining Ottoman Empire managed to tighten its indirect grip at the expense of the native landed nobility. With wars fought over their territory bringing destruction and hindering economic development, they came under periods of foreign occupation, and eventually lost chunks of Moldavia to Austria (northern Moldavia or Bukovina, in 1775) and to Russia (eastern Moldavia or Bessarabia, in 1812).

Too weak actually to take over Moldavia and Wallachia, the Porte had to tolerate constant shifts in allegiance by princes and aristocratic factions, so long as the sultan's suzerainty was not usurped by one or another of his enemies, and so long as it could retain the ability to manipulate and influence. A cordon of Ottoman fortresses with more and more dependent territory pushed the Principalities back from the Danube and the Black Sea, and the Porte increasingly influenced the choice of rulers.

After 1615 it made a point of investing individuals whose reliability was guaranteed by the upper-class Phanariot families in Constantinople. Then from 1711, it actually resorted to trusted Phanariots themselves, which was consistent with its readiness to strengthen Phanariot power generally to stabilize a tottering Ottoman economy. The princes could no longer play a part in the international relations of southeast Europe or have an independent armed force, but the clash of rival empires preserved their autonomy, however circumscribed.

Even at the time, the period of 'Phanariot rule' was perceived in the Principalities as one of decline. It was a value system of allegiance to the Porte with conservative Orthodoxy, which, true to its post-Byzantine tradition between the Ottoman Empire and Europe, also brought the princes into contact with enlightened despotism. They introduced reforms, although measures that directly favoured the peasants, culminating in the theoretical abolition of serfdom, could hardly be implemented because of opposition from the boiers who were the political class. These reforms, the prosecution of those who sought foreign assistance, and the promotion of fellow Phanariots, exacerbated hostility.

Economic exploitation intensified. The tribute to the Porte remained constant, but financial pressures generally increased. Apart from the devastations of war, the greatest financial burden was probably linked to the princes' investiture, which in practice came to be sold to the highest bidder. They arrived with debts, relatives, advisers and retainers. Ottoman demands for supplies grew and had a ruinous effect on the economy. Products that fell under the Ottoman right of pre-emption (including grain and cattle) went to Constantinople at prices that were fixed well below market value.

The princes had become little more than glorified high-ranking officials answerable to the sultan, who could depose them and even execute them for high treason. They reigned for a very short time, and their government lacked stability, but they still had absolute legal power within their territory. The assembly – the institution through which the boiers had elected rulers, resolved extraordinary problems and sought to influence government – had gone into decline, and no longer even met after the middle of the eighteenth century, not even formally for the election of princes. The entire government apparatus was by then used to wring as much money as possible out of the territory.

There was general boier disaffection with 'Greek' rule, with the limitations to their powers as an oligarchy generally, and more particularly with the disregard of their right to elect the princes. In their discontent, some sought assistance from Russia and Austria, others emigrated to southern Russia or to Transylvania, but no violent action ensued as the Phanariot régime was ultimately preferable to Austrian or Russian rule.

The two principalities of Moldavia and Wallachia had the same status, the same way of life, with the same transition from pastoral hills to agricultural plains, and the towns in between where boiers resided, though their estates were in the plains. The principality of Transylvania also had a majority Romanian Orthodox population, and a status which had oscillated between Hungarian and Ottoman suzerainty until 1688, when it finally reverted to the Hungarian crown. There, too, the nobility was the dominant class but the population was divided into a number of 'nations' and 'religions' to the exclusion of the majority group, made up almost entirely of enserfed peasants.

Protestantism had proved more enduring in Transylvania than elsewhere, and the Habsburg rulers faced the task of overcoming the largely Protestant Magyar nobility. They sought Catholic converts dependent on the Vienna court, thus giving Orthodox clergy the chance to improve their situation by accepting the terms of the Union of Florence. Nevertheless, the Uniate Church was not accepted as one of the established religions, nor was it viewed with favour by either the Hungarians or the mass of the Orthodox peasant faithful. It did, however, become the centre of a Romanian intellectual movement because of its Roman connexion and its Latin-educated clergy. With the reforms of Joseph II, the attempt to treat all Romanians as Uniates was abandoned, and the Orthodox in turn were tolerated, in Transylvania as elsewhere in the Monarchy.

The gradual retreat of the Ottoman Empire had benefited the Venetian and especially the Habsburg rulers more than local nobles and their vestigial institutions. Croatia was a kingdom linked to Hungary by a dynastic agreement which formally ensured the autonomy of its nobles' 'nation', but which varied in content with the balance of power between ruler and nobles, between war and peace. The efforts of the nobility to maintain their privileges and their autonomy had led them to accept the Pragmatic Sanction in return for a renewed guarantee of their autonomy, with a special emphasis on the protection of their privileges.

Authority was vested in the *ban* (or viceroy) who represented the crown, and in the *Sabor* (or diet of the estates) which included magnates, prelates and representatives of the lesser nobility and of the free towns. The predominant political influence was conservative, so that in order to stand up to imperial reforms, Croatia surrendered much of her power to the Hungarian diet. The reclaimed lands were kept apart from 'Civil Croatia', in a Military Frontier under direct imperial control. In Slavonia, redevelopment policies had assigned estates to German and Hungarian lords, and placed it halfway between autonomous Croatian and full Hungarian rule.

There was constant movement across a border that was difficult to hold, with raids on both sides by irregulars and bandits. The Habsburgs' use of these people, mostly Orthodox Serbs, by settling them as military colonists, was a source of friction with the Croatian diet. The nobility wanted to reimpose the old feudal order, and the Catholic Church opposed the freedom granted to the Orthodox. 'Military Croatia' was, in any case, one of the poorest regions of the Habsburg Monarchy and continued to provide men to fight for Austria. The emperor's Croats and Serbs were used extensively in the wars of the eighteenth century, and not only in the Balkans.

The shifting border between Venetian Dalmatia and the Ottoman Empire was likewise the scene of endemic fighting and of a steady influx of refugees from the hinterland. The latter completed the Slavicization of the coastal province by the end of the seventeenth century, although Venetian Italian speech had then entered the towns through political and cultural influences. Ragusa, even in decline, remained a window open on the west for the Balkans.

By the 1780s plans were being drawn up by Joseph II and Catherine II to partition the sultan's European provinces. They actually went to war with Turkey in 1787–92, but as the century drew to a close the partition projects crumbled. Even before the French Revolution, the western powers, who by then shared the Levant trade and had no aggressive aims in the Ottoman Empire, could not leave it to Russia and Austria.

The alarming prospect of further ventures that would make effective use of Christian grievances did, however, prompt the Porte to retaliatory action. This included the first officially encouraged forced conversions to Islam in particularly sensitive areas – essentially in the mountains of Albania and in adjoining Serb and Greek territory. Vigorous campaigns by loyal Albanian Muslim chieftains and grandees were successful but counterproductive. They exacerbated relations between Muslims and Christians, and opened the door more widely to the activities of Austrian and Russian agents in territories over which the Porte was unable to exercise control.

Elsewhere Ottoman reactions were less severe and tended to strengthen the power of leading Greek elements. The Phanariots were able to convince the Porte that the strength of their Orthodox millet would arrest subversion, and that Phanariot economic activity would bring in greater revenue. After their departure for Austria, the patriarch of Peć and his bishops were initially replaced with reliable Greek prelates, though eventually the autocephalous Orthodox centres – still nominally independent of Constantinople – were abolished altogether.

Collaboration with Austria and Russia by political forces in the Balkans was minimal even as late as the 1787–92 war, and the Porte's underpinning response to decline was reform. Ottoman reformist statesmen were closer to understanding the realities of change in the Balkans than Austrians and Russians. They were, however, unable to secure an understanding with the new forces emerging from their Christian Balkan population in the wake of the devastations of warfare and of the breakdown of authority over whole segments of territory.

Various trends of civilization had penetrated the Balkans in the Turkish period. The Byzantine trend, which was already essentially Hellenic at the time of the conquest, continued through the Greek-dominated Church, and later through Phanariot influence and Greek-dominated trade. The Turkish trend, which had been filtering in before the conquest, went hand in hand with the military and the administration, then spread through Islamization, and finally indirectly through Serb northward migrations. Truly western as opposed to central European influences had come by sea and were still felt along the western coasts. Habsburg expansion, wars and trade had brought in central European trends with Joseph II's version of Enlightenment. The European influences that would initiate far-reaching changes in outlook started to come timidly from France in the later eighteenth century, with trade, diplomacy, and even intellectual as opposed to administrative Enlightenment. The French Revolution then drew Habsburg attention away from the Balkans and injected the revolutionary ideas linked to the concept of 'nation'.

At the turn of the century, the Balkan peninsula dissolved into anarchy as powerful adventurers extended their personal ascendancy from estates to regions. Local governors, Albanian and Bosnian magnates, rebel janissary commanders and other warlords who lived off the land, refused orders from the imperial authorities, and inserted themselves between the sultan's rule and his Christian subjects. In so doing they used Christians against the Porte, as the Porte used Christians against them.

The introduction of new crops in response to growing European demand, and the attempts to reform the central administration and army on European models had contributed to the changes. Specialization in specific crops and livestock for foreign markets in the border areas disturbed the supply system of the Empire, where the large cities depended on Balkan agriculture. The difficulties were further aggravated by the wars, the loss of the rich Pannonian basin and the psychological impact of defeat by the Christian powers. Land was simply grabbed by those who could. The government no longer received service or revenue from an Ottoman caste which, in so far as it survived, broke away from any control.

The Church had served as a major vehicle of transmission of tradition, and the Ottoman authorities had never controlled Christian thought. There continued a popular literature, religious but not exclusively so, with folk traditions recounting tales from the lives of saints, martyrs, kings and heroes. The exploits of Byzantine warriors and the tragedy of the fall of Constantinople, the legends of Serbian kings, saints and knights, and their downfall, preserved the sense of a separate Orthodox identity, at the same time as a feeling of a historical community of related cultures.

Not all were Orthodox, even though there were Orthodox everywhere. Within the three faiths – 'Greek' Orthodox, 'Roman' Catholic and Islam – religion, geography and history produced segmented identities which both differed from and greatly resembled each other. Their differences were often reinforced by the scarcity of resources. In their similarities, they constituted a conglomerate of related cultures marked by common historical experiences that had touched them to varying degrees.

There had been an Ottoman order in the Balkans until the possibility of securing wealth by almost unlimited military means was brought to an end, but that order, while it separated the Balkans from the rest of Europe, had never been an 'iron curtain'. It had failed to impose a compact administration on a territory so open to the north and to the Mediterranean. The populations, mostly cut off from subsequent European cultural developments, had not been uprooted from the earlier joint heritage.

The Turks provided a rationale for rebellion by virtue of their alien faith. The theme of ridding the Balkans of the Infidel had been a leitmotiv of opponents of the Ottoman order ever since the conquest. By 1800 jacqueries had become more responsive to propaganda, as entire provinces came to be ruled by new landlords and warlords not sanctioned by law, who took over the land by force, imposed new taxes and terrorized Christian peasants and notables alike. In many areas, Christian peasants faced what had once been the military wing of the Ottoman order no longer as enforcers of the sultan's law, but as groups bent on achieving power at the expense of peasants and sultan alike. Those among the Christians who had not made a success of their undertakings in the new upheavals were most likely to be attracted by the revolutionary mood, but those whose very success attracted the spite of the new lords also felt threatened.

Traian Stoianovich has stressed the importance of millenarianism in the Balkans,[8] which reached its peak during the second half of the eighteenth century. To the beliefs in the coming of a liberating messiah, in the form of some ancestor or medieval hero, were added natural occurrences interpreted as portents of liberation and renovation to be achieved by war, epidemic and rebellion. These were expectations of a return to a golden age – a 're-volution' to use Stoianovich's term – but they were synchronized with the Revolution in France and its fallout throughout Europe, with the stirrings among the South Slavs and Romanians of the Habsburg dominions, and with the fears of anarchy and new oppression in the Ottoman lands.

In the Romanian Principalities, in Serbia, and among the urban Greeks, millenarianism yielded at least superficially to the Enlightenment. Despite the lawlessness, there was a commercial revival as the expanding economy of Europe stimulated the growth of a class of merchants and mariners, especially along the Habsburg border and in the maritime lands. Ottoman hostility had kept western European interests from gaining a direct commercial dominance, and the military orientation of the Ottomans had kept Muslims from entering commerce in a major way. Trade thus favoured Christian merchants, especially Greeks.

It was the merchants who controlled much of the trade with the rest of Europe who formed the nucleus of a new Balkan world more responsive to western influence, and even the beginnings of a secularized intelligentsia. Western civilization was no longer perceived as essentially dissenting and separated from Orthodoxy, but primarily secular under the name of Enlightenment. Secularism provided Orthodox Balkan merchants and intellectuals with an opportunity to identify with Europe at the level of everyday life.

Merchants in the Romanian Principalities, in southern Hungary, and in foreign cities across Europe were the main contributors to this awakening. In Europe, they were nourished partly by western political ideas and the classical revival, taking or acquiring pride in the Greek classical heritage. Scholars working mainly in the Habsburg Monarchy became engrossed in the cultural heritage of their native lands on both sides of the border, offering treasures of Balkan myth and poetry to the fascination of European writers of the romantic period. Philanthropists and dependent intellectuals all took an interest in promoting the cultural life of their native regions.

At the beginning of the nineteenth century, the peripheries were in a phase of transition, as they had been at the time of the Ottoman conquest. Enlightened and romantic Europe and Hellenism were rediscovering each other, but it was the Serb division between the advanced and strong Austrian Monarchy and

8 Stoianovich, 168–170.

the backward and weak Ottoman Empire that was destined to start the process of emancipation. The contact between the new ideas north of the Danube and the plight of peasants driven to desperation south of the river would eventually spark off revolution.

CHAPTER 2

The awakening of nationalities, 1804–30

From Phanariot Byzantinism to revolution. The successful revolts. The establishment of native rule in Serbia, in Greece and in the Romanian Principalities. Empires connected across peripheries.

FROM PHANARIOT BYZANTINISM TO REVOLUTION

At the dawn of the nineteenth century, in the ruins of the old Ottoman order, the surviving Byzantine tradition in its Phanariot and Russian interpretations faced the new ideas of the Enlightenment and of the French Revolution.

The Ottoman system had imposed neither a political integration nor a new culture. By largely isolating the Balkans, it had prevented the development of the countryside but enabled its survival and preserved old values. Living in the past blurred reality, but maintained hope. The intermediaries between the medieval past and village culture had been the Church and oral poetry. Individualism was absent.

The conservatism of the rural world was broken from time to time by the intrusion of armies, the agitation of foreign agents, the devastation of epidemics. Frightened and impulsive, peasants often responded to such shocks by turning to banditry. Local revolts were unsuccessful and provoked reprisals. However, the cumulative effect of warfare or insurrection generation after generation, along with the practical disappearance of the very basis of the Ottoman system, created a favourable terrain for rebellion against central power and for the emergence of parallel local hierarchies.

Over and above the new class of chiftlik owners, great warlords had come to control vast tracts of territory. All were eclipsed by Ali Pasha (1774–1822) of Janina (Ioannina), whose rule extended from Epirus and western Macedonia, across central Greece, even into the Peloponnese. In his desire for independence and European military expertise he was more akin to his contemporary fellow Albanian Mehemet Ali (1770–1849) who set himself up in Egypt. Below, at ground level, were all the outlaws, the paramilitaries and the pirates who provided manpower and leadership to fight on land and sea. The history of

23

flights, expulsions and migrations made for mobility, with echoes from one uprising to another.

As they extended their rôle, the Phanariots also steered the Byzantine tradition into new waters. They had come to be appointed to posts in the central Ottoman bureaucracy without converting to Islam, technically as 'interpreters', in fact as advisers to institutions dealing with the outside world. They supported the patriarchate with their money and their influence; they ran its finances and administration. In so doing, they politicized the patriarchate which, in turn, provided them not only with an identity, but with a sense of historical continuity through its unique relation to Byzantium.

The Phanariots combined wealth and position at the top of the Greek ethnic élite with actual territorial power in the Romanian Principalities where they formed real dynasties. There they reinforced existing Hellenic cultural influences; they favoured Greek traders, and they patronized a movement that led to a form of Orthodox-Byzantine political consciousness. From Bucharest and Jassy even more than from Constantinople, the Phanariots were able to move on to what can be termed – for want of a better description – proto-Hellenic 'nationalism', but they could also look to Europe and the Enlightenment from Bucharest and Jassy better than from Constantinople. Thus the princes of Wallachia and Moldavia were provided with inspiration to reform.

The model was first and foremost Austrian. The Habsburg Monarchy was a state of law whose enlightened imperial policy they could try and emulate, by granting legal freedom to serfs, by establishing in their capitals schools with a western type of education that included sciences and modern languages. All that went with a classical revival interpreted through western European perceptions, with increasing French cultural influence on the aristocracy. These late-eighteenth-century Romanian Phanariots were the first to be impregnated with the spirit of 'liberty' that emanated from France as the precursor of the concept of 'nation'.

At the same time, well-read people in the Principalities dissatisfied with Phanariot rule were prompted to turn to those who had replaced the hostile image of the Latin west by the friendlier one of Enlightened Europe. Byzantium had been Rome, and that renewed understanding came about more easily in the Romanian lands. By redefining their civilization in terms of Europe rather than Latin or western Christendom, the thinkers of the Enlightenment gave those in the Balkans who could, by their education and contacts, act as mediators, the opportunity to envisage their own return to a common European *oikoumene*. The Ottomans, however, failed to understand the attraction that the west could have for the Orthodox, or to what extent, beneath the forms that preserved the unchangeable foundations of Byzantine Orthodoxy, the idea of a return to a golden past had evolved as a result of Russian as well as western influences.

Russia had established for itself a rôle as successor to Byzantium. Under the partition planned with Austria, her sphere of Turkey-in-Europe would have been organized as a 'Dacia' (the Principalities) and a 'Byzantium' (Bulgaria,

Macedonia and the Greek lands with Constantinople). This design was never carried out, but one of Catherine II's grandsons had been conveniently called Constantine, and the new élites of the Balkan Christians had been impressed. 'New' southern Russia on the northwest coast of the Black Sea, the magnet for immigrants and refugees from all over the Balkans, was the breeding ground for such influences.

These projects had reinforced the dream of the Phanar oligarchy and of the patriarchate of a revival of Byzantium. It was clear to them that the Ottoman order was crumbling. With time, it would collapse, and with a little help from Russia, they would take over. They made no immediate plans; they did not find it particularly necessary; they had to be cautious because of their position. The patriarch swore allegiance to the sultan – who was still the Caesar to whom Christians had to render what was Caesar's – and guaranteed that his flock would not engage in treasonable activities, yet the patriarch was a Christian and, moreover, a Greek.

Both he, his prelates and his Phanariot backers were generally out of touch with the main body of Greek speakers in the provinces and their clerics. These were all rather suspicious of the glitter of the rich Greeks of the capital, and even of the Church hierarchy, which was often seen as neglecting the faithful except when it needed money. There was a certain split between the upper, Phanariot-influenced, reaches of the Orthodox Church and its rank-and-file in the provinces.[1]

Cultural changes moved down from the Phanariot gentleman-scholars to a wider spectrum – relatively educated wealthier merchants, secretaries, tutors, other dependent intellectuals and those whom they influenced. They, too, generally preferred reform to revolution, but a new spirit was coming from those doing business in Europe beyond the borders of the Ottoman Empire – Greeks, but also Slavs and Romanians. Vienna, with its 'Josephinist' rendering of Enlightenment, had become the centre of another kind of Hellenism, of Balkan Slavism, and even of a certain type of Romanianism.

The best-known representative of that spirit was Rigas (1760–98), born at Velestino in Thessaly, one-time secretary of Phanariot and boier magnates in Constantinople and in Bucharest, who had settled in Vienna in the last years of the eighteenth century. Before he was extradited to the Turks and put to death in Belgrade, his writings had provided the synthesis between the stirrings of an evolving Hellenism and the principles proclaimed by the French Revolution. He called on the inhabitants of Roumelia, Moldo-Wallachia, the islands and Asia Minor to rise, and to form a Hellenic republic on the principles of liberty, equality, fraternity and popular sovereignty.

---

1 Not to mention a certain reaction among western-educated intellectuals against the shackles of the Byzantine Orthodox past, seen as conservative and enmeshed in the Ottoman present. Adamantios Korais (1748–1833), of Smyrna, who studied and spent the best part of his life in France where he acquired a reputation as a classical scholar, believed in the need to emancipate his countrymen through education from both their Ottoman yoke and their Byzantine past.

A revolutionary mentality was set up as a new bond for the Christians of the Ottoman Empire. The ideas of the French Revolution became catalysts for the break-up of the Orthodox commonwealth, by providing the common denominator for the formation of nationalities, even though the links between the old concept of faith and the new one of ethnicity remained strong.

Returning to the top of the social hierarchy, one finds another version of that spirit emerging from a different environment with the Bucharest-educated Ypsilantis brothers. Their father had reigned over both Principalities before ending his days in exile in Russia. Alexandros (1792–1828) in particular, who had been an officer in the Russian army during the Napoleonic wars, aimed at the restoration of Byzantium through an appeal to all the Christians of the Balkans.

As exemplified by both Rigas and Ypsilantis, the space supposedly occupied by the 'nation' was still extensive in the Balkans. Only after the initial successes of rebellion would other ethnic communities react to Greek nationalism. The events in France and the way in which their meaning was spread throughout Europe by the armies of Napoleon forged new conceptions of society. They contributed to the emergence of what Benedict Anderson has called 'imagined communities'[2] – the conservation, creation and modification of the sense of community in response to specific historical circumstances.

In the universalist vision of French revolutionary Enlightenment, the nation was perceived as a means of freedom from tyranny and localism. Its first Balkan enthusiasts saw the Revolution as the confirmation that history could be made as well as endured. They organized themselves in the revolutionary societies that were typical of the times; they were influenced by freemasonry, and they influenced each other until the most famous of these groupings, the Philiki Etairia (Society of Friends), was formed in Odessa in 1814.

Since its foundation twenty years earlier, Odessa had developed into a great emporium with a population of Russians, Jews, people from all over the Balkans, Italians, French émigrés and others. It was a centre of political intrigue linking Russia to the Mediterranean. The ostensible purpose of the Etairia was the promotion of Greek culture, but its chief aim was the creation of a neo-Byzantine Greek empire. It spread to other radical groups in and around Odessa – Balkan exiles and Russian sympathizers – and then approached more influential and more conservative figures who embraced the objectives of a Christian pan-Balkan state. Eventually there emerged under its umbrella the project of a general insurrection as the focus of peasant disturbances, outlaws' actions, French and Russian influences, and neo-Byzantinist ideas. Its leaders, around Ypsilantis, were other Phanariots of the younger generation, linked to the Romanian aristocracy and westernized to a great extent.

Emancipation from Ottoman rule came from the periphery. The evolution of the process was gradual and irregular, determined by proximity to

2 Benedict Anderson, *Imagined Communities: Reflections on the Origins and Spread of Nationalism*, London: Verso Editions, 1983.

26

Europe in space or association. Two risings occurred in the first decade of the nineteenth century which merit the name of revolution – that of the Serbs of the province of Belgrade in 1804, and that of the Greeks centred in the Peloponnese and the islands in 1821. In both cases, the territories where they occurred had enjoyed a period of economic improvement at the turn of the century, followed by one of deterioration, with a radicalization of the population as a result of wars and disorders.

The Greek lands were both freer and more advanced. In particular, a merchant marine had grown in the Aegean from the middle of the eighteenth century as Orthodox merchants and mariners had been forced southwards by poverty, anarchy, war and the pressure of Muslim Albanians, and as warring European states drove off each other's craft. The end of the Napoleonic wars and the revival of European shipping confronted them with a crisis, which coincided with the several new views of Hellenism held by rural Peloponnesian notables, clergy and fighters, by intellectuals formed in Europe and by European philhellenes.

Once the fighting had started, the Phanariots' dream of Byzantium gave way to a new idea of Greece emerging from the War of Independence. However, this would occur only after the less well-endowed native rural notables, hajduks and peasants of the province of Belgrade had been driven to start the first rebellion that can be deemed in retrospect to have inaugurated, albeit inadvertently, a new era for the Balkans.

THE 'SERBIAN REVOLUTION'

The sanjak of Belgrade had benefited from being a distant border province, with two periods of Austrian occupation and administration (1718–39 and 1788–91), during which it had officially been termed 'Serbia' with the emperor as 'king of Serbia', and free exchange of persons and goods with the more developed left bank.

The restoration of Ottoman rule in 1791 came with an amnesty and with autonomy, to keep the province happy, as part of Sultan Selim III's general attempt to counter the breakdown of administration in Roumelia. Compared to adjacent provinces, the Belgrade sanjak was a haven. It largely administered itself as a federation of village communities; immigration from the south continued; links across the border were kept up. Chiftlik ownership and Muslim rebellion hardly affected it initially. It had garrisoned fortresses, a population of 300,000–400,000, of whom perhaps 20,000 were mostly Bosnian Slav, Serbian-speaking, urban Muslims, including some 900 sipahis, whose relations with the peasants were certainly better than those enjoyed by boiers in neighbouring Wallachia.

Selim III's reformist zeal did not hold up to Muslim rebellion. Chiftlik ownership and misrule soon crossed into Serbia, causing tension with the sipahis and spreading fear among peasants and notables alike. By the beginning of

1804, janissary bands had forcibly taken over. A massacre of elders led to an explosion, frightened notables organizing the terrified peasantry with hajduks and former Austrian servicemen.

This was not a rising against the sultan, but a revolt by some of his Christian subjects against Muslim usurpers. It tended to stick to legitimate 'Turks' and to look to Austria to restore the previous benevolent régime. Loyal Ottomans sided with insurgents. Yet in the woodland core of Šumadija, the armed men of Karageorge Petrović (1752–1817) had sparked off the rising by a real hajduks' gesture – setting fire to a janissary captain's quarters and killing all the Turks they could lay their hands on.

Karageorge's dominant personality and his background – that of a well-to-do peasant pig dealer, who had also been a hajduk and a commander of the native auxiliaries of the Austrian army – made him a natural leader. Under him, the captains were generally outlaws, whose bands stirred up rebellion. There were Christian Serbs, too, who fought for the janissaries and many more who hesitated. By the end of the first fighting season that autumn, the province had been freed from the janissaries, but the insurrection went on.

While it would be wrong to regard the First Serbian Rising as an offshoot of the French Revolution, the notion of a 'Serbian revolution' was accepted in Europe at the time.[3] In ridding the sanjak of the janissaries, the rebellion had also destroyed the foundations of Ottoman power there. The revolt of apparently loyal Christians had turned into a revolution, and an anti-Turkish one at that. Poll tax and tithe were no longer paid. The liberated territory was run by its own rudimentary government and defended by a local militia. From hajduks the insurgents had turned into the nucleus of a revolutionary army, and its commanders had all taken to dressing like Ottoman worthies, to make their victory obvious.

Their activities echoed in neighbouring provinces. They had links with other outlaws, attracted volunteers from the Habsburg Frontier, from Montenegro, Bosnia and Herzegovina, and also from further afield in the Balkans.[4] They obtained help from Serb merchants in Croatia and elsewhere, from Phanariots and diaspora Greeks. The Porte was in a difficult situation. Because of the general breakdown of authority, it could not muster enough troops to deal with both rebellious factions. The triangle was complicated and expanding.

3 By no less an authority than the German historian Leopold von Ranke, *Die serbische Revolution; aus serbischen Papieren und Mittheilungen*, Hamburg, 1829. Written from data provided by the historian, ethnographer and philologist Vuk Karadžić, this is a vivid contemporary study of the transformation of Serbia during the period. With a second edition in 1844, and a much expanded third one in 1879, *Serbien und Türkei im neunzehnten Jahrhundert*, it was a work of reference for European diplomats of the time. There was an English translation, *The History of Servia and the Servian Revolution*, London: Henry G. Bohn, 1853, but a complete Serbian edition did not appear until 1892, six years after Ranke's death. Karadžić was also the collector of Serb oral poetry, which along with Greek oral poetry did much, through German and French translations, to bring the Balkans to the knowledge of the writers of Europe at the time of romanticism.
4 Because it is not always easy to affix specific modern 'national' labels, Balkan historians have claimed as 'theirs' those among distinguished participants in the Serbian and in the later Greek risings men who were Serb/Macedonian/Bulgarian/Greek/Albanian.

By 1805 the rising had defeated an Ottoman army, and the Porte had proclaimed a *jihad* – a war waged on behalf of Islam.

Even though the Serb insurgents were rebellious peasants, they believed that only another emperor could deal with the sultan, and there were three of them – the Russian, the Austrian and the French. France had become a factor in the Balkans since the Treaty of Pressburg (Bratislava, the capital of present-day Slovakia) in 1805 after the battle of Austerlitz (Slavkov in Czech) had transferred the former Venetian dominions to Napoleon's Kingdom of Italy. Austria was apprehensive about a rebellion on her border which many of her own Serbs were going over to help. Russia, anxious to avoid an intervention by Napoleon, wanted the sultan's rule to be made tolerable.

The First Serbian Rising was caught in the ups and downs of Franco–Russian relations and of the Napoleonic wars. When Russian troops entered the Principalities and Turkey declared war on Russia in 1806, the French had encouraged, and the Russians discouraged, a settlement with Karageorge. Tsar Alexander offered his protection, with material help once his troops reached the Danube. They never crossed it because of Austrian opposition, and the war with Turkey stopped until 1809.

Left to their own devices, the insurgents discovered the outside world. Karageorge had gambled on going for full freedom. Realizing that Russia wanted to use rather than help him, he sounded out Vienna and Paris, convinced that he would benefit from the competition, while those of the captains and notables who opposed his autocratic rule continued to advocate complete dependence on Russia. Although generally supported by the combatants, he found the peasants diffident towards any form of power and was increasingly isolated. He was not as good a political leader as he was a military commander, and warfare had not been constant. The fighting season was generally limited to the summer, and by 1807 Serbia was completely free of Ottoman control.

Because of deteriorating relations with Napoleon, Russia hurriedly settled with Turkey in 1812 at the Treaty of Bucharest, kept Bessarabia, that part of Moldavia between Dniester and Prut (the present-day ex/post-Soviet Republic of Moldova), and obtained for Serbia a return to the conditions that had existed before the rebellion. Karageorge and not been consulted and did not accept. The Porte, fully expecting France to fall on Russia, hurried to crush the Serbs, treaty notwithstanding. As the powers were busy with Napoleon, the Turks got away with it and did so with a vengeance. In the summer of 1813 they invaded from three sides, crushed the insurgents, massacred, pillaged, burnt, deported and installed direct rule by terror. People fled to the woods, if not abroad. Many of the insurgents crossed into Austria. Some, including Karageorge, went on to Russian Bessarabia.

With no far-reaching intellectual background or political project, the 'Serbian revolution' had begun in an obscure territory at a time of general fermentation. For a while it seemed as if it might become a Balkan revolution, but it had attracted little attention in Europe and the price of that period of freedom had been high. It had, however, destroyed the old Ottoman system in the province of Belgrade, which rose again in April 1815, under Miloš Obrenović (1780–1860), one of the leaders who had not fled. Even though the Porte again proclaimed a jihad, the Second Serbian Rising was different. The Turks realized that, with the defeat of Napoleon, they would have to face Russia; Serbia's notables and peasants, tired and impoverished, went for what they could get. Miloš negotiated at the same time as he fought, fought only to be in a position to bargain, and by November had come to an agreement with the Ottoman troop commander.

Under the sultan's formal authority, the restored native hierarchy was headed by Miloš, who then exploited the prolonged crisis of the Ottoman Empire to obtain in 1830 formal recognition of all that he had achieved in fact. He, too, settled accounts with opponents who hesitated, who wanted to go for more, or who did not like his despotism. The Etairia wanted to profit from the new situation and had enlisted Karageorge. It smuggled him out of Russia in 1817, through the Principalities, to Serbia where he was promptly put to death. Miloš did not want a rival, nor did he want to gamble with the Etairia. His policy was to build gradually on what he could achieve, in his territory, in agreement with the Porte.

He used his position as Serbia's sole political representative with the Ottoman government to carve out more and more autonomy. Always giving the appearance of loyalty, he steadily eroded the sultan's authority. By the early 1830s the number of Turks in Serbia had shrunk to 15,000, living mainly in Belgrade – the military, a few officials, former landlords waiting to sell and a crowd of parasites.

The revenue on which Miloš was able to draw enabled him to bribe Ottoman officials on a large scale. It reflected growing economic activity – first and foremost the export of pigs. Rising prices on the Austrian market encouraged producers. The absence of serviceable roads on which the animals could be driven to Belgrade was compensated by the security to move about. Earnings more than kept pace with the taxes levied by the new native government to pay for itself and for its tribute to the Porte. Miloš took the largest share of the trade, until he became the richest man in the territory over which he ruled.

Once Napoleon had been dealt with, Tsar Alexander, on his return to Russia in 1816, decided to tackle the differences with Turkey. Once again, Serbia was entangled with other issues. This time, however, her status benefited from the international situation. Torn between his sympathy for the cause of the Eastern Orthodox Christians and his wish to preserve legitimistic stability, Alexander I had refrained from active intervention. There were other outstanding issues between Russia and the Ottoman Empire, from the Caucasus to the Aegean, as he tried to fit into the broader framework of international cooperation. His successor Nicholas I, however, enjoined the Porte in 1826 to implement fully all the provisions of Bucharest. The Greek lands were up in arms; the Ottoman military were in crisis following the implementation of army reforms; the Turks feared interventions from Serbia and the Principalities.

Russia was able to impose the Convention of Akkerman (Cetatea Alba, on the Russian border) which confirmed the 1812 Bucharest terms for Serbia. The war with Turkey over Greece in 1828 once again interrupted the implementation. The Porte also had to face revolts of anti-reformist Muslim nobles in Albania and Bosnia: it sued for peace. All existing differences with Russia were solved at the Peace of Adrianople (Edirne) in 1829. By a series of imperial acts in 1830–33, the political and legal position of Serbia and her borders were defined. The military fiefs were formally abolished. All Turks, except for the garrisons, were to dispose of their property and leave within a year. Miloš was recognized as hereditary prince of the autonomous and tributary Principality of Serbia – a territory of 38,000 sq. km within the Ottoman Empire. He went to Constantinople to be invested with his dignity by the sultan.

THE END OF PHANARIOT RULE IN THE PRINCIPALITIES

The Danubian Principalities stood apart from 'Turkey-in-Europe'. As 'treaty territories' they were caught between the growing pressure of European powers on the Ottoman Empire and the breakdown of administration in Roumelia. After the loss of the northern shores of the Black Sea, the Porte had come to rely on them as the 'granary of the Empire' through its right of pre-empting supplies for Constantinople and the military.

In theory absolute rulers under the sultan, the princes reigned increasingly in order to recoup the heavy outlay of their appointment, and they had to reckon with the nobility. The boiers were the first of the orders into which society was divided, the possession of land being the main condition for their status, although in the mid-eighteenth century, on the Russian model, state service was made the criterion.

The nobility was far from monolithic, and it was not all that numerous, for there were little more than 1,000 office-holding boiers in both Principalities at the beginning of the nineteenth century for a population of 1.5–2.3 million. Politics were dominated by the conflict between princes, who were trying to centralize government, and boiers, who clung to their privileges through office, intrigue and domination of the General Council. The boiers controlled more than half the land, living from it though not necessarily on it.

The clergy were even less homogeneous. Parish priests were recruited from the peasantry, whose life they generally shared. Most of the higher clergy were of boier birth or Greek, and prelates sat on the highest councils along with great boiers. Through donations, the Church had accumulated vast amounts of land. Most of it belonged to monasteries 'dedicated' by their donors to holy places in the East (the Holy Sepulchre, monasteries of Mount Athos, or Mount Sinai) for pious ends, and thus placed under outside local ecclesiastical jurisdictions. They had in effect been taken over by Greek monks who were sending to their superiors abroad larger and larger shares of their income. The dedicated monasteries notwithstanding, the Church provided population records, education and charity, for along with the genuine intellectual concern of part of the higher clergy at the turn of the century went a reinvigoration of monastic life.[5]

About two-thirds of the land was held by the princes, boiers and monasteries. Half the peasants were free smallholders at the time of the abolition of serfdom in the 1740s, but they had since lost much of their land. The once estate-bound peasants performed labour services for the use of their plots, and paid tithes. The cumulative result of Ottoman monopolies, wars, raids by neighbouring warlords and Carpathian hajduks (even if they were supposed to rob rich and Greek rather than poor and native), together with the boiers' efforts to get more out of their land, was that the mass of the Romanian population of the Principalities was worse off than those of the Serb or Greek peripheral areas that rose up in arms in 1804–21.

What little there was of a truly urban middle class had no sense of cohesion and no influence on events. Trade and the professions were still largely in the hands of Greeks and Jews, many of whom were 'protected' by the foreign consulates which had been opened since the 1780s. They were initially the subjects of powers with the privileges of extraterritoriality under the Capitulations system that regulated the rights of Christian foreigners in an Islamic empire. Greeks, i.e. Orthodox and at least partly Hellenized Ottoman subjects, and Ottoman Jews also made use of it. They were joined increasingly by Jewish immigrants from the neighbouring Austrian part of Poland, attracted by economic opportunities and relative toleration. Their number in Moldavia went up from 17,000 in 1803 to 37,000 in 1831, most of them urban and amounting to some 30 per cent of the population of Jassy (Iaşi). Many of them were, remained, or became Austrian subjects. They were less numerous in Wallachia, some 3,000 by 1831, mostly in Bucharest.

Conveniently situated between the Danube and the Carpathian passes into Hungary, Bucharest, the capital of Wallachia, was unique for its size, wealth and ethnic mix. Its prosperity and the style of its court set the tone for the boiers who came and built themselves town houses, generating jobs, services, trades and crafts. Its population of 60,000–70,000 in 1824 was half Greek, and also included Gypsies, Jews, Transylvanian Germans, Armenians, Bulgars and Serbs.

Land continued to attract investment. Demand for urban goods and services outside the towns was weak. Trade intensified as cities grew and foreign contacts developed, ingenuity and corruption allowed operations outside the bounds of Ottoman pre-emptions and Capitulations, but the princes and their administration had little or no control over foreign trade. The raising of animals

---

5 The influence of Paisy Velichkovsky (1722–94) highlights the continued supraterritorial character of Orthodoxy. His quest for a true life of the spirit took him from his native Ukraine to monasteries in the Principalities and to Mount Athos, before he returned to Moldavia and to Neamţ, where he became abbot and which he turned into a great spiritual centre. His translations of the Greek fathers into Slavonic, his emphasis on the practice of continual prayer and the need for obeisance to an elder were to have a great influence on Russian monasticism.

was the most important branch of agriculture. Warfare, Ottoman intervention in trade and a limited supply of labour had left boiers with little incentive to expand wheat growing. Peasants in the meanwhile had turned to corn, which was exempted from pre-emption and which fed animals and humans alike. As in Serbia, the value of pig exports to Habsburg lands matched that of the entire cereals export.

The years 1806–12 had been difficult. Princes had been appointed in 1802 under Russian influence, but deposed under French influence in 1806. Russia objected and moved troops in. There followed war and six years of Russian control. The princes were restored by Russia and the territories were administered without Ottoman ties until 1812, when they came fully under the sultan's authority once more and new princes were sent from the Bosphorus.

Russia regained its predominant influence after the fall of Napoleon, but people had been alienated by occupation. Most boiers tended to identify their interests with those of the country and they were closing ranks against newcomers, whatever their divisions otherwise. Their fear of the Turks had diminished. They sought a return to what they saw as the original relationship with the Porte, while admitting that they could only do it by seeking the 'protection' of Russia. Phanariot rule had reinforced links with the Russian Church as well as with the ecumenical patriarchate. The widespread influence of Greek culture had strengthened bonds with the Byzantine-Orthodox world and offered an opening to the west. The presence of Russian officers and their families had done wonders for French cultural influence.

The Etairia, which had spread during the Russian occupation, provided a strange mixture of inspirations – the principles behind the Holy Alliance under Russia's protection, the idea that Greece would lead all the Balkan Christians, freemasonry, French revolutionary ideology, and the liberal movements of Spain and Italy. It involved Romanian boiers, Greek and Serbian traders and exiles. Without a public programme, it meant different things to different people. The vital link between it, its Balkan supporters and Russia was the twenty-nine-year-old Alexandros Ypsilantis, who had agreed to lead the Etairia as its 'guardian'. Confused plans for a 'Greek' uprising were finalized in October 1820. The decisive encounter would be in the Peloponnese. Miloš's Serbia was a disappointment, but the Principalities provided a good starting point.

In Moldavia, Prince Michael Soutsos (Suţu) had been initiated. Although his kinsman of Wallachia, Alexander Soutsos, was not a supporter, the Etairia there had contacts with a number of great boiers and with Tudor Vladimirescu (1780–1821), whose background was not unlike that of Karageorge. He had acquired land and office to rank as a lesser boier in his native Oltenia. He had organized a local militia of pandours against marauding trans-Danubian gangs, and his men had fought with Austrian and Russian armies. As a livestock trader, he had travelled as far as Vienna. He was in touch with Ypsilantis and with the leading boiers who took over the regency when Prince Alexander Soutsos mysteriously died in January 1821. They commissioned him to start a rising to coincide with the advance of Ypsilantis's followers in Moldavia.

Oltenia was ripe. As in neighbouring Serbia, the better days of Austrian occupation had been followed by insecurity.

Vladimirescu told his pandours that the revolt was ordered by the tsar for 'our' freedom and that of the whole 'Greek' nation, to enable Ypsilantis to cross the Danube. He called on peasants to rise against the abuses of boiers and officials, but drew a distinction between bad lords and those who were with 'us'. His appeal was directed against the Phanariots rather than against the sultan. Thousands of peasants joined up. They also withheld tithes and services and swarmed over estates, looting and burning. Violence spread as pent-up grievances exploded.

In early March, Ypsilantis crossed into Moldavia and entered Jassy with a small band of followers from southern Russia. He took control of the government, announced a war for the liberation of all the Christians, and promised that 'a mighty power' would punish any Turkish violation of Moldavian territory. Together with the prince, he wrote to the tsar, who was at a European 'summit' congress at Laibach (Ljubljana, the capital of present-day Slovenia), asking for the immediate despatch of Russian troops.

The etairists seemed to have understood that they were creating a situation which justified Russian intervention. They misunderstood and overestimated both Russian and local support. No sooner had Ypsilantis left for Bucharest than it was learnt that the tsar had disavowed him. Panic ensued in Jassy. The prince abdicated and went to Transylvania. Both thrones were vacant. Boiers felt exposed to Turkish retribution; indifference turned to suspicion against the Greeks.

Vladimirescu was already in Bucharest, negotiating with the administration, appealing to the Porte and to the tsar, when Ypsilantis arrived. Both were in a difficult position, living off the country, causing anger as well as the flight of boier and merchant families. They were both compelled to turn to the boiers, they were afraid of one another, and they agreed to keep their forces separate. Ypsilantis, who could no longer cross the Danube, stayed in northeast Wallachia where he was brought into conflict with the locals, while Vladimirescu prepared for the defence of Bucharest, trying to restrain the social tensions he had unleashed. He strove to convince the Turks that he had nothing to do with the Greek Etairia, that he had risen against the Phanariots.

Ottoman troops moved into both Principalities at the end of May – without prior agreement with Russia. The Wallachian government fled to Transylvania. Vladimirescu and Ypsilantis retreated into the mountains. Suspected of being about to join the Turks, Vladimirescu was seized by etairists, tried and executed. His force disintegrated. Ypsilantis's retreating followers also dissolved, their remains routed in a last stand to cover their retreat to Austria and Russia. Ypsilantis himself escaped to Transylvania where the Austrians kept him interned until his death in 1828. By September the Turks were generally in control.

After the first reprisals, their occupation was more onerous than violent. The more important boiers had sought refuge across the borders, and the administration continued to function under Ottoman military governors. A politically active group of boiers entered into negotiations; they made the most of the difficult situation of the Porte which, alarmed at developments in Greece, wanted to keep the Romanian issue separate. It conceded native princes and reforms. Two new rulers were nominated who were conciliatory to the Porte – Gregory (Grigore) IV Ghica in Wallachia, and John Alexander (Ioniţa Sandu) Sturdza in Moldavia, but the Turks did not leave until the end of 1822.

The émigrés returned home between 1822 and 1826. Whether in Russian Bessarabia or in Habsburg Transylvania, they had been conscious of being still with fellow Romanians. With time on their hands, they had thought about the political future of their own homeland. For the first time, their increasingly French-influenced culture had encountered directly the Latinist culture of Romanian Uniates. This would provide the ruling class of the Principalities with the intellectual ferment for a Romanian identity. Many of them also wanted a measure of constitutional reform, if only to guarantee the nobility's political predominance.

Russia had not been consulted on the occupation or the princely appointments. She had protested but not reacted otherwise, until the new Tsar Nicholas I decided in 1826 to assert Russia's predominant influence in the Principalities, and obtained the Convention of Akkerman which reaffirmed Russia's prerogative as 'protecting power'. Russo–Turkish relations nevertheless deteriorated further with the Greek revolt. Russia declared war in 1828; her troops once again crossed the Prut. Sturdza of Moldavia was removed to Bessarabia, Ghica of Wallachia fled to Vienna, the governments of the Principalities were placed under a Russian administrator. Many boiers fled again to Transylvania, and Russian exertions caused discontent among all classes.

The Treaty of Adrianople in 1829 ended the war. All Ottoman installations and monopolies in the Principalities were abolished. The princes were to be elected for life, and they had to heed the advice of Russia on practically all aspects of government. The sultan was left with their investiture in Constantinople, a yearly tribute and the Capitulations régime. The Principalities were under a virtual Russian protectorate.

THE GREEK WAR OF INDEPENDENCE

The Greek revolt of 1821 was no less a revolution than the earlier Serbian risings, and it was much more significant. Derived from local conditions, it was backed by a broad spectrum of influences and it aroused remarkable European interest. The Ottoman way of grouping populations on the basis of religious faith, the perpetuation by the Church of the memory of Byzantium, and the continued input in some form of European influence on Greek culture, all combined to enable Greeks to formulate nationalism in the Balkans with the idea of uniting in a single polity all the compactly Greek populations of the Ottoman Empire. It remained to be seen who exactly were the

'Greeks'. Greek culture had spread in the Balkans under Turkish rule; elsewhere Orthodoxy continued even when the Greek language had gone.[6]

Much of this fermenting had taken place outside the Empire or on its fringes. The southern and insular part of present-day Greece had long been under the rule of Venice, and the Ionian Islands had continued as a self-ruled dependency until the French ended the Serenissima. The French interlude had disseminated new ideas before the Russians took over, and the British in 1815. Few in Europe cared about the other Balkan populations and their past, but the degree to which ancient Greece was revered was a vital factor in stimulating in Greeks a consciousness of their Hellenism and in exciting outside interest in their fate.

The Etairia had been able to target the Peloponnese (also known at the time as Morea) as a result of Mahmud II's determination to destroy Ali Pasha. That province had been allowed to run its own affairs after the war of 1768–74, like Serbia after 1791. Klephts preyed on both Christians and Muslims, but popular imagery saw them as defending oppressed Greeks against Turkish oppressors. In an effort to control them and to ensure the safety of passes, the Ottoman authorities made use of local Christian irregulars, even though the boundaries between these *armatoloi* and klephts were porous. The Ottoman military had mostly been withdrawn after 1819 to deal with Ali Pasha. Etairia agents nevertheless had to incite to rebellion. Local notables were loath to risk losing their privileged position; they feared Greek as much as Albanian warriors.

The fact that the initial leadership was provided by outsiders offered both advantages and disadvantages. An organization of sorts tapped a wide variety of support and resources, but such a ramified movement never really matched the aspirations and views of different regions and sections.

Its plans were pan-Balkan, but the leaders of Serbia and Montenegro did not want to be involved; in the Romanian Principalities, the rising took a turning of its own; and the revolt in the Peloponnese was sparked off by local events. Concerned with the possibility of mass Christian support for Ali Pasha, the authorities attempted to round up local leaders. There was an outburst of violence and, as usual, some of the first actions were taken against Turkish settlements. Such was the start to an ill-coordinated rising in April 1821 which spread from the Peloponnese to the islands and the mainland, and which also signalled the end of the Etairia and of Phanariot influence.

The Russian word *pogrom* – literally 'devastation', but in this context an incitement to murder by crowd manipulation – had not yet been spread around Europe, but what happened in Constantinople on Easter Day 1821 was a pogrom in all but name. The massacre of leading representatives of the Phanar élite in Constantinople, starting with the patriarch, who was hanged at the

6 How many thought of themselves as Greeks when they used Greek as a second, a 'higher' or a professional language, or when they used the Greek alphabet to write the Turkish that they spoke? The *karamanlides* were Turkish-speaking Greeks or Turkish-speaking Orthodox Christians who lived mainly in Asia Minor. They numbered some 400,000 at the time of the 1923 exchange of populations between Greece and Turkey.

gate to the patriarchate,[7] marked the end of the great age of the Phanariots. The Etairia faded into insignificance, but both left significant traces. The ideal of a Byzantine-inspired greater Greece would be adapted to the 'Great Idea' of a definitely Greek greater Greece. Many 'displaced' Phanariots and diaspora Greeks stayed on to take part in the Greek War of Independence, and to influence the constitutional forms of the emerging Greek state.

The insurgents scored initial successes. Commanded by klephtic chiefs and by Greek officers who had served in foreign armies, supported by merchant ships and pirates, they forced the few remaining Ottoman troops to withdraw to the coastal strongholds. The rising generated emotions throughout Europe. Philhellenes raised money, provided volunteers and lobbied their governments, but they had their fair share of do-gooders and cranks.

In contrast to the Serbian risings, which occurred on a small territory, where one outstanding local man was clearly in charge even in face of strong opposition, the Greek War of Independence was made up of several uncoordinated movements with no overall leader. Within three months, three regional authorities had been established. When Demetrios Ypsilantis arrived in June to take up the supreme command on behalf of the Etairia and of his brother Alexandros, whose fate was not yet known, he organized a Senate of the Peloponnese, but the Romanian failure all but destroyed him, as rival authorities appeared on the mainland. His nominally central government nevertheless summoned the first general meeting of delegates from the various parts of liberated Greece, at Epidaurus, to draw up a constitution which was proclaimed in January 1822. They left power in the hands of the notables, with a government that merely formed a cap over the regional authorities.

Each had its territory, its armed force, and a government headed by younger western-educated Phanariot aristocrats, ostentatiously dressed in Parisian fashion, trying to introduce methods of civilized warfare, diplomacy and government. With the help of their philhellenic friends, fund-raisers, advisers and volunteers, they more or less succeeded in setting up an embryonic government, equipped with the rhetoric of liberal constitutionalism and romantic nationalism, and empowered to raise a loan in London.

They were not popular with the captains who, like their Serbian counterparts, swaggered about in Turkish gold braid and an armoury of pistols and cutlasses, or the notables who, again like their Serbian counterparts, wanted to substitute their oligarchical rule for that of the Turks. By the end of 1823, the rising had degenerated into internecine war. Byron's arrival, with his reputation and the money of the Greek loan, nevertheless enabled the 'constitutional' government to be refloated.

---

7 Patriarch Gregory V, a noted opponent of Enlightenment and French revolutionary ideas, had done his best to condemn the Etairia rebels, but he had failed to ensure the loyalty of his flock. He was proclaimed a saint of the Orthodox Church a century after his death, and to this day the main gate to the patriarchal compound in the Fener (Phanar) district of Istanbul remains closed and painted black.

The formation of that government had coincided with the liquidation of Ali Pasha. The Turks had then gone on to subdue Epirus, Thessaly and Macedonia, in the first of three summer campaigns, when land forces moved into the Peloponnese, and sea forces succoured the coastal fortresses. The Ottoman army was no more than a roughly organized mass of men with a high proportion of Albanian irregulars who devastated the countryside. The insurgents dispersed, but soon gathered again to harass Ottoman troops, who withdrew at the end of the fighting season in the autumn. The Turks had recovered most of the mainland, partly through accommodations with local leaders, but failed to subdue the Peloponnese.

At the end of 1824, Mahmud II secured the help of Mehemet Ali, his nominal vassal of Egypt, in return for allowing him to take Crete and offering his son Ibrahim the governorship of the Peloponnese. The Egyptians had a French-trained army and navy. When early in 1825 they took over Crete and landed in the Peloponnese, the position of the Greek rebels, already badly weakened by their internecine struggle, became precarious. As the Egyptians were joined by Ottoman troops coming down from the mainland for their summer campaign in 1826, both employing Albanians, free Greece was reduced to the government at Nauplia, a few islands, Athens and Misolonghi on the continent.

Philhellenes did not represent official views; their governments – France, Great Britain and Russia – had thus far kept aloof. Russia did not want to be suspected of sympathy with rebels, but her authority and her interests were at stake. Where she was more directly concerned, she chose to negotiate alone with the Porte. In the case of Greece, she opted for close cooperation with the other interested powers. She liked the idea of autonomous Balkan governments under Ottoman sovereignty, and that is what she suggested for Greece as well.

The others feared that Russia might use events in Greece to extend her influence in the Ottoman Empire. In April 1826, as the Greeks formally asked the powers to intervene, Britain joined Russia to mediate on the basis of a Serbian-type settlement. France came along as the tsar demanded a combined naval intervention to press the Porte to accept. With the Treaty of London in July 1827, the three powers pledged themselves to mediate to stop the fighting and bring about a reconciliation between the Greeks and the sultan.

The nominal Greek government barely held on at Nauplia, but it was clear that the powers would intervene, and the assembly of delegates which had been convened, adjourned, re-convened and which had fallen apart since 1826, got together again to draw up a new constitution in May 1827, with a bicameral legislature and an executive 'governor' elected for seven years. He was an outsider, Ioannis Kapodistrias (1776–1831), a Corfiot patrician who had been in the diplomatic service of Russia.[8] British commanders would take over – Admiral Cochrane (a former British naval officer who had served in Chile and

8 Count Kapodistrias (Capodistria) had headed the local government of the Ionian Islands under the Russian protectorate. He had stayed on in the Russian diplomatic service, and had been in charge of the Near East at the foreign ministry until 1822 when he had withdrawn to Geneva.

Brazil) and General Church (who had commanded the Duke of York's Greek Light Infantry in the Ionian Islands and served in Naples).

The fact that the Greeks still held on, and the increased pressure of European opinion across political divides, forced the powers to step up their intervention. They instructed their Mediterranean squadrons to impose an armistice. In October 1827, as the joint fleet cruised off the Peloponnese, the atmosphere became tense with suspicion. The allied ships entered Navarino Bay where the Turkish–Egyptian fleet was anchored. An apparently unintended and still unexplained incident led to the destruction of some sixty Turkish and Egyptian vessels, and the loss of 6,000 seamen (many of them Greeks).[9]

Navarino was a turning point. The fleet had been sunk by powers who were not at war with the Ottoman Empire; there was a strong wave of anti-European feeling in Constantinople. As the powers had still not received any response to their proposals, they withdrew their ambassadors, the Porte denounced Akkerman, and the sultan pronounced a jihad against the Greeks. Eventually, in April 1828, the tsar declared war and invaded the Principalities. Great Britain and France agreed that an expedition be sent to the Peloponnese to obtain the Egyptians' evacuation. By the end of the year the Peloponnese and the Cyclades were in fact under a three-power protectorate.

In March 1829 the three powers agreed on a narrowly defined autonomous principality of Greece, paying an annual tribute to the sultan to include indemnity to Muslim landowners. After Adrianople had fallen to the Russians, the Porte gave in. It accepted the terms at the Treaty of Adrianople, but asked for further discussion on frontiers. The British now urged full independence, to reduce Russia's influence, but argued for a smaller territory to sweeten the pill for the Porte – all of which Russia accepted. In February 1830, a new Treaty of London turned Greece into the first independent state in the Balkans, sovereign but for the signatory powers who appointed themselves its 'protectors', with a territory extending to just north of the Isthmus.

In the meanwhile, Greece's first elected head of state had taken up his post in February 1828. He had arrived in a country whose independence had been secured, but whose frontiers had not been decided. He wanted to introduce a European-type centralized administration, but he did not have a base or a personal following. Like Prince Miloš in Serbia, he wanted peasant proprietors to form the backbone of the new state, but was up against the opposition of notables and captains. Unlike Miloš, he was not one of them and he badly needed money. Financial markets would do no more because of existing debts from the revolutionary period.

Believing the Etairia plans to be unrealistic, he had rejected their approaches. He had subsequently stood apart from the politics of the liberation struggle while promoting the Greek cause with his skills and contacts.
9 The classical account of the battle remains C.M. Woodhouse, *The Battle of Navarino*, London: Hodder & Stoughton, 1965, along with his lecture on the occasion of the one hundred and fiftieth anniversary of the event, edited as the introductory essay to Richard Clogg (ed.), *Balkan Society in the Age of Greek Independence*, London: Macmillan, 1981.

Without the support of the protecting powers or that of the factions at home, his plans were doomed to failure. He could not pay for the administration and the army through which he wanted to establish his government. He could not solve the problem of redistributing the lands that had been vacated by departing Turks before the greatest part was appropriated by notables. He also kept postponing the elections due under the constitution, with the excuse that they could not be held as long as Egyptian troops were in occupation, the frontiers were unsettled and there was no organized administration. He ended up by offending all factions and satisfying no one.

He carried on negotiations with the powers on the status of the Greek state which they had finally decided would be a hereditary constitutional monarchy. They were still debating the territorial limits and seeking a king. Kapodistrias suggested the British favourite, Leopold of Saxe-Coburg (1790–1865), hoping to appease the power most opposed to any extension of territory, and to encourage its candidate to work with him for better frontiers.

Prince Leopold was selected, and he did work hand in glove with Kapodistrias, but the ploy of withholding acceptance until better borders had been obtained misfired. He would later become king of the Belgians. Kapodistrias eventually secured a northern line running from Arta in the west to Volos in the east. In spite of this relative success, he had to face serious trouble in the extreme south of the Peloponnese, and was assassinated soon after he had at last felt obliged to call elections in 1831.

The chaos that followed was mitigated only by the presence of a residual French force. The elections produced an assembly that split into two rival governments, and factions fought. The powers started by recognizing the 'legitimate' government at Nauplia, then decided on a king in the person of Otto (to become King Othon), the younger son of the philhellenic king of Bavaria, who posed a series of conditions. Agreement was reached in May 1832; at the Treaty of Constantinople in July the sultan accepted both independence and the Arta–Volos line.

It was high time. Roumeliot guerrillas had invaded the Peloponnese, the writ of the Nauplia government did not extend beyond the town, and fighting continued until the end of the year. Styled *basileus* in Greek, like the Byzantine emperors, the new king finally landed in Nauplia in February 1833, protected by soldiers and ships of the three powers, to a kingdom of some 800,000 inhabitants (between a third and a quarter of all the Greeks of the Ottoman Empire), devastated by a decade of revolt, war and occupation, unable to survive without its protecting powers. Such were the small beginnings of modern Greece.

EMPIRES CONNECTED ACROSS PERIPHERIES

International treaties had by then acknowledged Moldavia, Wallachia and Serbia as self-governing principalities of the Ottoman Empire, and placed their status under the protection of Russia. Greece had become an independent kingdom, the first in the Balkans, but under three-power protection. Although there had been no general rising in the Balkans, the revolutionary period of the first three decades of the century had brought forth native leaderships in three peripheral areas that could negotiate with the Porte and with the powers. From the breakdown of the traditional Ottoman order, there had emerged the desire for self-rule to provide ordered government.

A period of violence had been necessary to achieve this. Risings started with the massacre of ordinary Muslim inhabitants, as hajduk acts of revenge, or as guerrilla tactics to compel the authorities to react. The insurgents' counter-terror in Serbia was such that the 'Turkish' population fled; the subsequent repression was mostly the work of those of them who returned. In Moldavia, Turkish civilians were killed by ill-disciplined etairists, and Ottoman troops coming ostensibly to restore order also turned to reprisals.

The Greek War of Independence was the bloodiest of all the uprisings. Nervous at having to cope at the same time with the Romanian adventure and with Muslim rebels, the Turks committed ruthless massacres and tolerated mob action, in Macedonia, Thrace, Cyprus, in Anatolia itself and in Constantinople. They relied on those very armed men who had initially sparked off the insur-rections. Greek fighters retaliated on liberated territory, particularly when the fortress towns fell with their refugee population. Perhaps as many as 15,000 of the 40,000 Muslims of the Peloponnese were killed over the period. It was soon assumed that Christians and 'Turks', could no longer live together, par-ticularly after the Muslims had been divested of their privileges. Revolutionaries also used cruel measures to force uncooperative notables or peasants to join them; the peasant jacquerie unleashed in Oltenia was even more violent.

In the province of Belgrade, local conditions had caused an uprising which the etairists' plans could not accommodate. In the Principalities, their plan-ning led only to the restoration of rule by the native nobility. It was in Greece, however, that ideals of a restored Byzantium or of an all-embracing democratic Hellenism foundered. Nevertheless, there had been links, and sparks ignited by the coming together of local conditions, broader programmes and outside influences. Eventually, in spite of the historical inspirations, there emerged nuclei of polities that aspired to the status of nation-states on the western European model.

In one manner or another, the whole peninsula had felt the effects of that revolutionary period. The whole of Turkey-in-Europe had suffered. Apart from the territorial losses represented by the Greek kingdom and by the now three Danubian Principalities, the clans of Montenegro considered that they had never been part of the Ottoman Empire. The Greek revolt had been of particular concern, because of the large Greek and Christian communities spread throughout the Empire, but Muslim lords had rebelled no less than peasants. They were difficult to deal with where they had local roots, as in Albania and Bosnia.

All established forces wanted to preserve the empire after its self-contained equilibrium had been upset; reformers and conservatives became adversaries

41

in a struggle for the same cause. Reacting to defeat and disintegration, reformers in government wanted to reorganize it, thus beginning the trend that would be known as *Tanzimat* or reorganization.[10] They faced the opposition of vested interests and ideological hard-liners.

The reformers' principal concern was to establish a modern army. Only those who had appropriated vast chunks of land, who had an old-established base in provinces undisturbed by central government, or who ran their own private armies, could provide levies for the sultan, and they opposed reform. In opposing rebellious Christians with such troops, the Porte was in danger of falling out of the frying-pan into the fire.

As he tackled Christian rebellion, along with that of Muslim warlords, and as he prepared to eliminate the dangerously useless janissaries, Mahmud II (1808–39) had no choice but to appeal to an even stronger yet still loyal vassal, Mehemet Ali. When in 1826 the janissaries actually staged a revolt, the sultan was able to destroy them in a bloodbath that took place all over the European provinces. One of their last bastions of resistance was Sarajevo. Conservative forces opposed to reform had lost a military auxiliary, but the Porte had not yet acquired an army. It had had to give in to the demands of the new native leaders and of the powers.

The Balkan peoples still moved in search of food and security, in war and peace, from lowland to upland and back, across provincial borders and across state borders. South Slavs and Romanians straddled the boundary between the Ottoman Empire and the Austrian Empire. The Habsburgs' Military Frontier took in a large part of Croatia and Transylvania. Its creation had been strategic and its agriculture was backward. Policy encouraged isolated and largely self-sufficient communal holdings, free from seigneurial obligations; heavy indirect taxation, after the initial tax-free period of settlement, and military service were a strain on the economy.

Thus shielded from an Ottoman Empire that no longer threatened it militarily, the Habsburg Monarchy was a state of law, its limitations and its authoritarianism notwithstanding; what ethnic grievances there were did not yet turn to revolution. Indeed, it was largely through Vienna that romantic Europe rediscovered the Southern Slavs. It was there that Jernej Kopitar (1780–1844), the polyglot Slovene scholar and imperial librarian, presided over a circle of Slav scholars. He urged them to study the language and poetry of their peoples, and he passed the results to the writers of western Europe.

Napoleon had also made his mark, by his acquisition between 1805 and 1809 of a string of territories on the eastern Adriatic, from Carinthia to the Bay of Cattaro (Kotor), administered from Ljubljana as the Illyrian Provinces of the French Empire. They all reverted to Austrian rule after Napoleon's fall, but French laws had tried to rationalize the messy mixture of the *ancien régime*,

---

10 The word has the same meaning as the Russian *perestroyka*. Once inner change and outside pressure had combined to destroy the self-contained polity and economy of the empire, Ottoman, just like later Soviet, reformers wanted to preserve it by reorganizing it.

introduced civil and religious equality, modern schools and the official use of the Slavonic vernacular. As in the Ionian Islands, the stimuli of the French interlude had a disturbing effect, and they acted retrospectively when the 'Illyrian' years came to be seen as an experiment which had brought Slovenes, Croats and Serbs together in one political unit removed from their traditional political masters.

The reverse of rule of law and scholarly research was that between 73 and 85 per cent of the South Slav and Romanian population of the Habsburg dominions outside the Military Frontier were dependent peasants on the estates of Germanic and, even more so, Hungarian lords, in peripheral, recently reconquered or acquired lands hardly integrated into the general economic life of the Empire. They were poorly represented in the nobility and in the commercial or industrial class.

The territory inhabited by the Slovenes was fully part of the hereditary Alpine domains of the Habsburgs, with direct access to the Vienna market and the expansion of Trieste. A growing Slovene element was joining the mainly German urban population, but the landholding nobility remained Germanic when it was not Italian. Dalmatia (with Dubrovnik) was also turned into an Austrian crown land after the fall of Napoleon. This was part of the Habsburg policy of juggling with its South Slav and other populations, to counter the attractions of liberal and nationalist ideas, of an autonomous Serbia, of a Montenegro which was autonomous in practice, and of Russian influence, and to prevent the strengthening of Hungary.

The link of inner Croatia and Slavonia with Hungary had been renewed or retained after the reconquest. The predominant class there was the landed nobility, 4 per cent of the population, concentrated in 'Civil' Croatia, where three-quarters of all arable land was held under a 'feudal' title, the greater part as crown grants, small to medium holdings of no more than 400 hectares, whose lords were dependent on the tithes and labour services they obtained from their peasants.

If the nobility remained Croat at its lower end, it became increasingly Hungarian or Magyarized in its upper reaches. Lagging behind the affluent estate-owners of inner Hungary, the nobles were attached to traditional institutions, primarily concerned with their position as the privileged order that dominated local government and the Sabor. The towns had a mixed population with a strong Germanic element. Apart from Zagreb which reached 15,000 in 1837, no town exceeded 5,000 inhabitants.

More specifically Croatian demands would come from the lower sections of the nobility, particularly from its educated young. They shared many of the ideas of their generation throughout Europe, and felt that Croatia had given in too much to Hungary for the sake of joint resistance to centralization from Vienna. Caught between the politically repressive measures adopted generally in the Austrian Empire after 1815 and the rising pressure of Hungarian nationalism, they began to question the nature of Croatia's association with Hungary. Their thoughts turned to a more extended Croatia that would incorporate 'Military' Croatia and Dalmatia, and to a wider South Slav cultural community based on similarities of speech.

Another territory associated with Hungary was Transylvania. Ringed on three sides by the Carpathians, it had been a sanctuary for emigrants, but few were attracted to it after it had been recovered from Turkish overlordship at the end of the seventeenth century. The autonomy of the principality had been limited. Tension had developed between Vienna and the predominantly Hungarian nobility, which had been strong enough to resist efforts to incorporate it fully into the Monarchy. Hungarians represented some 24 per cent of its population (with over 12 per cent Germans). The Romanians were over 63 per cent, the bulk of them peasants, but they were not one of the 'recognized nations' of Transylvania, and thus not part of its political order. Furthermore, they were divided religiously between Orthodox and Uniates. The demand to be acknowledged as a 'nation' would come from the better placed Uniate clergy, who borrowed arguments from their Roman contacts about their Roman origins, to counter Hungarian historical claims that the Romanians were newcomers to Transylvania.

The South Slavs and the Romanians under Habsburg rule thus found themselves in territories variously integrated, from the hereditary Alpine crown lands to Transylvania, through the recent acquisition of Dalmatia, the lands of the Military Border and Civil Croatia. Only the Croatian lower nobility and the Uniate Romanian clergy could as yet raise grievances linked more specifically to ethnic communities, at the time when native self-government was being set up in Serbia, in the Danubian Principalities and in Greece. There was considerable movement between the two empires. Romanian peasants crossed the Carpathians to the Principalities in order to escape religious harassment and the impositions of Hungarian lords in Transylvania or to the Habsburg Military Frontier in order to escape the impositions of Wallachian and Moldavian boiers. Merchants moved from the towns of Vojvodina and Transylvania to Belgrade and Bucharest. Serbian, Romanian and Greek writers went to Vienna. Serbian and Greek businessmen from Austria financed the insurgents; volunteers crossed the Save and the Danube to help them while rebels or boiers from Serbia and the Principalities sought refuge in the Habsburg lands.

CHAPTER 3

Self-rule, constitutions and revolutions, 1830–56

The emergence of the nuclei of nation-states in imitation of European models. The Principalities, autonomous Serbia and the Greek kingdom. Collective European guarantee. Reorganization and revolution in the empires.

Several self-governing territories had emerged after the Napoleonic wars on the Danubian border and on the maritime fringe of the Ottoman Empire. The Balkans were thus divided into three zones – the new so-called national states, the territories left under direct Ottoman rule, and the lands of the Habsburgs. The whole peninsula felt the consequences of that half-century of revolution framed by the French events of 1789 and 1830. The principle of legitimacy of the international order had been accommodated to the new realities by persuading the sultan to endorse them through treaties with the powers. Ottoman sovereignty over these territories was either abolished or reduced to little more than a fiction, replaced by the protection of one or more of the powers.

Serbia, Greece and the Danubian Principalities became states that tried to consolidate their internal régimes by adopting institutions inspired by those recently introduced in western Europe. In formulating principles of government, in limiting the powers of the ruler, in formalizing the supremacy of the oligarchy, they were influenced by the revised *Charte* of the French July Monarchy. Paradoxically, it was autocratic Russia who promoted constitutional government in the region, as she wanted more amenable, hence less powerful, rulers, and as she perceived ordered rule by the propertied class to be the most effective way of achieving her aims.[1]

In spite of distortions derived from grafting western models onto societies that had evolved in wholly different circumstances, one should not be unduly

---

1 Russia's reservations were semantic. She did not want the fundamental laws to be called anything which sounded like the French *constitution* (which would be the case in Russian or Romanian). In the Principalities, the *règlements organiques* were nevertheless the first effective Balkan constitutions. The Serbian *ustav* and Greek *syntagma* were acceptable, as they could be translated as 'rules', even though the Greek constitution was modelled on the most advanced constitution – the Belgian one of 1831.

critical of the institutional set-up of the Balkan states by the mid-nineteenth century as being no more than imitative trappings, without comparing them with other European states of the time. Their intentions were not democratic, even though Greece was the first to adopt virtual manhood suffrage, but the 'nation-state' was revolutionary in so far as it stood up against the principle of empire. Their nationalism was usually born of opposition to imperial rule. They were founded on a unity moulded out of varying doses of religion and language. They separated their ecclesiastical organization from the ecumenical patriarchate in Ottoman Constantinople, and subordinated it to the nation-state. They purified and differentiated their written language by going to the past or to the vernacular.

Everything inherited from the Ottoman masters became incompatible with the new national identity – except for a large, imponderable and unacknow-ledged measure of social and political mentality. All those who considered themselves Ottomans could not fit into the new states. Apart from those massacred and expelled in the initial violence, they left because they could not accept the new order or were made to feel unwelcome.

The nation-state implied a conceptualization of territory. The Principality of Serbia, the Kingdom of Greece and the United Principalities were the states of Serbs, Greeks and Romanians respectively. More precisely, they were the nuclei of such states, for they did not include all those who thought of them-selves as, or were thought to be, Serbs, Greeks and Romanians. The new centralized state that mobilized resources and projected a national idea was at variance with the old, local, parochial, provincial, intra- or even trans-imperial conceptions of the privileged but dependent Christian notables, who now had to serve or to lead the native government. It also offered peasants a framework to enable them to integrate into a national culture, a national economy and national politics, even if these were city-led and developed at the expense of their traditional values.

Balkan nationalism in the first half of the nineteenth century was primarily a cultural phenomenon, but in a world economy that was still essentially com-mercial, the state also responded to the need for a national market. Follow-ing their emancipation, the embryonic states embarked on an arduous struggle for markets, with long-term visions of a bigger territory embracing their whole ethnic community, independent of this or that power – essentially Russia and/or Austria.

Russia, once she had overcome Napoleon, found herself challenged by the emergence of the Balkan states and the threatened collapse of the Ottoman Empire, caught between her legitimist relations with other powers and her religious link with the Balkan populations. Nicholas I (1825–55) encapsulates the tension. After the Peace of Adrianople (1829), he embarked on a new policy of indirect ascendancy over the whole of the Ottoman Empire.

The dispute with Napoleon III's France over the Holy Places, which led to the Crimean War, originated with Nicholas I's wish to reaffirm Russia's author-ity in the area, as well as her reputation as an Orthodox and a conservative power. The defeat at the hands of the alliance between Turkey and western powers tarnished Russia's prestige in the Balkans. The Treaty of Paris (1856) that ended the war put an end to her unilateral guarantee; it placed Moldavia, Wallachia and Serbia under the collective guarantee of all the powers. Through their disagreement over the Romanian question, it also opened the door to the principle of self-determination by the decision to consult the wishes of the population.

When Russia was checked in the Balkans, both Turkey and Austria tried to push their way back. In the Ottoman Empire, the Tanzimat reform movement had taken a serious turn. The decline was checked, even though opposition continued, laws were diluted in their application, and the national states attracted increasing attention. In the Habsburg lands, efficient government prevented serious revolutionary outbursts until 1848, when conflicting ethnic aspirations were caught between the Hungarian nobility's compound of historic and ethnic claims, on the one hand, and the political and military acumen of the imperial court, on the other. The one lasting outcome, apart from an increased ethnic awareness across the borders, was the final abolition of peasant servitudes.

THE PRINCIPALITIES UNDER ORGANIC STATUTES

After Navarino had given an international dimension to the Greek revolt, Russia again occupied the Principalities until the Peace of Adrianople. The sultan agreed to abide by earlier treaties. Moldavia and Wallachia would each be granted an Organic Statute (*règlement organique*), and be ruled by an elected prince, confirmed by the two signatory powers. They were freed of the Porte's pre-emption of products and allowed to trade freely. The fortresses on the left bank of the Danube were returned; Muslims still holding property were given eighteen months to sell and leave. Turkey was to pay Russia a huge war indemnity; until that was done Russian troops would remain in occupation.

The war had all but destroyed what remained of pro-Russian feelings. With peace, however, the Russian military became enlightened. General Count Pavel Kiselev (1788–1872) was sent to Bucharest as commander of the army of occupation and 'president-plenipotentiary of the divans (or councils) of Moldavia and Wallachia', with responsibility for carrying out the peace terms. He found the land disorganized, prey to disease and famine. He solicited local help and took immediate steps to deal with urgent problems. His most important accomplishment was the introduction of the Statutes. Drafted by a joint Moldo-Wallachian commission, vetted in St Petersburg, endorsed by extraordinary assemblies in Jassy and Bucharest, they were promulgated, in 1831 for Wallachia, and in 1832 for Moldavia. They were the first effective Balkan constitutions.

They balanced the prince's authority against a General Assembly. The latter represented a narrow boier electorate (around forty members for some 3,000 voters in Wallachia; fewer in Moldavia). Elected every five years, it approved legislation and the budget; it had the right of representation to the prince, to the suzerain power, and to the protecting power, Russia. The prince was elected for life from among greater boiers by a somewhat larger Extraordinary Assembly that included delegates of merchants and artisans. He appointed ministers and officials, retained an absolute veto over legislation and the right to prorogue the Assembly with the assent of the two powers. A professional civil service, a uniform poll tax, an independent judiciary, a streamlined administration and state education were instituted.

Russia perceived ordered rule by the propertied class as the best way to ensure that the territories would remain a buffer under her influence. This approach fitted in with her new policy of indirect ascendancy over the Ottoman Empire, established with the Treaty of Hünkyar-Iskelesi in 1833. The Romanian arrangements were sanctioned in January 1834. The sultan issued the Statutes as acts of his own, the tsar agreed to evacuate, and they decided to appoint the first princes for a seven-year term – 'for this time only'. The Russian army began to withdraw; Kiselev left in April 1834.[2]

Russia's influence over the Principalities was more pervasive than any interference anywhere in the Balkans, even though she did not have the resources to invest in economic penetration. Her control was exercised through the consul general in Bucharest, assisted by his adjunct in Jassy. Factions revolved around the princes, the boier assemblies and the Russian consulates. This made government more open to interference, which aroused resentment.

So little did Russia trust the boiers that the two powers began by disregarding the Statutes in order to appoint the first princes – men who were affiliated to the Russian court, but determined to modernize. Alexander Ghica (1795–1862) of Wallachia was the eighth reigning prince of his family. Anxious to be a strong and a 'national' ruler, he chafed under tutelage and found it impossible to cooperate with his legislature. Michael Sturdza (1795–1884) of Moldavia, from an even more illustrious and richer family, cultivated relations with Russia and faced less opposition. The princes improved administration, roads, health and education.

No sooner had the Statutes been confirmed than Russia started to insist on an 'additional article' – to prevent any modification without the approval of the two courts. Sturdza easily obtained the consent of the Moldavian assembly, but not Ghica in Wallachia, who had to apply pressure. He antagonized liberals and nationalists, and lost the support of the two courts. Taking up complaints, they deposed him in 1842.

His regularly elected successor was George Bibescu (1805–75), Paris-educated and not devoid of romantic nationalism. The great achievement of his reign was to agree with Moldavia to abolish customs barriers, to adopt mutual citizenship laws, and the formal use of the name 'United Principalities'. The

2 He would later be the tsar's ambassador to Napoleon III from 1856 to 1862, and live on in Paris in retirement until his death. He had built the avenue into Bucharest that was in 1843 named in his honour the Chaussée Kiseleff, and that became the city's version of the Paris avenue now called after Marshal Foch.

occupation had dealt with the Principalities as a single unit, the Statutes explicitly referred to the '*fusion du peuple moldo-valaque*' and unification became almost an official programme. Otherwise there was no end to strife with the legislature, which made him more reliant on the Russians and cost him whatever esteem he might have started off with.

Nevertheless, the period was one of change. The removal of Ottoman restrictions made possible the full exploitation of the rich Danubian plains and their opening up to trade. The end of war and disorders, measures against disease, greater fiscal stability and a more orderly administration reduced emigration, and even attracted immigration. The population rose from a total of some three million around 1830 to over four million in the late 1850s. A flow of people from the countryside, where the land available for agriculture was no longer sufficient to feed the population, made the increase particularly noticeable in towns.

New cities developed and older ones expanded. The two ports at the mouths of the Danube – Galaţi for Moldavia and Brăila for Wallachia – reached a combined population of 40,000 by 1840. Bucharest was the biggest Balkan capital city, its population increasing from 70,000 at the beginning of the 1830s to 120,000 by 1859.[3] As the urban population grew, so its composition altered. By the middle of the century, businesses and crafts had become the dynamic force behind the development of towns.

An important part of the middle-class element was technically foreign, particularly in Moldavia. Greeks were losing ground to non-Ottomans – Jews and assorted Habsburg immigrants (including Romanians). The permissive provisions of Adrianople attracted Jews from Russia and Austria. Barred as foreigners from owning land and even from residing in the countryside as merchants or artisans, they settled in larger towns, or worked outside existing structures – running inns, for instance.

Boiers were keen to extend their control over as much land as possible, to produce wheat for export. The Statutes sanctioned their absolute proprietary rights over one-third of their estates. Dependent peasants' right to the use of land was limited to two-thirds, where landlords were still bound to provide land in exchange for tithes and labour services. Relations were defined, but the boiers in effect managed to reduce existing holdings, and most peasants had to lease more from the estate.

Production was increased, but agriculture could not satisfy both the growing demands of the international market and the needs of an expanding population, because there was no significant change in organization or methods. Industry remained modest, as capital accumulation was small, and used to purchase land, to finance trade or to spend on personal needs. Food processing was the most important branch, offering easy returns to merchants and estate lessees.

3 As figures differ quite widely, I go along with Lampe (86) in taking David Turnock's findings ('Bucharest: The Selection and Development of the Romanian Capital', in *Scottish Geographic Magazine*, 86, 1970, 59–62). Jassy was about half the size of Bucharest and equal to Salonika.

The bulk of grain continued to be produced by peasants, who cleared or rented additional land. By the middle of the century, about half of all estate land in Moldavia, and more in Wallachia, was leased out through managers. Landlords were satisfied to entrust production to their peasants, but were keen to extend their property rights, to take advantage of the rise in land values by leasing to the highest bidder. Accustomed to a predominantly cattle economy, peasants found it more difficult to benefit from a commercial grain economy.

In spite of its consolidated political power, the nobility was being undermined by social and cultural forces. Keith Hitchins speaks of an accelerated *embourgeoisement* of the lower-rank boiers who managed their own estates.[4] Within the great families the gap between generations continued to increase as more and more sons returned from study in the west.

The practice of sending their scions to be educated in France took a firm hold among the wealthy boiers. They had fluent French and saw themselves as being already part of Europe. Whereas their Greek and Serbian counterparts, on tight government grants and with only the rudiments of French, had to spend a couple of years studying hard to return with a degree that would provide them with employment, the Romanians had no such limitations. They had access to salons; they frequented literary circles, artistic cafés, left-wing political coteries. They met Polish exiles around Prince Adam Czartoryski who talked of Poland's mission to lead the struggle against Russia. They formed revolutionary circles; they struck a chord in urban society at home.

Modernization favoured the growth of a politicized national awareness, as government provided a framework of public education, with emphasis on teacher training and on higher education through the princely academies. The representative Romanian writers of the time came from the upper classes and believed that literature had a didactic value. The theory of Roman descent was accepted among the educated; history was drawn to past glories. Its best known practitioner was the future statesman Mihail Kogălniceanu (1817–91).[5]

Societies for the promotion of the Romanian language, literature and music brought together like-minded intellectuals, and veered to a political agenda. Their romantic ideals were matched by their remoteness from the 'people'; yet by 1840 they had moved from the old juridical conception of the 'nation' based on boier privileges to the idea of an all-embracing ethnic community, which led them to support the use of the Romanian language against the 'gallomania' of princes and aristocrats.

The young nobles returning from abroad were the prime movers of an opposition that linked independence, liberalism and a pro-western stance. By the late 1840s, the need for change was expressed in almost all political circles. As great boiers skirmished against the princes or tried to persuade them to initiate moderate reforms, peasants reacted with acts of violence against mounting

4 Keith Hitchins, *The Romanians 1774–1866*, Oxford: Clarendon Press, 1996, 178.
5 His *Histoire de la Valachie, de la Moldavie et des Valaques transdanubiens* was published in French in Berlin in 1837.

obligations compounded by natural calamities, with the French-educated young boiers somewhere in between. The European events provided the spark and the setting for the explosion of 1848.

All the Romanians in Paris participated in the demonstrations of late February there. When events in Pest and Vienna brought revolution closer to home, they returned, arriving in Bucharest and Jassy at the beginning of April. In Jassy it was all over in three days. A meeting drew up a petition proposing constitutional reforms, which the prince partly accepted before proceeding to arrests. In Bucharest action was delayed by the fear of Russia, the hope of winning over the prince, and the despatch of emissaries to reassure Constantinople, until a revolutionary committee decided to rally the peasants and impose a revolution.

A 'Charter of Romanian freedom' was read out on 21 June to a large crowd gathered at Islaz in Oltenia. It was an ambiguous mix of constitutional ideals and land reforms. The 'forty-eighters' went on to Bucharest, where they publicly burnt the Statute and the Book of the Nobility. The prince agreed to sign their charter and accepted their provisional government, but abdicated and left when told to do so by the Russian consul. The promise to end labour services, with its electrifying effect on the peasants, threatened an economic catastrophe. Left on its own, a divided provisional government took fright as rumours of Russian and Ottoman intervention increased. It gave up all talk of union and of agrarian reform, emphasized its loyalty to the Porte and turned to the western powers.

Under Russian pressure, Turkey agreed on a joint intervention. Ottoman troops entered Bucharest in late September; the revolutionary government collapsed. Russian troops followed, relegating the Turks to the position of observers. The two powers formalized their arrangements at Balta-Liman near Constantinople on 1 May 1849. They revised the Statutes: the princes were again to be designated for seven years by the two courts jointly; elected assemblies were replaced by appointed consultative councils. The occupation would continue until order had been restored.

Bibescu had abdicated and left Wallachia; Sturdza followed. Their successors were in Wallachia Bibescu's brother Barbu Ştirbei (1799–1869), who had taken his adoptive parents' surname, and in Moldavia another Ghica, Gregory V Alexander (1807–57). The Russians did not leave until 1851, only to return in 1853. Despite their handicap, the new princes, who were efficient administrators, pursued a programme of reform.

The wildfire of 1848 had extended as far as the Romanian Principalities because of the combined effects of events in Paris and in Transylvania. Ideally, for Romanian intellectuals it signified the triumph of the idea of 'nation', as they invoked the right of their ethnic community to self-determination – in Moldavia and Wallachia by throwing off the Russian protectorate and by merging; in Transylvania, Hungarian Banat and Austrian Bukovina by uniting all Romanians under the Habsburg crown into a single unit. They contemplated the possibility of uniting Romanians on both sides of the Carpathians.

51

There had, however, been more immediate and contradictory priorities in the different territories. In Transylvania, Romanian leaders came out on the side of the Habsburg emperor and of Russia, against the Hungarians. Even the 'smaller Romania' of the Principalities did not materialize under the young intellectuals who failed to implement anything of interest for the people in whose name they spoke.

Nevertheless, the idealism of the 'forty-eighters' persisted. They concentrated on the unification of the Principalities under a foreign prince. They recognized that rule by native princes led to instability, and that Russia rather than Turkey had become the chief obstacle. Most of them were gathered again in Paris. Their propaganda was intensive and successful; they aroused a good deal of sympathy in many European capitals. Yet their action affected little the course of events in their homeland until the Crimean War.

The great crisis over, Russia stepped up her policy of hegemony over the Ottoman Empire. Worsening relations came to focus on a dispute over Russia's right to intervene on behalf of the sultan's Orthodox subjects. When in 1853 Russia moved troops into the Principalities yet again, it was nothing to do with these territories, but it was to increase pressure on the Porte and reinforce her influence in the Balkans. Russian and Ottoman armies faced each other during six months of 'phoney war' on the Danube,[6] until Britain and France declared war in 1854 and real operations eventually started in the Crimea.

Russia had expected gratitude for the help she had given the Habsburgs in 1849, but the latter had viewed Russian action as a threat to their own interests. After trying to mediate, Austria had obtained from the Porte permission to secure the evacuation of the Principalities as best she knew. She demanded that the Russians evacuate; they complied by the end of September 1854.

The Porte, which had formally annulled Russia's special prerogative, tried to twist the agreement so as to restore its own position, and sent troops. Austria countered by moving in her own army under the formal umbrella of a joint occupation. Once the western powers had invaded the Crimea, Ottoman troops were transferred there, and Austria's cover that she was acting for Europe became a reality. Fearing their attraction for her own Romanian subjects, she was making a definite bid for supremacy over the Principalities. Although her efficient administration was seen as a lesser evil than Russia's, the princes were far from docile. Nor were Britain and France entirely happy with her rôle.

Exhaustion and the death of Tsar Nicholas I brought the war to an end. Russia accepted the terms put to her, and the peace congress opened in Paris. Some two hundred Romanians there lobbied hard for union. They had won over Napoleon III. Sardinia and Prussia backed France, and so, oddly enough, did Russia, to acquire French sympathy and recover some goodwill among the Romanians. Turkey was the firmest opponent, followed by Austria and Britain.

6 A French historian of the Balkans has applied the term retrospectively to this and other such *drôles de guerres* (Bernard Lory, 'La Serbie et la guerre de Crimée', in *Ilija Garašanin (1812–1874) – medjunarodni skup*, Belgrade: Serbian Academy, 1991, 83).

The treaty signed in Paris on 30 March 1856 reaffirmed Ottoman sovereignty and the privileges of the Principalities, and ended the exclusive Russian tutelage. The Congress established a procedure for revising the Organic Statutes, through the election of ad hoc advisory assemblies, made up of representatives of all interests, to express the wishes of the population. A European commission of enquiry would make recommendations on the future form of government, and advise the powers before they made a final decision. All foreign troops were to be withdrawn. Regulations were made for the navigation of the Danube; Russia had to cede her hold on the mouths of the river.

There were further delays. As both princes had placed themselves at the head of the movement for unity, Vienna and Constantinople did not want them reappointed. The Porte itself chose regents in yet another infringement of the Statutes. Austria made her withdrawal contingent on the satisfactory delimitation of the new Russo-Moldavian border. It was not before January 1857 that the powers settled the boundary dispute and called on Austria to withdraw. Final solutions regarding Moldavia and Wallachia had been postponed, but the right of self-determination had been tacitly recognized for the first time.

AUTONOMOUS SERBIA

Serbia, too, after 1830 was no longer insurgent territory. Smaller than the nominally independent Kingdom of Greece, it was an autonomous principality, its status protected by treaties between the Porte and Russia. This had been achieved by a native leader who had exploited, but kept out of, trouble elsewhere. A governor still resided as representative of the sultan's sovereignty, with direct authority over six garrisoned fortresses and over the remaining Turkish inhabitants. The latter were now given five years (and longer in Belgrade) to dispose of their property and leave, but they were under pressure: their numbers dwindled rapidly.

The risings had left the economy crippled. Rampaging Albanian and Bosnian troops had sacked the territory in the interval. The urban-based east–west transit trade had all but collapsed. The country was depopulated, but it was secure and there was plenty of land available. Peasants left the restrictive confines of the extended family community. They came into the lowlands from the hills and from surrounding provinces. Prince Miloš's offer of free land with three years' tax exemption caused a land rush.

Whereas there was continued emigration from independent Greece, autonomous Serbia went on attracting immigrants, who probably accounted for more than half the population increase to just under one million in 1854. The urban population in its broadest definition amounted to barely 50,000 out of a total of 700,000–800,000 in the late 1830s, with only two concentrations above 10,000, one of which was Belgrade, with a population of perhaps 18,000.

The spread of grain cultivation followed, as the population needed wheat to feed itself, and corn to feed the pigs for export once forests were cleared and acorns no longer available. Productivity, however, did not rise. There were no large estates to demonstrate more advanced techniques, even though local headmen had appropriated the best vacant and reclaimed lands, and availed themselves of free labour services formerly owed to local authorities. Together with traders and officials who had risen in Miloš's service, they formed something of an élite. Longing to model their way of living on that of the Wallachian boiers, they aspired to a restoration on their behalf of the Ottoman fiefs.

This was nipped in the bud by Miloš, who wanted no intermediaries between his paternalism and the people. Peasants had clung to the notion that the land belonged to the tillers, even when they were paying dues to sipahis. The disappearance of chiftlik ownership, followed in 1830 by the legal abolition of sipahi fiefs in return for compensation out of the annual tribute, meant that the peasants did not have to pay explicitly for their title to the land. Sipahi land was simply turned over to its tillers, and Miloš abolished labour services to officials. Smallholding remained the rule in Serbia, although peasants soon became indebted to small usurers.

The livestock-based export trade was Serb-dominated, but imports and what transit trade remained were still the preserve of Greeks and others. Yet towns were going native, as incoming Serbs became a clear majority of the urban population, of Belgrade in particular, with its officials, traders, craftsmen and smaller professionals.

Miloš was a 'new' man in that he had quickly halted the trend towards a native feudalism. He had also countered the peasants' anarchic self-centredness. He was ruthlessly building a permanent centralized authority, by taking from both inherited Ottoman and traditional local authority. Since the principality with its low degree of literacy could not supply many administrative personnel, he offered employment to Serbs from the Habsburg dominions. He was no Phanariot, Corfiot or Bavarian head of state, just an illiterate yet skilful local leader who had obtained authority in the same way as he had obtained autonomy. National hero, liberator and leader, he ruled with a household and with as few bureaucrats as possible. His political mentality remained that of a Turkish pasha.

Assemblies of notables continued to meet, not unlike early English parliaments, called by the prince twice a year to authorize taxation and expenditure. There were also extraordinary assemblies which could number several thousand, at which local officials brought with them delegations of notables, to give approval to some important measures or to transmit instructions from above.

As long as Serbia was insurgent, Miloš's paternalism was tolerated. He exploited popular dissatisfaction against the notables. The revolution had quickly come to be seen as a 'struggle for freedom', interpreted in a variety of ways – freedom from the Turks, but also freedom of full security of person, property and status, freedom to trade without monopolies or restrictions, and freedom to influence government. With territory and status settled, Miloš had to face opposition. New men were rising, some with more education and with other ideas. Dissatisfied at finding themselves under a native despotism, the notables carried the peasants along by promising legal security, freedom to trade and lower taxation.

They demanded that the prince's powers be limited by a constitution, and so the opposition came to be known as the 'constitutional' party. It disguised its principal demand, for a guaranteed participation in government, by coupling it to the peasants' wishes, and found support in Ottoman and Russian officialdom.

There had already been a number of notable-led local risings before a more serious revolt in 1835 decided Miloš to grant a constitution rather than provide Russia and the Porte with an excuse to intervene. Accepted without a debate by an assembly, it satisfied opinion at home – the political ambitions of the notables, the very simple wishes of the peasants, and those few educated persons who looked up to the more advanced polities of Europe. It formulated rights. A Council chosen by the prince would share with him legislative and executive powers. A National Assembly, elected from the most worthy citizens, would meet annually to approve the budget and make petitions. A special law would determine the electoral system.

The sovereign Ottoman Porte and the protecting Russian government raised objections. They wanted a fundamental law to circumscribe Miloš's power, not a constitution granted by the prince with attributes of statehood, that allowed him to manoeuvre between a council and an assembly. Miloš was only too happy to shelve it. Russia proposed to help draw up a statute on the lines of those introduced in the Romanian Principalities; the Porte invited him to come to Constantinople for talks.

During his visit to Constantinople in the summer of 1835, he saw something of the workings of the Porte and of power diplomacy. He already nurtured a vision of gathering areas of Slav settlement. He saw this, and his consequent raising to a higher dignity, as a way of escaping the threat of partition of the Ottoman Empire and as a way out of his domestic predicament. As the opposition enlisted the support of the Porte, of Russia and of Austria, he thought of France and Britain. For a while in the late 1830s, Palmerston envisaged using Serbia in a scheme to contain the advance of Russian influence over the Ottoman Empire. British diplomacy failed, but it nevertheless opened up Serbia for the interaction of European diplomacy in the future. It also led to the popular belief that Miloš had tried to sell Serbia to Great Britain.

The settlement worked out at the end of 1838 took the form of an act of the sultan's granting an organic statute to his province of Serbia. It gave the prince hereditary status, and reduced his prerogative to that of a modern constitutional monarch, by introducing what was virtually government by 'Prince in Council'. Every decision had to be taken in agreement with a Council of State of seventeen eminent and representative personalities chosen by the prince, and irremovable unless they contravened laws. There was no assembly.

55

The 'Turkish constitution' (as it was called in Serbia) was promulgated in Belgrade in February 1839. Four months later, Miloš abdicated and left for exile. Serbia was free from the liberator-prince who had freed her from direct Ottoman domination. The constitution and Miloš's departure marked the beginnings of the modern state, but of one that was still unable to stand against the Porte without turning for support either to Russia or to Austria.

Miloš's two sons followed him in quick succession. One died of tuberculosis and the other had to stand down in 1842 as he was not the expected malleable figurehead. An assembly then elected Prince Alexander Karadjordjević (Karageorgevitch, 1806–85), Karageorge's son. The politicians generally called the 'defenders of the constitution' or the 'constitutionals' were the real rulers until 1858. The Porte did not acknowledge their new prince as hereditary. He had no personal appeal or authority, but he did have a prestigious surname, and was accepted as the symbol of the state.

The constitutionals thought in terms of a state of law and rights. They viewed themselves as natural tutors to their ward – the people. They institutionalized their position by building a permanent bureaucratic oligarchy, which was their conception of an enlightened European government. They also provided legal guarantees for the peasants' recently acquired property. That was their strength, just as Miloš's had been to have turned the land over to the tillers.

They abolished all constraints on trade, which continued to grow, with a surplus based on the strength of cattle exports to the Habsburg dominions. The emerging class of exporters moved their operations to Belgrade and exerted a strong influence on government. The low Ottoman tariff on imports of 3 per cent ad valorem encouraged the inflow of foreign goods, as the rising bourgeoisie turned to European ways. Nevertheless, the absence of an organized credit system and of a domestic money supply placed limitations on the Serbian commercial sector. Various coins were in circulation, until the continued decline of Ottoman currency made Austrian coins the only ones generally accepted in trade.

The notables' perception of themselves was symbolized by the central European- and Russian-type titles and uniforms that they adopted. It was influenced by the Habsburg Serbs who poured in to man the new institutions. Their greatest achievement was the Civil Code of 1844 based on the Austrian (and thus twice removed from the Napoleonic) model. With it came the organization of a separate judiciary. Although the lack of trained personnel meant that it could not function properly for a long time, it was set up as a conscious standard to be attained and it contributed to the régime's initial popularity.

The constitutionals needed trained people; they did not want to depend on Habsburg imports for longer than was necessary. They spared no efforts to step up education, especially at higher level. The *Lycée*, a university in embryo founded in 1838, was expanded; schools for military, ecclesiastical, commercial, and even agricultural training were founded (the last of these was not a success as its students did not return to the land). All this was accompanied by a network of 'reading rooms' – in fact small libraries that would organize a range of events.

The government funded higher education abroad, mostly in Paris. The number of these students was inevitably small, reaching twenty a year by 1858. By 1848 there were about a hundred foreign-trained 'autochthonous' graduates, and the number doubled by 1858. They were the first native intelligentsia. Through them came French influence to rival and push back the Austrian influence of the Habsburg Serbs. The 'Parisians' were also appointed to the Lycée; Belgrade came to offer higher education to students from Montenegro and the Ottoman Empire.

These developments created a division between generations. Whereas the 'fathers' were the constitutional notables in high office who had set up a bureaucracy that people were expected to respect, the 'sons' were junior officials with foreign degrees and ideas of political freedom soon to be influenced by the movement of 1848. They did not just want to take over the system, but to change it. The new intelligentsia turned into a liberal opposition, advocating a representative government.

The oligarchs' base was the Council. They had come to power with Russian support, yet once in control they resisted Russian interference, but because Serbia was not yet independent, informal Ottoman influence was revived. They wanted to give the principality a solid institutional framework. They were also nationalists, in the sense that they thought of an ultimate aim – unity with other South Slav territories in case of a break-up of the Ottoman Empire.

An important figure in formulating this thinking, in linking the older constitutionals, the younger French-influenced liberals and other South Slav nationalists, was the prime minister Ilija Garašanin (1812–74). His formulation of Serbia's long-term foreign policy programme had been triggered off by advice from the Paris-based Polish Agency set up after the failure of the Polish insurrection of 1833, and whose activities extended to the Balkans as a potential base for action against Austria and Russia.

Garašanin's 'Project' of 1844 was a confidential memorandum of his thoughts on how to preserve and enhance independence to face a break-up of the Ottoman Empire. In order to be able to work for the unification of Serbs in the first place, Serbia should expand through the liberation of Bulgaria, Bosnia and Herzegovina, union with Montenegro, and the securing of an outlet to the Adriatic. This could only be done with the support of western powers, of Serbs outside Serbia, of other South Slavs, and of some Albanians. It was linked with the need to obtain international guarantees, and with the realization that Serbia would be economically subservient for as long as she was land-locked. Beyond lay the vision of a religiously tolerant South Slav state stretching from the Adriatic to the Black Sea.

The constitutionals, however, did not tackle the contradiction between the expansion of Serbia, and Serbia as a unifying factor for other South Slavs, or between diplomatic action which they favoured, and the necessity for revolutionary action. When the revolutionary fire of 1848 reached the Habsburg lands, the educated youth of Belgrade were deeply affected by the movement of South Slav solidarity across the border and pressed their government to provide help. The ferment in Belgrade brought together several strands – the call to join in the defence of the newly proclaimed Serb *Vojvodina* of southern Hungary, with outcries against the 'foreigners' (i.e. Habsburg Serbs) in the administration, for independence from Turkey and for freedoms at home.

The Porte and Russia were opposed to any move by Serbia, and so was the Habsburg court. The Serbian government remained neutral, but it had to summon an assembly to vent pent-up feelings, as money, arms and volunteers poured across the border. Its action helped to turn opinion away from domestic problems, but cost the régime much popularity. Even though he was afraid that so much emotion would spoil his long-term plans, Garašanin continued to envisage risings in the Slav lands of the Ottoman Empire. He kept up links with the continued double struggle in Bosnia, of Muslim nobles against the Porte's reforms and of Christian peasants against their lords.

Tensions resurfaced at the time of the Crimean War when opinion sided with Russia, but with Ottoman and Austrian troops on the border, the government once again remained neutral and kept popular pressure in check. The sultan had granted Serbia the right to remain neutral, and abolished the Russian guarantee. The Treaty of Paris then placed Serbia's autonomy, along with that of Wallachia and Moldavia, under the collective guarantee of all the powers.

Public opinion, however, knew only that the leaders had deserted Russia during the war, as they had deserted the Habsburg Slavs in 1848. Anyhow, the collective guarantee in immediate terms meant that Austria replaced Russia. France and Great Britain had needed Austria to keep Russia in check in the Balkans during the war, and so they let her look after Serbia.

The Russophiles' position in the Council had been weakened. Prince Alexander saw his chance at last to assert some authority with Austrian support, but he overreached himself and his attempt failed. As he had stopped being a malleable figurehead, the constitutionals tried to get rid of him. In order to do so, they had to get popular backing through an assembly, and discovered that they had all, prince and Council, become unpopular together. The new political generation was both nationalistic and liberal. Behind it emerged a popular demand for Miloš's return. The peasants had the land, they were free to trade, but they did not have the money to make the best of it. They were indebted and were getting poorer. The combination would bring the whole régime to an end in 1858. The rule of the constitutionals had laid the basis for liberalism among the urban educated, but through unsettling times for the peasantry, it had also laid the basis for the later rise of radicalism.

OTHO'S GREEK KINGDOM

The three powers had put an end to the fighting in Greece, imposed a solution, defined a territory of 47,500 sq. km, found a monarch and guaranteed a loan. The king of Bavaria had been empowered to appoint a council of regency that would rule on behalf of the underage King Otho (1815–67) until he was twenty. Greece had not been a party to the settlement, and her king brought with him in 1833 a virtually foreign administration – three Bavarian regents with a host of German officials.

Their immediate concern was to create an institutional infrastructure and to repair the ravages of war. In spite of vague assurances made by the king of Bavaria about a constitution, the regents just sought to introduce what they considered to be enlightened European government. They were dealing with a complex society, which they viewed as primitive. In so far as it was – and some of it was as underdeveloped as Montenegro – it could not take the Bavarian model. At the same time, some Greeks – Phanariots in particular – were more sophisticated than the foreign officials. Between the two were traditions of local government that had survived to preserve what little semblance of organized life the Bavarians found, and ignored.

A Napoleonic-German mould was imposed on the Church as well. To the extent that it looked to any Orthodox precedent, it was to Petrine Russia, hardly a good point of reference. The separation from the patriarchate in Constantinople was confirmed, once again unilaterally and hence uncanonically, and the streamlined hierarchy was placed under a crown-appointed synod. This was an unpopular move, all the more so for being carried out by non-Orthodox foreigners. The powers had arranged for the king and regents to have a force of 4,000 Bavarian soldiers, to whom would be added a thousand Greeks (the navy being completely Greek). The land was teeming with embarrassing guerrillas from the War of Independence, most of whom came from regions that were still Ottoman and were therefore uprooted; many relapsed into brigandage. The major question to be settled was that of the land.

Most of the 65,000 Muslim landlords had left, and they had controlled over half the land. Much of the rest had been held by Christian notables, while the peasants, who formed the bulk of the population, usually worked on share-cropping arrangements. The revolutionary government had nationalized the formerly Ottoman-held lands, amounting to 721,000 hectares, so as to be able to receive income pending a settlement by sale and by distribution to the landless. Since it had hardly been able to enforce its property rights, or to implement its promises, 300,000 hectares had actually been taken over by notables, but also by peasants, one-sixth of whom did 'own' their land by 1833.

The regency favoured the formation of a smallholding class, but was prevented from carrying out a settlement because of the hopeless financial situation it had inherited. There was little pressure from below. The position of the peasants had improved, there were other means of livelihood (the sea, crafts, cattle), and emigration continued from the kingdom to Ottoman provinces.

To finance the long war, the insurgents had borrowed abroad. Their lack of experience had led them to accept unfavourable terms. The amounts received were in real terms below the nominal value of the loans, and they were not always put to best use. By 1827 repayments had been interrupted. In their

1832 settlement, the powers had come up with a guarantee to a 600-million franc 'Independence Loan'.

The regency did a great deal to organize the state, but it was hampered by the gap between its ambitions and its aims, as much as by the fact that it practically excluded the notables from government. By going along with the war, they had been able to participate in revolutionary power with military leaders, prelates, philhellenes, patriotic bandits, enlightened Phanariots, ship-owners, pirates, diaspora businessmen and peasant community leaders. At independence they found themselves excluded from a foreign-run monarchy unrestrained by a constitution. Not clearly differentiated politically or socially, they grouped themselves around powerful individuals, into factions reflecting regional rivalries and the influence of the protecting states.

The Peloponnesian notables and the clergy looked up to that old political and military hand, the one-time Klepht, Theodoros Kolokotronis (1770–1843), and to Russia. The veterans of continental Greece, along with the 'intellectuals', sought the patronage of France, and gathered around the Epirote Ioannis Kolettis (1788–1847). He had led the guerrillas from north of the Isthmus, and controlled the loyalty of the warriors whose cause he espoused. The 'English party' was that of the islanders and merchants around Alexandros Mavrokordatos (1791–1865), a Phanariot aristocrat who had presided over the Epidaurus assembly.

As even the regents disagreed among themselves, the residents (or representatives) of the three powers had ample opportunity to interfere, for they all believed, like the British representative, that 'a truly independent Greece is an absurdity'. At the end of 1834 the small political scene of 'independent' Greece was transferred to Athens for reasons of prestige. A big ruined village, it symbolized the classical pedigree of Greece. A new capital was laid out in a style blending neo-classical with official Munich; it respected ancient ruins but ignored the remains of intervening centuries.

Discontent with Bavarian rule had become widespread, and so was insecurity, until Kolettis was called to the home ministry in 1834 to deal with it. He did so by employing his Roumeliot followers as auxiliary gendarmes. Since they went off again into the mountains and woods once they had been disbanded, local authorities were empowered to enrol veterans against brigands on a more regular basis.

After the regency had come to an end in 1835, King Otho became his own ruler, especially after his marriage in 1836 to the beautiful and ambitious Amalia of Oldenburg. He soon had Greek ministers, but had to play with the 'Russian', 'English' and 'French' parties, who manipulated their patrons as much as they were manipulated by them. He also had a Greek army, as the bulk of Bavarian troops left in 1838, but the native military offered no reliable backing. Although not an authoritarian, he remained an absolute monarch.

Not all the problems went away with the Bavarians. Discontent soon coalesced on the lack of a constitution and of an Orthodox succession. Catholic Otho and Protestant Amalia had agreed that the heir would be brought up as an Orthodox, but none appeared. The Russian party wanted at least a future Orthodox king, a canonically correct Church, and more amenable rulers throughout the Balkans. The British feared that Otho might move away from their influence and they joined the French in supporting demands for a limitation of royal powers.

The demand for a constitution expressed the discontent of native-born notables and veterans at being kept out of power, first by a foreign-dominated administration, then by an absolute monarch, but also by the presence of many better-qualified Greeks who had come from elsewhere to take their share of office. The residents joined in a conspiracy; the conditions imposed for a further tranche of loan culminated in the coup of September 1843.

A group of politicians, with military backing, went to the king to demand a constitution. Contrary to expectations, he agreed to summon an assembly to draw one up, and to appoint an all-Greek, all-party cabinet.[7] This was the first assembly with strict criteria for attendance. Previously, no distinction had been made between representatives of liberated and of unliberated territory: all who could attend were welcomed. Now the only delegates from outside the kingdom were from Epirus, Macedonia and Thessaly, and the assembly itself, when it met, voted to exclude from office Greeks from the Ottoman Empire who had not been active in the war. All parties collaborated in drafting the constitution, to which the king took the oath in March 1844.

Modelled on the Belgian constitution of 1831, it set up a bicameral legislature, with a Senate of members appointed by the crown for life and a Chamber elected for three years by virtual manhood suffrage. It retained a wide prerogative for the ruler, whose heir would be his nearest Orthodox male relative.[8] However, although a constitutional monarchy had been established for Greece, it did not change her monarch's views, it did not solve her problems nor did it emancipate her from the tutelage of the three powers.

The cooperation between them and their parties ended as soon as the constitution came into force. University graduates increasingly formed the French party as the products of foreign, generally French, schools were joined by those of Athens University. Founded in 1837 (a year before the Belgrade Lycée) with the idea that enlightened Greece had the duty to pass on her lights to the 'Greek Orient', it attracted students from the whole Greek world.

Two politicians towered over the crowd. Mavrokordatos, the leader of the English party, believed that the first business of the state was to make the kingdom a model polity, a nucleus to which other Greek territory would gradually be added. He also happened to be sincere in his ideas of good government. For Kolettis, who led the French party, the top priority was to gain more

7 Since then, the square in front of the royal palace in Athens, now the parliament building, has been called Constitution Square.
8 The comparison with the Belgian constitution is interesting. Greek senators were appointed for life by the king from among specified categories of citizens, like the French peers of the July Monarchy, and representatives were elected by direct manhood suffrage qualified only by *some* property, movable or immovable. In Belgium, senators were elected from among older and richer citizens, and representatives by an electorate which satisfied property qualifications.

territory, since the nucleus was poor, dependent and did not encompass any of the better regions or centres. Greece such as it was needed cereal lands and maritime routes. As Kolettis declined to join in a coalition government, it was to Mavrokordatos that the king turned to be the first constitutional prime minister.

The proof of Mavrokordatos's honesty is that he was defeated in the first elections held under the constitution. Kolettis took over and remained prime minister until his death. He worked closely with Otho, and organized the 'system', which consisted in using the resources of the state for his own associates, and the state apparatus to ensure the return of his party at elections. To remain in power was almost the sum total of his domestic policy. The institution of regular tax collectors put an end to the farming of revenue. More of the national domain was distributed through legislation granting land to veterans and to settlers from unliberated regions, and through legal recognition of squatters' rights.

In foreign policy Kolettis stood for expansion, but since the powers opposed it, he could achieve no concrete gains. The régime was nevertheless popular. Kolettis's party was associated with French-influenced democratic traditions, now imbued with a rhetoric of love for the people and the unredeemed territory. The opposition came from conservative 'English' business people and 'Russian' rural notables, who had no consistent programme and were unlikely to support any threat to existing order. It was Kolettis who coined and publicized the term *Megali Idea*, the 'Great Idea', one of a Greece of all the Greeks associated with Greek history, and which immediately captured imaginations.[9]

After Kolettis's death in 1847, retired war heroes continued the system less successfully. The economy managed to make progress despite the government's hopeless financial situation and the ups and downs of security in the countryside. The powers' guarantee of the Independence Loan was spread out over twelve years, during which time they used it as a means of influencing Greece's foreign policy. Forced in 1836 to suspend regular servicing, the government made irregular repayments. On each occasion the powers guaranteed a further tranche to enable part repayment of the former tranche, the issue of new obligations to make due repayments reducing most of the value the initial loan could have had as an instrument of reconstruction.

It was not until 1841 that a National Bank of Greece was set up, as a private enterprise. As the apex of the existing traditional credit structure, it attracted native capital, perpetuated the notables' domination of credit and blocked off any chance of real industrialization. In the meanwhile, the crafts that had survived the war found it difficult to compete with British manufacture. As more peasants had enough land to support themselves, agriculture picked up in the Peloponnese, with intensive crops, requiring much labour and little land (grapes, olives, citrus, tobacco), trying to generate enough exportable produce to pay for grain imports. The population grew, in spite of continued

9 This was in 1844, when Kolettis became prime minister, the same year when Garašanin wrote his *Načertanije*, which, however, was not a public document and was hardly known at the time.

emigration, exceeding a million by 1856, when that of Athens had also increased to 35,000.

The continued growth of shipping after independence, far from being a sign of prosperity, reflected the lack of prospects for the island community. Propelled by sail, operated by cooperatives, unable to adapt to structural changes in sea transport, it had reacted defensively, encouraged by short-term benefits and false expectations. Widespread male suffrage favoured the more populous agricultural areas; the islanders found it hard to integrate into the system.

With an underdeveloped Greek state almost an enclave in Ottoman territory, expansion to neighbouring Greek-inhabited areas was the main idea behind foreign policy. The Megali Idea was more than a vote catcher. It linked the continuation of the national liberation movement centred on independent Greece with the economic superiority of Hellenism outside it. This was accompanied by a change in the nature of Hellenism. After 1843, the Greek state linked language and religion to advance the union of all Greek-speaking Orthodox Ottoman subjects to independent Greece as its long-term foreign policy aim. Peace was made with the patriarchate, which recognized the autocephalous status of the Church of Greece in 1850.

Dreams and long-term aims notwithstanding, the financial situation of the kingdom and its protected status limited its foreign policy to the activities of secret patriotic societies and of armed bands across the border. Both aroused Turkish protests and countermeasures, in particular against Ottoman Greeks. There were serious frontier incidents. A full-blown diplomatic crisis in 1847 added to military expenses and caused the British to vent their anger.

Palmerston decided to humiliate Greece. He needed a pretext, which came in the shape of the Don Pacifico affair in 1850. Various outstanding claims by British subjects were brought out and presented in an ultimatum backed by a naval blockade.[10] The brutality of this action helped Otho. He resisted with dignity; the country remained calm. Russia and France intervened, but the Greek government had to give in.

The net effect was to forge a real link between the king and public opinion, and to push him towards Russia. Anglo-Greek relations were further strained by the Crimean War, when King Otho reached a new height of popularity. When hostilities started between Russia and Turkey, Epirus, Thessaly, Macedonia and Cyprus flared up. Volunteers hurried to join the insurgents. The Porte broke off relations and took retaliatory measures. Greek leaders were divided on the wisdom of actually going to war. Sustained by popular enthusiasm in his vision of Greece allied to Russia in the liquidation of the Ottoman Empire, the king continued to prepare for war, until the insurrections faltered and the western powers decided to enforce neutrality.

10 The biggest claim, for £27,000, was that of the Gibraltar-born businessman, David Pacifico, for property in Piraeus damaged by a mob at the time of the 1847 disturbances. It was later reduced to £150 by the mixed commission that assessed the claims. Another, more modest, claim was from the historian and philhellene George Finlay for land enclosed in the grounds of the royal palace.

Resorting to the pretext that money earmarked for loan repayment had been diverted to war aims, British and French troops landed in Piraeus. The king had to accept an 'occupation cabinet' under Mavrokordatos, already retired from politics, who accepted the thankless task. Relations with the Ottoman Empire were resumed, but Greece was excluded from the Paris Peace of 1856. The occupation continued until 1857, when a financial control commission was imposed.

Mavrokordatos retired permanently in 1855. As in Serbia, a new generation was coming to maturity who had received a university education in western Europe or in Athens. Too young to have been involved in the War of Independence, they felt alienated from the ruthless pursuit and retention of office for the sole sake of dispensing patronage. They were imbued with liberal ideas, and saw genuine parliamentary government as the remedy to political stagnation. They were also anxious to obtain posts, and were beginning to turn against the king.

When Otho celebrated the twenty-fifth anniversary of his accession in 1858, he was more popular than ever, yet four years later he was overthrown. The War of Independence had helped to establish a sense of nationhood that went beyond those who wielded pen or musket, but as yet there was no great sense of loyalty to the kingdom, perceived as an arbitrarily defined territory which contained only a minority of the Greek population.

While early nationalists had looked exclusively to the classical past, by the middle of the century nationalists were beginning to argue that they were part of an unbroken continuum as justification for their aspiration to unify all Greek settlements in the Near East within the boundaries of a single state. The obsession with past glories remained, to compensate for present poverty and to enhance the aspiration to be part of Europe again.

Access to the sea had helped establish contacts with the continent, yet Greece's identity as a European country was uncertain. The state that emerged did not make much economic sense. It remained divided into enclaves almost independent of one another, and often still more turned towards the Ottoman Empire. The trading classes, whose very development had contributed to the revolution, continued to a large extent to function at the level of the Ottoman Empire. The bigger traders abandoned the Greek market for more international activities. The upper crust of notables in the kingdom were poorer, with narrower horizons, threatened by the power of their own state and by the emerging smaller bourgeoisie linked to the government and the tertiary sector. Pushed into alliance with the lower strata, the notables took up democratic demands in their struggle against royal power.

TANZIMAT AND REVOLUTION IN THE EMPIRES

In the period between the Treaty of Adrianople and the Crimean War, the Porte had to cope with the rebellion of Mehemet Ali and to accept the protection of a defensive alliance with Russia. Facing yet more trouble in his

European dominions, the sultan responded with reforms and concessions. In 1832, the Aegean island of Samos obtained the status of an autonomous principality under a Christian prince appointed by the sultan. There were risings in Crete linked to Mehemet Ali's campaigns against his suzerain: native Muslim lords defied the more stringent Egyptian administration and were defied in turn by their Christian peasants.

The Muslim nobles of Bosnia and Albania rose against tax and army reforms, appealing to Prince Miloš for help. He gave them money, just in time to round off his principality with a few additional border districts that had been part of Karageorge's territory, and to blackmail the Porte into accepting this in 1832.

The Tanzimat ministers wanted to reassert the authority of the central government over what was left, a functional government that would provide security of life and property for all. A modern drafted army dependent on an efficient fiscal system, and a land system that provided agricultural exports to pay for manufactured imports, were two important means for reaching these ends. Ottoman statesmen had a clear grasp of the problems, but they were powerless to change overnight institutions and practices that had separated social and religious groups from each other for centuries.

Military tenures were abolished in 1834; those sipahis who had fulfilled their military obligations were allowed to keep their fiefs outright. Tax collecting was farmed out to new contractors. Forced labour rents were abolished. The first of a series of solemn acts promising equal rights to all the sultan's subjects was issued in 1839. Whatever else that meant or did not mean in real terms, it did mean the legal right of Christians to own land, and with it went the removal of all monopolies.

The results were disappointing in the core chiftlik belt of the central Balkans, where agricultural exports stagnated in spite of increased exploitation of the sharecropping peasantry. In Bulgaria, however, developments were in many ways comparable to what had happened in Serbia, except that they occurred nearer the centre of Ottoman power, and that they flowered under reformed Ottoman rule, not despite Ottoman misrule.

The restoration of order, the reforms, and the growing European demand for wheat brought about a revival in what had long been a very backward region, particularly in the grain-producing lowlands. Turkish owners, who lost the possibility of supplementing their income with tax collecting, began to sell out to Christians and to leave. The poorest peasants who had suffered most from the disorders of earlier years, continued to lose out through indebtedness, and joined in the endemic peasant unrest of the period in the Balkan provinces of Turkey and Austria.

With rent in kind and money replacing labour rent, the better off were able to produce a market surplus. A top layer involved in the livestock trade started to buy land from departing Turks. They were the village elders whose families had, as in Serbia or the Peloponnese, performed administrative functions, and who went by the quaint name of *chorbadzhii*, usually referred to in

English as chorbadjis (from the janissary *chorbadjibasha*, the senior man of the smallest unit who had originally ladled out the *chorba* or soup). Their installation as local officials and tax collectors after the reforms of the 1830s was often the formalization of functions they already performed. Tax farming and money lending had enabled many of them to accumulate land by foreclosing on indebted peasants even before acquiring Turkish land.

The new regular army meant garrisons and contracts. With extensive sheep raising in a region where there had been no large-scale rebellion, and which was close to Constantinople, the government entrusted orders for uniform cloth and leather to Bulgarian wool and livestock merchants. Along with traditional metal work, this ensured the survival and indeed the development of traditional crafts well past the middle of the century. It was an added advantage for Bulgaria over the other Ottoman provinces of the Balkans.

Trade relations created a class of itinerant merchants, who travelled in the Ottoman provinces and across the Danube, to the principalities and to southern Russia.[11] There they met and joined compatriots who had settled earlier, refugees from the wars, and the many who had enlisted as volunteers with the Russian armies and left in 1830. They were usually gardeners, tailors, other craftsmen and smaller merchants. With peace and relative prosperity, many returned. The population doubled between then and 1875 within the territory of 1914 Bulgaria, from 1.5 million to 3 million.

The urban population grew accordingly, accounting for one-fifth of the total, but scattered in twenty or so towns of over 5,000 inhabitants, who gradually went native. Peasants who had lost their land moved there at a time when their crafts were in demand, and so did chorbadjis who became the nucleus of a native bourgeoisie – one that was closely associated with the Ottoman system, and opposed to any further reforms that would undermine their acquired position.

What has come to be called the 'Bulgarian Revival' was not due to the chorbadjis, even less so to the peasantry. Yet the very backwardness of the peasants meant that they were unaffected by the Hellenization of whatever culture there was. Those active in the Revival came from among the merchants and craftsmen, especially those who had settled abroad, and particularly the teachers and writers dependent on them, as had been the case in the Greek and Serbian cultural revivals.

The Ottoman guild structure provided political apprenticeship. There were guild representatives on the new municipal councils which began setting up Bulgarian-speaking primary vocational schools, even before millet representatives were promised seats on the new provincial councils set up in 1840. Chorbadjis had a strong position on local councils, but their token presence

---

11 It is estimated that by the mid-nineteenth century more than half a million Bulgars lived in Wallachia (including over 10,000 in Bucharest) and the southern Russian provinces, some as far as the Habsburg empire. A further 50,000 lived in Constantinople (J.R. Lampe, *The Bulgarian Economy in the Twentieth Century*, London: Croom Helm, 1986, 140).

on provincial councils allowed Muslims and Greek clergy to dominate these until the 1860s. It was the relative prosperity of artisans and merchants which gave substance to a movement that instilled ethnic consciousness through a school system and local government.

The romantic movement enabled Europe to discover the Balkans, and the 'intellectuals' of the Balkans – those who had some education, who read and who wrote – to discover Europe and themselves. In the Habsburg dominions, the Herderian view of a nation defined by its language and customs was the prime factor in getting South Slavs and Romanians to see themselves as ethnic entities.

To face the pressure for the official use of Hungarian in the lands of the Hungarian crown, Croat intellectuals moved to standardize a native literary language, and carried the 'Illyrian' idea over from Napoleon's Empire to 1848. Its foremost exponent was Ljudevit Gaj (1809–72), who had studied in both Hungary and Austria. He knew the work of Karadžić, and was keen to un- cover the substratum of a unified Slav culture that could be used to counter German and Hungarian claims to pre-eminence. The classical name of the 'Illyrians' was adopted as that of the presumed common ancestors of Slovenes, Croats, Serbs and Bulgars.

Likewise among the Romanians of Transylvania, excluded from politics by virtue of their class and religion, a recent crop of urban professionals, acknow- ledged as 'intellectuals' in a largely illiterate society, sought to define their nation by their history as descendants of the Roman settlers of Dacia and by the Latinity of their language. In both Croatia and Transylvania, the move- ment was translated into political terms in the 1840s.

The aim of the Illyrian party, which became 'national' when the former name was banned, was to reorganize the Empire into ethnic units. It kept in touch with Belgrade, even though it was an essentially Croat movement, whose outlook was 'Yugoslav' or pan-South-Slav as it needed a broader base to counter the more narrowly Croatian pro-Hungarian 'Magyarones'. The nationals attracted the very small nobles; they were not to the liking of the more traditionalist members of the clergy and the nobility. They also had adherents in Slavonia, in Dalmatia, among the Serbs of Vojvodina and the Franciscans of Bosnia, but most educated Slovenes were not keen to be associ- ated with a movement that was more relevant to a Hungarian context.

When in 1848 the revolutionary fever had moved from Paris to Pest, Prague and Vienna, the all-German parliament convened in Frankfurt found itself at odds with the Czech-influenced Slav Congress in Prague and with the new Hungarian parliament. South Slavs and Romanians reacted to events in Hungary once she had obtained her own government from the emperor. They reacted to the extension of the Hungarian language and institutions to the associated territories and to the non-Magyar majority.[12]

12 Magyars amounted to less than 40 per cent of the 14.6 million population of the Hungarian lands, which included 2.5 million Romanians, 1.3 million Croats and over 1 million Serbs.

While the constitution granted in Vienna in April for the non-Hungarian lands, with its income-based franchise, and the abolition of peasant labour obligations, satisfied most politicized Slovenes, revolutionary demands were made in Zagreb concerning territorial reorganization, feudal relationships and links with Hungary. Emperor Ferdinand (1793–1875) appointed a *ban* without going through the Hungarian government. He was a popular and 'Illyrian' Croat general, Baron Josip Jellačić (1801–59), who was acclaimed by a general gathering that requested territorial unification and the abolition of estates representation. When the regular diet met to endorse his appointment in the absence of the Catholic bishop of Zagreb, his swearing in was administered by the Orthodox metropolitan of Sremski Karlovci, the religious head of the Serbs of Hungary. 'We are all one people; we have left behind both Serbs and Croats,' he told the Sabor, and Bishop Peter II of Montenegro acclaimed him as the saviour of the South Slavs.[13]

The Serb townsfolk of southern Hungary had also started by making language and local demands. In May a general gathering of delegates at Sremski Karlovci acclaimed Metropolitan Josif (Rajačić, 1785–1861) as 'Serb patriarch', and elected as military voyvod a Serb Frontier colonel then serving in Italy, over a territorially defined Serb Vojvodina, under the house of Austria and the crown of Hungary, and in alliance with the reunited Triune Kingdom of Croatia, Slavonia and Dalmatia – all of which was unacceptable to the government in Pest. The fact that in the Serbian Vojvodina Serbs amounted to no more than 29 per cent of a population that included almost as many Romanians illustrates the difficulty the leaders of the different nationalities faced in 1848 when seeking territorial autonomy on an ethnic basis.

Zagreb had asked its king, the emperor, for a revival of the Triune Kingdom (defined as Croatia and Slavonia, with Dalmatia, and bits of purely Hungarian territory, including the port of Rijeka) and for a federal ethnic reorganization of the Empire. The nationals even hoped for the inclusion of Vojvodina into a single kingdom of Illyria under the constitutional rule of the Habsburgs.

In Transylvania, a general gathering of Romanian delegates also met in May outside Blaj (Blasendorf/Bálazsfalva) to demand recognition of their nation and language within a territorial framework. They asserted their loyalty to the emperor, and set up a permanent Romanian National Committee at Sibiu (Hermannstadt/Nagyszeben) under the moderate Orthodox Bishop Andrei (Şaguna, 1809–73). Relations deteriorated when the Transylvanian diet, dominated by Hungarian nobles, voted for full incorporation with Hungary, and the Hungarian government ignored Romanian demands.

---

13 The modern spelling is Jelačić, but he used the form 'Jellačić'. Because of his popularity, he was kept at his post after the revolutionary years until his death, and made a count. The most picturesque square in Zagreb bears his name and is adorned with an equestrian statue of him. Both name and statue were removed by the communist authorities after the Second World War, and restored when Croatia proclaimed its independence in 1991.

For as long as the Hungarian government did not break with the imperial court, Croats, Serbs and Romanians under the guidance of conservative leaders were also looking for a settlement. The court remained neutral; it had left revolutionary Vienna, and its largely South Slav army was tied up in northern Italy; but after Prague had been put down and Piedmont defeated, the military were anxious to stop the Hungarians. Over the summer, fighting broke out, as Kossuth took over a radicalized Hungarian government.

There had not been much unity between the Romanians and South Slavs, caught as they were between Pest and Vienna during the long summer of 1848. Bucharest and Jassy were having their own revolution. The constitutionals of the Belgrade government had mixed feelings. They were in touch with Zagreb; they tried to see whether Serbo-Croat cooperation could be linked up with insurrections in Ottoman territory; they aimed for a federal link with Bulgaria under the suzerainty of the sultan. But they were also anxious to protect their relations with their suzerain Porte and their protector, Russia. On the other hand, the educated young in Belgrade, who simply thought in terms of a revolutionary democratic movement from Croatia to Bulgaria, pressed for open support.

In Croatia, Jellačić was careful both to remain loyal to the emperor and to take account of the mood of his Serb soldiers. There, too, the urban intelligentsia pressed for a broader front with Serbs, with others, and even with revolutionary Hungarians for a thorough reorganization of the Empire. Gaj talked of the long-term objective of a Belgrade-centred Yugoslavia, and the exiled Miloš Obrenović turned up in Zagreb. Hungarian influence remained strong in Slavonia, while in Dalmatia the more politically conscious urban element was generally not keen on union with Croatia. The Vojvodina Serbs were also divided between nationals and Magyarophiles, conservative notables and younger radicals. Romanians were not united on the question of autonomy, and in southern Hungary there was tension with Serbs, particularly in Banat (where Romanians largely outnumbered Serbs).

As the Hungarian government became more radical in its demands, and more intransigent in its attitude towards the non-Magyars, pro-Vienna conservatives gained the upper hand among the latter. The court having definitely returned to Vienna, Ferdinand abdicated in December in favour of his nephew Francis Joseph (1830–1916). Jellačić, who had helped to retake Vienna, was appointed governor of Dalmatia and of Rijeka as well; the Serb patriarch and voyvod were confirmed. Only then did the Romanian Committee of Transylvania call for a Romanian duchy (similar to the Vojvodina), and the union of all the Romanians of the Empire under the emperor as grand duke of the Romanians.

The imperial government with a loyal army had by then restored control everywhere except in Hungary, and Romanians, Serbs and Croats were fighting alongside imperial forces against the Hungarians. In March 1849 a new imperial constitution took them all by surprise by keeping the established provinces.

In April, the Hungarian diet deposed the Habsburg dynasty. Francis Joseph requested the intervention of Russian troops from the Danubian Principalities. A series of defeats brought Hungarian resistance to an end and imperial rule was re-established in Hungary.

The year 1848 had for the first time seen something like a popular Yugoslav movement, but it was inchoate and uncoordinated. The idea of individual and ethnic rights as opposed to historic rights had become important, but not to the point of abandoning historic arguments. The intransigence of the Hungarian nobility had prevented a united action of the nationalities against Vienna, and the more radical the Hungarian movement became, the more it insisted that Hungary should be a unitary state. All were admitted to the Hungarian 'nation' provided they considered themselves as Magyars and spoke the language. Croats, Serbs and Romanians had had much sympathy with Hungarian nationalism until it became clear that its programme clashed with their own aspirations for national recognition and territorial autonomy.

The failure of the movements of 1848 restored centralization for all. Romanians and South Slavs were not rewarded for their services to the Habsburg cause. There was no ethnic reorganization of the Monarchy. Transylvania and Croatia-Slavonia remained separate from Hungary, and so did the Military Border, as well as a reduced Vojvodina. The period that followed was an attempt to return to a more or less enlightened absolutism that would give maximum efficiency to the state. A centralist and authoritarian régime was introduced. Historic crown lands were kept as administrative entities, emptied of substance. The smaller 'Voyvody of Serbia' (*Vojvodstvo*, or duchy) was Serb in name only. Its 300,000 Serbs were outnumbered by Germans and Romanians; German was the official language. The emperor took the title of 'grand voyvod of Serbia'.

The reforms enacted everywhere in 1848 had abolished what remained of peasant seigneurial servitudes; there was no going back on that. At times this was little more than the legal acknowledgement of an accomplished fact, for the higher nobility had long wanted an end to this antiquated régime. Peasants became owners of the plots they tilled, in return for compensation, while the lords kept the rest. As a result, a generally alien aristocracy was left with consolidated landed estates, and the peasantry with little opportunity to influence developments. Small nobles and small peasants were affected, particularly in the Hungarian lands. By 1848, half the peasants had been rendered landless there as a result of selling land to reduce their labour obligations and to pay taxes. Now the lower nobles lost out. Inefficient labour services was all that they had to generate a grain crop, as peasants had tended to use their own land for livestock rather than grain so as to avoid paying the tithe.

In the decade of centralism that followed, the abolition of the old order of 'nations' in Transylvania at least made the Romanians in that respect equal to Hungarians and Germans. The 'forty-eighters' withdrew from public life, or joined their counterparts from the Principalities in exile, but the idea of a Romanian nation remained. On the South Slav side, the promoters of genuine

Yugoslavism had been recruited from the intellectual élite and the youthful idealists. In Zagreb, they extolled South Slav cultural unity as a boost to Croatian aspirations. In Belgrade, many of the educated young also took up and popularized the idea of a common language, but their conception of a common nation was centred on autonomous Serbia. They were reluctant to give up a name already upheld by their rising statehood, for the ambiguous Illyrian name. The nationals in Zagreb soon adopted 'Yugoslav', and many of Gaj's followers eventually preferred 'Croat'. There were variations, misunderstandings and disagreements. The secularized idea of a linguistic community over and above religious affiliations was often difficult to accept, yet representative writers on both sides did agree on one common literary language, in March 1850 in Vienna.

CHAPTER 4

The Balkan states under loosened power control, 1856–78

The Balkan states take advantage of the divisions among powers. From King Otho to King George I. From Alexander Karadjordjević to Michael Obrenović. The union of the Principalities.

Legitimacy had been the principle underlying the international order of the post-Napoleonic era. Revolutionary outbursts had been contained until the Greek War of Independence, but legitimacy had been well and truly breached with the de facto separation of a Greek state from the Ottoman Empire. When Belgium in turn separated from the Netherlands, the powers (or the 'international community' in today's parlance) decided to save the principle by regulating changes to it, including the appointment of new legitimate rulers.

Great Britain, France, Austria, Prussia and Russia were Belgium's guarantors; Britain, France and Russia were Greece's guarantors and protectors. The Congress of Paris in 1856 extended the principle to the autonomous Principalities of the Balkans. Earlier endorsed in bilateral treaties between the tsar and their legitimate sovereign the sultan, their status was now guaranteed by seven powers, Piedmont-Sardinia being the new member of the Concert of Europe.

The two decades that followed saw the disarray of the Concert, though not the abandonment of the system. The divisions among the seven powers allowed the protected to take disturbing initiatives. Prussia and Piedmont were engaged in the task of unifying respectively Germany and Italy in the name of another (and subversive) principle – that of nationality. While Prussia at least took account of the existence of the other German rulers, Piedmont's attitude towards the sovereigns of other Italian states was revolutionary. Austria and Russia faced increased conspiracy and rebellion from Hungarian and Polish nobles, also in the name of the principle of nationality.

The movement for Italian unification enthused South Slav, Hellenic and Romanian nationalists. Of the great powers, France under Napoleon III was ready to support the aspirations of emerging nationalities and to redraw maps, for reasons that pertained to both ideology and prestige. The Second Empire was a respectable, though not so 'legitimate', member of the Concert of Europe. It wanted to play a major rôle, and it was initially seconded by Russia, who hoped in that way to regain the influence she had lost in the Balkans after her defeat in the Crimean War.

Russia, however, did not have a clear-cut policy towards the Balkans. After the Polish insurrection of 1863, her relations with France cooled as she turned to Prussia instead, and one can hardly speak of a 'Russian policy' comparable to a British or a French policy. Ministers, ambassadors and generals contended for the tsar's attention, forming antagonistic cliques, even acting on their own, and such internal rivalries weakened the Empire's international position. While pan-Slavists circulated agents, ideas and assistance, even at the level of the Constantinople embassy, those at the highest level in the foreign ministry were unwilling to take action without support from another power.

Austria was the most consistent champion of the status quo and of the sultan's sovereign rights, always wanting to intervene when these were infringed, but prevented from doing so by France and Russia, and hampered by her many problems. She was losing the struggle for hegemony over Germany and Italy, weakened by military defeats, and by constitutional experiments which always came up against the Hungarian problem. The Balkan peninsula in the 1860s was the centre of activity for Italian, Hungarian and Polish nationalists, Russian pan-Slavists, Italian, French and Prussian diplomats. They all hoped to create diversions which would facilitate the attainment of their respective goals. All were in touch with various governments and movements in the Balkans, as these were in touch with one another. 1866 was the year that provided the best chance, but it was not acted upon, as the various Balkan actors were not ready, united, or bold enough for the wider schemes they had envisaged.

Nevertheless, they were taking things into their own hands. They already had their diplomacies and they were distorting the international protectorate to suit themselves. By deposing and choosing rulers, and by introducing new constitutional arrangements, they signalled that they were no longer willing to accept their institutions as grants from the suzerain Porte or from the protecting powers. Like Italy for the visionaries of the Risorgimento, the Balkans were adopting a *farà da sè* (do it alone) attitude, through rulers, through emboldened political groups in assemblies, or through plebiscites. Divided as they were, the powers were willing to defer to local verdicts as a way of overcoming their divisions.

Balkan states were intent on acting as though they were sovereign, their rulers adopting European bearings, accrediting or receiving quasi-diplomatic agents, concluding alliances, joining international technical organizations and issuing their own coinage. The symbolic importance was as great as the practical advantages.[1] Agreements were concluded around the core of a Graeco-Serbian

1 When Napoleon III launched the Latin Monetary Union with France, Belgium, Italy and Switzerland, the LMU (a veritable forerunner of the EMU) failed to cross the Channel or the Rhine. Great Britain chose to keep out and Prussia wanted first to unify Germany politically and

alliance in 1867, to cooperate on the preparation of uprisings in the Ottoman Empire, spheres of military operations and common diplomatic moves. Each party sought support for its own aspirations. They did not resolve territorial issues beyond indicating minimums and maximums. Yet they did envisage considering the wishes of the populations and establishing a Bulgarian state.

The new states legalized the results of rebellions and revolutions, and began to organize the framework for further development. They grew out of ethnicity, but the forms were introduced from Europe, by Serbs, Greeks and Romanians who had been formed abroad, and by foreign advisers. Wars and revolutions had strengthened the tendency towards centralized bureaucratic monarchies, albeit with the vocabulary of liberalism, but the constitutional issue remained essentially whether to have a strong monarch or an oligarchy. Although the new bureaucratic establishment increasingly alienated village and peasant from city and state, monarch and oligarchy had to vie with each other for peasant support. This was particularly the case in the more egalitarian societies that had emerged from direct Ottoman rule, where those who worked the land had obtained possession of it, where the oligarchy had risen from the village, and where the peasant soon obtained the vote. Equality before the law obviously did not abolish economic inequalities anywhere, for the population explosion after 1860 left the peasants with less and less land as they became 'more and more equal'.[2]

Otho of Greece, while accepting a Belgian-type constitution, so distorted it in practice that he came to rule through patronage as head of a king's party. Michael Obrenović of Serbia and Alexander John Cuza of Moldavia-Wallachia looked to the Second Empire model. They wanted constitutional instruments that concentrated power in the ruler's hands, for they considered that only enlightened despotism could overcome the self-centredness of the oligarchy, and raise material and cultural standards. As benevolent autocrats, their aims were greater than their abilities.

They were hostages to, and shared, the nationalism of public opinion. The capacities of their states were not adequate for their expensive foreign policies. They had to face a new, broader and better educated political generation that was both nationalist and liberal; authoritarianism came to an end. Although they had acceded on a wave of popularity and were never perceived as tyrants, Otho was deposed in 1862, Cuza had to abdicate in 1866 and Michael Obrenović was assassinated in 1868.

After them there was a return, at least on paper, to a more liberal constitutional model. It often operated through nepotism, patronage and manipulation,

---

monetarily. Romania, however, pegged her new currency to the French franc by adhering with her leu (lion) to the fixed exchange ratio in 1867, and Serbia acceded with her dinar in 1873. This was meant as a defence against the continued destabilizing effect of Ottoman denominations, but even more so as a symbol of sovereignty, since the new Romanian or Serbian coins represented but a fraction of the Austrian and Ottoman coinage in circulation in these countries.
2 Traian Stoianovich, *Balkan Worlds: The First and Last Europe*, Armonk, NY, & London: M.E. Sharpe, 205.

but it did gradually introduce some of the practices of parliamentary government. This did not necessarily always happen with liberals in power, but at times through conservatives who had previously been in opposition and who used parliamentarianism for the sake of Europeanism and order. The crown also retained an important rôle as a stabilizer.

Nationalism was first and foremost an urban phenomenon, which derived from cultural identification. National consciousness was formulated as a re-awakening, which called for a sense of a national past as well of a national future, even if it meant manufacturing modern myths from medieval history. The correlation of ethnic identity and religion brought about the subordination of the Church to the new states, by western-trained élites with little feeling for Eastern Orthodox traditions. As the modern states separated from the Ottoman Empire, it was felt that the local bishops could no longer remain under the jurisdiction of the ecumenical patriarchate, situated in the sultan's capital, which was part of the Ottoman system of government, and which in any case had become an embodiment of Hellenism.

The irony was that the Greek state was the first to impose separation from Constantinople. Although canonical relations were eventually restored and autocephaly was formally granted, governments took over the Church according to a model that was more Lutheran than Orthodox, along with a new interpretation of autocephaly modelled on political independence.[3] A sort of *cujus regio ejus religio* principle was adopted, following on a long heritage of population transfers in the Balkans, until the Treaty of Berlin in 1878 moderated it in favour of religious minorities in the newly recognized independent states. The principle was linked to political power, but perhaps even more so to land ownership, since it was usually Christian peasants who were subordinated to Muslim landowners in the Ottoman territories that the Balkan states saw as their *irredenta*.

THE FALL OF OTHO AND THE ADVENT OF GEORGE I

Otho's popularity in Greece went into rapid decline after the celebrations of his silver jubilee. He had turned the constitution into an instrument of royal autocracy; any pretence of constitutional government had been abandoned. The remaining politicians of any standing had been sent to diplomatic posts abroad, the prime ministers were mere figureheads, yet the king, absorbed as he was in details, was unable to arrive at rapid decisions. To a younger and better educated political generation he could offer neither foreign policy gains nor participation in government.

---

3 Autocephaly was usually imposed by the state, and later accepted by the ecumenical patriarchate (in 1850 for the Church of Greece, in 1885 for Romania, and as late as 1945 for Bulgaria). Only Serbia managed to have her own way in 1879 without facing the ecumenical patriarchate with the fait accompli of modern autocephaly. The evolution of the status of the Church of Serbia, which followed that of the Principality, to autonomy and to independence, was achieved canonically, but it subordinated the Church no less to the state than in Greece and Romania.

By the early 1860s opposition had accrued, but had Otho found an Orthodox heir, he might well have been forgiven much. He had no children, and his Bavarian younger brothers did not think that it was worth giving up their Catholicism for the sake of the Greek succession. In the absence of male heirs, the king had the constitutional right to nominate a successor to parliament, but he took no action. Greece would not really have been able to do anything during the war in Lombardy in 1859, but it so happened that king and the people no longer shared the same sympathies when the battles of Solferino and Magenta were fought. Whereas popular opinion enthusiastically endorsed the cause of Italian unification, Otho the Bavarian favoured Austria.

The elections of 1860 were so manipulated that when the new Chamber met in February 1861, it had no authority. There was a rapid turnover of cabinets against a background of student demonstrations and military plots. That was an eventful year in the Balkans, when the continued presence of Ottoman garrisons in Serbia led to the bombardment of Belgrade, and when Prince Nicholas of Montenegro (1841–1921)[4] was at war with the Ottomans of Herzegovina.

Otho hoped that he could once again divert opinion to the Great Idea and save himself by involvement in foreign ventures. He had talks with Serbia, with Montenegro and even with Garibaldians. Great Britain tried to bribe him with the offer of the Ionian Islands. She would thus have killed two birds with one stone, unburdened herself of the islands, which had become ungovernable, and committed Otho to not 'raising the Eastern Question' – the question of taking over from a shrinking Ottoman Empire. He refused, turned to Russia, displeased the British and did not convince the opposition.

His diversionary contacts came to nothing, as Michael of Serbia accepted the settlement offered by the powers, Nicholas of Montenegro had to make his peace with Turkey, and Garibaldi did not get involved. King Otho had incurred the hostility of all three protecting powers: the British distrusted his anti-Ottoman moves, the French were disturbed by his Austrian sympathies, the Russians were worried by the lack of an Orthodox heir. Ironically, Greek opinion regarded him as a liability once he had fallen out of favour with the protectors; it agreed with much of their criticism.

Otho went on a tour of the country in October, to counter a widespread movement of urban disturbance organized by politicians, veterans and students with the connivance of the army, but only succeeded in accelerating it. In his absence from the capital, the Athens garrison rebelled and the government concluded that the king's deposition was inevitable. As his yacht returned, a provisional government was already in place. Otho was deposed; a Constituent Assembly was summoned to draft a new constitution. The representatives of the powers advised Otho to accept: he transferred to a British cruiser, from

---

4 Prince Danilo had on his accession in 1851 separated the princely office from that of the metropolitan bishop. He was succeeded by his nephew Nicholas in 1860.

where he issued a proclamation that, in order to avoid bloodshed, he was leaving the land he loved.[5]

Even though the overthrow of Otho had upset the arrangements made by the three powers, the latter had helped it by clearly signalling that they had lost interest in him. The provisional government organized what can only be described as a semi-official plebiscite, to back its strong preference for Queen Victoria's second son, Alfred (future Duke of Edinburgh and future reigning duke of Saxe-Coburg and Gotha). The gesture was symbolic, as the prince was disqualified by being a member of the reigning house of one of the protectors, who reasserted their authority by choosing Prince William of Denmark (1845–1913), whose sister Alexandra had just married the Prince of Wales. The throne was formally offered to him by the Greek Constituent Assembly when it met; he was declared of age although he was not yet eighteen. He thus landed in October 1863 without regents, to reign as King George I (the last and only one of his baptismal names translatable into Greek).

Great Britain made her accession gift of the Ionian Islands in March 1864 – to rid herself graciously of them, to dampen Greece's irredentist fervour, and to check the spread of Russian influence. This was the first accretion to independent Greece, with 50,211 sq. km and a quarter of a million inhabitants who had been more exposed to western influences than any part of the kingdom. The new monarch visited the islands, whose deputies joined the Constituent Assembly in Athens.

Greece then placed herself at the forefront of constitutionalism in the Balkans, not only by going back for inspiration to the original Belgian model, but being one of the first states (not only in the Balkans) to adopt full manhood suffrage. The Constituent Assembly had been at work since the end of 1862, led by its merchants and landowners, but with a vocal radical participation reinforced by the arrival of the Ionians. The constitution of 1864, to which King George took an oath in November, introduced a parliamentary régime, based on a single Chamber of Deputies, elected for four years by direct and secret voting.

The crown nevertheless retained an important prerogative, through the authority to appoint and dismiss ministers, and to dissolve parliament. Both the new monarch and the new constitution would be long-lasting. King George, personally and through his marriage in 1866 to Grand Duchess Olga of Russia, contributed valuable dynastic links to a reign that extended over the next half-century. The previous era of parties and politicians tied to the British, French and Russian legations came to an end, even though parties were still little more than groupings around prominent politicians engaged in the pursuit of office. Office provided prestige and gave access to patronage. The state was important as a source of employment, and elections were fiercely

---

5 He spent the last four years of his life 'in exile' in his native Bavaria, often wearing Greek dress, and surrounded by a small court of loyal Greeks.

contested. Shifting coalitions, that could not provide stable parliamentary majorities, strengthened the importance of the crown.

Originally a defence against the arbitrariness of late Ottoman misrule, patron–client relations were adapted to the parliamentary system. The electoral participation of the masses strengthened the old cliental networks through the deputies' obligations to their voters, even if transitory state service was usually the most that could be provided. A constant process of filtering up through such recruitment reinforced the hold of the upper classes on clientèles, although the state did not give them much in return beyond patronage and prestige. The demands made on politicians were such that relatively few prospered at public expense. This precocious and rough democratization created a balanced relationship between social layers in an essentially open society, while a lively press acted as check against the most flagrant abuses of the system.

Social stability in the countryside improved with the agrarian reform of 1871. The objections of foreign creditors to the disposal of the national domain without their consent having been overcome, the distribution of public lands was finally legalized and completed. In spite of a greater emphasis on commercial products, the weak surplus from agriculture was not sufficient to provide capital for its restructuring. Part of it was used to deforest or to improve the national lands that had lain fallow, or to invest in increased production; there was little change in structure, ownership or modes of production.

The economy was dominated by financial networks. This was on the whole small-scale capitalism gathered around local hierarchies, whose profits were reinvested in trade and commercial credit. They were linked to diaspora Greek entrepreneurs from the Ottoman Empire and elsewhere, who started investing massively in the kingdom from the late 1860s. They tended to invest conservatively (in the tertiary sector, in the National Bank, in urban buildings) or speculatively (in property, in stock, in exchange dealings). They contributed to modernization, to the development of Athens, and even to the quantitative expansion of agricultural production, but not to industrialization. The traditional credit system was a closed one, with very little capital going out to long-term credit or direct industrial investment.

Yet slow and steady economic progress continued. After the Crimean War, British and French interests in the Near East expanded, producing an economic movement without precedent. Greek entrepreneurs benefited, in spite of tension with the Ottoman Empire and the development of nationalism in the Balkans. Ethnic Greeks still had an important stake in the trade of Balkan countries, with much of the Black Sea and Danube traffic. In Egypt and the Ottoman Empire of the Tanzimat era, Greek communities developed economically, acting as bankers and associates of western firms.

This was felt in the kingdom through tighter relations with outside Hellenism. Investment now grew with immigration into the kingdom, from the Balkans and from the Ottoman Empire, so that the population rose from 850,000 in 1840 to over a million at the end of Otho's reign. Athens was by that time a city of some 30,000, concentrating government services and a large part of the country's economic activities, with many public buildings contributed by diaspora benefactors. It had also definitely become the cultural centre for Hellenism, even if Constantinople was its economic centre.

Although Greece was still excluded from the major financial markets, she had access to those of the Levant and the government was generally satisfied with what the National Bank could provide. Ports and roads improved, but insufficiently. Irredentism continued to swallow a major part of the resources of the state and to feed the public debt. It served the Great Idea, which offered a synthesis between classical antiquity, Byzantium and modern Greece. The Great Idea was an ideology, comparable to that of the Risorgimento. As the latter was the credo of those who in Italy after 1861 identified themselves with the completion of the unification process, so the former provided a grandiose vision for the governing class of Greece. It was susceptible of various interpretations, but it also had real foundations in the Hellenic population of several regions of the Ottoman Empire, the economic expansion of whose business élite was a constant reminder of how small Greece was.

Russia's influence as the power most likely to assist in such ambitions had waned, but Athens still counted on Russian support when the great Cretan rebellion broke out in the summer of 1866. Periodic risings followed by repression in the island, whose union with Greece the powers would not hear of, had led Athens to draw nearer to Belgrade in the 1860s, to plan a common effort for the emancipation of all the peninsula from Ottoman rule.

When in September 1866, a Cretan assembly proclaimed union, there was excitement throughout the Balkans. The Greek government allowed the despatch of aid, arms and volunteers, including army officers. Risings were also provoked to the north, in Epirus, Thessaly and Macedonia, to ease the pressure on Crete. Greece, however, was not allowed to go to war, and Crete was devastated by the repression. Greece had incurred great expenses and gained nothing but tens of thousands of refugees from Crete. Turkey had also suffered huge losses, financial and military. At the beginning of 1869, Greece had to agree to refrain from sending any more aid to rebels in Ottoman territory, the insurrection finally collapsed, and the powers decided that Crete should be a privileged province of the Ottoman Empire, with a special status.

FROM ALEXANDER KARADJORDJEVIĆ TO MICHAEL OBRENOVIĆ

With Russian influence much reduced after the Treaty of Paris, and Austrian influence in the ascendancy, Prince Alexander tried to assert his power in Serbia. When he attempted to purge the Council in 1857, his opponents took advantage of the principality's new international status to appeal to the representatives of the powers. His manoeuvre backfired on him, he lost all prestige. The constitutionals determined to overthrow him, but in order to remove their chosen prince, they needed public support through an assembly.

This meant obtaining the help of the young Belgrade intelligentsia, who, like their counterparts in Athens, were both liberal and nationalist. The liberals believed that a nation such as theirs, one with a glorious medieval past, should have its own independent state and be a modern sovereign nation within it. They, too, wanted an assembly, in the form of an institutionalized representative body, and they were backed by the hard-core Obrenovićist notables who wanted to settle all grievances.

A law for the National Assembly was enacted that specified the composition and the electoral procedure for what had hitherto been a traditional gathering summoned when the government felt the need for it. It was a law for that one assembly only, whose task was simply to give an opinion on questions that would be put to it. Garašanin and the oligarchs, the liberals and the Obrenovićists were not united on what they wanted beyond removing Alexander.

Meeting in a revolutionary mood in December 1858, with its proceedings taken over by the liberals, the Assembly asked for the prince's abdication. Once Garašanin had in practice removed him by getting him to the safety of the Ottoman citadel, the Assembly went on to proclaim Miloš Obrenović. Taken by surprise, the government could only insist on a transitional regency pending acceptance by the Porte. The liberal-led Assembly had brought the rule of the constitutional oligarchy to an end. Austria wanted to intervene and restore order, France and Russia opposed her; Miloš waited for more than a year in Bucharest to be confirmed by the Porte.

Just before Miloš's return, the liberals managed to obtain a law turning the National Assembly into a regular institution, elected by all taxpayers, but with a purely consultative rôle. Duly confirmed, Miloš was back in January 1859. After an absence of nearly two decades, and almost eighty, he had been forgiven everything, but had forgotten nothing, learnt nothing, and found it convenient to have the system of 1838 destroyed for him by the 'people'. He appointed liberals to high office, not because he agreed with their ideas, but to reward those who had engineered his restoration. He was in a hurry to consolidate again the ruler's authority and give some satisfaction to the peasants.

Although he had obtained hereditary status from the sultan as far back as 1830, his successors and he again had all been confirmed by the Porte. He had the Assembly pass a law on the hereditary succession and took up the question once more in Constantinople. He was genuinely concerned that usury might undermine peasant ownership. As liberals and the one-time constitutionals, now called conservatives, disputed over a solution but did not provide the quick answer that he needed, he resorted to short-term measures, such as providing credit facilities from local authority funds at the fixed and relatively low interest rate of 12 per cent, on the guarantee of two reputable citizens.

Miloš's restoration had turned into a popular movement against bureaucrats and usurers; he welcomed this as he needed support to free himself from the Porte and from the bureaucrats. By the time of his death in the autumn of 1860, he had not delivered the miracles people had expected from the peasant prince, yet he was still a legend, even if for both conservatives and liberals he was but an arbitrary despot grown old.

Michael M. Obrenović III[6] (1823–68) was thirty-seven on his second accession. Highly educated and well travelled as a result of sixteen years in exile, he shared the aspirations of those South Slavs who, aroused by events in Italy, dreamt of freeing themselves from foreign rule and of uniting. He wanted to make his principality fit to play the part of a Yugoslav Piedmont and to unite the Balkans for a final war of liberation. Appalled by Serbia's underdevelopment, he considered that only enlightened despotism could bring about the required preconditions for the rule of law and material welfare.

Failing to obtain a government of united conservatives and liberals, he started with a ministry of technocrats to reform the institutions according to his views. He then turned to the experienced Garašanin, who in 1861 returned to head a government of conservatives, with the liberals in loyal opposition. These labels did not mean much except to educated Belgraders. In the country at large, people of some influence had come to think of themselves in terms of dynastic loyalties. Prince Michael's policy of reconciliation, followed by that of ruling with the best available ministers, whatever their past affiliations, was not generally understood. He was seen to rule with Karadjordjevićists who had overthrown Obrenović princes, but who were viewed as renegades by Karadjordjevićists because they served an Obrenović.

The Porte did not mind him altering the constitution, as long as he did it by courtesy of the sultan, which was precisely what Michael did not want. He got his own way by not formally amending the constitution of 1838, but by enacting a series of so-called organic laws that did in fact fundamentally alter it. A new law on the National Assembly replaced that of 1859. With the same electorate and the same consultative rôle, it was smaller and more tightly controlled. The three assemblies of his reign were docile affairs and attracted little electoral interest.

The Council was turned into a legal and financial watchdog under the prince, while retaining its legislative functions, thus in fact handing legislation over to the ruler. The cabinet was institutionalized as a Council of Ministers, at the head of a bureaucracy that served, and no longer ruled, the state. The introduction of monarchical trappings and of court protocol symbolized the fact that Michael Obrenović carried the weight of the state, although his rule was based on law.

He sought no outside support, with the result that, initially acclaimed as saviour by a country in need of order, he gradually lost his popularity. The institutional strengthening of the ruler's position was not what the liberals had hoped for. As their disaffection was denied the freedom of expression, they turned against the prince. In time, conservatives, too, became discontented with the authoritarianism of ministers too long in office. Dissatisfaction spread

---

6 As he was styled, being the third Obrenović prince of Serbia.

to the whole intelligentsia, and even to the peasants who paid and served for a war that never came. Yet for eight years Michael ruled with no limitations.

His greatest achievement was the introduction of the militia in 1861. The innovation was to bring instruction to the peasant on the spot rather than take him away from work on the land, but even if it needed neither uniforms nor barracks, the 'people's army' had to be armed. As Turkey and Austria would not allow Serbia to import them, arms had to be smuggled through Romania. Prince Michael believed he had created an army. The romantic idea that it was sufficient to give each peasant a rifle and a minimum of training held fast until put to the test in 1876. Meanwhile the militia made a great impression. On paper, it numbered 50,000 men of twenty-five to thirty-five years of age, and 40,000 in the reserve. Foreign experts believed Serbia could raise 150,000 men in time of war. Her military strength was taken seriously by the Porte, by the powers, and even more so by Serbian opinion which turned again to thoughts of liberation.

With a state structure established over a defined territory, and changed social and educational conditions, the informed young had become more receptive to the sense of identity developed across the border among the ecclesiastical, trade and intellectual élite of the Serb community in the Habsburg lands. Although religious difference could mobilize the peasantry against Ottoman rule, nationalism began as a secular and cultural movement among the urban educated. Intellectuals blended language, folk culture, memories of the pre-Ottoman past and religious symbols in an identity expressed through the nation-state. Religion was just one of the ingredients, which helps to explain the links between Belgrade and Zagreb across the Orthodox–Catholic divide.

Michael had public support as he made Serbia the centre for nationalist activity in the Balkans. Serbia was still part of the Ottoman Empire in terms of international law, but apart from despatching imperial commissioners to make that point in times of crisis, the Porte did little to influence internal affairs. The militia was another matter. Although Michael had not publicized his ultimate bellicose intentions, the Ottoman government knew what he was aiming at, and applied diplomatic and military pressure.

Increased tension caused incidents. In June 1862, one such incident in Belgrade led to the death of a child: the Turks were attacked by the population and driven into the citadel, which fired its guns at the town. Whether intended to frighten the Serbian government into submission, or the result of panic in an overcrowded fortress, the bombardment caused more alarm than damage, and was a godsend to Prince Michael, who ordered mobilization and demanded the immediate evacuation of all Turks.

The ambassadors of the powers met in Constantinople: Britain and Austria stood by the Porte, France and Russia backed Serbia, and a compromise was devised. All Ottoman civilians would leave, two smaller forts would be destroyed, the four main fortresses would remain, there would be mutual compensation for damages caused. There followed five years of armed peace, during which the smuggling of arms through Romania became more discreet, the Turks strengthened what remained of their military presence, and Prince Michael continued with his pan-Balkan plans.

Serbia's policies were directed towards the preparation of a general rising against Turkish rule, particularly in Bulgaria and in Bosnia where her military intervention would be prompted. Michael believed in the right of nationalities to self-determination, in their intrinsic strength and in the decadence of the Ottoman Empire. These preparations remained essentially amateurish in character, they had no meaningful economic and social appeal for the peasant masses, and they did not take account of the ethnic complexities of the territories to be divided.

It was in any case only from 1866 that the pace quickened. Austria was anxious that Serbia should not raise the 'Eastern Question'. Turkey, facing a formidable revolt in Crete and possible war with Greece, feared the spread of rebellion to the Balkan mainland provinces where Serbia was considered influential. It was then that Michael Obrenović put it to the sultan that he might entrust the citadels to his safekeeping, and a formula was agreed. While remaining formally the sultan's, the fortresses were handed over to the prince of Serbia who, in return, went to pay homage to the sultan to symbolize his vassalage. When the garrisons evacuated Serbia in April 1867, the only tokens of Ottoman sovereignty left were the tribute and the Ottoman flag next to Serbia's over the citadel of Belgrade. Serbia was a vassal in name only, so much so that it immediately went on to mint its own small coinage and to conclude alliances.

Prince Michael could put the finishing touches to his Balkan plans. Garašanin's discussions with the Croat Catholic Bishop Josip Juraj Strossmayer (1815–95) for a common Yugoslav entity independent of Austria and Turkey, with Serbia taking on responsibility for the conduct of diplomatic and military activities, were accepted by the National Party in Zagreb. A mutual defence agreement was concluded with Greece in case of war with the Ottoman Empire, together with partition plans according to which Serbia would look after Bosnia and Herzegovina and Greece would look after Epirus and Thessaly. Treaties were also made with Montenegro and with Romania.

Meanwhile at home the régime was losing popularity. In 1864 a number of hard-core Karadjordjevićists, sentenced for plotting against the government in the wake of popular opposition to the recently introduced income tax, had had their sentences quashed on appeal. A shocked government had reacted with a retroactive law on the legal responsibility of judges; such an infringement of the independence of the judiciary had not gone down well.

The intelligentsia was losing faith. Michael's rule was meant to concentrate its efforts on a nationalist foreign policy, but it had so far produced little by way of liberation and was expensive. The army and diplomacy had been responsible for most of the 61 per cent rise in government expenditure between 1858 and 1868. Revenue could only increase with population, as taxation was still based on the traditional poll tax. In 1861 a bold move had been made to bring in progressive income tax, abandoned three years later in the face of general resistance. Deficits continued to be met from state reserves. At the very end of his reign, Michael thought of raising a loan in London guaranteed by his private fortune (inherited from Prince Miloš).

Economically and culturally, Serbia still lacked strength. In 1862 the liberals' idea of state credit was taken up to help with peasant indebtedness. All the trust funds maintained in the treasury were placed under a Central Administration of Funds, out of which 6 per cent mortgage loans were issued. As there were no branches outside the capital, Belgrade traders benefited more than poor peasants, but a way forward had been found.

Although many other economic and financial projects were considered, they went no further for lack of money. Serbia's capacities were not adequate for her foreign policy. Industry was virtually inexistent but for one gun foundry. Only the growth of foreign trade really indicated Serbia's modernization, in spite of the continued limitations suffered by the commercial sector. Urbanization was its most visible sign. Belgrade, which had only 17,000 inhabitants after the departure of the Turks in 1864, had increased to 25,000 by 1867, and the 8–9 per cent of town dwellers were the country's political, economic and cultural vanguard.

Culturally, too, the principality lagged behind the Serb urban centres of southern Hungary. Yet literacy did rise from 4.2 per cent in 1866 to 6.7 in 1874, as the numbers of schools, teachers and pupils rose steadily. The Lycée gave way to the new proto-university High School with its thirty to forty, predominantly law, students. More important perhaps than the setting up of a National Library in 1858 was the continued encouragement given to reading rooms.

However, the great Balkan dénouement rapidly turned to anticlimax. The best time for war and rebellion would have been 1866, when Serbia obtained the fortresses. Like most people with inside knowledge, Prince Michael believed that Austria would defeat Prussia. France and Russia pressed him to keep quiet, which he did for he was not quite ready. When he and his allies were ready, the time had passed. After the Austro-Prussian war, France drew nearer to Austria, and Russia was no longer so keen to back Serbia. The Austro-Hungarian Compromise of 1867 which gave a new lease of life to the Habsburg Monarchy coincided with a political crisis in Serbia.

The immediate issue was that of the possible remarriage of the prince, who was separated and had no direct heir. Garašanin's opposition led to his fall. As the country expected Michael Obrenović to make critical decisions – to remarry, to go to war, to grant liberal reforms – and all Belgrade talked of plots, he was assassinated in June 1868, when out on a walk, by isolated plotters. Opinion was shocked.[7] The prince had not deserved such an end, even though he had successfully brought political life to an end. There was no

7 Prince Michael Obrenović is commemorated by an equestrian statue erected in Belgrade in 1882 on what was Theatre Square. The square has since been renamed Republic Square, but the statue has never been removed.

declared heir; the only male Obrenović was Michael's ward Milan, a fourth-degree cousin at school in Paris. Garašanin, who had no official position, called the government together to summon a National Assembly to elect a provisional regency, but Colonel Milivoje Blaznavac (1824–73), the Austrian- and French-trained army minister, had Milan acclaimed by his troops. The Assembly subsequently merely proclaimed Milan M. Obrenović IV, at the same time as it elected a regency.

Blaznavac shared the regency with Jovan Ristić (1831–99), a Heidelberg- and Sorbonne-trained diplomat who had been the liberals' failed alternative to Garašanin in 1867. What followed was the result of a compromise between the regency and the liberals. A show trial of Michael's murderers satisfied the public demand for quick retribution; it was politically correct in so far as it blamed Karadjordjevićists and exonerated liberals.

A representative advisory committee was appointed to draft a new constitution. Ristić's brainchild, it was passed by a National Assembly and promulgated in 1869. It defined Serbia as 'a hereditary constitutional monarchy with a national representation'. The latter was an elected house of representatives and an appointed senate rolled into one National Assembly. Two-thirds of the members were elected by all taxpayers (which left out a small number of landless peasants and servants, along with army personnel), and one-third were chosen by the prince from citizens 'distinguished by their learning or experience of public affairs'. It met annually and shared legislative power with the prince.

Romanticism gave way to realism. Since leaderless Serbia could no longer lead, the Balkan league disintegrated as the regency strove to strike a diplomatic balance between Austria and Russia, and a political balance between conservatives and liberals. It got away with the constitution, which was not granted by the sultan. The regency prosecuted those it considered subversive of its line of controlled moderation – in dynastic terms those dubbed 'Karadjordjevićists', and in political terms those labelled 'radicals' or 'socialists' who appeared to the left of the liberals.

Political life really took off when parties had to go to the country. The constitution made the liberals the controlling force in the Assembly, as the conservatives were a party of the past, but after Milan had come of age in 1872, he tried to govern with the latter. The results were interesting. The permissive political atmosphere, a new generation of the intelligentsia, and the conservatives' experience of opposition had rejuvenated them. Under Paris-educated Jovan Marinović (1821–93), the government embarked on a series of reforms, ranging from the press to the metric system, from penal procedure to education, from improved land protection and credit facilities for peasants to introducing a silver currency unit.

In the course of these reforms, and because the conservatives did not control the National Assembly, Marinović gave the Assembly a taste of parliamentary government to carry it along in his concern for European standards of legality. The same atmosphere also saw the seeds of socialism being intro-duced by Svetozar Marković (1846–75). On his return from studies in Russia and Switzerland in 1870, he brought with him a brand of ideology to get Serbia to socialism through peasant communalism, and thus avoid capitalism.

He lashed out at the centralized bureaucratic monarchical state, and de-nounced the nationalism of liberals that could not liberate Serbia yet planned South Slav unification. He died of advanced tuberculosis at twenty-eight in 1875, after an eighteen-month prison sentence, but not before he had gathered angry young men from the left-liberal fringe and had a couple of his followers elected to the Assembly. In their call for more realism in politics, and for measures to tackle the dissatisfaction of peasants paying the price of economic progress that seemed to benefit mainly the towns, they were the precursors of what would become the Radical Party.

THE UNION OF THE PRINCIPALITIES

The Treaty of Paris had an even greater effect on the Danubian Principalities, where at the beginning of 1857 the sultan summoned the ad hoc assemblies. The last Austrian and Ottoman troops left, the exiles returned, the six-power commission arrived and the unionist movement gained momentum.

Thirteen thousand voters were enfranchised for the purpose, divided into electoral colleges. Unionist sentiment was weaker in Moldavia, where reac-tionary regents,[8] with Ottoman and Austrian backing, made the most of the absence of statistics to manipulate the lists, thus obtaining an anti-unionist majority in July. The validity of the ballot was challenged. A meeting be-tween Emperor Napoleon III and Queen Victoria agreed that Britain would advise the Porte to annul the Moldavian elections in return for France not pressing for complete unification. In September, new elections in Moldavia and elections in Wallachia returned assemblies that requested the union of the two principalities under a foreign prince (because of many native contenders).

The guarantors were back in Paris in May. Supported by Russia, Prussia and Sardinia, France was willing to accede to the Romanian desires. With Austria and the Porte opposed, and the British attitude not clear-cut, negoti-ations resulted in the Convention of Paris of August 1858, a hybrid best sym-bolized by the name of the 'United Principalities of Moldavia and Wallachia'.

The Convention reaffirmed the collective guarantee of their status under the sultan's sovereignty, expressed through his formal investiture of the princes and an increased tribute. It introduced new parallel institutions for the two

8 The last of these was Nicolae Vogoride (or Vogorides, or Bogoridi), the son of Stephanos Vogorides, nicknamed 'le Talleyrand de l'Orient'. This Phanariot of Bulgarian origin brought up in Bucharest, who had held various posts in the Danubian Principalities, had been appointed the first prince of Samos, but he had combined the position in the 1830s with that of agent in Constantinople for the then prince of Moldavia, his son-in-law, as well as being confidential adviser to various Ottoman ministers. Naturalized in Moldavia in 1846, Nicolae aspired to become prince in the old Phanariot mould. His brother Aleko, who served in the Ottoman foreign service, became governor-general of Eastern Roumelia in 1878.

Principalities. Each would be governed by an elected prince. Boier ranks and privileges were abolished. Chosen for life by the Assembly from citizens of either principality, the prince ruled with a Council of Ministers responsible to the legislative Assembly, elected by a few thousand income-qualified voters divided into colleges. As a concession to unionist feelings, a central commission considered common legislation. The settlement emancipated the Principalities from exclusive Russian influence, but kept formally separate the two entities whose union all accepted as inevitable.

The supporters of union were emboldened by the news from Belgrade, where the liberals had just changed the prince through the Assembly. In Moldavia, they held a caucus to decide on a single candidate – Alexandru Ioan Cuza (1820–73). A 'forty-eighter' who had studied in Paris, he had attracted attention by resigning as prefect of Galaţi to protest against the manipulation of electoral lists. 'Gentlemen, I fear you will not be satisfied with me,' he was reported to have said, but he accepted the nomination as a mandate to achieve union under a foreign prince, and was unanimously elected prince of Moldavia in January 1859.

The idea of electing the same prince was quickly accepted in Bucharest as a show of support for union. Again Cuza accepted with tact. Taken by surprise, the powers met and, after an interruption due to the war between France and Austria in Italy, accepted the British formula that made a virtue of necessity – to recognize the double election as an exception.

Cuza was a well-meaning patriot, a self-indulgent individual and a poor politician. Whatever his personal failings, his reign was a period of great changes. With two sets of institutions that pressed him to adopt a new unitary constitution, he dared not go too fast. He thought like his Obrenović counterpart that his countrymen's political culture was not sufficiently advanced for parliamentary government and immediately asked the powers and the Porte for changes. He made a good impression when he went to Constantinople in October 1860 for his investiture. By the following spring, the Porte had assented to most of his demands, but would go no further than a personal union for his reign only.

Meanwhile Cuza was criticized at home for not achieving anything. Parties competed in unionist fervour to the point of threatening a joint meeting of the two assemblies to depose him and proclaim union. The sultan's act of December 1861 came just in time: for the duration of Cuza's reign it acquiesced to a single government and a single Assembly. In order not to be accused of having linked union to his person, Cuza delayed the publication of the act itself, merely announcing that the union had been 'fulfilled': 'The Romanian nationality is founded . . . Long live Romania!'. 'Romania' was already being used in official documents when the text was released in 1862.

Alexander John I (as he now called himself) Cuza had achieved union in practice, but public confidence in him had waned. He did not succeed in forming his own party to hold the middle ground between the two broad groupings of gentry coteries identified as conservatives and liberals. Boier status had been abolished with almost no opposition. Most of the 5,400 or so boiers belonged to the lower non-hereditary ranks which no longer had the income of office. By contrast, the hereditary boiers retained considerable influence based on estates which had increased their income at the expense of worsened social relations. Several hundred families made up the core of the conservatives, who stood for rule by the landed class. Their leaders, conscious of their limited base, tried to attract support from the free peasantry and even the commercial element.

Many boiers and better-off free peasants were, however, being drawn to industry and commerce, adding to a bourgeoisie of industrialists, master crafts-men, professionals and civil servants which nevertheless remained small. Eco-nomic changes and the functioning of representative institutions helped to propagate the liberal spirit. The liberals, still largely boier-based, were the heirs to all the reformist and radical aspirations since the 1830s. They sup-ported the development of industry, a widening of the franchise and land reform. Their leaders, conscious of the imbalance of Romania's social struc-ture, and of the lack of a strong industrial and commercial class, envisaged the support of the peasantry after careful instruction.

Confronted in 1862 with a unified legislature dominated by conservatives, Cuza tried to rule with them, but relations worsened as he determined to push ahead with his reform programme. Nationalist issues initially united all shades of opinion, as they did in Serbia. In the arms-to-Serbia affair, a blind eye was turned to consignments going through the Principalities. Rendered nervous by Serbia's actions, by agitation in Greece and by Romania's disregard of her obligations, the Porte demanded that the arms be sequestered and the cul-prits punished. The Romanian government objected to any move that would infringe its autonomy, and played for time until the arms were safely out of the country.

In October 1863, Cuza asked the liberal leader, the historian Kogălniceanu, to head a government that would activate the reforms, starting with the estates of the Greek-held dedicated monasteries. They amounted to between a quarter and a third of all arable land, but with Russia as their champion, these com-munities obstructed the settlement procedure stipulated by the Convention. No sooner in office than Kogălniceanu took the bull by the horns, with enthusi-astic support from boiers and peasants alike. A nationalization law was enacted, with the award of a sizeable indemnity. The powers recognized it. Since, however, the patriarch of Constantinople and the Greek monks rejected the very principle as well as any indemnity, in 1867 the offer was declared to have lapsed.

Cuza went on to challenge the legislature with reform proposals. In March 1864 a well-publicized bill was tabled that granted dependent peasants owner-ship of the land they were using, and offered landlords the capitalized value of dues and services. As they dared not reject it, the conservatives amended it, granting the peasants land from the state rather than from estates, and voted a motion of censure of the government. Cuza forced the issue with an electoral reform bill. As the Assembly refused to discuss with a ministry against whom it had already passed a vote of no confidence, it was forcibly dissolved in May. The prince assumed full powers, and submitted an electoral law and a Statute to a plebiscite of all those who met the voting requirements for local elections – all male taxpayers over twenty-five.

Approved by 682,621 votes against 1,307, with 70,220 abstentions, the Statute set up a bicameral legislature subordinated to the executive, with an increased franchise, offset by the division into electoral colleges and two-tier voting for the peasantry.[9] Cuza went again to Constantinople where he convinced the Porte that graceful acceptance was preferable to the risk of international complications.

The powers agreed with the Porte on an 'Additional Act to the Convention of 1858' which, in return for a few minor changes, not only embodied the Statute, but left the Principalities free henceforth to modify their internal administration as they wished. Again Cuza chose not to publish the act, but to explain that it had been necessary to obtain the assent of the powers to the changes approved by the plebiscite.

Cuza's coup, which had left everyone gasping, cleared the way for the reforms on which he had set his heart. The agrarian reform was enacted by decree in August 1864 and came into effect a year later. Dependent peasants were freed of all dues and services. They were given holdings in full ownership – up to a maximum of two-thirds of the lords' arable land, for which they made compensation payments to an indemnity fund. Landlords were issued with treasury bonds ten times the value of yearly dues.

The act was greeted with jubilation. For Cuza, Romania was more than her boiers. He looked to the peasants as his potential allies, and genuinely endeavoured to help them. Perhaps as much as 2 million hectares was handed over to half a million families. Yet the reform did not solve the land question. Not only did boiers and the state retain 70 per cent of arable land and pasture, but the boiers, who controlled the local administration, were able to carry out the distribution so as to retain the best lands. Most peasants received too little, compensation payments were heavy, and the benefits of redistribution were largely wiped out by demographic growth.

The large landowners were in a good position to benefit from the rise in foreign demand for agricultural products. Absenteeism intensified social tensions. Properties were leased to entrepreneurs who sublet to peasants in need of land, or continued to be worked by peasants in need of supplementary income. Romania remained a country with large estates and a depressed peasantry, in contrast to Serbia and Greece.

9 For Cuza as for Michael Obrenović, the model was no longer the Belgian constitution of 1831, but the French one, presidential, then imperial, of 1852. The name was taken from the *Statuto* granted in 1848 to his Kingdom of Sardinia by King Charles Albert, and which became the fundamental law of the united Kingdom of Italy in 1861. The prince initiated legislation that had been drafted by the Council of State whose members he appointed. Bills were debated by an elected Assembly before being sent on to a Senate of ex-officio members and of senators appointed by the prince from lists presented by districts from certain categories.

Cuza's other major reform of 1864 was the law on public instruction, which set up a complete education system, from a free and obligatory primary school to the two universities of Bucharest and Jassy, with bursaries enabling the brightest poor students to go right through. Although much would remain on paper for lack of funds, it set out standards for future progress. Legal codes were introduced on the French model, as well as the metric system.

Still in order to increase the modernizing power of the state, the Church was shorn of its civil powers and brought under government supervision. The Gregorian calendar was introduced (for the first time in an Orthodox country), and an integrated hierarchy set up unilaterally. The patriarchate was unpopular because of the dedicated monasteries, and Romania's élite, while not denying its Orthodox heritage, felt separated from Greeks and Slavs by its 'Latin' affinities.

Cuza's foreign policy sought to obtain recognition of union and to strengthen autonomy. With support from Napoleon III and Cavour, who thought of using Romania as a threat to Austria's back, he sought to take advantage of Hungarian discontent to gain concessions from Vienna. Attempted talks with Hungarian leaders broke down over the rights of ethnic Romanians in Transylvania. Careful not to allow himself to be used as a tool, and acting in full solidarity only with Michael Obrenović of Serbia, he achieved much in limiting the remains of the sultan's suzerainty and of the powers' tutelage.

Uneasy about links with the leaders of Transylvania's Romanians and with Hungarian émigrés, Austria received Cuza's overtures coolly, and failed to take advantage of opportunities to penetrate the Romanian economy. She was still in 1865 the second largest outlet for Romanian exports with 18 per cent, the Ottoman Empire accounting for 78 per cent. The growth of wheat exports to western European markets came only as a consequence of the land reform and of the development of the transport infrastructure. Cuza had ambitious plans, but was disappointed in his hopes of a massive inflow of French and British capital. For the time being, deficits and loans gave an impression of prosperity. The contours of modern Romania had been shaped. The political and intellectual élite had been endowed with a sense of mission to extend ultimately the frontiers of the state to their ethnic limits.

Cuza's benevolent authoritarianism had achieved much, but his position had been gradually undermined. Discontent grew rapidly in 1865 as his disorderly private life played into the hands of his enemies. Feeling overshadowed, he forced a disillusioned Kogălniceanu to resign over a desperate financial situation. Cuza had antagonized the great boier landowners, the liberals with his dictatorial style, the clergy in one way or another. He had disappointed the countryside with the muddled implementation of his reforms, and even lost favour with the powers.

It seems that Cuza chose that moment to think of heredity through an adopted illegitimate son. He went in the summer on a western European tour, presumed to be linked to his dynastic plans. Thrown into each other's arms by the fear of disorders and of dictatorship, the parties decided to force his abdication and find a foreign prince. They sent emissaries to counteract Cuza's action and obtain foreign support.

Cuza returned in haste but had lost the will to soldier on. To the new parliamentary session, he renewed his offer to retire in favour of a foreign prince. Led by radical liberals under Ion Brătianu (1821–91), who already had a full curriculum vitae as a 'forty-eighter' and a conspirator in Paris and in Bucharest, the opposition decided on a swift coup, with support from the Bucharest garrison. On the night of 22 February 1866, conspirators broke into the palace, Cuza calmly signed his abdication and went abroad.

A three-man regency and a provisional government were set up, to include the most prominent moderates of both parties, with five ex-candidates for the princedoms. The situation was serious. The Principalities should have separated again, and a certain feeling of resentment in Moldavia of playing a subordinate rôle to Wallachia received encouragement from abroad. The treasury was empty. All agreed on the need for a foreign prince for a variety of reasons – for foreign support, for stability, against despotism, against radicalism. Parliament met, and elected the Count of Flanders, younger brother of King Leopold II of the Belgians, to be Philip I of Romania.[10] He declined; the move had been meant as an urgent demonstration of unity. Parliament was dissolved, and elections called for a Constituent Assembly. The sultan protested, convened the powers and massed troops.

Luckily, the powers still had their differences over the Principalities and more pressing concerns, as Europe was on the eve of war between Prussia and Austria for hegemony in Germany. The powers met in Paris but did nothing, while Brătianu was busy searching for a real prince with the connivance of Napoleon III, and sounding out Prince Charles of Hohenzollern-Sigmaringen (1839–1914) – a twenty-seven-year-old Prussian army officer, more than half-French and well educated. Before he had even clearly accepted, he was put to a plebiscite, and approved by 685,969 to 224. In May he was Romanianized to Carol I, reigning prince of Romania, by the newly elected Constituent Assembly which also pronounced Romania 'one and indivisible'. Charles, who had travelled to Bucharest incognito, took the oath in the Assembly amid jubilation.

He appointed a representative government, whose urgent task was the new constitution, accepted unanimously by parliament in June: Belgium once again provided the inspiration. Romania's existence and her neutrality were guaranteed by the powers. She would have liked to be the 'Belgium of the East', hence the initial choice of a Belgian prince. The state was a hereditary monarchy with a bicameral legislature. The prince was given a strong prerogative: he appointed ministers, commanded the army and concluded treaties (a clause that ignored the fact that Romania was still only an autonomous principality within the Ottoman Empire); he could veto legislation and dissolve parliament.

---

10 He was thus a son of King Leopold I who, as Prince Leopold of Saxe-Coburg thirty-six years earlier, had not become king of Greece.

Legislative power was shared between the prince and the two houses of parliament: all three could initiate legislation. An elected Senate of worthies had equal rights with the Chamber of Deputies. Elected for four years, they met annually. A system of electoral colleges divided voters according to income and residence, and assured the predominance of the educated and propertied.[11] The constitution of 1866 had numerous contemporary precedents in entrenching rights that were not quite as equal as it seemed at first sight, yet it was a manifesto of independence and union for 'Romania', with no reference to the Ottoman Empire and without the participation of the powers.

Napoleon III invited the powers to Paris in March. The Porte protested at Charles's unapproved acceptance, claimed that the union was dissolved and demanded permission to occupy the Principalities. This was refused, but in view of the war between Prussia and Austria, the Cretan rising and tension in Serbia, no other action was taken. The powers in effect acquiesced to what had happened. Romania's coalition government, formed after the first elections under the new constitution, negotiated with the Porte.

With problems elsewhere, the Ottoman government was ready for concessions, but insisted on symbols of suzerainty. In October, Charles was recognized as hereditary prince of a territory which the Porte referred to as 'the United Principalities',[12] paying an increased tribute. He was formally invested in Constantinople; recognition by the powers followed. Since the sultan's suzerainty manifested itself essentially in symbols, so Romania's struggle for affirmation was primarily one of symbols – the name Romania, the avoidance of reference to vassalage, the recognized signs of European statehood (from court étiquette to international relations), and carefully selected native traditions. Prince Charles publicly participated in Orthodox rites, his Catholicism notwithstanding, and agreed to Orthodox children after his marriage in 1869 to the Lutheran Elizabeth of Wied.

He quickly learnt to act with the reality of opposing factions and individuals, playing an important rôle through his rights of appointment and dissolution. He did it with moderation, generally conforming to the majority opinion emerging in the small political élite through parliament, the press and public meetings. There was a rapid turnover of cabinets and parliaments before 1871. Conservatives dominated parliament but had no clear programme. Among the liberals, Ion Brătianu's radical faction set about creating a broadly based organization.

Relations between them and the prince were, however, soured when they tried to use him as an instrument of policies that turned most powers against them – attempts to throw off the vestiges of Ottoman sovereignty, supporting the Romanians of Hungary or Bulgarian revolutionaries, limiting the economic activities of foreign Jews. They reached crisis point at the time of the

11 In 1883, fewer than 7,000 voters, the great majority being large landowners, elected senators. Deputies were returned by some 650,000 electors; 96 per cent of these were the peasants of the fourth college who voted indirectly for 30 out of 118 deputies.
12 There was until recently in Paris an Hôtel des Principautés-Unies in the rue de Vaugirard.

Franco-German war, when the liberals openly supported the power that had been Romania's principal backer, with anti-German demonstrations aimed at Charles. He contemplated abdication, before the political leaders acted to calm the storm, and a conservative leader formed a ministry in March 1871 which remained in office for the next five years.

Indeed, it was those years of stable conservative government that made the liberals take the final step towards the formalization of the National Liberal party in 1875. When the conservatives fell at the beginning of 1876, Brătianu formed a liberal government, and remained prime minister until 1888 (except for a short interlude in 1881).

Charles and the leaders of both parties agreed in their quest for independence and security, but differed on how to achieve it. Liberals wanted an openly anti-Ottoman policy, and closer ties with Russia, though not with France. They had come to view Austria rather than Russia as the main threat. The conservatives, quite a few of whom had studied in German-speaking countries and many of whom were from Moldavia, still saw Russia as the main danger. Trade agreements were signed with both Austria-Hungary in 1875 and with Russia in 1876, to protests by the Porte. They were seen as promoting independence as well as economic development, like the silver currency that Romania introduced three years ahead of Serbia.

The plans for continued liberation and unification were linked to the question of land ownership; revolutionary organizations and nationalist propaganda were exported from the Balkan states to the Ottoman provinces to exploit agrarian discontent. The Ottoman system had discriminated in favour of Muslims, both with regard to political power and to land ownership. Most of the land in the Ottoman Balkans was still in Muslim hands. Although the idea of a general rising of Christian peasants was not realized, the atmosphere was favourable to regional movements that occurred for local reasons, and influenced by propaganda from across the borders.

The rebellion of the peasantry of Herzegovina in 1875 was one such movement. It extended to Bosnia, to parts of Macedonia, to Bulgaria, even to Albania, and turned into the great Eastern Crisis. The revolt moved quickly from the social to the political and the national level, into one of the greatest guerrilla wars of modern European history.

By 1875 the action of the 1860s had indeed aroused the South Slavs. The rebellion had a great echo in the Habsburg Balkan lands of Dalmatia, Croatia and Vojvodina. Serbia and Montenegro went to war against the Ottoman Empire, of which they were still nominally part. Sympathy had also been aroused in Romania, even though she was affected only by the fact that she was placed between Russia and the Ottoman Empire. When Russia decided on war, Romania offered cooperation in exchange for recognition of status and territory, and she, too, fought against her suzerain. Greece's involvement was more marginal. The government did not respond to Serbia's overtures to go back to the alliance of 1867. Although it eventually had to give way to the pressure of opinion, its eleventh-hour intervention in the revolt of Thessaly came too late.

The Eastern Crisis ended with the wholesale revision of Balkan boundaries. The Treaty of Berlin in July 1879 brought formal independence to Romania, Serbia and Montenegro. All that Greece obtained was an intervention by the powers to prevent Turkey from declaring war on her, and the recommendation of frontier adjustments to the north. Cyprus meanwhile had been transferred to British administration. Serbia and Montenegro obtained more Ottoman territory, but not as much as they had conquered. They were kept separate, and they had to accept the transfer of the administration of Bosnia and Hezegovina to Austria-Hungary. Romania did not quite obtain the territorial integrity she had expected. In spite of gains, illusions in all three states, about Russia in particular, had been shattered for years to come.

CHAPTER 5

The imperial Balkans through crises and reforms, 1856–78

The Austro-Hungarian Ausgleich *and the Hungaro-Croatian* Nagodba. *The renewed Tanzimat and the Bulgarian exarchate. The Eastern Crisis, the Treaty of San Stefano and the Congress of Berlin.*

HABSBURG COMPROMISES: *AUSGLEICH* AND *NAGODBA*

The house of Habsburg had ruled over a conglomerate of dominions without a name until 1804, when the decision was taken to call it the Empire of Austria. This apparent realism separated it from other European monarchies which, as they became constitutional, also became identified with nations, something the Habsburgs could not do. Even though most of their nationalities remained loyal for a long time to come, there were particular problems in Italy and Hungary. The Italian national movement looked outside the Empire to a united Italy. The Hungarian national movement aspired to its independent constitutional state, which could be under the Habsburg dynasty but not in the Empire of Austria.

Having survived the revolutionary storm, Emperor Francis Joseph went on trying both to be ruler of an 'Austrian' Empire of many nationalities, and to remain at the head of all Germans. He had to juggle at home, confronting the dangers of liberalism (essentially Germanic) and of nationalism (principally Magyar), while facing challenges in Germany and Italy. After the defeat in Italy in 1859, Vienna started a period of constitutional experimentation to restore its standing and maintain the cohesion of the Empire. The October Diploma of 1860 and the February Patent of 1861 veered towards a constitution, by first accepting a measure of decentralization through a reorganization of the provincial structure, then capping it with centralist liberalism.

With the Diploma, the equalized crown lands all obtained diets, elected indirectly and publicly by a very limited number of voters, who were divided into colleges and rarely exceeded 8 per cent of the population. The Patent extended the old appointed *Reichsrat* or Council of the Empire, to become a central legislature whose lower house was made up of representatives of the diets. Only through concessions, fudges and a fleeting cooperation with the non-Magyars of Hungary was the court able to overcome Hungarian opposition.

South Slavs lived in the crown lands of Dalmatia, Istria, Gorizia, Carniola, Carinthia and Styria, as well as in Croatia and in Hungary proper; Romanians lived mainly in Transylvania, as well as in inner Hungary and in Bukovina. Meeting in 1861, the Croatian Sabor (which did not represent more than 2 per cent of the population) discussed conditions for renewed links with Hungary. The only results were that representatives of Military Croatia (Krajina) came to the Sabor, so that Serbs for the first time entered the legal political structure of Croatia, and that the Sabor voted to call 'Yugoslav' the language it now used.[1] The next diet, however, opted for 'Croatian' as the official name of the language in Croatia, this being only one of the several names used for Serbo-Croat.

The 1860s were an important decade for the ideological development of the South Slav movement in the Habsburg lands. The successors of the Illyrians gathered around Strossmayer[2] in their search for a broad South Slav programme of cultural and political ties. He led the National Party in the early 1860s in its pursuit of the political aim of a larger Croatia – to include not only Slavonia and Military Croatia (that separated Civil Croatia from Slavonia) but also Dalmatia and even Slovenia. In the late 1860s, in anticipation of a break-up of the Austrian Empire, he also elaborated with Garašanin plans for a Yugoslav confederation to include Bulgaria. The idealism of the accord covered up a more complex reality, for while they kept in close touch with Belgrade, Croatia's nationals also hesitated between Vienna and Buda.

The National Party, which had been more a 'front' than a party, and a joint movement with the representatives of Croatia's 26 per cent Serbs, split on the issue of cooperation with Vienna at the time of the February Patent. As Hungary boycotted participation in the Reichsrat, most of the nationals supported the Hungarian stand, but a splinter Independent National Party supported Vienna. In 1865, the two sets of nationals together won a majority in the Sabor, but the unionists (as the Magyarones had come to call themselves) remained active. A new group also appeared, the Rights Party, so called because it stood for Croatia's 'state' rights – true Croat nationalists under Ante Starčević (1823–96), a disillusioned Illyrian who had come to oppose the Yugoslav orientation of the nationals, who wanted no permanent partnership with either Vienna or Hungary, and who argued that all South Slavs were really Croats.

---

1 It did so after considering four options: national (neutral but populist), Croato-Slavonian (from the official name of the territory), Croatian or Serbian (ethnically correct), and Yugoslav (ideological).

2 Nominated by Jellačić in 1849 to the large and well-endowed diocese of Djakovo in Slavonia, his jurisdiction extended to Bosnia, and to the Catholics of Serbia after his appointment in 1851 as apostolic vicar there. He founded the Yugoslav (now Croatian) Academy in Zagreb in 1866. The multiplicity and the depth of his activities has given rise to a variety of interpretations and misinterpretations, for he was a Catholic prelate who wanted close links with the Orthodox, who was opposed to the dogma of Infallibility but remained loyal to the pope, simultaneously Croat and Yugoslav, idealistic and realistic.

Initially kept on as a separate province, the 'Serbian Voyvody' was abolished in December 1860 as part of the court's attempts to placate Hungary. The Serb community there had to fall back on its traditional Church assemblies of representatives of clergy, military and laity, which looked after parishes and schools, but had no political significance.

With the Habsburg Monarchy going through constitutional difficulties, and plans afoot for a rising of the Ottoman Slavs, Yugoslavism faced the dilemma of coming to fruition in or out of the Monarchy. The first choice presumed the federal restructuring of the Habsburg lands and the cultural supremacy of Zagreb; the second, their revolutionary dissolution and the political supremacy of Belgrade. Its difficulties notwithstanding, there was no early disintegration of the Habsburg Empire; Yugoslavism emerged as a supranational ideology, in support of the particular struggles of various communities and regions.

As an ideology it could be amended, interpreted, questioned. It had ups and downs, in part explained by the tension between its two poles, Zagreb and Belgrade, but it challenged 'historical' rights, and stood for 'natural' rights based on ethnic and linguistic entities. The Yugoslav idea, however fluid, was seen as a danger by all who relied on the rights of history, established or imagined. It was at the root of Austria's distrust of Serbia and of its relief at developments there after Prince Michael's death.

For the Romanians, as for the South Slavs, the experiments of the early 1860s provided some hope, followed by disappointment. The October Diploma kept Transylvania, where spirited debates and an active press contributed to two trends of Romanian opinion. While Church leaders under Bishop Andrei Şaguna, still the dominant figure, urged cooperation with Vienna on the basis of equality for all communities within existing crown lands, younger lay intellectuals advocated federalization on ethnic lines.

Cooperation was rewarded after the February Patent through an extended franchise which produced slightly more Romanian than Hungarian members in the diet. As a result of the Hungarians' boycott, the diet of 1863 recognized the Romanians' claims to equality with the other 'nations'. The achievements were, however, short-lived; the necessary formalities of enactment had not been carried out by the time the court had started to negotiate with Hungary's leaders. The Transylvanian diet met for one last time, at the beginning of 1866, with Hungarian members in attendance – to vote union with Hungary.

When the court realized that only a compromise with a moderate Hungarian programme could solve the constitutional impasse, it abandoned the other nationalities. The 1866 defeat by Prussia in the contest for supremacy in Germany, as a result of which Austria also lost Venetia, prompted the *Ausgleich* or Compromise of 1867, which satisfied the Hungarians – the Hungarian gentry – at the expense of the smaller nationalities.

Each of the two sides overestimated the other, hence the compromise to maintain what each considered essential – the Habsburgs their empire, and the Hungarians their state. With no foreign support, the Hungarians gave up their quest for total independence, in exchange for the safeguard of their historical territory. They were liberals in their own way, trying to reconcile the irreconcilable – independence, a constitutional monarchy under the imperial dynasty and the integrity of a territory.

The family conglomerate ruled over by the Habsburgs was turned into two constitutional entities with a common monarch and some other joint institutions. The Hungarians interpreted the 'Austro-Hungarian' Compromise as an arrangement to share certain affairs between their state and a neighbouring state called Austria. Austria, however, remained very much what it had been previously, but without Hungary – officially 'the lands and realms represented in the Council of Empire'. It thus not only kept an empire for the emperor of Austria, but also until 1871 the illusory hope that it could somehow find again a dominating position in the German world.

The Ausgleich had a shattering effect on the political development of the other nationalities. For both poles of the South Slavs, for Belgrade and Zagreb, the scheming and dreaming came to an end. Just when the Balkan states were more or less ready to launch their onslaught on the Ottoman Empire and expected at least some disruptions in the Austrian Empire, the latter reorganized itself into the Dual Monarchy, and the disappearance of Prince Michael of Serbia signalled an end to all plans of rebellion and war.

Hungary became a highly centralized state. Its new government felt the need for a sub-compromise only towards Croatia, which was its main domestic problem. Elections for a new Sabor, under a new electoral law, a new ban, and administrative measures against the National Party, produced a unionist majority which sent a delegation to Buda (which was not united with Pest until 1872) to negotiate a settlement, and the result was the *Nagodba* (compromise) of September 1868. Croatia-Slavonia was an 'adjacent territory' of Hungary, with a measure of autonomy in running its administration, judiciary and education, with its Sabor and its local executive, under a ban appointed by the Hungarian prime minister. Otherwise it shared with the rest of Hungary a common king, government and parliament.

It was then that Bishop Strossmayer retired from active political life, even though he retained a great personal influence until his death in 1905. South Slav solidarity did not come to an end, but it became realistic. Opinion in Croatia in the 1860s had placed great hopes on Serbia, and then turned to South Slav solidarity within the Habsburg Monarchy for a while. By the 1870s, dualism was accepted as a return to stability, and its framework as a reality with little likelihood of change. The 1868 settlement did mean initially a measure of autonomy, a barrier against Magyarization measures, and in 1881 the full integration of Military Croatia. The National Party accepted the limited reforms in order to become the governing party in Croatia.

Croatia was the only exception in an otherwise unitary Hungarian state. The territory of Fiume (Rijeka), Vojvodina and Transylvania were fully reintegrated, but Hungary's new leaders were liberals in their declared intentions as far as 'nationalities' were concerned. A Nationalities Law was enacted in 1868 which distinguished the political Magyar 'nation' of citizens from the 'nationalities' – communities allowed the use of their native language in the lower levels of the administration, the courts and schools.[3]

The divisions in the leadership of Transylvania's Romanians were reinforced; the urban élite split between an 'active' and a 'passive' trend. When the Orthodox Church of the Habsburg lands was reorganized as a result of dualism, the Romanians' Church organization in Hungary was reinforced by the elevation of the Orthodox bishopric of Sibiu to a metropolitanate separated from that of Sremski Karlovci which was Serb-dominated. Şaguna, now Metropolitan Andrei, favoured loyal participation in the constitutional system, so as to be able to lean on Vienna, but a new generation of intellectuals advocated passive resistance – a complete withdrawal from political life. Under Ioan Raţiu (1828–1902), a lawyer and ex-'forty-eighter', they believed that dualism would fail, and made the restoration of Transylvania's autonomy their objective, which they linked to the promotion of Romanian national rights. They confronted the metropolitan, whose policy in the meanwhile did at least make it possible for an enhanced Church organization to become a stronghold of Romanian identity in Transylvania. Its Uniate and Orthodox branches operated denominational Romanian-language schools.

Both tendencies were nevertheless reduced to being political bystanders, and by 1875 passivism had been strengthened. Şaguna died in 1873. The very restrictive electoral law of 1874 brought Count Kálmán Tisza's (1830–1902) new Liberal Party to power in Hungary the following year, with a policy aimed at strengthening Magyar predominance. Similar divisions appeared in the Serb leadership. The nationals of Vojvodina divided, as conservative prelates, landowners and field officers relied on the court and existing Church privileges, but the lawyer Svetozar Miletić (1829–1901) founded the Serb National Liberal Party, which called for equal citizenship within a democratic constitutional Hungary.

Romanians and South Slavs remained divided in the reorganized Dual Monarchy. By the end of the century, there were approximately 2.8 million ethnic Romanians (20 per cent of the population) in the Kingdom of Hungary, with another 230,000 in Austrian Bukovina, which had been cut off from Moldavia in 1774,[4] as well as some 2.6 million South Slavs (Serbs and Croats) in Hungary (including Croatia), and 1.1 million (Slovenes, Croats and Serbs) in the Austrian provinces.

What remained of Austria would have been a strange crescent-shaped geographical expression, lacking even territorial continuity along the Adriatic coast, with a heterogeneous population, four-fifths of whom were non-Germanic, had it not been kept together by the old principle of dynasticism. By 1871, however, with the setting up of the Prussian-led German Empire, the dynasty, and with it the Austro-Germans, had lost all hope of playing a

---

3 That distinction would be taken over by Soviet and, later, Yugoslav communist constitutionalism.
4 Not to mention perhaps another million in Bessarabia, that other part of Moldavia cut off in 1812 by Russia, where they were certainly not able to participate distinctly in political life, and where they were subjected to intense Russification.

rôle of any sort in Germany. At the same time, a Hungarian veto had prevented a dynastic sub-compromise with Bohemia, which affected the loyalty of the Czechs and, more generally, of all Slavs. Serbs looked to Serbia, Italians to Italy, and all wondered why Hungarians had been rewarded for their doubtful dynastic loyalty in 1848–49.

After that, the various groups and territories, kept carefully apart, fought uncoordinated struggles that varied according to local conditions. In Dalmatia, the essentially urban National Party which had been a joint movement of Croats and Serbs (the latter about 16 per cent of the population), obtained a majority in the provincial diet in 1870. While it came to see union with Croatia as being no longer feasible, it also became more Croat, acting through reading rooms and bilingual newspapers. The vernacular (here called 'Illyrian–Dalmatian') had been official alongside Italian since the Napoleonic interlude. The Orthodox Church organization for the Austrian lands, restructured as the metropolitanate of Bukovina-Dalmatia, made a significant contribution to the cultural life of both Romanians and Serbs, but being common to all the Orthodox, could not be used as an ethnic framework, as was the case with the metropolitanates in Hungary.

Scattered among six Austrian provinces, with a majority in only two, and pressed by Germanization, the one million or so Slovenes formed a largely peasant society. Their intelligentsia, including Catholic clerics, made the most of the Austrian constitutional régime to work at a linguistic and cultural revival through newspapers, reading rooms and public meetings. Since they could not turn to any 'historical' rights, they asked for separate ethnic electoral colleges in every province by reason of 'natural' rights.

These provinces were actually the first of the South Slav or Romanian-inhabited lands to undergo modern industrialization, as the percentage of the peasantry there declined gradually from 83 per cent in 1857 to 73 per cent by the end of the century. There were significant deposits of iron and coal and extraction was expanded to meet the needs of the Vienna–Trieste railway and of Trieste's construction trade, with the beginnings of local manufacture of rail and ship parts, of sawmills and paper making. Industrialization, however, went with Germanization, as the Slovene bourgeoisie was still predominantly mercantile and professional.

At the other end of the scale was Dalmatia, isolated both geographically and administratively. Divided between Italianate towns and a backward countryside, 90 per cent of its population was still rural and in some dependent relationship, engaging in traditional Mediterranean cultivation on extremely parcelled land. Only caravans went into Ottoman Bosnia, there were no trade links with Croatia, and even sea trade was lost to Trieste and Fiume.

Generally speaking, the two parts of the Monarchy remained economically separate. Even the Hungarian free port of Fiume suffered from the fact that the border was only sixteen kilometres away, and had no access to a nearby supply of iron ore and to markets. Croatia's capacity to industrialize was restricted by the rivalry between the two parts of the Monarchy in rail construction. It was also hampered by the maintenance until 1881 of the Military Frontier, whose viability Hungary took every opportunity to undermine as it had not forgotten the rôle played in 1849 by Jellačić's regiments.

The peasants' emancipation had little immediate effect on agriculture in the Hungarian part of the Monarchy. Roads were bad, railways generally still beyond Hungarian resources, Austrian lines ignored east–west trade, so that the kingdom remained compartmentalized. Only late in the century would access to rail and credit and the adoption of more efficient techniques by the great landlords of northern Hungary start an expansion of the agricultural sector. Even then, the lack of direct rail links with Austrian markets, as well as the border, prevented Romanian or Croat smallholders from selling their grains and livestock elsewhere than in Hungary.

With the Habsburgs cut off from their rôle in Germany and Italy, a Balkan mission would be invented as a substitute by the aristocracy, the military and the bureaucracy which identified with the dynasty. It was meant to be a new lease of life, but it was also a way of escaping from the gradual accumulation of problems and conflicts into a foreign policy of prestige. It made the Monarchy ready for involvement in the Eastern Crisis, particularly in so far as it affected the Ottoman provinces of Bosnia and Herzegovina wedged into its territories.

OTTOMAN REFORMS: RENEWED TANZIMAT AND EXARCHATE

In the Ottoman Empire, the Tanzimat had started up again more vigorously after 1856 under French-inspired ministers, with measures to achieve the promised equality between Christians and Muslims and to consolidate and modernize the central administration. Their aim was to satisfy the powers that now guaranteed the integrity of the sultan's remaining territories, but also that the Empire should take its rightful place on the European scene. Their assumption was that, once individual rights had been guaranteed by law, both domestic and diplomatic progress would automatically follow, that a relatively secularized sense of Ottoman loyalty would both counter the threat of nationalism and prevent religious strife.

The millet system was reformed as the state assumed a series of responsibilities that had belonged to the ethnic-religious groups. The existing millets were reorganized between 1862 and 1868, starting with the largest, the *Rum* or Eastern Orthodox. New statutes brought in lay representatives of regions and professions, so that power effectively passed from the religious hierarchy to the upper urban élite (usually Greek or Hellenized in the case of the Orthodox). The Porte then went on to set up a series of new, smaller, millets, until there were nine altogether by 1875.

A European-type budget was introduced, secular schools were established for the élite, and a land code enacted in 1858 which safeguarded holders' and users' interests. In 1864 a comprehensive plan was drawn up, to be introduced gradually, to reorganize the provincial administration, tighten control, redraw the provinces and reduce their number.

The Ottoman bureaucracy did not find it too difficult to accept the principle of religious equality, but the reformers nevertheless met with opposition from all sides. 'Young Ottoman' intellectuals, already brought up in the spirit of the Tanzimat, accused the reformers of merely copying what they liked from the west, in effect freeing the arbitrary will of the sultan from the restraints of traditional Ottoman institutions. They wanted to move on to constitutional government that would base political rights on the concept of defence of the fatherland, and associate them with the law of Islam. The mass of the Muslim population simply balked at westernization, and the intelligentsia in particular saw it as a threat to what remained of its special position. With their élites largely left out of the market economy, as a result of the growing power of non-Muslim commercial and professional groups, the political and military spheres were seen as the remaining and essential preserves of Muslims.

The reforms satisfied few; the momentum of the Tanzimat was lost by the early 1870s. It had undermined the traditional organization of non-Muslim religious communities, but the effect had been different from that intended. The political system had turned into a quasi-modern imitation of European central government, but without social, cultural, or even ideological cohesion, and increasingly identified with the Muslim majority. By facilitating communications between social classes belonging to the same community, by limiting the power of the higher clergy and increasing that of the lay élite, by forming new communities, the reform of the millets accelerated the differentiation between Christians and Muslims. Religion continued to be an important factor in determining an individual's position, but 'millet' began to take on a secondary meaning, its modern Turkish one of 'nation'.

The nationalism of the middle classes filtered down to the peasants, as they were influenced by the preoccupations of their respective millets and by the nation-states of their own ethnicity, and as they reacted to the very shortcomings of the Ottoman state. In order to avoid having to increase direct taxation, the latter increasingly turned to borrowing, which led it to bankruptcy at the end of the period, and advances from tax collectors, which stimulated devaluation and increased the pressure on taxpayers. Raised state harvest tithes and labour services for railway construction added to an atmosphere flashed through with local jacqueries, and receptive to the action of secret organizations.

Islam was still dominant. Muslims remained in top posts. Conscription did not work, the government had to introduce an exemption tax and military service remained generally confined to Muslims – mainly Turks. In the Ottoman Balkans, Muslims still held sway in a variety of ways. Their numbers had been increased, and their anti-Orthodox attitude often hardened, by many of those who had left the independent and autonomous territories. Officials and military were generally Muslim; much of the land was still in Muslim hands.

The large estates whose existence had been favoured by the proximity of Constantinople predominated between the Balkan mountains and the Aegean coast. In Macedonia too, the landowners were generally Turks, as opposed to the few Muslim peasants who were Slavs. There were many more such native Slavs who had accepted Islam in Bulgaria, where they were known as 'Pomaks' ('those who had left'). Perhaps over a million Muslim Circassians had emigrated to the Ottoman Empire in the 1860s after the Russian conquest of the Caucasus. The authorities had planted 100,000–200,000 of them across a sensitive belt of territory in the Balkans, concentrated in Dobrudja and northeastern Bulgaria, but extending right across Macedonia to Prizren. Their implantation caused disruption. Neither well integrated nor well received, they lived miserably and many turned to banditry. If the idea of a general rising of Christian peasants was not realized, the general atmosphere was favourable to local outbreaks that could influence each other.

The reforms had come up against resistance in Bosnia and Albania, where historical circumstances had added special twists to the advantages of conversion to the dominant faith. Albanians were spread across the three newly redefined provinces of Scutari (Shkodër/Skadar), Janina and Monastir (Bitolj/Bitola). Timars had been turned into chiftliks. The mountainous areas escaped almost totally from the competence of the regular administration, and the north was organized into clans. Muslims made up some 70 per cent of Albanians, estimated at over one million. The Christian minority was divided between 20 per cent Orthodox, concentrated in the south, and 10 per cent Catholics, mostly around Scutari.

Albanians spoke various dialects of their own language, which was not used in any official or educational capacity, except in Austrian- or Italian-supported Catholic schools. Ottoman Turkish was the language of government, Arabic that of Islam, Greek the medium of worship and instruction for the Orthodox. In the late 1860s, the Serbian government had managed to involve some north Albanian magnates in its anti-Ottoman plans, and although these were no more than uncertain arrangements, they had left the impression in the region that a wider Slav state around Serbia was in the offing.

In Macedonia, the towns continued to be a mosaic, to give no lead and to be separate from the surrounding countryside. None had a population of more than 30,000, except Salonika, of whose 60,000 inhabitants, 40,000 were Jews – 'the curious instance of a city historically Greek, politically Turkish, geographically Bulgarian, and ethnically Jewish'.[5] The Muslim urban population had dropped behind the Christian component, but some of the latter were moving out to neighbouring regions to become super-Greeks, super-Bulgars and super-Serbs. As they set up Serb and Bulgarian schools to rival

5 As described by Miss Muir Mackenzie and Miss Irby after their visit there in 1863; quoted from the 5th edition (2 vols) of G. Muir Mackenzie and A.P. Irby, *Travels in the Slavonic Provinces of Turkey in Europe*, with a preface by W.E. Gladstone, London: Daldy, Isbister & Co., 1877, 57.

the Greek schools, urban Christians tended to divide ethnically – occasionally in the same family – according to the schools they had attended.

The restoration of political order in Bulgaria, with its concomitant economic 'revival', had led to a parallel cultural phenomenon,[6] as teachers subsidized by the Bulgarian communities in Romania and southern Russia began to set up Bulgarian schools on the model of Greek schools. The movement had to overcome the lack of a standardized vernacular, opposition from the Church hierarchy (which did not like the Greek vernacular, let alone the Bulgarian), and the dearth of books in Bulgarian.

By the middle of the century, most sizeable communities had schools teaching in Bulgarian, supported by local councils and guilds. An important feature of the revival was the reading rooms, with their multiple activities characteristic of all such South Slav revivals from the Habsburg Alps to the Ottoman Black Sea. The ablest students from the larger towns were frequently sent abroad, again at the expense of local merchants, guilds and councils, or with grants from Russian Slavophile organizations. Most of those who returned went on to work as teachers, with ideas in conflict with those of the notables who employed them. There were perhaps 2,000–3,000 in the 1860s, working in some 2,000 schools and in a few teachers' and priests' training colleges.

The region chosen by the Porte to be the showpiece of its reformed provincial administration, right from the start in 1864 was the *vilayet* of the Danube. It extended from the Black Sea to the mountains of Albania, and included the core Bulgarian region south of the Danube. One of the most prosperous of Ottoman territories, it could be made to yield tax revenues to impress European creditors, if efficiently collected. Midhat Pasha (1822–84), one of the chief planners of the reform and the Ottoman government's most able administrator, was appointed governor. The son of Pomak parents, he remained in the post until 1867, and in these four years did much for the material improvement of the province. He also achieved the goal that had been assigned to him, of improving fiscal revenue above the average, which effectively meant raising the tax burden.

Bulgaria's relative prosperity had generated rising expectations, which the Ottoman authorities met with a better administration that included the obligation to contribute more. Legal reforms enabled the recognition of ownership, the purchase of land from departing Turks, and even a network of agricultural savings banks providing a restricted line of credit. By the 1870s most peasants had become, to all intents and purposes, proprietors of the land they worked.

6 One of its pioneers had been the monk Paiisi of Hilandar monastery on Mount Athos in the middle of the eighteenth century. Reading in the monastery library, he had learnt of the old Bulgarian realm, and taken pride in the history of his people. He wrote 'A Slavonic-Bulgarian history of the people, tsars and saints, and of their deeds, and of the Bulgarian way of life' in a form of Church Slavonic. His work did more than extol a Bulgarian past; it placed its glory above that of all other Slavs, as being the first to have kings, patriarchs, and Christianity, and as having had the largest territory. With praise of the Bulgars went scorn for Greek culture. Paiisi's history was copied in samizdat until its first printed edition appeared in Hungary in 1844.

The number of private chiftlik estates with peasant sharecroppers, still dominant in Macedonia and Thessaly, had been constantly decreasing.[7] There was no rural overpopulation, and the household manufacture of textiles, leather and ironware provided supplementary cash income.

Yet improved material conditions had disappointed expectations and increased peasant disaffection towards local authorities and their Bulgarian agents. Bulgarian native trade remained dependent on major Ottoman markets, without support from the imperial authorities, facing more efficient impositions and continued monetary depreciation. In that sector, too, Ottoman reforms had created and disappointed expectations.

More Bulgars pressed to be acknowledged as an ethnic group within the Ottoman Empire. A notable success had been obtained by the 30,000-strong Bulgarian community in Constantinople, when the Porte had agreed to their building a church where they could worship in their own language. Consecrated in 1849 (and still in existence), St Stephen's in the Phanar spearheaded the movement for a separate church organization. The reform of the Orthodox millet had led to increased Hellenism, which made it more difficult for Bulgars to expect a greater participation. As city guilds split into Greek and Bulgar sections with the approval of the authorities, thoughts turned to Rome. Catholic and Protestant missionary activities were making the most of Bulgarian discontent, with the particular appeal of uniatism linked to a Slavonic liturgy.

The patriarchate was sensitive to the issue of Orthodox unity, for its own sake, but also to help the Greek participation in Michael Obrenović's schemes and to ward off the fear of union with Rome. The patriarch appointed some Bulgarian bishops, and also convened a number of meetings to discuss Bulgarian grievances, but he faced increased intransigence from both Greeks and Bulgars. On Easter Sunday 1860, St Stephen's in Constantinople omitted the name of the patriarch from its intercessions, and so did a number of dioceses. This was tantamount to withdrawing from his authority. Acting as though they were outside his jurisdiction, Bulgarian bishops were demanding more than mere participation or autonomy; they wanted a separate status.

The Russian ambassador to the Porte, General Nikolay Ignatiev (1832–1907), worked hard for a compromise that would avoid a schism and inter-Balkan nationalist conflicts, satisfy the Bulgars and not alienate the Greeks. He influenced the election of Patriarch Gregory VI in 1867, who offered an autonomous jurisdiction over a definite territory between the Danube and the Balkan mountains, under the authority of a Bulgarian archbishop resident in Constantinople, with the title of 'exarch' or patriarch's representative. As the plan was being negotiated, the Porte took it upon itself to end the dispute by an act of the sultan's in February 1871 – a declaration of intent to recognize a separate Bulgarian millet under the authority of an exarch. A number of

---

7 The land survey carried out by Russian officials in 1878 before the mass departure of Turks found about 200 chifliks. Of those recorded, about 59 per cent were in Turkish hands (33 per cent unrecorded ownership), and only 15 per cent were over 50 hectares (48 per cent unrecorded).

dioceses would immediately be transferred to his jurisdiction, others would be split up, and there were provisions for sees to join if at least two-thirds of their faithful expressed the wish to do so.

Nevertheless, negotiations continued under Ignatiev's backstage mediation, as the patriarchate wanted specific territorial dioceses, with no ethnic divisions and no expansion, and the Bulgarian side tried to get more dioceses immediately. When the talks became deadlocked over the two Macedonian sees of Skopje (Üsküb) and Ohrid, the Porte proceeded to organize plebiscites. Most Slavs voted for a Slavonic liturgy and bishops were appointed without the authority of the patriarch, who summoned a council.

Attended by senior Greek prelates of the Ottoman Empire, including the heads of the autocephalous Churches of Alexandria, Antioch and Cyprus, the Council of Constantinople in September 1872 condemned the heresy of phyletism (the determination of ecclesiastical jurisdictions within the Orthodox Church on an ethnic rather than on a territorial basis), and declared its instigators to be schismatics, singling out the Bulgarian bishops and their followers.[8]

The patriarchal compromise had come too late. The Bulgars wanted more by then. The Porte encouraged them, anxious that they should not line up with the Greeks. The issue was one of nationalism; it had nothing to do with religion. The Bulgarian notables had obtained recognition as a separate millet, and they now had a framework within which to develop. Once established, the exarchate became a leading force, representing Bulgarian interests at the Porte, and sponsoring Bulgarian churches and schools in mixed dioceses. As it expanded southwards and eastwards, it fuelled Greek anti-Slav feelings and alarmed the Serbs.

The élite had their millet, which was not turned against Ottoman rule, and peasant discontent was not transformed into an anti-Turkish uprising for lack of adequate leadership. Individual Bulgars had taken part in movements elsewhere in the Balkans and in Russian wars, but political activists had been few and ineffective. The first stirrings of armed rebellion against Ottoman rule came from left-wing revolutionaries abroad. These were 'intellectuals', many of them educated in Russia, bent on direct action, with economic backing from Bulgarian settlers and sympathizers abroad.

They first operated from Serbia, which provided a model, an incentive and a haven, help and books for students, and a base from which to send armed bands or chetas. After Michael Obrenović's assassination and Cuza's fall, the centre moved to Bucharest, where Romanian liberals and a large Bulgarian community provided support. Political committees represented various tendencies, increasingly bent on causing peasant risings and provoking the Turks to reprisals which would affect European opinion.

8 The Moscow Synod had been invited to send representatives, and then to sign the Council document. It failed to do either, neither supporting nor condemning the exarchate. Only in 1945 would the Church of Bulgaria be reconciled.

Russia (particularly the Slavophile lobby) was showing increasing interest in Bulgaria, with more grants for students who fell under the influence of the Russian left. In spite of the concentration of militant tendencies under an umbrella Bulgarian Revolutionary Central Committee in Bucharest, revolutionaries found it difficult to organize action. Their radicalism did not win them many allies in Bulgaria, personalities clashed, the Ottoman authorities quickly dismantled various attempts across the Danube, and yet the initiative was taken to launch an insurrection in September 1875.

By that time Herzegovina was up in arms, followed by Bosnia. In 1850–51, Omer Latas Pasha (1806–71), a Serb convert from Krajina who had been in command of the Ottoman occupation army in the Danubian Principalities in 1848–49, had broken the political and military power of the old landowning nobility, as a preliminary to the introduction of the Tanzimat. The seven districts of Bosnia and Herzegovina had been reorganized into one large vilayet of Bosnia, the administrative framework and the legal order had improved. Christian churches had undergone a period of renewal and provided their own local communities with schools, as links with Serbia and Croatia were tolerated. Russia protected the Orthodox; Austria-Hungary did the same for the Catholics.

While the 1860s were in many ways an improvement for Bosnia, the province was still a 'Turkey-in-Europe'. Wedged between Austrian Dalmatia, Hungarian Croatia and autonomous Serbia, Bosnia and Herzegovina remained one of the most backward areas of the Balkans. Population estimates vary and should be treated cautiously. Out of a total population of some 1.3 million, there were perhaps 400,000 Muslims, of whom 7,000–10,000 formed the landowning élite, where a particularly strong autochthonous Slav element had been able to assimilate more recently settled Turks and other Muslims. They tended to reside in towns rather than on their estates, and not all were rich. Most were Serbo-Croat speakers, few of them knew any Arabic or Ottoman Turkish, most felt 'Ottoman' yet were disillusioned with the way they had been treated by the Ottoman government and disliked Turks. Many retained traces of Christian customs. Relations with Christians varied from paternalistic or friendly to jealous or fanatical. The distribution of the Muslim settlement tended to coincide with its control of towns, plains and valleys.

There were about half a million Orthodox – the overwhelming majority of whom were peasant sharecroppers on the estates of Muslim lords. Indeed, over half of all the peasants were dependent sharecroppers, almost all of them Christian (74 per cent Orthodox, with 21 per cent Catholic), owing between a third and a half of their crop to the landlord. Catholics ('Latins') totalled some 250,000, mostly peasants and without much of an élite. A small but developing Orthodox urban commercial class was the first segment of the population to modernize on European–Ottoman lines, alongside a prosperous Sephardic Jewish community concentrated in Sarajevo. The seat of the Ottoman administration, this was a city of some 50,000 inhabitants, dominated by

Muslims as were all towns. It had more schools than any other city in the province, but still no bookshop in 1878.

The merchants and some of the Christians who had acquired land had advanced, yet the mass of the peasantry not only paid its tithe of produce to the lords, but the money equivalent of a tenth of the crop in tax to the state, and a new tax in lieu of military service. Once again, administrative efficiency had both increased the expectations and lowered the living standards of the peasants, most of whom, affected by the propaganda of the 1860s, looked emotionally to Serbia.

THE EASTERN CRISIS AND THE CONGRESS OF BERLIN

The peasant revolt in Herzegovina and in Bosnia was a spontaneous one. Not only did the Porte find it difficult to impose its legal reforms on the local nobility, but paradoxically the very modernization of the state, in so far as it reached those provinces, added to the peasants' fiscal constraints. The bad harvest of 1873 in Anatolia, followed by a severe winter and floods, had put pressure on the European provinces. Herzegovina suffered a disastrous harvest in 1874 and tax collectors resorted to violent measures to gather the state tithe. The Christian peasants of its eastern tip bordering on Montenegro took to the mountains to resist payment.

The revolt was separate from any propaganda put about by Montenegro or Serbia, yet receptive to it. The sultan's rule had never been effective over minute mountainous Montenegro. Recognizing no political borders in their pastoral (and cattle-rustling) activities or in their blood relationships, her clans were a constant threat to Ottoman hold over adjacent territories as they forayed into Herzegovina and northern Albania. Her rulers considered themselves Serb, were generally supportive of a 'Serb' cause and willing to cooperate with Serbia, but nevertheless gave priority to their own territorial objectives.

The Serbian government had supported local committees in its planning of a rising which Serbia and Montenegro would have joined by assuming responsibility for military operations against Ottoman troops. Quite apart from Montenegro's objectives, there were also 'non-governmental organizations' operating in the region. Serb propaganda was far from being monolithic. It generally did not advocate radical social reforms. All its strands played down religious differences so as to integrate the three faiths in their action, not only the Catholic peasants and their Franciscan clergy, but also the Muslims and their nobility in particular.

The rising quickly spread without a central organization. Villagers whose pastoral way of life regularly took them to the uplands knew where to take refuge, and how to survive with more meat than bread. Mountainous clans joined rebellious sharecroppers. Within the first two months, they had isolated garrisons in Herzegovina, destroyed lines of communication and defeated Ottoman reinforcements. By the end of August the rebellion had spread to

Bosnia, particularly along the Austrian border. There it was generally limited to the Orthodox, whereas Catholics took part in Herzegovina, but the Muslim areas of central and northeast Bosnia remained loyal.

It was guerrilla warfare, with insurgents operating from uplands that were almost immune to counter-insurgency. Military operations ceased with the advent of winter and resumed in the spring. The pattern was in many ways reminiscent of the Serbian and Greek uprisings at the beginning of the century, but the extent and the violence were far greater. By the spring, there were perhaps 25,000 armed insurgents facing 30,000 Ottoman soldiers. Atrocities were committed on both sides as refugees were pushed around and abandoned villages pillaged or destroyed. It is estimated that 200,000 refugees crossed into Austrian territory and that 150,000 lives were lost.

Montenegro was influential in Herzegovina. Much of the direction in Bosnia came from a committee in Belgrade – chaired by the archbishop, with financial support from the Serbian government – that gathered and channelled equipment, supplies, money, arms, propaganda and volunteers, and took care of refugees. The rebellion found a response in Habsburg territories, with aid committees active in Vojvodina, in Dalmatia, in Croatia, and even in Slovenia. It attracted socialist groups and sundry other volunteers, including Peter Karadjordjević (1844–1921).[9]

With the Ottoman Balkans destabilized as a result of the revolt and Bulgarian volunteers joining in, a renewed leadership of the Bulgarian committee in Bucharest had decided to take advantage of the upheaval to provoke an insurrection in Bulgaria in September 1875 – which failed. Undeterred, they planned another for the following spring, to coincide with the rekindling of the Bosnian guerrilla war and the expected intervention of Serbia and Montenegro.

The 'April Uprising' was another disaster. Although it later became one of the major events in Bulgaria's interpretation of her history, it would have attracted little attention but for its suppression. Unable to elicit a popular response, the leaders had to concentrate on a few mountain towns. Most of the participants were schoolmasters, priests, students and artisans. The majority of the population wanted nothing to do with the uprising even after it had started, and a significant proportion actually supported Ottoman rule. The wealthier Christian layer did not want a revolutionary adventure, the Islamic element even less so. There was treachery and mutual recrimination.

The Porte was determined to crush any attempted rising in this sensitive region. Since it could not spare regular troops, most of whom were either in Bosnia or facing Serbia, it resorted to recruiting *bashi-bozuk* irregulars from the Muslim population. Local Turks, Pomaks, Circassians and refugees from 'infidel' rule wreaked a fearful vengeance on Christian peasants, usually innocent of the earlier killings of Muslim civilians that had accompanied the rising.

---

9 The Geneva- and Paris-educated son of ex-Prince Alexander had been through French military schools and taken part in the Franco-German war. Hitherto something of a playboy in spite of his military exploits, he turned up in Bosnia from Paris to improve his political rating. His participation stood him in good stead as he was to become king of Serbia, though not until 1903.

The excesses were often carried out by people who had themselves been victims – villagers whose relatives had been killed or miserable Circassians. Not only were most of the actual insurgents wiped out, but whole villages were plundered and burnt, and perhaps as many as 30,000 people died (although numbers were inflated or reduced according to sympathies). In a few weeks, the rising had come to an end.

Meanwhile, there had been developments at other levels. Austria-Hungary was taking up its new rôle in the Balkans. Russia, in order to regain her influence there, particularly with regard to the Straits, was ready to acknowledge Austria-Hungary's share, if and when necessary. Since the leaders of the Bosnian insurgents had rejected a reform plan initiated by Austria-Hungary, fighting had resumed in the spring of 1876, as expected. Opinion in Serbia and Montenegro demanded intervention. As for the 'Bulgarian atrocities', not only did they incense and increase a Bulgarian consciousness, but they caused an international reaction. Hitherto unknown Bulgaria became almost overnight a household word, its fate the concern of philanthropists and liberal politicians.

In what became known as the year of three sultans, Abdülaziz was deposed in a coup that brought to power a coalition of Ottoman opponents under Midhat Pasha. In June, Serbia and Montenegro effectively went to war against their suzerain by sending their troops into Bosnia and Herzegovina, with Yugoslav, Romanian, Bulgarian, Greek, Russian and other European volunteers, thus dashing hopes of a local settlement through diplomatic mediation. Official propaganda stressed the Yugoslav aspect of the war, which was neither religious nor social, and tried to reassure Muslims. In Croatia, where the mainstream National Party favoured leaving Bosnia to unite with Serbia so as to create the nucleus of a future Yugoslav federation, the Sabor had to be threatened before it would give up its support for the rebels. Russian opinion pressed for intervention, as an Ottoman counteroffensive moved into Serbia.

Romania had acted cautiously, trying to use the crisis for her own benefit. Brătianu's liberal government that had come to power in June 1876 maintained an official attitude of neutrality, in return for which it asked the Porte and the powers to recognize the 'individuality of the Romanian state'. It also asked Russia, should it go to war through Romania, to recognize the country's independence, to guarantee its territorial integrity and to accept its military participation.

Russia then obtained Austria-Hungary's agreement, in exchange for a free hand in Bosnia, to a move to stop the Turks from defeating Serbia and Montenegro. The Serbian militia was no match for the reformed Ottoman army in terms of experience, officer training and weaponry. There was talk of war fever in Belgrade, but peasant soldiers deserted to bring the harvest in. Serbia could not maintain its effort for any length of time. A Russian ultimatum to the Porte in October 1876 brought an end to hostilities and saved Serbia from total defeat. She had to accept Russia's advice to settle for a return to the prewar situation, and to withdraw from any further action on Ottoman territory.

Russia was gearing up for war, but she was also anxious to obtain a European mandate to press for reform by hook or by crook. There was a final diplomatic attempt to work out a scheme that would restore order in the rebellious provinces. The Conference of Ambassadors that met in Constantinople produced a protocol in January 1877 – to set up districts according to religious majorities, and to regroup them into two large vilayets with a measure of autonomy and assemblies elected by all property holders.

Ottoman opinion reacted against dictation by the powers. Thus backed, the new government in Constantinople countered with the promulgation of a constitution by Sultan Abdülhamid II. The move strengthened the hand of the political élite, gave satisfaction to the reformers, proclaimed the unity of the Ottoman Empire and warded off foreign intervention in its internal affairs. In April, sensing British reticence to go along with any European mandate to exert additional pressure, the Porte rejected the proposals of the conference; an elected parliament would solve all problems on the basis of direct representation. Russia took the rejection as a cue to declare war.

She had cleared the way for the expected failure of the conference by another secret arrangement with Austria-Hungary in January. In case of a Russo-Turkish war, Austria-Hungary would adopt an attitude of benevolent neutrality towards Russia; Russia would limit her operations to the eastern Balkans; Austria-Hungary could, at the end of the crisis, help herself to Bosnia and Herzegovina; no large state would emerge in the Balkans.

In April, Russia had agreed with Romania on the logistics and the political implications of stationing troops in and transporting them through her territory. Romania would provide unhindered access and full cooperation; Russia would respect her 'political rights' and her territorial integrity. No sooner had Russia declared war and her troops crossed into Romania, than parliament in Bucharest declared a state of war on the Ottoman Empire and the country's 'absolute independence'. Participation in the war was seen as a way to obtain recognition of this independence.

Sultan Abdülhamid took advantage of the war to reveal his true colours, to dismiss Midhat and to shelve the constitution, which would only be restored with the Young Turks' revolt in 1908. In June, the Russians eventually crossed the Danube. They were received by the Bulgarian population as liberators, but Ottoman resistance was stiff. The advance was stopped both at the Balkan mountains and by the long siege of Plevna. Montenegro had also gone into action again at the same time, moving towards the coast and Scutari.

Serbia followed suit in December, with an offensive aimed at Niš which helped the Russians. Even more decisive, however, was the intervention of the Romanian army. Russia had been categorically opposed to any active Romanian participation, until the stalemate of the summer, when the tone changed. Prince Charles was first requested to provide troops to hold prisoners and occupy territory, so as to release the Russians for action, and then to take a full part in operations with overall command at Plevna. The tenacity and endurance of the Romanians made a decisive contribution to victory, but casualties were heavy on all sides.

The fall of Plevna opened up Bulgaria, Ottoman defences crumbled and the Russian army moved on rapidly. In January 1878 Sofia and Adrianople fell, Constantinople itself was under threat and the Turks obtained an armistice. Russia hurried to impose peace terms, to face the powers with a fait accompli. Under the terms of the 'peace preliminaries' signed on 3 March at San Stefano on the outskirts of Constantinople,[10] Serbia and Montenegro were recognized as independent states and obtained additional territory, the former gaining the upper valley of the Morava, the latter access to the Adriatic. Romania, likewise recognized as independent, received part of Dobrudja in compensation for the southern Bessarabian districts which Russia had had to return in 1856, and was now taking back.

Reforms were to be introduced in Bosnia and Herzegovina, but the most momentous clauses affected Bulgaria. San Stefano created an autonomous Principality of Bulgaria with an area of 172,000 sq. kms from the Danube to the Aegean (even though Salonika was left out), and from the Black Sea coast to the Albanian mountains, including Skopje and the whole of the Vardar valley. It went beyond the most fervent dreams of Bulgarian patriots, and the most alarmist expectations of European diplomats. Russian troops would remain in occupation of the new principality for two years. At one stroke, directly ruled Ottoman territory would become an autonomous principality with the whole of Macedonia and a frontage on two seas – a 'greater Bulgaria' that was to become the 'Great Idea' of Bulgarian nationalists.

Of Romania, Serbia and Montenegro, not one had been party to the negotiations, and all three were dissatisfied with the results. Romania felt betrayed. To add insult to injury, she was required to maintain the supply routes through her territory for the Russian occupation army in Bulgaria, and threatened with occupation herself if she did not accept. Greece had not joined in the fray, although nationalists had sent aid, arms and volunteers across the border and to Crete. In the summer of 1877, fearing for Greek interests in Epirus, Macedonia and Thessaly, the government itself prepared to organize risings among the Greek population there. The Ottoman government took special measures, including the mobilization of Muslim Albanians. The revolt gained momentum after the fall of Plevna. Athens eventually ordered its troops across the border on the eve of the Russo-Turkish armistice that brought the war to an end. The Turks were free to turn on the Greeks, who had to withdraw. Russia stopped any further action and the revolts ended in May.

The dominant feeling in Europe was that 'autonomous' Bulgaria would be a protectorate under Russia, who would thus gain control over Constantinople

10 San Stefano or Yeşilköy, a pleasant village of villas near the Sea of Marmara, 14 km to the east of the present-day city, is now also the site of Istanbul international airport.

and the Straits. Russia's negotiator Ignatiev, the architect of the peace preliminaries, had probably taken more than he expected Russia to keep, in order to
give her a surplus to bargain for changes in the Paris settlement of 1856. San
Stefano infringed the terms of the Paris settlement, which had introduced the
principle of consensus between Turkey's guarantors. San Stefano could not be
more than a set of preliminary terms, pending a final European settlement.
Russia immediately agreed to attend a European congress. By June, Austro-
Russian and Anglo-Russian agreements had prepared the ground for the Congress of Berlin.

The Treaty of Berlin, signed on 13 July 1878, confirmed the setting up of
an autonomous and tributary Principality of Bulgaria under the suzerainty of
the sultan. It would be ruled by an elected prince, who would not be from the
reigning house of any of the powers, but would be approved by them and
confirmed by the Porte. Alarmed at the thought of a Russian-dominated greater
Bulgaria, the powers gathered in Berlin drastically reduced the territory to
64,500 sq. kms between the Danube and the Balkan range.

South of the Danube would be a province called Eastern Roumelia (rather
than southern Bulgaria), governed by a Christian governor-general nominated for five years by the powers, with an Assembly, and a gendarmerie
reflecting the size of the various ethnic groups. Arrangements were made for
a Russian provisional administration and occupation of both Bulgaria and
Eastern Roumelia (reduced to nine months), in consultation with the Porte
and the consuls of the powers. During that time, an Assembly of Notables
would meet in Bulgaria to decide on a constitution and elect a prince. The
composition and the competence of the assembly of Eastern Roumelia, as well
as the authority of its governor, would be defined by a European commission.

The formal recognition of independence for Serbia, Montenegro and
Romania was ratified. Serbia lost about half of the new territory she would
have obtained under San Stefano, and Montenegro two-thirds. Romania's disappointing exchange of territory was confirmed. Macedonia remained under
direct rule from Constantinople, with the promise of administrative reforms.
Bosnia and Herzegovina, although remaining formally Ottoman, were entrusted to Austria-Hungary, to occupy and administer provisionally. Austria-
Hungary was additionally authorized to garrison the sanjak of Novi Pazar,
which separated Serbia and Montenegro. As for Greece, the Porte was simply
invited to come to terms with the government in Athens on frontier changes.

Notwithstanding the procedure established by the Congress of Paris in
1856 to consult the population of the Danubian Principalities through the election of special advisory assemblies, and the dubious plebiscites of the unification of Italy between 1859 and 1870, there was still no international concept
of self-determination. The Treaty of Berlin did, however, try to cope with
the problem of religious minorities in the new nation-states that had emerged
from the Ottoman Empire.

It stated explicitly that the Bulgarian constitution should guarantee freedom
of worship, and specified the elimination of all religious restrictions on the

exercise of civil and political rights from the legislation of the newly recognized independent states. Likewise, the powers decided to observe how the Porte carried out its obligations under the treaty. These were steps in the direction of trying to anticipate the multiple problems encountered by the new states as they faced new realities – some stemming from the old Ottoman complexity they had inherited, others implicit in the new European order they were joining.

Many illusions were shattered. Of the powers, Russia, although allowed to keep most of her acquisitions in Asia, had not expected so much mutilation of the preliminary settlement, nor did Austria-Hungary anticipate the difficulties she was about to face in Bosnia-Herzegovina. In spite of formal international acknowledgement and territorial accretion, all the Balkan states were embittered, and, perhaps more particularly, disappointed by Russia of whom they had expected more.

The oldest of them all, Greece, had obtained nothing but Slav advances into territories she viewed as Greek, and a fear of pan-Slavism. The youngest, Bulgaria, after San Stefano had dangled before her eyes a dream that would become a nightmare, saw herself as having been 'partitioned' at birth, but was nonetheless regarded with suspicion by the other powers and with jealousy by her neighbours. She would not even be grateful to her liberators for long. Romania, after having provided so much help to Russia, had been made to accept an economically backward and ethnically alien Dobrudja for the retrocession of ancient Moldavian districts. Serbia and Montenegro were forcibly kept separate, and out of Bosnia and Herzegovina.

The settlement would embitter all the territories kept really or formally under Ottoman rule. The transfer of Bosnia and Herzegovina to Austro-Hungarian administration would raise new tensions there. As it was placed out of bounds for Serbia, it ended illusions that all Serbs could be unified in an independent Serbia, or that Bosnia could become a bridge for a future Yugoslavia. Serbia had to turn her attention southward, entering the three-cornered struggle that would poison inter-Balkan relations and foment bloodshed in unpartitioned Ottoman Macedonia. Eastern Roumelia would not rest until it had undone the restraints that kept it from joining Bulgaria.

Yet another blow was inflicted to the ecumenical character and the spiritual heritage of the Eastern Orthodox Church with the phyletism that went a step further towards linking the local churches to state and nation. At the top of the Ottoman Empire there was a reaction away from the Tanzimat and the attempts at developing an all-Ottoman citizenship, as Sultan Abdülhamid II turned to autocratic rule with a pan-Islamic policy.

CHAPTER 6

From the Congress of Berlin to 1900 – Part 1

Southern Slavs and Romanians under the Dual Monarchy. Progressive and radical governments in independent Serbia. Liberal and conservative governments in independent Romania.

The Eastern Crisis and its aftermath had again brought great changes to the Balkans, as the powers took it upon themselves to bring some order to the final crumbling of Ottoman rule in large areas of Turkey-in-Europe.

Whatever might have been thought in some circles, Russia had not gone to war against Turkey in 1877 for pan-Slavist motives. Pan-Slavism had never been as great as its supporters hoped or its enemies feared. The war and the diplomatic crisis had been caused by internal conditions coalescing with Austro-Russian rivalry, when the Habsburgs and Russia both turned to the Balkans again. Antagonism between them continued after 1878, in spite of the implicit division of spheres between these two imperial powers, but they nevertheless cooperated to maintain calm in the peninsula: neither wished to be distracted by Balkan events.

Russia gained a strong position in the eastern half, Austria-Hungary in the west, but neither lasted. To Russia it appeared that the real winners were the Habsburgs (and the British). Austria-Hungary took over a large chunk of Turkey-in-Europe which rounded off her South Slav possessions. She also wanted to monitor her now fully independent Balkan neighbours, the kingdoms of Serbia and Romania, through diplomatic and trade links. They were building their national statehood and could affect the Dual Monarchy's stability and balance through its South Slav and Romanian subjects, most of whom were in Hungary.

The Ottoman Empire came out of the crisis seriously weakened. Bulgaria, the latest addition to the Balkan states, went on to overcome as best she could most of the limitations imposed upon her by the Berlin settlement – the immediate division into two provinces with different degrees of attachment to Constantinople, Russian control and the practical effects of the sultan's residual sovereignty. She did not forget the greater Bulgarian vision of San

Stefano which took in Macedonia. Ottoman control over that central Balkan province was increasingly difficult, as rival nationalisms fought over it, and it was no easier to control Albania.

At the southern end of the Balkans, Greece bordered on Ottoman lands. The kingdom encompassed only a minority of ethnic Greeks, most of whom remained under Turkish rule. Although the oldest of the Balkan states, her independence was nevertheless hedged in and frustrated, not only by Turkey, but by the powers generally and by Britain particularly.

When Austria-Hungary took over the administration of Bosnia and Herzegovina after centuries of Ottoman rule, the occupation almost turned into a conquest. One-third of the Monarchy's fully mobilized combat capability (mostly made up of Krajina Serbs and Croats) was committed in three years of intermittent warfare to overcome the fierce resistance of Muslims who could not face the idea of finding themselves under a Christian government.[1] Muslim fighters received unexpected support from part of the Serb population that would not exchange Ottoman for Habsburg rule.

Neither the Porte nor the Serbian government was in any way involved. The initial resistance to the power transfer in central and northern Bosnia was due to the fact that most of the Ottoman soldiery there at the time consisted of local conscripts, who took over much of the matériel. Serb leaders and agitators cooperated with Muslim activists.

The guerrilla war had almost come to a halt with the end of the 1878 'season', when another rebellion, this time Serb-led and Muslim-supported, started up in 1879 in Herzegovina, where dissatisfied former insurgents turned police auxiliaries took to the uplands. Then conscription, when introduced in 1881, provoked a veritable revolt which spread to southern Bosnia as deserters threatened Sarajevo. This was not put down until the spring of 1882 and lingered on in eastern Herzegovina until the autumn.

Only then did the region settle down. Formally still part of the Ottoman Empire, Bosnia and Herzegovina were kept as one unit, Germanically hyphenated as Bosnia-Herzegovina. They were treated as a colony, even though Ottoman legislation remained in force until superseded by enactments of the new administration. All chances of union with Serbia having collapsed, only Croat opinion favoured the takeover in the hope that the new territory could be joined to Croatia.

A request to that effect had indeed been put forward by the Sabor, but neither Budapest nor Vienna wanted to strengthen Croatia, and in terms of international law the takeover was no more than a 'mandate' from the powers. Since Austria-Hungary had to provide the funds and the troops, the local

1 The best account in English of the Austro-Hungarian 'conquest' of Bosnia and Herzegovina is Robert Donia, 'The Battle for Bosnia: Habsburg Military Strategy in 1878', in Akademija nauka i umjetnosti Bosne i Hercegovine, *Posebna izdanja*, XLIII, Sarajevo, 1979.

government was placed under the joint finance ministry and entrusted to the commanding general in Sarajevo. Under Benjámin Kállay's (1839–1903) long tenure of that ministry,[2] Habsburg rule moved efficiently but carefully, so as not to upset any further the balance between the three religious communities, which in 1879 was 43 per cent Orthodox (496,000), 39 per cent Muslim (448,000) and 18 per cent Catholic (209,000). Muslims had immediately started leaving in large numbers for other parts of the Ottoman Empire, even when they were not Turkish speakers, and they went on emigrating for the remainder of the Austro-Hungarian period – perhaps as many as 100,000–140,000 in the period leading up to 1910.[3]

Kállay tried to win over the Muslim nobility and to exploit Serbo-Croat rivalry. With ever greater emphasis on ethnic definition, both Serbs and Croats claimed the Muslims so as to become the majority, while the administration promoted the idea of a Bosnian identity (and of a 'Bosnian' or 'local' language), to insulate the province from nationalist movements. This only appealed to some Muslims, as most of them wanted to be neither Serb nor Croat, and still considered themselves to be Ottoman (which all the inhabitants of Bosnia-Herzegovina formally were). The Muslim gentry were gradually reconciled by the fact that the social structure of the countryside was left untouched.

The Habsburg period contributed to the creation of a Bosnian Muslim identity, increasingly separated in fact from the Ottoman Empire (as from the rest of Islam) and adapted to new European ways. Its élite learnt how to use these to preserve its position, through compromises with Serbs, Croats and the Austro-Hungarian administration.

The religious organizations were streamlined, regulated and subsidized, to discourage political activism. With the approval of the Holy See, a Catholic hierarchy was set up, appointed by the emperor, under an archbishop in Sarajevo and clergy imported from Croatia, to replace the predominant Franciscan influence which the Habsburg régime did not trust. The ecumenical patriarch conceded the right to appoint Orthodox bishops. The Muslims obtained an organization of their own, with control over religious and educational foundations. Autonomous educational and cultural movements thus developed in towns.

A much-improved civil service was put in place, necessarily more numerous, 'colonial' in that it was generally staffed by officials from all over the Monarchy, and backed by garrisons. Refugees and newcomers were successfully

2 A diplomat and Balkan specialist, Kállay had been consul general in Belgrade, where he had learnt the language and written a history of the Serbs. He kept the ministry from 1882 until his death.
3 Figures vary from 60,000 to 300,000. Noel Malcolm's 'likely guess' is in the region of 100,000 all told, including Orthodox emigrants (*Bosnia: A Short History*, London: Macmillan, 1994, 140); Milorad Ekmečić accepts the figure of 140,000 Muslims, with another 40,000 Orthodox (*Stvaranje Jugoslavije, 1790–1918*, Belgrade: Prosveta, 1989, II, 86). Serbs also went, for both political and economic reasons. By 1910, the Muslim population was down to 33 per cent, the Catholic had increased to 23 per cent, and the Orthodox remained at 43 per cent.

resettled. Infrastructures were improved, and the exploitation of natural resources encouraged, but only by enterprises under state control, and for fiscal and military motives. The principle that the territory should be self-supporting meant that it had to pay for its own modernization, as well as defray as much as possible the costs of occupation and administration. In spite of tax increases, there were limits to what could be achieved, and what was achieved was often of no direct value to peasant taxpayers.

Agriculture was the branch of the economy in which the great majority of the population was engaged; it remained largely static in spite of some measures to assist dependent peasants to buy their land. In 1878, 85,000 sharecropping peasant families, mostly Orthodox, worked on 6,000–7,000 Muslim-owned estates. By the end of the century the free smallholders – with generally unconsolidated plots totalling under five hectares – had come to outnumber the dependent sharecroppers, but they spent what they earned on indemnifying their lords under the terms of an *in extremis* Ottoman law of 1876.

Population growth absorbed most of the production. The marketable surplus was too small to take real advantage of the wider Austro-Hungarian market or to tempt even Muslim landlords away from their anti-commercial mentality. The only way out for the peasantry was emigration, seasonal (to Hungary, Serbia or Romania), temporary or permanent (essentially to the United States). Muslim peasants emigrated to remaining Ottoman possessions.

The joint finance ministry was, with foreign affairs and war, one of the three common ministries of Austria and Hungary. Hungary ruled over the great majority of South Slavs and Romanians, whereas in the Austrian lands the South Slavs were only a little more than 7 per cent of the population. In Dalmatia, economic and cultural predominance remained in the hands of the Italian-speaking urban element, who represented no more than 2 per cent of the population, but whose position in the diet had initially been ensured by a very limited franchise. With the unification of Italy, as more and more Italian speakers came to consider themselves ethnically Italian, Vienna was less favourable to their domination in Dalmatia, nor did it want any more talk of unification with Croatia.

The Venetian context had weakened separate Croat and Serb traditions in that coastal province, where both had to assert their common Slavism against the predominant Italian element, and where ethnic divisions did not entirely coincide with religious adherence.[4] As the National Party of Dalmatia took on a more Croatian hue, however, educated urban and Catholic-led Serb representatives felt they had to remain closer to the official line and began to cooperate with the autonomists, who opposed any thought of administrative union with Croatia.

The tension was exploited by the authorities, but at the same time and in line with Austrian policy in all the provinces, the local majority language had

4 There were Serbs who retained their ethnic feeling even though their forebears had become Catholic.

become official in 1883 as 'Croatian or Serbian'. Austro-Hungarian rivalry denied the coast any railway except between the Austrian port of Trieste and the Hungarian port of Fiume. Wine production was hard hit by phylloxera as well as by Italian competition. Dalmatia remained a land that could not support its population and was a source of emigration.

The Slovenes of the Alpine provinces were a Catholic, highly literate, relatively prosperous and conservative peasantry, which generally owned its land and whose clerical activists aimed at getting the best of existing circumstances. With some thirteen deputies in the Vienna parliament after 1879, the Slovene People's Party concentrated on obtaining greater use of their language in education and administration, and secured considerable cultural concessions. From the 1890s, it developed a modern Christian social movement.

Slovene peasant cooperatives were the most successful in the Balkans. It was in the 1880s that smallholders started getting together to avoid borrowing at high interest rates usually from non-Slovene operators. By 1910, with professional management and party backing, they had involved more than 10 per cent of the population in their association. Small timber mills provided an industrial sector.

The province of Bukovina contained Austria's ethnic Romanians. Once the most numerous group there, by 1880 they had fallen behind the Ruthenes and represented no more than a third of the population. Over 80 per cent were dependent on agriculture, most of them surviving on plots of less than five hectares. Bukovina was a land of large estates, but only a small fraction still belonged to the descendants of Moldavian boiers. Educated Romanians were on the defensive. They feared that they would be submerged by the steady immigration from neighbouring Austrian Galicia. They distrusted Ruthenes in the Orthodox Church, Germans in the administration and education, Jews in the economy, and even their own peasantry.

Hungary was politically blocked by the very spirit of the Compromise. She could not advance on the road to social change, or to a more widely representative legislature, or to independence, as her ruling class went on trying to set up a unitary Hungarian national state over a territory where the Magyar population was not a majority. Only 5.9 per cent of the population had the vote under a system of electoral qualifications that effectively excluded most Slavs and Romanians. Political control remained in the hands of some 3,000 landowners who held half the land. The implementation of the Nationalities Law was ever more restricted, as Magyarization was gradually pushed through schools, public signs, place-names and even surnames.

The Kingdom of Croatia-Slavonia, with Military Croatia fully integrated in 1881, did have its own language and institutions. Count Károly Khuen-Héderváry (1848–1918), ban from 1883 to 1903, nevertheless ran an efficient Hungarian-dominated régime by exploiting ethnic, regional and political differences. He controlled a cooperative Sabor that included official members and hereditary nobles, and whose elected members represented no more than 2 per cent of the population. As the proportion of Serbs edged up to 25 per

119

cent after the incorporation of the Frontier, and as independent Serbia became a satellite of Austria-Hungary, Serbs were encouraged to enter the administration and were granted various facilities. Slavonian particularism was also stimulated.

The Croatian political spectrum changed, as the National Party continued to split and then drew closer to the Rights Party. The latter, originally backed by Khuen-Héderváry, was in the ascendancy, but faced difficulties in applying its nationalism to an ideal Croatian 'state' that would have contained many 'Orthodox Croats', 'Muslim Croats', perhaps even 'Mountain Croats' (Slovenes). As it veered to left and right, it, too, split in 1894. Josip Frank's (1844–1911) 'Pure Rights' Party was more favourable to the Monarchy, but even more suspicious of Serbs, who had by then set up their own Serbian Independent Party.

The Hungarian government pushed through as much Magyarization as it could get away with in Croatia. In Hungary proper it applied much greater pressure, which led to the division of the Serb National Liberal Party into 'liberals' and 'radicals'. The latter formed themselves into the Serb Radical Party of Hungary in 1891 on the model of the radicals of Serbia, to advocate universal suffrage and local ethnic autonomy within districts.

Even fewer of the ethnic Romanians in Hungary had a vote. In 1881, representatives of their electoral organizations – mostly lawyers and landowners – met in Sibiu to set up the Romanian National Party. Their programme called for a restoration of Transylvania's autonomy on the Croatian model, a widening of the franchise and the official use of Romanian where it was the majority language. They refrained from raising any social issue, but remained divided on the question of political participation, until they finally gave up passivism in 1890.

When their president Raţiu then took a delegation to Vienna to explain to the emperor the point of view of his Romanian subjects, the sovereign declined to receive them or accept their memorandum on constitutional grounds. It was passed on unopened to the Budapest government, which responded harshly: the leaders of the Romanian National Party were tried in 1894 and imprisoned; the party was dissolved. The trial aroused opinion in favour of the defendants, not only on both sides of the Carpathians but also in Paris and London.

Hungarian policy drew Romanians and Slavs together. In 1895 Romanian, Serb and Slovak activists met in Budapest, to call for a reorganization of the Monarchy along 'natural' ethnic rather than historical lines. Again, the government banned the Romanian National Party, which nevertheless continued to function, as its educated members became more prominent in the cultural sphere, and formed close links with their counterparts in Romania. The Orthodox and Uniate churches, as the Romanians' only legal 'national' institutions, also successfully preserved the autonomy of their ecclesiastical and educational cadres.

Agriculture did not respond to the opportunities offered by the large imperial markets in the South Slav and Romanian-inhabited periphery, which lagged behind the revolution that the fertile plains of northern and western Hungary were going through. There were fewer big estates in Croatia-Slavonia, Vojvodina and Transylvania; inner Hungary was an obstacle to their moving into production for the Austrian and Czech urban markets. The total grain output per head remained lower than Serbia's, not to mention Romania's, and the predominant crop continued to be corn. The share of livestock in production increased, however, especially in Croatia, to fill an opening left by the Hungarian magnates' concentration on wheat.

Hungary's agricultural revolution was fraught with economic difficulties that forced the pace of change in the countryside. Subsidies, protective tariffs and support for the introduction of more modern methods had benefited the large landowners, but smallholders found it difficult to survive competition. They were still paying off the acquisition of their plots, and suffered from both bad and good harvests. When a bad harvest did not provide them with enough grain for the whole year, they suffered from higher food prices; a good year meant that the price for their surplus was forced down. By the 1890s many smallholders in Croatia were trapped in negative equity, becoming landless labourers or emigrating.

In Transylvania, competition from Hungary proper led to the sale of estate lands to smaller owners, to urban businessmen turned lessors, and to over 400,000 Romanian peasant families with the help of long-term credit. Nevertheless, most smallholders who owned less than five hectares had to use estate land in exchange for days of labour, to work as paid labourers or to emigrate. In Vojvodina, German colonists bought land from indebted Serb peasants and established middle-sized holdings. Shortage of land was the peasants' heaviest burden throughout the Hungarian lands, particularly among Slavs and Romanians of the borderlands, with over 30 per cent landless in Vojvodina, in Transylvania and in Croatia by 1900.

From 1880 there was a wave of emigration from the Hungarian part of the Monarchy, with the minorities overrepresented. Most went overseas, others simply to the more developed Austrian lands, or from the countryside to towns. Between 1890 and 1914 190,000–250,000 (6 per cent of the population) emigrated to America from Croatia-Slavonia, as did over 200,000 from Transylvania, with another 100,000 going to Romania (altogether 8 per cent of the population).

The Austrian stock-market crash of 1873 had ended the era of private railway building, which was thereafter hampered by Austro-Hungarian competition, and state-led by a combination of geostrategic and fiscal needs. Viennese banks showed little interest in that part of the Monarchy, except for the coal and ferrous metals of Transyslvania, industries which developed with railway construction and the growth of Budapest, but with little modernizing investment after 1870. Although timber products dominated light industry in all the region, most enterprises remained rudimentary.

There was growing dissatisfaction among the South Slav and Romanian populations after 1880, when cultural Magyarization was added to political control. What economic development there was hardly benefited them. The great landowners, the bourgeoisie and the bureaucracy were mostly alien, even in Croatia. Indeed, developments increased the number of people coming from elsewhere in the Monarchy.[5]

Throughout Austria-Hungary, South Slavs and Romanians generally failed in their major efforts to improve their position after the Compromise, for acceding to their demands would have meant thwarting the dynasty's Magyar partners. Their leaders and their representatives thus developed a way of struggling for small advantages.

SERBIA OF THE PROGRESSIVES AND RADICALS

On the European periphery of the Ottoman Empire and exposed to central Europe, Serbia had developed an autonomous form of statehood before Bulgaria. Looking both westwards and southwards, she had nourished the dream of being the Piedmont of South Slav unification, at the very least of Ottoman Slav territories, but when the revolt in Herzegovina started the Eastern Crisis, she was in no position to give a lead.

The more nationalist and popular liberals were nevertheless entrusted with the government, and Serbia went to war along with Montenegro. Military defeat by the Turks before Russia took up arms revealed the gap between the dream and the capacity to realize it. The loss of Russian support and the setting up of an autonomous Bulgaria provoked a rude awakening, as they signalled the end of the leadership rôle Serbia had assumed among the Balkan Slavs. The international settlement placed her and all the western Balkans in the Habsburg sphere. Not only Bosnia and Herzegovina, but also the sanjak of Novi Pazar that separated Serbia from Montenegro, were out of bounds. Russia made it clear that Austria-Hungary would be taking up the position of Serbia's patron.

The newly independent state ceased to be in form a tributary of the Ottoman Empire to become in fact a vassal of Austria-Hungary. At the Congress of Berlin, Habsburg diplomacy had provided Serbia with the best support that she could hope for in the circumstances, but in exchange imposed on Prince Milan the 1881 agreements that turned his principality into a satellite. A new ministry was appointed, which agreed to a commercial convention that made Serbia an agrarian dependency of the Dual Monarchy. Even more significant was a secret political convention by which Milan agreed not to conclude treaties without the approval of Austria-Hungary. Only after he had signed it did he inform three of his ministers who were sworn to prevent disclosure.

The Liberal Party had come to the end of its rôle. The younger intelligentsia had turned away from it when it had nothing more to offer, and so had the peasants who had had to pay for the war. In the elections of 1880, the liberals

5 German was usually the language of upper classes in Croatia, and a quarter of Zagreb's (or Agram's) 40,000 inhabitants in 1890 were (mostly German-speaking) 'foreigners'.

were defeated by two new parties, right and left, that had formally established themselves that year. The progressives were a left-wing offshoot from the old conservatives, and it was to them that Milan turned to form a government that could accept at least the commercial convention. They were admirers of western European constitutional forms who believed that the modernization of Serbia's underdeveloped society should be initiated by its educated élite, in cooperation with the crown. Although quick to organize themselves as a modern party, they retained the spirit of a political club of like-minded gentlemen.

It was the radicals who actually set up the first mass party and involved the peasantry in the political process. Inspired initially by Russian socialism and populism, but also and increasingly by the French republican left (not forgetting Swiss radicalism), their programme aimed at limiting the powers of the crown and of the bureaucracy, calling for full manhood suffrage and the dominance of the legislative over the executive. The liberals, as they faded out, were the last to turn into a structured body.

In exchange for linking himself to Austria-Hungary, Prince Milan obtained support to elevate his principality to the status of kingdom in 1882, following Romania's example the previous year. The proclamation of the kingdom was accompanied by the institution of orders of knighthood, modelled on the French Légion d'honneur – the Order of the White Eagle (of Serbia's coat of arms) and the Order of Saint Sava (Serbia's patron saint). This symbolized and enhanced its new status as an independent state, and diverted attention from opposition to increasing subservience to Vienna.

Milan's progressive ministers were more reformist than their constitutional and conservative predecessors, and more enlightened than the liberals, but without strong popular support they were forced to work closely with the palace. The elections of 1883 were the first that involved electioneering by organized political parties, and the radicals won by a two-to-one majority. The progressive cabinet resigned, but King Milan refused to accept the rule of the new majority. He appointed a ministry of old conservatives, who immediately adjourned the newly elected Assembly and decreed the confiscation of all privately held weapons from the days of the militia. Disarming the peasantry was meant as a protective measure; it caused an explosion.

It was resisted in eastern Serbia by a widespread peasant rebellion, incited by radical agitation in a region that had suffered from the war with Turkey. The army crushed it; its leaders were tried and sentenced, or fled to Bulgaria. Executed, gaoled, exiled, dispersed or cowed, the radicals were neutralized, but Milan had to call back the progressives.

The integration of the new triangle of territory to the south posed problems. Not only had it suffered from the war, but it was generally below Serbian standards. There were Muslim property owners, some of whom still had Christian tenants. In Niš, which had been an important Ottoman administrative and military centre, Orthodox Serbs amounted to no more than half the population on the eve of its 'liberation', with Muslims about a third. Serbia was bound by the Treaty of Berlin to respect their rights. In order to get Muslim landlords to sell and leave, tenants were pressed to buy up, under a temporary military administration. Speculators bought property at cheap prices. Many public buildings, including mosques, were subsequently neglected and destroyed to make way for new ones, even if they were of architectural value, as they were felt to be reminders of Turkish times and of past humiliations.[6]

The new southern frontier bordered in part on Bulgaria – an additional and Slav rival in the struggle for the remaining Ottoman territories, which intensified once the western *irredenta* had been blocked by Austria-Hungary. After the 1883 rebellion, Bulgaria had also become a haven for Serbian émigrés, who came and went with ease, provoking border incidents. When Bulgaria declared union with Eastern Roumelia in 1885, King Milan saw it as a breach of the Treaty of Berlin, a step back towards San Stefano, a change in the Balkan balance of power.

He was obsessed with Bulgaria's next moves – a possible takeover of Macedonia, perhaps a war against Serbia similar to that of Prussia against Austria in 1866. He launched a preventive war, to yield compensation, to bring about a European intervention, to destroy for ever the dream of San Stefano and to divert attention from his internal problems. Milan did not realize that his war of prestige was seen in Serbia as practically a civil war against brothers, against allies in a common cause. Even the conservatives did not understand why Serbia could not come to an understanding with Bulgaria over spheres of influence in Macedonia. Serbia's reluctant conscripts performed badly in a war that brought the young kingdom defeat and humiliation.

Austria intervened to spare Serbia from being invaded by Bulgaria, but Milan's position had become untenable. It was also tarred by his tempestuous relationship with Queen Nathalie, the daughter of a Moldavian boier. He began to prepare for his withdrawal, accepted a new radical-dominated Assembly, and had a new constitution drawn up by an all-party commission, after experts had been sent to France, Belgium, Denmark and Greece.

Adopted by the Assembly, the fourth constitution of Serbia was a considerable step forward. It spelt out civil liberties, strengthened local government and enhanced the powers of the Assembly. All its members were henceforth elected by direct and secret ballot of an electorate still restricted to taxpayers. Educational qualification survived only in the form of an obligation for each department to elect at least two graduates. The crown retained an important prerogative as active moderator and watchdog.

No sooner had he promulgated the new constitution at the beginning of 1889 than the thirty-five-year-old King Milan abdicated, though not before he

---

6 By 1867, when the Ottoman garrison left Belgrade, there was only one mosque left in Belgrade. Built in the seventeenth century, it was restored by the Serbian government for use by Muslim worshippers, restored again in 1893, and has survived to this day as a place of worship. The first steps towards granting Jews civil rights had been taken by Prince Michael, before they were fully extended according to the requirements of the Treaty of Berlin and enshrined in the constitution of 1888.

had been granted a divorce. He was succeeded by his thirteen-year-old son Alexander (1876–1903), under a regency council. The Radical Party had won all elections since its foundation, and with all its remaining rebels of 1883 amnestied, it was asked to form a government.

Soon, however, the young monarch was showing the same authoritarian tendencies as his father. By a series of coups, beginning when he was not yet seventeen, he turned constitutional government into a farce, by abolishing, restoring, granting and suspending constitutions. He exploited divided party leaderships and obtained parliamentary sanction of sorts. His quarrelling parents took turns to return to Belgrade and exercise their influence. In 1893 he arrested and dismissed regents and ministers at a palace dinner party, and assumed royal powers. In 1894 he abolished the constitution of 1888 and restored that of 1869. In 1900 he married his mistress, an older widow with an intriguing past.

His reign was one of weak government. The radicals were the most popular party, their strength rested on their peasant voters, but their leaders were bourgeois politicians and professors who introduced few radical changes after 1889. The king managed to have a court faction within each party. Alexander became adept at playing factions against each other and at manipulating elections through administrative pressure. In 1901, as a compromise with radicals who were looking for a way back to a more parliamentary régime, he was able to change the constitution yet again. He granted a new one on his own authority, with a bicameral legislature, three-fifths of whose Senate were crown appointees. King Alexander had turned his kingdom into an object of international fun.

Serbia at the time of independence found herself wedged between Austro-Hungarian and Ottoman territory,[7] a landlocked state of 48,500 sq. km with 1.9 million inhabitants. Over 87 per cent of them were statistically rural, and some of the town dwellers were still agricultural producers. With Niš, Serbia had acquired a second town of over 10,000 inhabitants, but it was in Belgrade that rapid change was taking place. Its population doubled between 1874 and 1890, from 27,600 to 54,200 (only 34 per cent of whom were born in the city), with 73.25 per cent literacy by 1900. The 1880s were years of chaotic development for the capital, halfway between an Ottoman town and a European capital, with prestigious new buildings, a royal palace, a theatre and a university.

The urban population, most of it born in the countryside, had become the carrier of development, mainly through its merchants, civil servants, officers and teachers, whose thin upper crust was turning into a European-type bourgeoisie. It was, however, very much a *Bildungsbürgentum* – an educated bourgeoisie destined for state service or for state-controlled professions. Still divided into the one-time Ottoman guilds and facing increasing competition from abroad, craftsmen formed a transition between bourgeois and workers. Apprentices,

7 She had a short common border with independent Romania, and the Principality of Bulgaria was nominally part of the Ottoman Empire.

shop assistants, students and older pupils provided the manpower for anti-government demonstrations.

The peasant mass of the population was distinguished by mistrust of the towns and of the state apparatus which benefited mainly towns. They fed essentially on low-protein maize bread, milk products and vegetables. What they resented most was the fiscal pressure, more than doubled between 1879 and 1883 as a result of military expenditure and railway building. Essentially interested in material and local questions, they were not very nationalistic. 'If we take Bosnia, that won't make my field any bigger,' commented one peasant deputy in the National Assembly in 1876.

The success of the Radical Party came from its call for a radical cutting down of the bureaucracy and for the devolution of power to local government. It was a populist party with an ear for what its electorate wanted and an eye for the realities of power. After the great setback suffered in 1883, it had started to move away from the left. While there is no doubt about its contribution to the democratization of political life, its rôle in the modernization of Serbia is subject to controversy.

It was at independence that modernization took off with a conscious effort. Like all Balkan societies, Serbia was poor and had only a small élite. Competition was limited, and with it the quest for solutions capable of providing a transition to an open society. Although compulsory by law, primary education was limited by the lack of schools and teachers, and parents' reluctance to lose labour. Secondary schooling was available in towns only, and involved 5,600 pupils in 1885/86. The intelligentsia was recruited from university graduates. The 1880s were years of intense development in cultural life, as the Belgrade High School was extended and reorganized into a fully fledged university in 1880, when the state also spent 119,000 dinars on grants for study abroad (which was more than on parliament).

There was a general realization that a turning point had been reached. Part of the élite took it up as a challenge, to prove that Serbia had come of age. The progressives were intent on moving away from what they viewed as romantic pseudo-liberal ideals, to tackle the real task of setting up a European state. Serbia not only had the duty to raise herself to the standards of the family of modern states which she had joined, she actually had to modernize in order to survive as an independent country. Theirs was a view shared to a certain extent by King Milan in his less cynical moments. While he directed his energies, as monarch and later as 'king-father' and commander-in-chief, to organizing a modern army to take over from his predecessor's failed romantic 'nation-in-arms' militia, the progressives thought more in terms of a war on backwardness.

In its period of office between 1880 and 1883, the progressive cabinet of Milan Piroćanac (1837–97) – the Paris-trained lawyer who had accepted Prince Milan's conventions of 1881 with Austria-Hungary – carried out reforms of fundamental importance. The freedoms of press, speech and association were strengthened, as well as the independence of the judiciary; taxes and schools were reformed; a regular army and a note-issuing National Bank were set up; the first railways were built.

French influence in modernizing Serbia was important, both through the schooling of Serbian students in France and through French advisers in Serbia, but Austrian and German influence should not be forgotten. Germany was particularly influential from the 1870s, especially on the military, and through the military in such fields as medicine, sanitation and engineering. Nor should Russian influence be overlooked.

Modernization was a process that was accompanied by the fear of change and uncertainty, and by resistance to the price that had to be paid. Associating the progressives' élitist Europeanism with the monarch's conservative political leanings and with his attachment to Austria-Hungary, the radicals saw it as a threat to, rather than as a condition of, Serbia's independence. They linked the remains of their early Russian socialist and populist ideas with elements of Slavophilism.

Even though they had fully turned to popular sovereignty and parliamentary government under French influence, their leader Nikola Pašić (1845–1926)[8] opposed the systematic adoption of a western model that uprooted Serbia's peasants and turned the country into a colony. He advocated a policy that would borrow from the west only the technology to build upon what he viewed as traditional Slav peasant institutions (such as local self-government), that fostered Slav links (notably with Bulgaria), and that relied on Russia. The radicals tended at the time to see the west ('Europe' in the general Balkan parlance at the time) and Russia as two worlds, and to look at the west through Austria-Hungary. Borrowing the technology to build upon traditional institutions was one way of envisaging development; it was (and is) to be found in all developing societies.

In fact, the 1880s began a period of expansion that eventually enabled Serbia to resist dependence on Austria-Hungary. Agriculture continued to be the main economic activity, with 73 per cent of agricultural land in units of less than five hectares. Land under grain cultivation had doubled from the 1860s to the 1890s. The main crop was maize, followed by wheat, and although woodland had been mercilessly exploited, it still amounted to about 30 per cent of the total area.

Ordered government and predictable money taxes enabled peasants to produce a marketable surplus, more quickly earned with crops than with livestock. The domestic urban market took a faster-rising share, so that by the end of the century little more than 12 per cent of the total harvest was exported, and cereals never accounted for more than 30 per cent of Serbia's export value before 1905.

Dependence on livestock exports to the Habsburg lands continued as before. The 1881 treaty, by establishing almost a customs union with Austria-Hungary,

---

8 He had studied engineering in Zurich, and had been in exile in Bulgaria and in Romania from 1883 to 1889.

helped Serbia's agricultural exports, to the point where her trade balance became favourable from 1887. Improved breeding on large Hungarian estates did, however, put an end to the simple export of acorn-fed lean pigs. Serbian breeders were forced to fatten their pigs for the bacon and lard market, and to find new and better corn-growing pastures. Constraints nevertheless increased as Hungarian interests called for protective tariffs, and eventually led to tariff wars with Romania and Serbia.

The beginnings of manufacture were slow because of the lack of capital, and the boost given to Austrian imports in 1881. The ordnance factory at Kragujevac was still the largest enterprise, with over 2,000 employees by 1900. A few breweries in the larger towns, flour and sawmills, and the start of mining with Austrian and Belgian capital completed Serbia's industrial sector.

The lack of proper communications was, with the lack of capital, the main obstacle to quicker development. In 1884 there were no more than 400 km of roads, mostly unusable when it rained. The completion that year of the Belgrade–Niš line, linked by the Save bridge to Zemun in Hungary, and in 1888 with the Ottoman and Bulgarian railways, left Montenegro as the only European country with no railway. The rail link was not only a commitment imposed by the Treaty of Berlin, it was a crying need. The railway carried 272,000 passengers in 1888, opening new possibilities for the development of Belgrade, then already an important river port with a 41,000-tonne traffic.[9]

As elsewhere, the birth of rail travel was attended by suspicion. Railway contracts were turned into an emotional issue in the parliamentary debates of 1880, as the radicals used it against the progressive government, exploiting fears of foreign interests that would reduce the country to economic bondage again, and destroy a native culture embedded in equality and local government.

Railway building and armaments certainly increased public spending, and caused budgetary deficits from 1880 as interest payments to European creditors replaced the tribute to the sultan. From 27 million dinars in 1879, the budget went up to 44.7 million in 1887. That year, over 34 per cent of it went to servicing the foreign debt and over 31 was earmarked for armaments, leaving 34 per cent for the rest of government expenditure. Whatever radicals said of state bureaucracy, 'the rest' was not all that much, and much less than in some other Balkan states.[10]

In spite of undeniable progress, the image of independent Serbia in the last quarter of the nineteenth century was not an attractive one even for Serbs outside the kingdom, let alone for the other Yugoslavs – because of the vagaries of her Obrenović kings and her diplomatic attachment to Austria-Hungary. Montenegro had affirmed herself under a succession of able rulers, but could not make up for the decline in prestige of the larger Serb state, and neither was able to play a decisive rôle in the movements of the South Slav subjects of the Habsburgs.

9 The railway station in Belgrade is still the original one, built in 1884.
10 12 dinars (francs) per head in Serbia in 1879, 22.79 in Romania, 32.18 in Greece.

ROMANIA OF THE LIBERALS AND CONSERVATIVES

The logical consequence of Romania's independence was the proclamation of the kingdom in 1881. Other symbols marked the formal termination of Ottoman suzerainty. The first law passed after independence was to set up an order of knighthood, the Order of the Star of Romania, followed by that of the Crown of Romania. The Hohenzollern colours and motto (*Nihil sine Deo*) were incorporated into the coat of arms of the kingdom, to link dynasty and state. The crown for the king's coronation was made of the metal of a Turkish cannon captured during what was called the 'War of Independence'. Charles's only child having died, his nephew Ferdinand (1865–1927) was adopted as crown prince.[11]

The Treaty of Berlin had imposed the return to Russia of southern Bessarabia which had been Romanian (or Moldavian) again since the Treaty of Paris, in exchange for 15,600 sq. km of Ottoman Dobrudja up to and including the Danube delta. Bessarabia as a whole continued to be subjected to relentless Russification. The old Moldavian boier community was gradually absorbed into Russian society; the Romanian part of the population fell from 74 per cent in 1874 to 56 per cent in 1896. Dobrudja had known extensive settlement by Turks, Tartars and Bulgars. It had suffered from the war, it was backward in every respect and its integration was not easy. Although it eventually brought benefits as agriculture and the port of Costanţa developed, there was at the time little enthusiasm for the exchange, which was a condition of independence.

Another condition of de jure recognition was the abolition of all legal religious discrimination. Article 7 of the constitution excluded non-Christians from naturalization. This concerned the newly acquired Muslims of Dobrudja, but mostly affected immigrant Jews. Russia and Austria-Hungary quickly recognized Romania unconditionally to soothe her feelings, but France, Germany and Great Britain did not do so until 1880, when the revision had been carried out, in an atmosphere of fear of the Jews' economic competitiveness and of resentment at interference in Romania's internal affairs.

Jews had already been moving into Moldavia from the Austrian part of Poland, but it was in the second half of the nineteenth century that Russian Jews left in ever-increasing numbers for the Habsburg lands and Romania, and also moved from Austria-Hungary to Romania, grasping the economic advantages offered by their adopted country's exposure to Europe. Modest steps had been taken under Cuza towards emancipation and individual naturalization, but the coming to power of the liberals had brought about a new tightening of rules.

Various restraints made Jews gather in towns, where they were in business, while in the countryside they were innkeeper-moneylenders and estate managers. By the turn of the century they numbered 250,000 – 3.3 per cent of the total population, 14.6 per cent of town dwellers, 32 per cent of the urban

11 In 1893 he married Princess Marie of Edinburgh, a granddaughter of Queen Victoria and of Tsar Alexander II.

population of Moldavia, and up to 42 per cent in Jassy. Generally unassimilated, they became scapegoats for the evils of land distribution, and were perceived as a threat to the rising native urban classes. The issue had become an international one. Romanian Jews had gained the support of Jewish organizations abroad which, through sympathetic western European politicians, brought pressure to bear on the Romanian government, culminating in the requirement of the Congress of Berlin for a revision of the constitution.

Romania grudgingly complied in October 1879: Jews could apply for naturalization, with a ten-year probation period, and only Romanian-born citizens could own land. This satisfied the powers formally, but as Russian emigration increased, anti-Semitism became a feature of political life. No more than one thousand Jews managed to obtain citizenship under the new procedures before the First World War, and liberal legislation in economic matters discriminated against foreigners. The issue was one that could be used profitably by Romanian politicians, and by foreign powers when they wanted something out of Romania.[12]

In spite of this and other problems, independent Romania during the reign of King Charles I had the most stable political framework and the most advanced economy in the Balkans. Brătianu, who had steered the country through the Eastern Crisis, the war with Turkey and the Congress of Berlin, remained in office until 1888. Under his liberal administration, not only did Romania become an independent kingdom, but much modernizing legislation was passed affecting every aspect of government, education, the army and the economy.

Elections were held in 1883 for parliament to revise the constitution. Brătianu calculated that moderate electoral reform would not only avoid a breakaway of his left, but provide more support for the Liberal Party by increasing the influence of the bourgeoisie and reducing that of the landowners. The king recognized that electoral reform was unavoidable, and trusted Brătianu to keep it within bounds. All levers were used to prevent the conservatives from gaining the necessary third of deputies and senators to thwart his proposals; the liberals obtained an overwhelming majority.

By reducing the number of electoral colleges to three, the reform strengthened the political influence of the middle classes at the expense of the large landowners. The first two colleges together returned 145 deputies, whereas the third, which represented the peasantry, returned 38 – slightly more than before. The total number of voters increased somewhat, and would continue to do so with economic development, from just under 60,000 in 1888 to 94,000 in 1905 – out of a total population of nearly 6 million. The Senate remained a conservative stronghold because its electoral body was still less than 25,000 in 1905.

Whereas the Conservative Party continued to represent the interests of large landowners, the liberals stood for the growing commercial, industrial and

12 Powers also used it out of fear of having to absorb an unprecedented number of Jews when, at the turn of the century, Romania became a source of Jewish emigration as well as a land of immigration.

professional middle classes. Even so, such divisions were blurred. Landed property began to pass from old boier families to the new wealthy bourgeoisie, either directly or through being mortgaged to liberal-controlled credit institutions. The bankers and merchants who bought land adopted the outlook of landowners, while the latter who had sold or lost land entered the bourgeoisie. Conservatives favoured free trade on behalf of landed interests which exported grain and cattle, whereas liberals favoured protective tariffs for industry. Even though they acquired modern structures, both parties were still coteries of men connected by personal loyalties, common interests and the desire to hold power.

The king played a key rôle in determining the outcome of elections through his authority to appoint the prime minister and to dissolve parliament. When he had obtained the resignation of the council of ministers, he consulted political leaders before selecting one of them to form the new government. The first task of the incoming prime minister, after he had formed the cabinet, was to organize elections. The government had the advantage of controlling patronage and the state apparatus. The procedure gave the monarch a pivotal rôle between the parties, whose leaders competed for the guarantee of stability that he provided.

The liberals were dominant for a decade after the War of Independence. Having established a congenial working relationship with King Charles and parted with some of the more radical liberals, Brătianu became increasingly authoritarian. Strains appeared with the monarch after 1884, when the opposition turned to criticizing him for giving too much support to the liberals.

In disarray as their supporters drifted away, the conservatives had been held together in opposition by their aversion to those who wooed the lower classes. After the 1888 elections, King Charles understood that Brătianu had outlived his usefulness, and the liberal leader realized that he had lost the monarch's confidence. Splits within his party allowed a series of short-term conservative governments. Under pressure from their own Junimist ('Youth') group to show concern for the peasant issue, and to present themselves to the bourgeoisie as advocates of reasoned change, the conservatives eventually produced an enlightened administration which remained in office until 1895.

The demise of historic leaders, internal divisions and the financial difficulties resulting from the public debt caused more frequent changes of government at the turn of the century. Useful legislation was carried out under both parties, as the system offered freedom of assembly, of association and of expression. The press flourished, stimulating political life and contributing to the moulding of public opinion, even though the majority of citizens were given little opportunity to manage their own affairs.

'Nation building' absorbed the energies of Romania's political and intellectual élite. It meant providing the country with a modern structure. As in Serbia, the west was the model, generally to be followed, but also to be wary of. For 'nation building' additionally meant forming a nation-state that would encompass all Romanians. The kingdom provided a powerful cultural stimulus for the Romanians of Hungary, with writers, scholars, artists and journals, two universities (Bucharest and Jassy) since the 1860s, and the Romanian Academy set up in 1879 along the lines of the French Academy to regulate the language. Even more than in Serbia this cultural expansion concealed the low level of attainment of a peasant society where no amount of legally compulsory primary education could make up for the short supply of teachers and schools.

In spite of the secularization of political institutions, the Church continued to serve as a bulwark of national consciousness – under the control of the state, which in 1885 obtained the assent of the ecumenical patriarch for its status of autocephaly. Orthodoxy, however, was not sufficient to build a specific Romanian identity. Historians searched for a glorious past as a guarantee of a glorious future.[13] As with their Balkan neighbours, their recovered past had to give Romanians their due place among the nations of Europe, but in their case their 'Romanity' set them apart from Slavs and Greeks. As opposed to the latter's domination by Turkey, it was the Greek 'Phanariot epoch' that they set up as the dark age of Romanian history.

Again more than anywhere else in the Balkans, intellectuals embarked on a wide-ranging debate between Europeanists and traditionalists. Europeanists emulated not only the political model, but the industrial and banking system, and aspired to the wholesale reception of French culture. They were met with objections that they adopted forms that touched only the surface of their society. Their critics at the time were no less western-educated; usually more German-influenced, they subscribed to historicist and evolutionist ideas. They also wanted to bring Romania into closer contact with Europe but on her own terms, with respect for her traditions and structures. Such debates were echoed among politicians and economists.

Since the middle of the century, the population had increased by two million to almost 6 million in 1899, with town dwellers almost doubling to just over one million. By 1916 Bucharest had 381,000 inhabitants. People moved to the capital which was also the industrial centre, to the two Danubian ports of Galaţi and Brăila, and to Ploeşti, the site of the new oil industry.

In spite of all the changes, at the very end of the century, half the agricultural land was owned by 6,500 individuals with estates of over 100 hectares, 38 per cent held by 2,000 of them with more than 500 hectares each. Most leased their estates, lived in Bucharest and other cities, or spent much time abroad. Their neglect of agriculture, their traditional source of income and the basis of their position, accelerated the dissolution of their class, as their place in the countryside was taken by the leaseholders. These were moneylenders, shopkeepers and grain brokers who had thus invested their accumulated capital, some of them in very large-scale commercial leasing.

---

13 In the words of the noted historian Alexandru Xenopol (1847–1920), in the introduction to his 'History of the Romanians for primary schools of both sexes', 'National history is most important for us Romanians, because it gives us an understanding of our nation [people], of what it can become in the future.' (*Istoria Romanilor pentru clasele primare de ambele sexe*, 2nd edn., Bucharest 1879, 4.)

A prosperous class of small independent proprietors did not develop, as most peasants had too little land for that. The 1864 agrarian reform had still not been completed by independence, and within twenty years, the majority of those who had received land had lost at least part of it through sales and mortgages. The peasantry was not a homogeneous class. There were some 200,000 completely landless labourers (14 per cent of the active agricultural population), with another 100,000 who rented but did own some land. 750,000 owners of less than five hectares had to supplement their income by working on estates, and 176,000 with five to ten hectares occasionally had to hire themselves out. At the top, 36,000 with ten to fifty hectares formed the upper layer of village society at the beginning of the twentieth century.

Romania's advance in grain cultivation was impressive. By the end of the century, grain (mainly wheat) accounted for nearly 85 per cent of the total value of exports, and by 1910 Romania was the world's fourth wheat exporter. The cultivated area for grains doubled from 1860 to 1890, resulting in a cultivated area per head that was 40–75 per cent above Greece, Bulgaria or Serbia.

Large estates played a decisive rôle in the expansion of grain cultivation. Some of them did emulate modern Austro-Hungarian practices, though not sufficiently to initiate an agricultural revolution, because of the maintenance of, and indeed the rise in, sharecropping. Given too little land in 1864, peasants contracted for more land to supplement their needs, working one section of the estate in return for another leased in part through a share of its crop. This avoided additional monetary obligations, but multiplied misunderstandings. When world grain prices turned upwards after 1896, more estate owners turned to this system to increase crop and labour requirements still further.

The distress of peasants thus deepened at a time of unprecedented agricultural expansion. Fed on a corn-based diet, generally lacking even in dairy products, burdened by debt and crushing contracts, always on the edge of poverty, they were more often than not ignored by politicians. Deteriorating economic conditions and the use of military force against those who failed to carry out the terms of their contracts, led to violence in the 1880s. Collective responsibility for non-fulfilment was abolished in 1882 and the use of force forbidden, but abuses continued. Uncoordinated but serious disturbances in 1888 brought the plight of peasants forcibly to the attention of politicians.

An Agricultural Credit Bank had been established in 1881, and reorganized in 1892 to target peasants more specifically, but the majority was too poor even to qualify for help. In 1889 legislation was passed for the sale of state land in small plots, with the provision of credit, and for the protection of smallholdings. The legislators dealt with specific issues as they arose; they did not want to tamper with existing structures and their primary interest was always to increase production. Furthermore, for the liberals agriculture was always secondary to industry.

An urban middle class of merchants, industrialists, lawyers, teachers and civil servants had generally replaced the largely foreign commercial and money-lending class of old. It was topped by an upper bourgeoisie that came into its own in the last two decades of the century, with a nucleus investing in industry and exerting an influence on the economic policies of the state.

When the traditional guilds were abolished in 1873, the law had simply recognized a fait accompli. The old urban artisans were replaced by a new industrial working class of wage labourers in food-processing and other consumer industries, in mining, oil and transport – 200,000 by 1914, or 20 per cent of the active population, over half of them in enterprises of more than 100 workers. Most of them were unskilled, coming from the countryside, and continuing to obtain part of their income from agriculture. A persistent oversupply of such labour kept wages and working conditions depressed.

Industry benefited enormously from the liberals' comprehensive programme to sustain industrial growth. The state placed itself on the side of modern industry, which nevertheless remained tied to the land, as the processing of foodstuffs, forestry products and oil predominated. As soon as Romania had been freed from her commercial convention with Austria-Hungary, the General Tariff Law of 1886 was enacted to shield her leading industry, the processing of agricultural products – mainly sugar refining and tobacco. The liberals then embarked on a wider programme to create a viable national industrial sector, by offering entrepreneurs encouragement and protection, a decade ahead of similar measures in Serbia or Bulgaria.

Investment capital had accumulated from a variety of sources – the more intensive exploitation of land, compensation payments for the agrarian reform, the leasing of estates, and trade. The rapid growth of foreign trade stimulated economic activity and attracted investment from abroad. This came in substantial amounts after independence, through loans to the Romanian government for ambitious public works programmes, as well as in banking and insurance, commerce and industry.

The 1895 Mines Law, which opened the way for foreign capital, marked a turning point in the oil sector which became the most dynamic industry. Romanian oilfields were closer to the major European markets than existing Russian or American sources. Petroleum deposits north of Bucharest and around Ploeşti had been discovered in the 1860s, but were little exploited until the 1890s. Oil production rose from 1,188 tonnes in 1850 to 250,000 in 1900. Most of the refineries were by then controlled by German, Dutch, British and American capital. Over half of the production was exported. The state was the largest domestic consumer through the replacement of coal by oil in railway engines at the end of the century.

The Romanian state provided the infrastructure for economic development with a modern system of currency and measures, transport and banks. State-aided credit banks had been set up as well as private banks specializing in commercial transactions, but none of these could meet the rising demand for credit after independence which called for the setting up of the National Bank of Romania in 1880. Modelled on that of Belgium, with the monopoly of note issue, it also acted as a central commercial bank. A limited company with exclusively native capital, and state participation until 1901, its private shares were snapped up by the leaders of the Liberal Party, who made no secret of their intention to direct it to play a key rôle in their industrial policy.[14]

Romania enjoyed a head start among Balkan states in railway construction, which had begun in 1857. By 1880, when the government had had to give in to Bismarck (who had tied the issue to recognition of independence) and buy up the shares of German bankers who had gone bankrupt, there were already 921 km of track, compared to 224 km in Bulgaria, 12 km in Greece, and none in Serbia. Fully nationalized by 1889, Romanian State Railways were the country's largest industrial enterprise with 23,000 employees. By 1900 the network had expanded to 3,100 km, and so had the roads, from 1,800 km in 1871 to 24,800 km in 1900.

This was an expensive advantage. By 1879, the annual repayment of the loans from capital markets already accounted for more than 20 per cent of state expenses. As the landed interest in both parties imposed political limits on direct taxes, and the urban sector set economic limits on indirect ones, budget increases were impossible without repeated access to these markets. Budgets almost doubled between independence and the end of the century.

There was a significant shift in foreign trade from east to west. In the first instance, as for Serbia, Austria-Hungary took the top place, as a market for Romania's agricultural products and as provider of her imported manufactures. Commercial conventions with the Dual Monarchy, but also with Russia, France, Great Britain, Italy and Germany, resulted in striking increases, with favourable balances. The relative openness of Romania's market until the 1886 legislation had nevertheless dealt a severe blow to local industry. When Austria-Hungary responded with a tariff war, Britain took over as Romania's best customer, and Germany as supplier.

What had hitherto been a policy of balance between her two powerful neighbours, tilted in favour of Austria-Hungary, was upset by the bitterness felt towards Russia, who again became public enemy N°1, for the politicians as well as for the general public. The prime diplomatic objective of Romania's leaders was protection against Russia. Popular opinion favoured France, but Paris showed even less interest than London and was perceived as being diplomatically isolated.

With no real alternative in sight, in 1883 Brătianu's liberal government concluded a defensive treaty with Austria-Hungary against Russia, to which Germany adhered, followed by Italy. In pushing for the treaty, Bismarck's objective had been to strengthen Austria-Hungary's position in the Balkans. As in the case of Serbia, this was a secret arrangement, known only to the king, Brătianu and a few ministers. If made public, it would have caused a storm in Romania's overwhelmingly pro-French opinion. Renewed until the First World War, the treaty linked Romania to the Triple Alliance.

14 The only private bank in the Balkans that had both the capital and the initiative to promote a broad range of industrial ventures was the Bucharest Banca Marmarosch, Blank & Co., founded as far back as 1848 by Habsburg Jewish immigrants who in 1890 joined with the princely boier Iancu Cantacuzino (1847–1911), a Paris-trained engineer and industrialist.

Although it ended Romania's diplomatic isolation, and backed up the economic advantages of the opening of central European markets, the agreement was nevertheless perceived as going against the long-term national interest. Relations with Austria-Hungary were not warm. Unable to obtain a revision of the 1875 trade convention, which, however favourable, still taxed her agricultural exports, while it allowed Austro-Hungarian manufactured imports to enter the country almost tax-free, Romania did not renew it in 1885. The protectionist tariffs which she then introduced led to a customs war from 1886 to 1893. Austria-Hungary was the real loser; Romanian agriculture found new markets further west, her industry grew, and her public hostility to the Habsburg Monarchy too.

There was not much foreign policy otherwise. Romania's hands were tied, the *irredenta* were under the control of Austria-Hungary and Russia, and there was little interest as yet in any Balkan diplomacy. Relations with the Porte were almost non-existent; with Bulgaria they were cold because of Dobrudja; with Greece they were poor as Bucharest tried to develop a Romanian awareness among the Vlachs. Relations were friendly only with Serbia, who was in a similar position.

As Hungary's Magyarization policy gradually made Romanian opinion more and more sensitive to the question of Transylvania, parties used it to embarrass each other. With the rebirth of France at the end of the century, pro-French feelings exploded again. A gradual diplomatic reorientation could begin, especially when Italy showed signs of wanting to do the same.

CHAPTER 7

From the Congress of Berlin to 1900 – Part 2

Bulgaria's difficult beginnings. The Cretan revolt of 1897. The Macedonian road to anarchy. The League of Prizren. Greece between Trikoupis and Deligiannis. Unmixing and building nations.

BULGARIA'S DIFFICULT BEGINNINGS

The Russian victory had brought virtual independence, but a bitter one, as Bulgaria emerged in two pieces. The Principality of Bulgaria and the province of Eastern Roumelia were both technically part of the Ottoman Empire. They were sponsored by Russia and regarded with suspicion by all states. Russia had also dangled before the eyes of the Bulgarian élite the vision of the 'Bulgaria of San Stefano' – which encompassed the whole of Macedonia.

The task of setting up the government was entrusted to a Russian imperial commissioner. As Kiselev had tried to do for the Romanian Principalities earlier in the century, so Prince Aleksandr Dondukov-Korsakov (1820–93) wanted a model Bulgaria. With his advisers, he drafted a constitution (called thus, in accordance with the provisions of Berlin), which was vetted in Saint Petersburg before it was submitted to the Assembly of Notables that met at Tŭrnovo, the medieval capital, in February 1879.

Less than a third of these 'notables' were elected. The others represented the administrative, legal and ecclesiastical apparatus. Delegates of Bulgarian communities outside the principality were admitted, to counter the threat of a boycott by members who argued that it was better to remain united under the Turkish yoke than to be divided by a *diktat* from Berlin. Realism prevailed, after debates which moulded the emerging political class into conservatives and liberals. Although more established and even more representative, the conservatives were discredited as they had once advocated a settlement with the Turks. The liberals were young idealists catapulted into power by the Russian victory.

The 1879 'Tŭrnovo constitution' owed as much to the liberals as to the Russian advisers. It was among the most advanced in Europe. A National

Assembly of salaried deputies, literate and over thirty years of age, was elected by direct manhood suffrage. Although a vassal of the sultan, the prince represented the principality in its relations with foreign states. He appointed ministers and shared legislative power with the Assembly. Individual rights were enshrined. Orthodoxy was the official religion, but the first ruler was exempted from it. As the Bulgarian exarchate faithful outside the principality outnumbered those within it, the exarch was left in Constantinople, while the governing synod was transferred to Sofia.

On the recommendation of the Russian government, the twenty-two-year-old Prince Alexander of Battenberg (1857–93) was offered the throne, and had to be pressed to accept it, for he was not keen on the constitution.[1] He started off with a purely conservative ministry which did not have parliamentary confidence, but in 1880, after failing to obtain Russian approval for a change of constitution, he appointed a liberal government headed by Dragan Tsankov (1828–1911). Not only was there no trust between them, but Alexander and Tsankov irritated the Russians by trying to out-do each other in nationalism. An increasing number of educated Bulgars were getting tired of Russian interference, exerted through the consul general in Sofia and through the army – where the war minister and all officers above the rank of captain were seconded from Russia.

After Tsar Alexander II's assassination in 1881, his successor Alexander III was more disposed to listen to his client's suggestions. The prince summoned a Constituent Assembly to consider changes. The liberals acquiesced, believing that they would win, but the elections were so conducted (by a purged administration, with public support from the tsar, and Russian-controlled polls) that only two liberals were returned. Meeting in Svishtov, the Assembly instantly approved the proposals. Alexander had shown skill in staging the coup. The peasantry was devoted to Russia and disappointed by the liberals, but the more politically conscious would not accept rule by the conservative oligarchy, and the prince would not tolerate the liberals.

He had to make do with a government of conservatives and Russian generals, and called for elections with the newly restricted franchise in the autumn of 1882. The result emboldened the conservatives to free themselves of their dependence on Russian generals. In 1883 prince and party leaders reached a compromise. Alexander would restore the Tŭrnovo constitution in the first instance; the liberals would envisage agreed reforms in a second stage. The generals left and Tsankov formed a coalition cabinet.

No one had benefited from the interval. In the eyes of the peasantry, Alexander and the politicians had angered the tsar. The relatively free elections of 1884 were a contest between the right and the left of the Liberal Party. Tsankov's willingness to consider constitutional reform, and to pay apparently too high a price for the purchase of the British-owned Russe–Varna

---

1 A nephew of the tsarina and the offspring of the morganatic marriage of a prince of the house of Hesse who was an Austrian general, he had himself served with the Russian army in Bulgaria. His elder brother Louis was a lieutenant in the Royal Navy.

railway, led to the defeat of his right-wing liberals by the 28 per cent of the electorate that had bothered to vote. Petko Karavelov (1843–1903) was appointed to head a left-wing liberal cabinet. The split was eventually formalized as the Karavelists became democrats.

Important questions of 'national unity' returned to the fore. In Eastern Roumelia, an international commission had produced an elaborate Organic Statute, with regional institutions in Plovdiv (Philippopoli), and safeguards to ensure the representation of non-Bulgars. The sultan retained the ultimate right of veto over legislation.[2] Bulgars made up 70 per cent of the population. Their supremacy was established at the 1879 elections, which returned thirty-one Bulgars out of the thirty-six elected members of the Regional Assembly.

Politicians in the southern province considered union with the north to be a matter of time. So did the Russians, but they were not ready to approve it yet, whereas Prince Alexander saw in nationalist aspirations a way to re-establish his influence. Even if this was not the view of Serbs and Greeks, the Slav population of Macedonia was considered to be Bulgarian. Many of those who did indeed consider themselves to be so had settled in Bulgaria, where they formed a disruptive lobby on the democratic left.

A new Revolutionary Central Committee was set up to foment risings. As the Porte tightened its control over Macedonia, and the Karavelov government blocked wider endeavours, the committee went for a more limited aim. It organized a military coup in Plovdiv that proclaimed the union of Eastern Roumelia with Bulgaria in September 1885. Alexander and Karavelov were caught between the danger of defying Russia by accepting union, and that of defying opinion if they did not. The liberal president of the National Assembly, Stefan Stambolov (1854–95), forced the issue by telling the prince that his choice lay between going to Plovdiv and returning to Darmstadt. Alexander went to Plovdiv and endorsed the union.

There was an explosion of enthusiasm among Bulgars and adverse reactions elsewhere. The tsar recalled all Russian officers from Bulgaria and Eastern Roumelia. Greece and Serbia protested against the violation of the Berlin settlement; British pressure prevented the Greeks from siding with Serbia, who went to war. With no officers above the rank of captain, the Bulgarian army stopped the Serbian offensive in a three-day battle. Bulgarian public opinion had stood behind its army; Serbian public opinion had not accepted the war; scars were left to be exploited in the future.

The newcomer in the Balkans had emerged from the battle of Slivnitsa with Eastern Roumelia, an enhanced reputation, and the confidence that it could take on its neighbours. In the spring of 1886, power-brokered compromises restored the *status quo ante bellum* between Serbia and Bulgaria, and had 'the prince of Bulgaria' (not mentioned by name) appointed governor-general of Eastern Roumelia for five years.

2 The first governor-general was Aleko Bogoridi Pasha, a Phanariot Ottoman civil servant of Bulgarian origin (one of the sons of 'le Talleyrand de l'Orient') who had endowed St Stephen's church in Constantinople.

Bulgaria was made to understand that union was acceptable to Russia only with another prince. People were worried about the limited nature of what had been achieved. Even Eastern Roumelia caused problems. The politicians from Plovdiv resented being treated as auxiliaries by their less sophisticated colleagues in Sofia. The departure of Russian officers and the integration of the southern militia politicized promotions in the army.

Elections for the first united assembly were held in 1886. The issue turned out to be the Russe–Varna railway, for which Karavelov was now willing to pay a higher price than that which he had considered exorbitant in 1884. Debates and demonstrations turned against Prince Alexander. In the space of a fortnight from August to September, he was deposed by a group of Russian-trained officers, escorted out of the country, restored by Stambolov, and seen off again in deference to the tsar's wish.[3]

Stambolov was left at the head of a princely lieutenancy, which appointed a coalition government and summoned an assembly to elect a new prince. All Russian officials left. A prince was desperately needed. Various solutions were envisaged and found wanting, until Ferdinand of Saxe-Coburg and Gotha (1861–1948) was discovered. He took office in August 1887, unrecognized for the next nine years.[4] The new ruler took on as prime minister the man who had brought him to the throne. Linked by nothing more than common interests, Ferdinand and Stambolov in tandem had to prove that they were de facto rulers of an ordered state if they were to have any hope of receiving de jure recognition. The turning point came in 1890, when a thwarted conspiracy to remove Ferdinand showed both the extent of discontent and the resilience of the régime.

People were worried for the future of Bulgaria and for her influence in Macedonia. Turks, Greeks and Serbs had been put on their guard. Stambolov believed that the only way to secure the whole of Macedonia, was to Bulgarianize it gradually while it was under Ottoman control. He persuaded the Turks that any alternative to Ferdinand would be worse for them, and secured exarchist bishops for three important sees in Macedonia – Ohrid, Skopje and Bitola.

Stambolov's subsequent electoral triumph of 1890 was thus obtained with relatively little pressure. The following year, however, there was an attempt on his life, which he took to be Russian-backed. He responded with repression of the Macedonian lobby, and by pressing for a good dynastic match to strengthen Ferdinand's case. Marie-Louise of Bourbon-Parma was in the wings, but her family would not marry her off to the Balkans without a guarantee that the children would be no less Catholic than their parents.

Ferdinand had already been exempted from the constitutional requirement of Orthodoxy by being accepted as another 'first prince'. Stambolov had an

3 He joined the Austrian army, married an opera singer, died at the age of thirty-six and was buried in Sofia.
4 A Vienna-born Catholic, he too was the son of an Austrian general. His mother was a daughter of King Louis-Philippe, and he was related to Saxe-Coburg-Gotha monarchs and monarch's consorts in Belgium, Britain and Portugal.

amendment passed to extend the exception to the 'first prince and his heir', hoping that popular joy would outweigh clerical objections. The wedding took place in Italy, the exarch relented, and nine months later the birth of a son was an even more popular event. Boris (1894–1943) was named after Bulgaria's medieval ruler who had converted to Christianity.

In between the two happy events, Stambolov had secured another victory at the polls, but his position was weaker. Peasant resentment led to sporadic outbursts. Most of the 200,000 refugees could not accept a gradualist strategy on Macedonia. Stambolov turned to ridiculing Ferdinand's European ceremonial. A clash over the appointment of a new war minister in 1894 led to his resignation. A year later, he was brutally murdered by vindictive Macedonians. Stambolov had shown that Bulgaria could survive as an international pariah, but he had done so at the cost of distorting the Tŭrnovo constitution. His electoral malpractices had been worse than anything ever done in neighbouring countries. He had left a legacy where parties had become little more than fragmented groups in pursuit of patronage from an increasingly powerful executive.

Prince Ferdinand had found an alternative prime minister in Konstantin Stoilov (1853–1901), a moderate conservative, educated in Germany and France, anxious to reach an accommodation with Russia. Once in office, he formed his National Party with a programme of 'Freedom and Legality, Order and Recognition', which secured an unconvincing majority through the usual, though now less brutal, methods.

Its place in the slogan notwithstanding, recognition came first. The death of Tsar Alexander III in November 1894 removed the main obstacle. Ferdinand's condolences were answered by Nicholas II. The ice was broken, but a number of issues were still at stake, the most important of which was the heir's religion. Ferdinand pleaded in vain with the pope, and in February 1895 announced that Prince Boris would be received into the Orthodox Church.

Nicholas II agreed to act as godfather. The sultan confirmed Ferdinand as prince of Bulgaria and governor-general of Eastern Roumelia. Recognition by the other powers followed. Prince Ferdinand first went to Constantinople to pay homage to the sultan, then on a tour of European capitals, and finally to the tsar's coronation. Bulgaria functioned as an independent state, although its double status under the sultan's suzerainty had been reaffirmed and Ferdinand had incurred the pope's condemnation.

The prince assumed control of the political system, helped by his domination of the war and foreign ministries, and by the splintering of the parties into competing factions. Recognition had not solved all problems. The Stoilov government had shown interest in modernizing and in relieving repression, but it could hardly advance the cause of Macedonia in the face of European opposition and of its own financial problems.

The situation in Macedonia was getting worse. At the end of 1894, a number of activists gathered in Sofia and set up yet another Central Committee, to organize raids across the border. The government connived at this, so as not to oppose a popular enterprise, and to have at least some control over it. Other bands, however, were operating with their own agenda. In March 1897, in view of Greece's deteriorating relations with Turkey over Crete, Bulgaria concluded a secret understanding with Serbia, to ensure that they would not steal a march on each other in Macedonia during the forthcoming conflict. Baffled by the government's attitude, many Macedonian activists turned away from commitment to Bulgaria, to the liberation of a Macedonia that would not be embroiled in the rivalries between states, and that would be the starting point of a Balkan federation.

The Stoilov government came to an end in 1899, followed by a series of short-lived cabinets, as the search for revenue precipitated the worst domestic crisis since liberation. By 1901 the public debt had grown to over 250 million gold francs, and its charges absorbed 30 per cent of the revenue. The government had no option but to accept whatever terms its foreign creditors chose to dictate. Commerce and industry were not developed enough; only the land could provide revenue. In 1899, the land tax that Stoilov had finally introduced was replaced by a tithe in kind. However financially attractive to the government, such a reversion was in stark contrast to the modernization that the post-Stambolov administration had been anxious to promote.

The return to the tithe, coming on top of bad harvests and phylloxera, provided ideal material for a new political movement – the product of increasing alienation of the countryside in the 1890s, and of the government's failure to do anything about it. Committed to improving the lot of the peasants, the Bulgarian Agrarian National Union held its first congress in December 1899. The constitution had been made by 'intellectuals' (meaning people with some education) for idealized peasants who did not even bother to participate. No more than half the electorate voted. Peasants did not understand why Bulgaria should be at odds with Russia. The modernization undertaken by the post-Stambolov governments meant nothing to them.

Some 150,000 Muslims had fled during the war, and the seizure of vacant lands effectively amounted to a popular liquidation of Ottoman landed property, both private and public. Although over half the refugees had returned after the war, they soon began to drift away again, even from Eastern Roumelia. The government had taken over all former state lands and forests, together with private land left vacant for three years, much of which it rented or sold. In 1880 the occupation of former chiftlik land was regularized by redemption payments over fifteen years, with later easing of terms.

It is estimated that by 1880, in both Bulgaria and Eastern Roumelia, no more than 25 per cent of arable land was still in Turkish hands, and less than 15 per cent by 1900. In the end, the Bulgarian peasants acquired the land, after payments to the state, which paid some compensation to the original owners. The decline in the Muslim population enabled the self-sufficient smallholder to remain the predominant figure in the country, even in the face of population growth. With no restrictions on forest clearing until 1907, the area of available land went on increasing. Most families had enough for their needs.

Even though the extended family was in constant decline, as in Serbia, in many areas working the land, as opposed to owning it, was still regulated by communal councils of heads of households. There was no surplus labour available for commercial agriculture, and little need for anything but backward farming methods. Peasants grew their own food and depended on the outside world for very little. The main crops were cereals; sheep provided meat and milk.

As the gap had noticeably widened between the countryside and the towns, which were no longer inhabited by Greeks or Turks, country people focused their resentment on urban Bulgarians who benefited from the services provided by increased taxation. Although their income had generally kept ahead of tax increases, peasants had borrowed to purchase. As taxes increased, together with the price of land from the mid-1890s when it was no longer in such plentiful supply, their dependence on credit grew.

Credit was generally obtained from private usurers, whose rates of interest were never below 25 per cent, and could be as high as 200 per cent. The banking system offered as yet no alternative source of credit. Foreign banks did not become really involved in Bulgaria until the 1890s, nor did Bulgarian capital succeed in establishing private banks. The National Bank had no branches outside larger towns. Neither Midhat's inadequate agricultural savings banks, which had suffered badly from the war, nor the beginnings of credit cooperatives could prevent the agrarian crisis of the last years of the century.

Urban dwellers accounted for a fifth of the population by the end of the century, but only eight towns had more than 20,000 inhabitants. Urbanization was mostly the result of an expanded bureaucracy, particularly in Sofia. With 20,000 inhabitants in 1880, it was smaller than Plovdiv, Ruse, Varna and Shumen. It had been made the capital because it was nearer to Macedonia and at the intersection of important routes. By 1905 it had grown to almost 83,000 inhabitants (of whom 39 per cent were native), and its Turkish-style small houses and crooked alleys had largely given way to western-type grid planning, government buildings and housing.

A quarter of Sofia's working citizens were government employees. The 2,000-odd Bulgarians employed by the Russian Provisional Administration had grown to 20,000 by the turn of the century. Initially, high salaries had been offered, to prevent corruption, and to attract the best of native, expatriate and diaspora Bulgars, but eventually they deprived all other professions of able recruits. Only to a very limited extent can the growth of towns be attributed to industry. The war had destroyed most of what industry had existed. Ten years later, there were about ninety mills, tobacco-processing plants, breweries and distilleries, textile and leather works, classed as 'factories' because they used machinery, and thus did not come under the jurisdiction of established guilds. The larger enterprises were foreign-owned and managed.

The government, which operated the railways and the Pernik coal mine complex, did show some sense of wanting to encourage industry through subsidies, monopolies and concessions, but its involvement came mostly in response to emergencies. Even though the 1,566 km of railways in 1900 compared favourably with Greece's 1,033 km, let alone Serbia's 571 km, they had been built at vast expense less to promote economic development than to meet international or political needs.

Because the Capitulations remained, Bulgaria had little freedom in tariff policy. Her exports were agricultural, grain being the chief commodity, while imports were mainly manufactured goods. Bulgaria's largest customer in the period 1891–95 was the Ottoman Empire (with 29 per cent of trade), followed by France, and her chief source of imports Austria-Hungary (with 36 per cent) followed by Great Britain. Although a specific Bulgarian currency, the lev, on a par with the French franc, had been created in 1881, Ottoman and Russian currency continued in circulation to the end of the century. An indication of the low level of economic development was the fact that in the same period, only two million levs' worth of notes were issued.

TURKEY-IN-EUROPE

The Ottoman Empire had come out of the Eastern Crisis seriously weakened – territorially, politically and economically. In Europe it retained Thrace, Thessaly, Epirus, Macedonia and Albania. Thessaly and part of Epirus were ceded to Greece only a few years later in 1881, as an addendum to the Berlin settlement. Although they were still technically part of the Empire, nobody believed that Bulgaria, Eastern Roumelia (or northern Thrace, but already in fact southern Bulgaria), Bosnia and Herzegovina would ever revert to Ottoman control.

The revolt in Herzegovina had coincided with a serious economic crisis, as a result of which the Porte was unable to pay its debts. The problem was made worse by initial relief for many of the refugees from the lost territories. In the confusion that followed, Midhat's 1876 constitution (with senators appointed for life and deputies elected by male suffrage) seemed to promise magical results. Elections were held for a parliament which met in 1877, but a year later Abdülhamid II removed the reformer, dissolved parliament and shelved the constitution. The Tanzimat era was thus closed by a sultan who was to rule at the head of an autocratic régime for the next thirty years, but who had to accept the setting up in 1881 of the Administration of the Ottoman Public Debt.

He also used his position as caliph to enhance the power of the Ottoman Empire as spokesman for the Muslim world, and to link the embryonic feeling of Turkish nationalism with non-Turkish Muslims. It was at the very end of the century that the political élite began to identify with the Turkish ethnic group, and that the Ottoman government increasingly came to be called 'Turkish'. Nationalism emerged among Balkan Turks from the psychological background of Islam as a frontier religion. The insistence on Islam actually helped to lessen reactions against the continued introduction of technological innovations.

Western military training and modern schools had given voice to feelings of Turkish nationalism, stimulated by the rise of Balkan Christian nationalism and by economic factors. The political cadres strove to identify with the Muslim majority on religious and cultural grounds. Aiming to preserve the dominance of the old Ottoman bureaucratic and military élite, they were aggrieved by the ever-increasing economic control exercised by western interests and their largely non-Muslim intermediaries. The constitutionalist ideal of the Young Ottomans survived through clandestine circles in the officer corps and in the universities. One such group was the 1899 Committee for Union and Progress (CUP), known as the 'Young Turks'.

The emphasis on Islam and the beginnings of Turkish nationalism further contributed to the alienation of non-Muslims. The support given to the Bulgarian schism, by eliminating the largest Slav-speaking group from the Orthodox millet, sharpened the ethnic consciousness of the remaining Greek-speaking Orthodox population. Its establishment had invested heavily in identifying with the rank-and-file on religious and cultural grounds. At the same time, the aspiration to unite with the Greek kingdom, taken up by westernized intellectuals, went against the hegemony that the traditional élite had enjoyed since the Tanzimat.

In British-administered Cyprus (still formally Ottoman until 1914) with its 74 per cent Greek Orthodox majority, modern Greek nationalism was clearly seen as undermining the old order – but that was henceforth a British problem. If the established Orthodox élite in Cyprus was adapting to British rule, rather as the Muslim élite of Bosnia-Herzegovina adjusted to Austro-Hungarian rule, a different parallel with Bosnia was to be found in Crete, where the upper crust of its 20 per cent Muslim minority held large estates and the best positions in the administration.

Until 1841 Crete had been a dependency of the governor of Egypt. Since the return to direct Ottoman rule, repeated risings of the Christian population had resulted in the enactment and the suspension of reforms. Continued unrest and repression had led to segregation; Christians from the cities sought refuge in the countryside and fearful Muslims congregated in the cities. The appointment as governor in 1895 of Alexandros Karatheodori Pasha, a Phanariot who had been the Porte's chief representative at the Congress of Berlin, satisfied no one. It infuriated the Muslims and did not prevent another rising of the Greeks in 1896.

Reports of massacres so inflamed popular opinion that the Athens government was forced to send troops and ships in 1897. The powers stepped in, dispatched international units, made the Greek force withdraw and brokered a status of autonomy. Far from abating, the rising spread to the Greek-inhabited mainland provinces of the Ottoman Empire and led to a disastrous Greco-Turkish war. Greece was saved from total defeat by the powers, who frustrated union and imposed autonomy under their protection. The last Ottoman troops left Crete in 1898; the international force stayed on until 1909. Prince George of Greece (1869–1957), the second son of King George, arrived at the very end of 1898, to be high commissioner under the new constitution. A National Assembly was elected in 1899; the emigration of Muslims followed.

Located in the centre of the Balkans, Macedonia, formed by the three vilayets of Salonika, Monastir (Bitola) and Üsküb (Skopje, called the vilayet of Kosovo from 1877), was the focus of competing nationalisms. Its population was made up of several ethnic groups that met and overlapped – Greeks, Bulgars, Serbs, Albanians, Turks and Vlachs, not to mention the peasant majority that spoke a range of South Slav dialects. Taking on a specific identity depended on time, location, schooling, family ties, personal affinities and the action of neighbouring states. The Muslim element was perhaps almost half the population (Turks, Albanians, Muslim Slavs, and those who had come from Russia and the lost Balkan provinces).

The majority of peasants were sharecroppers on chiftliks whose ownership was concentrated in the hands of Ottoman – Turkish and Albanian – officials, although a number of estates around Salonika were owned by Greek and Jewish merchants. Most chiftliks were under 200 hectares and made up of unconsolidated plots. The landlords took half the crop and at least ten days' labour, with the help of gangs of Albanians and immigrants.

During the war and following the Berlin settlement, there was a series of local peasant risings. That of 1880 was more particularly the consequence of the resettlement in Macedonia of Muslims leaving the lost areas. Intimidated and with little incentive to expand cultivation, Christian peasants emigrated to the rest of the Balkans and to the United States. Soil and climate favoured wheat, with a yield which nevertheless did not even match Serbia's by 1910, although it covered twice the area. Tobacco, which produced nearly ten times the export value of wheat and flour, went to the Italian and Austro-Hungarian monopolies.

An industrial labour force of some 10,000 worked mainly in seventy odd 'factories' with mechanical power – most of them flour mills and tobacco plants. More than twenty were located in Salonika, which had grown to 130,000 inhabitants by the turn of the century, and which could hope to attract capital. An assortment of foreign and local interests founded in 1888 the Banque de Salonique, which helped the port's Mediterranean commerce, but offered scant stimulus to the hinterland. The railways out of the port owed their existence to non-economic motives. Concessions had been granted with the thought of moving troops. The line to Skopje had been completed before the crisis, but not until 1888 did it meet the Serbian one coming from Belgrade. Concessions to Bitola and to Constantinople were granted in the 1890s.

Prince Michael's Serbia had been a source of hope, but she had concentrated her action on Bosnia, and Bulgarian nationalism had been the first to challenge the position of Hellenism in Macedonia. The creation of the exarchate had weakened Greek dominance of the Church hierarchy and created bitter rivalries, initially played out in terms of ecclesiastical, educational and cultural propaganda. Once Serbia's attention had shifted away from Bosnia, she also joined in towards the end of the century. Expansion southwards was seen partly as a way of fending off an Austrian takeover, and the Serbian cause in Macedonia progressed.

Greece, Bulgaria and Serbia were staking as much as possible of the crumbling Ottoman possessions in the Balkans, even though they appeared at times to support the idea of a Macedonian entity. As the war of words slid into the armed struggle of guerrilla bands, another response to external pressures was a regional Macedonian particularism which began to favour a self-help emancipation effort. It originated in the young urban intelligentsia, influenced by Bulgarian and Serbian socialists. With its emphasis on an egalitarian social order, it eventually recruited peasants who were reacting to the abuses of landlords and authorities, but also to the cross-fire of nationalists.

In 1893 militants set up in Salonika the Macedonian Revolutionary Organization, which agitated for an autonomous undivided 'Macedonia for Macedonians', but had ties with Sofia. When the following year, a Supreme Committee was set up by Macedonian émigrés in Bulgaria who disliked the stance adopted by the Salonika-based organization, the latter prefixed 'Internal' to its name and thus became IMRO. The actions of their more-or-less Bulgarian-supported but rival bands were followed by those of Greek and Serbian-backed bands, and precipitated Ottoman reprisals. The anarchy that ensued made mockery of Prince Michael's plans for a combination of Balkan forces to drive the Turks out of the Balkans.

The Ottoman government even found it difficult to enforce its will on, or protect the interests of, the 70 per cent Muslim Albanian region. Only with the end of the Greek War of Independence had it been free to settle accounts with the great lords of Albania. Having in the late 1860s toyed with the idea of a single vilayet of Albania to restrain Slav nationalism, it had reorganized the territory into three, then four vilayets, which all took in non-Albanian populations as well. Like their counterparts in Bosnia, Albania's lords opposed the Tanzimat and resented centrally appointed officials. Tribal highlands continued to run their own affairs; large estates remained in the lowlands. As in Macedonia, bad rural conditions caused emigration to Constantinople, Egypt, Bulgaria, Romania, southern Italy and the United States.

The Albanian problem emerged as a result of the Treaty of San Stefano, which assigned Albanian-inhabited territory to neighbouring Christian states. Local leaders, with the support of Ottoman governors, wrote appeals and raised armed followers. In the spring of 1878, against the favourable background of a war party in Constantinople, a number of prominent Albanians in the capital came together to work against those clauses affecting 'the region of Albania' (*Arnavutluk* in Turkish). They called for delegates of all four vilayets to meet at Prizren as the representatives of the powers gathered in Berlin.

Some fifty to eighty individuals, mostly Muslim notables from the affected northern regions, gathered in June to form the League of Prizren. Several Muslim lords from Bosnia had also come, hoping to form an alliance with the Albanians, some of whom did indeed want to emphasize Ottoman–Muslim unity. Others preferred to stress the union of all Albanians, Muslim and Christian. They set up a committee to supervise activities and raise money, together with an armed force. They asked the Porte for support, while stating that 'above all else we are Albanians'. They addressed a memorandum to the Congress of Berlin to demand the 'integrity of Albanian territory'. The Porte initially supported the league, to influence the congress to review San Stefano.

The powers had been made aware of the existence of Albanians, so much so that Bismarck had to state rather bluntly that there was no such thing as an Albanian nationality. At Berlin, the Ottoman Empire was left with more territory than under San Stefano, but there was still strong local opposition to the settlement with Montenegro, and concern about the future settlement with Greece. The Porte used dilatory tactics on the delimitation of the new Montenegrin–Ottoman border.[5] When Ottoman troops eventually left, the league's forces took their place, to resist the Montenegrins but also the Porte which had to enforce the decisions of the powers. There was the same resistance to ceding anything to Greece in Epirus, the same mixed motives of protecting the integrity of the Ottoman Empire and of safeguarding local privileges, and the same Ottoman stalling. Eventually, most of Epirus remained Ottoman.

Early in 1881, Kosovo notables (i.e. from the northwestern mountainous part of the Ottoman province of that name) took to open rebellion, and with league forces the movement spread as far as Skopje. A large Ottoman army, sent out in the spring, received assistance from loyal Albanians, and the league collapsed. Its leaders were arrested or exiled to other parts of the Empire, but there were no further reprisals.

The three years of the league's existence had been important. It had been the work of the three Frashëri brothers,[6] who typically had served both the Ottoman government and the embryonic Albanian movement. They were highly educated, influenced by European nationalist movements, and part of the important Albanian community of Constantinople. One should not over-emphasize the nationalist orientation of the League of Prizren which, although widespread, was loosely knit and dominated by Muslim traditionalists. Most of those who went along did so to keep their lands within the Ottoman

---

5 A strange situation prevailed in that area, where Christian clans had for long clashed with Muslim lords. While some of the latter were Albanians, others were proud of their noble Serbian ancestry, spoke the same language as their peasants, and considered themselves 'Turks'. The atmosphere of the time and place is vividly rendered in Milovan Djilas's historical novel, *Izgubljene bitke* (Belgrade: Prosveta, 1994). Podgorica, the present-day capital of that republic in what is left of Yugoslavia, was in the territory awarded to Montenegro in 1878.

6 The eldest, Abdyl Frashëri (1839–92), its true organizer, had been a deputy in the Ottoman parliament in 1877. His death sentence was commuted to life, before he was released and allowed to live in Constantinople without taking part in political activity.

Empire, or out of frustration over harsh economic conditions. Albanian troops had participated in the wars against Serbia and Montenegro; many soldiers went on to fight for the league; many later fought alongside Turkish regulars against the league.

Muslim Albanians fitted into the Islamic orientation of Abdülhamid's rule. The Porte took measures to base the sultan's rule in the Balkans on them. Albanians from the ceded territories resettled in the Kosovo area, where they took reprisals on local Serbs for the estates and lands they had lost. The Ottoman authorities encouraged the colonization by Albanian hillsmen of the fertile plains, thus reinforcing their presence in Kosovo, Macedonia and Epirus. Full use was thereafter made of the Albanian military. Propaganda was used to stress that the prosperity, even the very existence of Albania, depended on the Ottoman Empire. Much was done to develop Muslim education in Albania. Influence was exercised through important families, whose members became provincial governors, ministers, advisers.

The deteriorating situation in the European provinces at the turn of the century then altered the Porte's Albanian policy. As southern Albanians fought loyally in the Greco-Turkish war of 1897, northern Albanians joined in the increased activities of armed bands of various ethnic groups, even clashing with regular troops. The Kosovo area once again became a major security problem, as a semblance of Ottoman order survived in the mountainous areas only at the price of buying the loyalty and irregular military service of mercurial and pillaging individuals with favours, titles and money. Muslim–Christian relations worsened.

Austria-Hungary and Italy entered the arena. Vienna supported the trend for an autonomous Albania as a bulwark against the spread of Serbian and Montenegrin influence to the Adriatic; Rome wanted to check Austria-Hungary. They competed in education, as the superior Christian- (particulary Catholic-) sponsored schools attracted pupils of all faiths. The League of Prizren had in 1879 established in Constantinople a Society for the Printing of Albanian Books. It was influenced by the work of German scholars on the Albanian language, taken up by Italo-Albanian writers. These descendants of Albanians who had emigrated to southern Italy played a major cultural rôle, as they focused interest in the use of history and language as evidence of an Albanian identity, distinct from Turkish, Greek and Slav.

Within the context of the Porte's Albanian policy, permission had been obtained for an Albanian periodical in Constantinople, and the first all-Albanian school in Korçë in 1887. The Porte was interested in countering Greek influences through the Orthodox Church, but not in promoting an Albanian identity. The Society for the Printing of Albanian Books was closed in 1881, as part of the repression of the League of Prizren. Fearing that the language movement was becoming subversive, the government in 1902 imposed a general ban on Albanian schools and publications. By that time, however, links had been well established, not only with Italo-Albanians, but with more recent émigrés in Romania, in Europe generally, in Egypt and in the United States.

Few Albanians wanted to see the Ottoman Empire collapse. Rather they tended to see Albania (in the words of Sami Frashëri, the scholar brother) as 'our special homeland' within 'our general [Ottoman] homeland'. By the turn of the century, the idea of autonomy had taken root in the more developed south, among those with a European education, but the clans of northern Albania, the lords of Kosovo and the landowners of central Albania also wanted it in order to preserve existing structures.

GREECE BETWEEN TRIKOUPIS AND DELIGIANNIS

Like their counterparts elsewhere in the Balkans, Greek political leaders would have liked to run both an expansionist foreign policy and a programme of internal development, but their country seemed at times not to be able to afford either. By the time of the Eastern Crisis, they had come to realize that they could not have both. A turning point was reached in 1875 when King George accepted the principle that he would call on the leader enjoying the support of a majority of deputies to form the government. This captured the mood of increasing public dissatisfaction with what Richard Clogg has called 'issueless politics'.[7] Two blocs formed, and for much of the last two decades of the century something like a two-party system operated.

Kharilaos Trikoupis (1832–96), the proponent of reforms, secured a majority in 1881 and was prime minister for most of the decade. Representing the modernizing trend, he believed that the state had to be strengthened before it could contemplate an active foreign policy, let alone embark on irredentist enterprises. He sought to improve Greece's infrastructure, her creditworthiness and her armed forces, all of which necessitated tax increases. Crete and the coveted provinces to the north were, however, a permanent reminder of the kingdom's limits, and such 'foreign' issues tended to dominate domestic politics. Public prejudices were somewhat better reflected, and reinforced, by Theodoros Deligiannis's (1824–1905) demagogic championing of a 'greater Greece'. His policies placed an additional strain on the economy, not to mention the tension in relations with the powers.

The 1878 Cyprus Convention had entrusted the administration of that island to Great Britain. The Congress of Berlin, while of the opinion that Thessaly and part of Epirus should be ceded to Greece, had formally done no more than invite the Ottoman Empire to revise its frontiers in favour of the Hellenic kingdom. Power mediation resulted in the cession of Thessaly and the Arta district of Epirus, an additional 13,400 sq. km with half a million inhabitants, thus bringing the population of Greece to 2,187,000 in 1889. This was the second extension of territory after the acquisition of the

7 Clogg, 65.

Ionian Islands; it brought the borders of the kingdom up to the confines of Macedonia.

Like others in the Balkans, Greece had been deeply disturbed by the Treaty of San Stefano. The new Bulgarian principality challenged Greek claims on territory regarded as part of a historical legacy. The Bulgarian exarchate was in a good position to dispute the authority of the patriarch of Constantinople in lands that were still under Ottoman control. The appearance of an Albanian movement extending to Macedonia and Epirus was another worry.

Schoolbooks from 1870 not only defined Greeks in opposition to 'others', but integrated into Hellenism all that it could possibly embrace, in particular Byzantium and ancient Macedonia, which had previously been ignored. Geography followed. As the end of the Eastern Crisis seemed to announce the break-up of Turkey in favour of the Slavs, the Bulgars went up the scale of enemies. A National Society was set up in 1894 to promote 'national' aims, by sending propaganda, arms and volunteers across the border to the north, and across the sea to Crete. When Serbia went to war against Bulgaria in 1885, there was considerable pressure in Greece for similar action, but it led to no more than a 'phoney war'. The powers stopped it, by imposing a naval blockade in May 1886; Deligiannis had to resign.

Attention had focused on the north. It was considered that Crete, with no other claimant, would sooner or later come to Greece. In May 1896, the island flared up again and its leaders declared union with the kingdom. Nationalists in Greece provided enthusiastic support. Although once again under Deligiannis since 1895, the government was cautious after the 1885 experience, but in response to intense popular pressure it reluctantly sent soldiers and ships to Crete. In spite of intervention by the powers, the uprising continued. Greece prepared for war, stoked up insurrection over the border and ordered a general mobilization. In April 1897, the Porte responded by declaring war – a thirty days' war that ended in disaster for the Greeks. Troops under Crown Prince Constantine were defeated in Thessaly and Epirus; the Ottoman army invaded Greece.

As with Serbia in 1885, only the intervention of the powers saved Greece from anything worse. The Peace of Constantinople practically restored the *status quo ante bellum*, and imposed on Greece a war indemnity of 100 million gold francs. The sultan accepted the special status of autonomy for Crete. The humiliating defeat had not only highlighted the gulf between Greece's irredentist aspirations and her modest military capabilities, but effectively bankrupted her. Ever since 1878, when a compromise settlement had been achieved with foreign bondholders over loans that went back to the War of Independence, Greece had overstretched herself in new loans, to the point where the servicing of her foreign debt of nearly 600 million gold francs consumed a third of state revenues.

Revenues did not increase in line with defence spending or with public investments in infrastructures. The latest burdens resulted in a serious breach of Greek sovereignty – the enforcement of foreign financial control in 1898.

At the insistence of the powers, the government had to accept the appointment of a European Financial Commission representing their bondholders, to monitor the budget and oversee the servicing of the external debt. Repayment was to be assured by the revenues of customs and monopolies.

The defeat ushered in a period of self-doubt. Politicians realized that the Great Idea could not be pursued single-mindedly or single-handedly. Strenuous efforts were made to impart a sense of Hellenic identity to the Orthodox inhabitants of Macedonia and to the large and often Turkish-speaking Orthodox population of Asia Minor. The sultan's Greek subjects were still the majority of Greeks. Some intellectuals even discussed the possibility of some sort of condominium with the Turks, to benefit from the extent to which the Greek élite in the Ottoman Empire had managed to re-establish much of its economic power.

There was a return to advocating the build-up of national resources as an essential precondition of expansion, since the economy of the kingdom also underwent a transformation in the last decades of the century. As less than 20 per cent of the territory was arable, limited cultivation goes a long way towards explaining the lowest population growth rate and the highest emigration rate in the Balkans. Nevertheless, there was an increase, essentially quantitative, in agricultural production.

The acquisition of the wheat-growing plains of Thessaly raised the grain area from 7 per cent to two-thirds of the total under cultivation. Greek merchants had already acquired some of the larger chiftliks there before 1881. In 1907 perhaps as much as half the peasantry of that province still worked on estates with traditional sharecropping contracts. Smallholding prevailed outside Thessaly and cereal production was largely for family consumption. With not enough moisture for corn, cattle production was not even sufficient to meet domestic needs, let alone generate export earnings.

Stimulated by increased demand from foreign markets and by the rise in prices, vineyard cultivation occupied much of the countryside from the 1860s. The Mediterranean phylloxera epidemic, which reached even Serbia and Bulgaria, left Greece untouched. The destruction of French vineyards coincided with the distribution of national lands in Greece after 1871. Peasants planted more vineyards to supply European producers with grapes; when France recovered in the early 1890s, the Greeks turned to drying grapes. Plots that would not yield enough grain or support enough livestock for subsistence were converted to vineyards for the raisin market.

Greece became the biggest producer of raisins. By 1875 they represented over 50 per cent of the value of her exports and provided half the total world output. The uncontrolled overproduction of raisins for inelastic European markets led in the 1890s to huge unsold surpluses and a collapse of prices. From the 1880s the general fall in agricultural prices caused a slowing down of agricultural growth and accelerated emigration.

In the 1870s, there was something of an industrial growth, benefiting from the coincidence of a relative expansion of primary production with a relative pause in technological innovation.[8] Mechanical power was introduced to a range of manufactures, from food processing to textiles. Such establishments doubled from 107 in 1875 to 220 in 1900, with the total number of industrial workers going up from 4,750 to 15,000. Minerals provided 28 per cent of Greek exports by 1885, inflated by the output of one enterprise – the Compagnie Française des Mines du Laurium in Attica, which in 1864 had reactivated the ancient argentiferous lead mines of classical antiquity. The abundance of locally treated iron ore did not, however, provide the basis for any advanced industry. Local markets were restricted and exports hampered by insufficient infrastructures and the high cost of sea transport.

Important public works were carried out, and much of that development was associated with Trikoupis. The network of roads suitable for wheeled traffic was increased threefold during the 1880s. The rail network was established during the last two decades of the century, expanding from the 12 km of the Athens–Piraeus line in 1882 to 1,033 km by 1900 (even though the Greek system was still not connected to the rest of Europe). The Corinth Canal, built between 1882 and 1893, was a major feat of engineering, which shortened by half the sea route between Piraeus and Italy. Even so, port infrastructure did not develop sufficiently to keep up with export needs, in particular with those of Patras, the raisin capital.

Industrial growth benefited from no more than a brief transition between two phases of the evolution of techniques. Furthermore, it did not attract enough investment or manpower. The benefits of credit and commerce were high compared to the modest returns and high risks of capital locked in industry. State bonds, Greek and Ottoman, were also more interesting. The domestic public debt in 1897 amounted to 200 million gold francs (compared to a budget revenue of less than 100 million francs, and a total capital of all companies of no more than 29 million francs).

The National Bank of Greece was the oldest of all banks. It had been founded in 1842 as a private joint-stock enterprise with diaspora Greeks, led by some Swiss, English and French stockholders, and with state participation, but the state never contributed its full quota, and in 1871 publicly sold its shares. The bank was accepted by notables only on conditions that made it impossible for it to compete with them. It granted credit almost exclusively to the traders and financiers of the main cities at rates of around 8 per cent, which they channelled down at higher rates. Only in 1891 did the National Bank begin to grant mortgage loans on agricultural land, increasing that share

8 The case of Syra in the Cyclades is characteristic. The island had attracted (mostly Roman Catholic) refugees from other islands at the time of the War of Independence. These merchants and artisans had developed there their traditional activities, and provided half a century of prosperity based on the wheat trade. Textiles, leather, wrought iron and other crafts flourished in small industries. Shipbuilding employed 1,500 workers in 1850 and was dispersed in small yards operated by the old association between the trader-shipowner-skipper, who provided the capital, and the builder and his workers. Hard-hit by the obsolescence of steam, the Corinth Canal and direct access of European entrepreneurs to the Ottoman Empire, Syra went into slow decline from the 1880s. Its architectural heritage is a testimony to that era.

of its credit operations very gradually, from over 9 per cent in 1893 to more than 18 per cent by 1900.

The National Bank had repeatedly granted the government loans in unsecured note issues. With heavy borrowing of gold-backed European denominations, and trade and budget deficits, this had forced the silver-backed drachma to slip badly by the 1890s; it could be exchanged for gold only at a huge premium. The European Financial Commission in 1898 imposed measures to return to par value and aim at the gold standard. Other banks also operated in trade, private loans and state bonds, all easier solutions than industrial investment. There was very little direct foreign investment. Every crisis signalled a flight of capital out of industry. After 1880 diaspora Greek capital benefited almost exclusively a flourishing merchant fleet, which was very slow to adapt to steam.

Greek industry also suffered from a lack of manpower. The countryside generally resisted the call of nascent urban industries. Urban growth was slow. Although urban dwellers had increased to 28 per cent of the population by 1879, towns of over 5,000 inhabitants accounted for just 18 per cent. The real growth of Athens and of its port, Piraeus, came later, as their joint population expanded from 55,000 in 1870 to 240,000 in 1907, with the proliferation of services and small trades, but also with the growth of state administration. Patras, the second-largest town, numbered only 38,000 in 1907.

The smallholding structure and emigration kept down population density and growth. Faced with shrinking holdings of poor land, peasants looked elsewhere for work. Seasonal work was an outlet that protected from absolute poverty, but it was emigration that cushioned the peasantry and absorbed the bulk of the labour surplus. Some went to Athens where they worked for several years as craftsmen or labourers, but the great majority went abroad, again often on a temporary basis, and principally to the United States. Out of an average annual emigration of 7,795 in the five years between 1896 and 1907, 2,238 went to the USA. Altogether between 1890 and 1914, some 350,000 emigrated – nearly one-sixth of the entire population, and almost all of them males. Their remittances not only helped their families in the countryside, but were a key element – however unpredictable – in the balance of payments.

The education system, although widespread, valued patriotic ideology rather than technical meritocracy. Industry had to import its engineers, technicians and specialized workers. Even less qualified labour came from Albania, Italy or Spain. Refugees from Crete and elsewhere were practically the only permanent Greek industrial workers. Whereas raisin exports and public works had increased wages up to the mid-1880s, the agricultural crisis and the devaluation of the drachma that followed prevented any further incentive to mechanical innovations. By the end of the century, industry was stagnating in a small-scale and labour-intensive structure manned by the leftovers from emigration.

Although Greece had achieved independence half a century and more before the other Balkan states, she was still in fact under the trusteeship of the powers, as much if not more than Serbia and Romania. Her more adventurous and usually frustrated endeavours had been costly in terms of both pride and growth.

UNMIXING, BUILDING AND INVENTING NATIONS

As Christians had been moving into self-governing territories from provinces that were still under Ottoman rule, so Muslims left regions that fell to Christian rule. Whatever their rights, they would not adapt to being second-rate citizens, or they found their land occupied, or they were encouraged to leave. They went from Bulgaria and Eastern Roumelia, from the territories ceded to Serbia and to Montenegro, and from the part of Dobrudja that became Romanian. They left Thessaly after 1881 when it became Greek, and Crete from 1897 when it became autonomous. They went from Bosnia-Herzegovina, where they did not lose their possessions or their social position. They left even when they spoke little or no Turkish. Many settled as near as possible to where they had lived previously, to reinforce the Muslim presence in mixed areas where they vented their feelings on the Christians.

That was part of the 'unmixing of peoples' that occurs at the time of the collapse of empires,[9] but people also left for other reasons. Impoverished peasants from the Hungarian lands, from Austrian Dalmatia and even Slovenia, from Ottoman Albania and from independent Greece left for the New World, and so did Macedonians of all sorts as Christian peasants clashed with Muslim lords and their refugee tithe and labour enforcers, and as various 'Christian' nationalist bands clashed with each other and with Ottoman forces.

When real warfare occurred between states, it was still 'phoney' to a certain extent. They did not have the capacity to realize dreams of liberation, or to alter the local balance of power against the sultan's modernized armies and the collective will of Europe. Balkan peasant conscripts were better at defending their soil than at fighting Ottoman soldiers, let alone one another, even when they were not actually stopped by the powers. The Balkan states also found it difficult to integrate the new territories they were allowed to acquire, as these had been longer under Turkish rule and had developed regional differences of one kind or another.

The Tanzimat had encouraged the privatization of property. This generally meant initially the legal recognition of what peasants regarded as an illegal appropriation of their ancestral rights, but also the possibility for richer peasants to buy land. In liberated territories, spontaneous agrarian reforms took place, belatedly legalized, as the estates of departed Muslim landowners in fact disappeared. Estates remained where they were already in the hands of native Christians, where direct Ottoman rule continued, where native Muslims adapted to foreign rule, and in the older Habsburg dominions.

---

9 Roger Brubaker, 'Aftermath of Empire and the Unmixing of Peoples: Historical and Comparative Perspectives', in *Ethnic and Racial Studies*, 18/2, London, 1995.

Regions where estates remained generally produced little marketable surplus and much emigration from the countryside. Peasants emigrated when they lost what little land they had, or when they could no longer live from it or from working on the land of others, particularly when lawlessness was added to poverty. Emigration was lowest from Romania, a land of large estates with greatly expanded grain cultivation, and highest from Greece, where peasants did own the land but often could not subsist on the produce of their tiny plots.

Where land was available and smallholders could survive on it, even when they owned less than the five hectares estimated to be the minimum to support a family of five, they generally stayed in the countryside. Political and social changes encouraged them to bring more land under cultivation, with initially higher yields, however primitive the methods. Order, security, urban expansion and the spur to private property pushed peasants back into long underpopulated and undercultivated lowlands, and into producing some marketable surplus. The population grew during the second half of the nineteenth century, to rural densities never previously attained – 30–50 per sq. km. This was achieved by the control of epidemics, but even more by the development of a cereal economy in the lowlands, which could sustain a larger population than a meat-based diet in the uplands.

The end of the century marked a faster tempo of economic development, but a commercialized cereal economy occurred in the Balkans later than elsewhere in Europe. Peasants had no access to credit at reasonable rates of interest. At the very moment when systematic investments should have made sense, from the 1870s, the fall in farm prices turned capital away from agriculture, except in the highly privileged Danubian basin.

Balkan society was rooted in the village. Before the middle of the century, there was no city apart from Constantinople with more than 100,000 inhabitants. Bucharest reached that level around 1850, Athens by 1880, Salonika rose to 130,000 by 1900, and all the capitals quickly became centres of national life. Their population had a much higher standard of living than the rest of the country – and eventually services not far behind western Europe, as they adopted all the newest all at once. The élites wanted their capitals to resemble Napoleon III's transformed Paris. They built royal palaces, ministries, universities, libraries, theatres, cathedrals, banks and hotels (although western visitors and guidebooks usually looked down on them).

Cities grew, more because of the expansion of the state than because of the expansion of industry. All four Balkan states, along with Austria-Hungary and the Ottoman Empire in their Balkan peripheries, developed infrastructures, and especially railways, but more for political, military and fiscal reasons. Their advent was not always welcome. A common view was that they would be paid for chiefly by the peasant taxpayers and be of advantage mainly to the most developed European states.

All these efforts had some success, but there was no industrial takeoff except in Romania. Balkan governments initially favoured low tariffs, to help the export of their agricultural surpluses and to please the powers. When falling grain prices led them to imitate the post-1880 European pattern of helping industrialization by tariff barriers, they were thwarted in their aspirations. They could not create a home market rapidly enough for their manufactures, or protect them adequately enough. European interests set impediments in their way in order to continue the policy of the Capitulations – to keep the Balkans as a reservoir of raw materials.

The last in Europe to try and lift their economies, the Balkans could not compete in the world market, except in a few commodities. In the words of Traian Stoianovich, they fell behind economically while moving ahead.[10] Only in Romania was there investment capital available locally. Foreign capital was invested for political reasons, or to foster transport, mining, and the drainage of easily accessible fertile marshland, but did little to promote industry.

Private capital favoured trade and credit. Budget deficits were financed largely by the issue of treasury bonds, at rates and volumes which drew in private capital. The public debt was the result of expenditure on infrastructure and foreign policy expenses. Manpower was no more available than capital, for it stayed on the land as long as possible. Where and when there was a rural surplus, it could not be absorbed by, or could not be attracted to, the urban sector. When it had to go, it emigrated to the New World.

Even after the cities had been appropriated by the natives, and their élites were busy making the transition from Ottoman patterns to European models, the urban population was still attached to the countryside. The contrast has often been emphasized between the form and the substance of political life. Constitutional forms were implemented by men who believed that modernization should be carried out by the educated élite, and by others who idealized the peasantry and its way of life.

By 1880, direct 'universal' (or nearly 'universal') suffrage was the norm in all Balkan constitutions except in Romania.[11] Peasants, however, were not as yet very interested and distrusted town-based politicians who flattered them in order to obtain their votes. Parties had come into existence everywhere, but only Serbia's radicals had a truly national network and something like a platform that could attract the peasantry. They all had trends and factions, ready to compromise on principles to get into government. Central government was important. It was the apex of the bureaucratic régime, adopted because it was considered modern, and it provided the tools to implement policies.

The crown represented sovereignty and legitimacy. The monarch played an important rôle, as arbiter, as guarantor of the constitution (even when he distorted or suspended it), and as symbol of the state's international status (even when he alienated it through secret deals). He appointed the government,

---

10 Traian Stoianovich, *Balkan Worlds: The First and Last Europe*, Armonk, NY, & London: M.E. Sharpe, 1994, 215.
11 The French notion of *suffrage universel* extended the franchise to all citizens (with few exclusions), who were the adult males. Serbia's franchise, restricted to taxpayers, left out very few adult males.

even if he accepted the parliamentary principle, and often chose the ministers of war and foreign affairs. Romania, with the most limited electorate, had the most stable political framework in the Balkans. Bulgaria, with the most democratic of constitutions, was also the country with the greatest electoral malpractices.

Two contradictory principles opposed each other within the constitutional quasi-parliamentary system. 'European culture' extolled the positivist ideas of order and progress. Its adherents believed in the authority of the state to modernize, that is to modify continuity, so as to draw the masses away from their local tribal instincts and up to the universal goals of their common humanity. In their modernization policy of opening windows to Europe, they came up against the reaction of those who wanted to preserve the advantages of continuity.

The modernizers were opposed by the collectivists. These were socialists, especially young Serbs and Bulgars, who sought a Balkan form of utopian socialism which would omit the stage of capitalism by developing in a rural milieu. Linking national and social issues, they sought the basis of a new order in the peasant community incorporated into the framework of a South Slav or Balkan federation. Other, not necessarily socialist, particularly Romanian and Greek, intellectuals also sought to build on the old local communities, with nostalgia for an idealized world that no longer existed, if it had ever done so. They knew that in France too, as in England, the idea of the village as good opposed to the town as evil also appealed to late nineteenth-century romanticism.

Those politicians who had idealized the extended family and the village community as forms of native democracy, and those who had related freedom at home to freedom abroad, not to mention historicist intellectuals, had been unsuccessful in penetrating the villages. Peasants were in general more interested in their economic situation than in their political rights. It was only when and where the middle-class political left linked urban liberalism with rural opposition to the expense and burden of state bureaucracy that it managed to mobilize the countryside.

The peasants responded. The gradual acceptance of the principle that the prime minister appointed by the monarch should be able to form a government enjoying the support of a majority of deputies, the enlargement of the electoral body and the establishment of modern political parties, enabled peasants to take a real part in the policy-making process during the last two decades of the century, through force of numbers. They had to be taken into account, even though their involvement reflected, but did not solve, their problems. Barbara Jelavich believes it is unfair to make comparisons with the most advanced parts of Europe that had provided the models.[12] The situation was not as bleak as is often made to appear by contrast. Institutions had been introduced, ideals accepted, standards set.

12 Barbara Jelavich, *History of the Balkans, II: Twentieth Century*, Cambridge: Cambridge University Press, 1983, 4.

Political emancipation had first come from European influences on the periphery of the peninsula, and then travelled back again from the centre of the national states to their periphery. The programmes were formulated outside the rural community even when they were based on it. They needed to impose discipline on the peasants, who had been and could still be rebels, but who had to be turned into taxpayers and soldiers even before they became citizens. As the struggle for emancipation was essentially nationalist, all political trends exploited nationalism – conservatives who preached a strong state and domestic unity for the sake of a successful foreign policy of national emancipation; liberals who related freedom from autocratic rule at home and freedom from foreign rule abroad; even socialists who fused the national and social revolutions. Few had a social and economic programme that would attract the peasants.

Peasants remained suspicious of those in power, who failed to satisfy their aspirations and deal with their discontents. Whatever their voting power, they lacked autonomy in their relations with cities and officialdom. For them, the capitals, which concentrated money and power, were almost a new enemy, as states failed to eradicate a problem inherited from Ottoman times, that of the non-generative urban state, which diverted resources from the peasants to the governments, the cities, and, in the case of Romania, the estate owners.

As compared to western Europe, political activity was distorted. In the west, it had to establish a modern state of citizens within an existing framework; in the Balkans, it had to destroy and reconstruct frameworks. Ethnic communities had come to a degree of self-consciousness in an often structureless environment, and in transitional zones of blurred religious and linguistic borders. The enlightened notion of the state survived, but it was transferred to small and weak states which aspired to territories of neighbouring empires. They had to confront, and eventually to submit to the dictates of, the international community of powers.

They looked beyond their treaty borders to territories where people lived who were linked to them by language, religion and other feelings, but also to places inhabited by historical memories. Ethnic territory was not necessarily the same as historical territory, even if either could be defined. They found it difficult to make themselves altogether acceptable or believable nations, because they were emerging from two once rival and neighbouring empires, and they always feared for their existence, as states or as collective entities. To encompass whole ethnic communities and to recover the past were not necessarily compatible. As both aims were pursued simultaneously with the building of a modern enlightened state, ethnicity and historicity impinged on enlightenment in the complex enterprise of nation building.

The new states fortified their national identities by the use of religion and language. Political authorities all over the Balkans took over or obtained the right to appoint religious authorities. They used organized religious communities as channels for the promotion of cultural and political identity. Orthodoxy was placed in the service of state nationalism by westernized or westernizing élites who imposed autocephaly on their territorial churches, no longer in the traditional ecclesiological sense of interdependence of local churches, but in the new political sense of independence from outside jurisdiction. The Church was to be as independent of the patriarch in Constantinople as the state was of the sultan, but it was not to be independent of the state.

The decentralization of the Orthodox Church made it responsive to local conditions, but it also weakened its ability to stand up to secular authority. In spite of the ideal, the trend had, in practical terms in the nineteenth century, been away from the ecumenical to the regional and the ethnic, blurring distinctions between 'Church', 'state' and 'nation'. Imagined, imaginary, budding and even real Balkan westerners naturally looked west for their modern rendering of Orthodoxy. If they were inspired by the Gallicanism and Anglicanism of western Catholic monarchs of old, their organizational model was Lutheran, imported via Russia and pioneered by Greece. The national state made the Church into a national institution, and used it, along with school and army, to propagate a national ideal that often skirted the teaching of the Gospels.

Conditioned by the confrontation between Christian peasant and Muslim landlord (and overlord), early nationalism had had aspects of a 'holy war', reinforced by the fact that European wars against the Turks had also been presented in these terms. They continued to be present in uprisings and wars against Turkey throughout the nineteenth century and later. In its initial stage, this religious nationalism combined with the peasant desire for landowner-ship offered a broader basis for cooperation among movements, but it was gradually superseded by a narrower nationalism based on, and nourished by, historical memories. Peasant revolutions were rendered respectable by historians, Muslim minorities gradually left, many blurred religious–ethnic identities became purely ethnic.

Other models were found in Europe. The geostrategic interests of Balkan states, even when advanced as historical claims, replaced ethnicity in seeking to establish boundaries in ambiguous mixed areas. This they eventually did – when necessary, at the expense of neighbouring states of their own sort, even at the expense of their own long-term national interests. The influence of Hungary was also felt, in the Dual Monarchy, in applying the modern notion of nation-state to a historical territory 'greater' than the ethnic community, in holding on to rights, in opposing participation.

As spoken languages were fluid, scholars, educationalists and politicians altered and codified the literary and official languages. Schools and armies then taught teachers and officers, who in turn taught pupils and conscripts, to speak and write in a uniform manner.[13] Nations were defined in opposition to

---

13 Romania abandoned the Cyrillic script and continued to purge the language of much Slav, Greek and Turkish vocabulary. Greece favoured a universal, 'purified', literary language accept-able to all Greeks, but with competition from those who urged the adoption of 'demotic' Greek. Croats and Serbs somehow managed to fuse the two, by giving up various literary variants in favour of a demotic, if pure, variant, deemed to be the core of joint Serbo-Croatian in its

others near at hand, or in imitation of others far away. Grand narratives were constructed of a country once free, culturally elevated and usually egalitarian, until the greed of its decadent élite had delivered it to the greed of foreign conquerors.

This was a sublimation of one's own history, practised all over Europe at the time, but potentially dangerous if turned violently against reality by 'intellectuals' who had had too much of an education too quickly. Society was not developed enough for them to find much independence outside state employment. Impatient of long-term action over generations, once in control of state institutions, they wanted to carry out the ideals of their youth in their own lifetime.

But for all that, their foreign policies went no further than looking for or resisting a patron power, and pushing their individual claim to some more Ottoman territory. Greece had obtained formal independence long before any other state in the Balkans. Yet her 'sovereignty' was limited right from the start by her protecting powers, and by the financial control imposed on her at the very end of the century. The most recent addition to the Balkan states, Bulgaria, which was not even formally independent, managed at times to defy her liberator and protector, Russia, and to behave more independently than Greece. Romania, Serbia and Montenegro, promoted to full independence in 1878, either found that independence hedged in by their powerful neighbour Austria-Hungary, or found it advantageous to accept such informal patronage.

All at times exploited the mutual jealousies of the powers and enjoyed some freedom of action in spite of their financial constraints. Imperialism contained so many internal contradictions, and was weakened by such rivalries, that it did not result in the renewed subjugation, political or even economic, of the peninsula.

---

slight regional varieties. This left out Bulgarian, which was free to develop on its own. The few literate Albanians employed several scripts until the turn of the century, when a move was made in favour of a compromise spoken variety with Latin script.

CHAPTER 8

The tail end of the nineteenth century, 1900–14 – Part 1

The foundations of the Ausgleich *undermined. The Young Turks behind the Porte. The Albanian movement and the Macedonian question. King Peter's Serbia. King Ferdinand's Bulgaria.*

Historians have said that the nineteenth century ended in 1914. 'The last of old Europe'[1] came to an end on 28 June 1914, in Sarajevo, the administrative centre of Bosnia-Herzegovina, a part of the Balkan peninsula which, although formally part of Austria-Hungary since 1908, was still very much a legacy of the Ottoman Empire. For the Balkans as a whole, but more particularly for the independent states, 1900–14 is indeed the last period of a century that started around 1800, when in the ruins of the old Ottoman order, the surviving Byzantine tradition faced the new ideas of the Enlightenment and of the French Revolution.

Since then five states (six, if one includes a formally independent Albania set up in 1912) had squeezed out of the Ottoman Empire, which had done much to restore itself, to the point of surviving for another hundred years or so. Their aim was to join Europe as latecomers, a Europe which may appear to us as 'old Europe', but which was new to them, even when they sought their inspiration in a (largely mythical) Europe that predated their imperial conquerors. By 1914 they had achieved much. In many ways, they were part of Europe again, if not by the standards of the Belgian constitutional model or of the French parliamentary politics that they so admired, at least by less demanding comparisons with some of the continent's less-developed southern parts, or of the great mass of people in France a generation or two earlier.

THE FOUNDATIONS OF THE *AUSGLEICH* UNDERMINED

The Habsburg Monarchy went through a new crisis. The Hungarian opposition won the elections of 1905, but was unable to form a government until it

1 To borrow the title of A.J.P. Taylor's admirably selected photographic album (New York: Quadrangle/The New York Times Book Co., 1976).

had given in to the sovereign over not altering the *Ausgleich*. Demonstrations in favour of universal suffrage were used to scare it into backing down. For a while it had sought support in the Balkans, but Serbia's agricultural exports which threatened Hungarian interests were another reason to overcome the constitutional crisis.

Never introduced in Hungary, universal male suffrage did come to Austria in 1907; the Slovenian People's party – the 'clericals' – won seventeen representatives in the Vienna parliament to the liberals' (the National Progressive Party) four. It subsequently increased its share to the point where it practically had a political monopoly among the 1.2 million Slovene-speakers (4 per cent of the population of the Austrian crown lands). Slovenian clericals usually cooperated with the Croat 'rightists' of Dalmatia; neither at that time were keen on union with the Orthodox Serbs. Economic conditions in the Slovene lands were relatively good. Peasants usually owned land. Although it did not provide great profit for Vienna banks, the flow of capital into coal mines and iron works was important for the receiving economy.

It was in Austria's coastal province of Dalmatia that the first steps were taken to bring together again Croat and Serb activists. Antagonisms had never been deep between the 81 per cent Croats and 16 per cent Serbs that together made up 610,000 of the province's 635,000 inhabitants. It was there that their political leaders in 1905 first decided to exploit the crisis in Budapest, by offering support to the Hungarian Independence Party in exchange for the integration of Dalmatia into a Triune Croatia with more autonomy. On the other side of the Austrian lands, there was little irredentism among the Romanians of Bukovina, where the relative decency of the administration contrasted with the way in which minorities were treated in Hungary.

In 1908, Budapest had agreed to the annexation of Bosnia-Herzegovina, on condition that the territory would not be joined to Croatia. The continued condominium brought a good deal of modernization, along with (at times divisive) incentives to the three communities. Dependent peasants were offered help to buy themselves out, although interest on loans available through the Privileged Agrarian Bank was generally too high, and landlords preferred to keep their more profitable rent arrangements. There was little change in economic and social conditions. Muslims made up 91 per cent of landowners with dependent peasants, and 57 per cent of free peasants; 74 per cent of dependent peasants were Serbs. Seventy-seven per cent of peasant proprietors owned less than five hectares. No more than 13,300 people worked in manufacturing firms employing more than twenty workers.

Eventually, in 1910, Francis Joseph granted a constitution to Bosnia-Herzegovina. A general was placed at the head of the administration, flanked by an advisory diet, with official members, and deputies elected through a restricted franchise and a system of electoral colleges divided according to social position and religious denomination.

The coincidence of the Monarchy's internal crisis and of the changes in Serbia favoured a considerable improvement in Croatia's political climate, although the franchise was restricted to 1.8 per cent of the population. A small trades union movement came into being, with social democrats demanding more autonomy and universal suffrage to implement social reforms. It achieved some success in down-to-earth questions such as wages and working hours. A Croat Peasant Party, formed in 1904 with the aim of bringing the peasant masses to politics, also called for universal suffrage, with agrarian reform and a federalization of the Monarchy on the basis of nationalities. Its first deputies were elected in 1910.

Intellectuals and politicians in Zagreb and Belgrade had been in touch with each other intermittently, and kept the mystique of South Slav or Yugoslav unification as an ultimate aim. Visits, congresses and exhibitions brought together Slovenes, Croats, Serbs and Bulgars, and Croatian students attended Belgrade University. This fuelled the Dual Monarchy's distrust of Serbia. A new generation brought about a regrouping of political forces in Croatia. When the conflict between the dynasty and Hungary escalated in 1903, Croatian politicians were at first disposed to cooperate with Vienna, but when the offer was rejected, the opposition swung round. The decisions taken in 1905 brought together most of the opposition parties of Croatia, both Croat and Serb, in an offer to support Hungarian demands in return for changes in the *Nagodba*.

That offer, too, was ignored, but a move had definitely been made from the more limited stand on Croatia's 'rights' to broader South Slav interests that encompassed the 25 per cent Serb population of Croatia-Slavonia: the Croato-Serb Coalition was born. On a liberal platform aiming at bringing together the people of Croatia, Slavonia and Dalmatia, it won the 1906 elections with 43 out of 88 seats and thereafter dominated the Sabor. It remained united, and as such the major political force in Croatia.

The annexation of Bosnia-Herzegovina and its consequences ensured that Croat discontent would turn to solidarity with Serbs. Unable to govern Croatia with the elected Sabor, the Hungarian government resorted to ruling without it in 1908. There were arrests, treason trials of Serb politicians, even anti-Serb pogroms. As part of the campaign against Serbia, a Vienna 'historian' came up with incriminating evidence to show that Croato-Serb Coalition leaders had conspired with the Belgrade government, evidence that was proved to have been fabricated. Unrest increased to the point where the authorities had to come to terms with the coalition.

Constitutional rule was restored in 1910, and the franchise extended to 7.3 per cent of the 2.6 million population. The attitude of the Budapest government and Serbia's new prestige strengthened the aspiration towards South Slav solidarity and reform. The moderation of the coalition met with criticism from younger people no longer willing to accept legal action for piecemeal reforms. Constitutional arrangements were again suspended as the situation worsened in 1912.

On the eve of the First World War, the strongest political grouping in Croatia stood for Croat-Serb cooperation within the Monarchy. Smaller parties to right and left sought its radical reorganization, usually with an enlarged Croatia. In Dalmatia, the young were entirely won over to a united Yugoslavia. Even the students of Slovenia had turned to radical activity in favour of unity. Solidarity was particularly reflected among the young in Bosnia-Herzegovina, where agricultural unrest and the neighbourhood of Serbia fed the rebellious ferment. The Sarajevo conspiracy was not born in isolation. It was linked with turmoil throughout the South Slav territories of the Habsburgs – students' and workers' strikes, demonstrations, a dozen or so plots against dignitaries, links with students, parties and secret societies in Serbia.

Yet openly anti-Habsburg aspirations were limited to a fringe. Archduke Francis Ferdinand let it be said that he would consider giving the South Slavs equal status with the Hungarians on his accession. The Budapest government reverted to constitutional government in Croatia at the end of 1913. The Croato-Serb Coalition was returned to the Sabor with its greatest majority ever. In 1914, politicians could once again entertain hopes of reforms within the Habsburg framework. As for the vast majority of the predominantly rural population, it remained loyal to the Monarchy until the end of the First World War.

The rural percentage of the population had fallen from 84 per cent in 1900 to 78.5 per cent in 1910. Livestock increased significantly, to 842 pigs and cattle per 1,000 inhabitants, compared with Serbia's 626. They were sold to large urban markets; local banks could draw on Vienna and Budapest capital to issue mortgage bonds that financed estate, if not smallholder, breeding. Manufacture, essentially light industry, employed no more than 9.6 per cent of the population, but in value, capital and mechanical horsepower it surpassed Serbia's. Although there was obviously no protection against Austrian and Czech manufacture, Croatia had better rail access to the Monarchy's markets, local financial institutions that provided short-term credit, and a literacy rate more than double Serbia's. Yet livestock raising and light industry were unable to absorb rural overpopulation; 230,000 pauperized peasants emigrated between 1900 and 1914, mostly to America.

All told, the population of the Hungarian part of the Monarchy numbered 9 per cent Croats and 5 per cent Serbs. The 14 per cent Romanians were its largest ethnic minority. Outside Croatia-Slavonia, the South Slavs – mostly Serbs – were concentrated in Vojvodina where they formed 34.7 per cent of the 1.3 million population (followed by Magyars and Germans). The 2.9 million Romanians were concentrated in Transylvania where they formed 53.8 per cent of the 5.3 million population (again followed by Magyars and Germans). Hungary's education laws were gradually replacing minority-language teaching, thus effectively keeping these overwhelmingly peasant populations with a low level of literacy.

Eighty-six per cent of ethnic Romanians lived in the countryside. No town in Transylvania had a Romanian majority. A thin layer of small entrepreneurs, artisans, shop owners, professionals and public employees made up its bourgeoisie. At opposite ends of the Monarchy's borderlands, and all differences notwithstanding, Transylvania and Slovenia had the richest coal and iron ore deposits in the Balkans; they could benefit from better railways, with capital and entrepreneurs from the more developed areas. Even so, of the 87,000 emigrants that left Hungary between 1908 and 1913, 19 per cent were Romanians, mostly agricultural labourers heading for the United States.

The government in Budapest after 1910 wanted a comprehensive settlement of the nationality problem in order to consolidate the existing constitutional structure. It needed to convince Serbia and Romania that they had no chance of ever satisfying irredentist ambitions at the expense of Hungary, and to draw them once and for all into Austria-Hungary's orbit. For all its concern with the consequences of Hungary's nationality policy, the Bucharest government was worried about preserving its alliance with Austria-Hungary.

In 1905 the Romanian National Party changed its aim to that of ethnic autonomy for all areas inhabited by Romanians. As they opted for constitutional means, eight of them, including their leader Iuliu Maniu (1873–1953), were elected to parliament in Budapest that year. In 1906 they increased their representation, and, together with Serbs and Slovaks, formed a minorities parliamentary group committed to autonomy, democracy and federalization.

Both the Hungarian government and the Romanian National Party were ready for talks in 1910, but the Romanians asked for too much and the government offered too little. Pressure from Vienna and Bucharest to settle for the sake of regional stability and of Romania's link with the Triple Alliance, resulted in a second round of talks in 1913. The refusal of the prime minister, Count István Tisza (1861–1918), to admit that the Hungarian state was in fact polyethnic led to the talks being broken off again in the summer of 1914. Maniu and his colleagues were not separatists, but the middle ground between assimilation of the minorities and the dissolution of historical Hungary gradually disappeared.

The Monarchy in 1914 was in crisis. Unable to compete economically with industrialized western Europe, it was losing its leverage in Balkan affairs. It faced the exacerbation of the South Slav question, new militancy from its Romanians, Italian irredentism and demands from Hungary. The attitude of its rulers towards the nationalities hindered the development of the Hungarian state. By not extending the franchise so as not to increase the influence of non-Magyars, it also kept the majority of Magyars out of politics.

Not only were the foundations of the *Ausgleich* undermined, but Archduke Francis Ferdinand (1863–1914), the heir to the Habsburg crowns, intended to change everything. A showdown was expected on the death of the aged emperor-king between his heir and the Hungarian ruling class. Both were preparing for it by trying to win over the other nationalities. Whatever his real intentions, Francis Ferdinand let it be known that he wanted all nationalities under the dynasty to be equal. No major leader or party among them called for the destruction of the Monarchy. They acted as spokesmen for their nationalities, but came from, and were elected by, a small section only. What the people really thought has yet to be discovered.

There was in the new generation of South Slav youth a shift from political to terrorist action. Secret student societies indulged in overt revolutionary propaganda from 1913 onwards. Mistrusting elected political leaders and lacking confidence in the revolutionary zeal of peasants, they turned to individual terrorism. They sought support in Belgrade, particularly among the 'Unification or Death' group of officers, which thought that Serbia's government was too timid. And yet, tensions and crises notwithstanding, on the eve of the First World War, the Habsburg Monarchy was still intact with dynastic loyalty barely impaired. By contrast, the sultan's European possessions were reduced to a protective strip around Constantinople, and a Turkish identity was being built under a military dictatorship in what remained of the Ottoman Empire.

THE YOUNG TURKS BEHIND THE PORTE

In 1900, however, Turkey was still an important power. Leaving aside the provinces only theoretically subject to his sovereignty, Sultan Abdülhamid II ruled over 19 million subjects, from a capital that was the biggest city in the Balkans.[2] Its size notwithstanding, the Empire's financial weakness effectively blocked endeavours to attain centralized control and military strength.

Opposition to the Hamidian régime had been forced underground or abroad, coalescing around those who had been in Paris since the suspension of the constitution, and who were known as 'Young Turks' from their journal *La Jeune Turquie*. As the Committee for Union and Progress (CUP), they had in 1902 held a first congress of various groups, which included Turks, Albanians, Kurds, Greeks, Armenians and Jews, united by their wish to remove Abdülhamid, restore the constitution and save the Ottoman Empire from foreign interference. They had links throughout the Empire, were strong in the towns of the European provinces, and associated with disgruntled army officers.

The threat of foreign intervention was particularly strong in Macedonia. The term was used vaguely for a region extending from the Šar mountain in the north to the Aegean, Mount Olympus and the Pindus in the south, and from the Rhodope mountains in the east to Lake Ohrid in the west, but it referred also to the much wider territory covered by three vilayets of Turkey-in-Europe – Salonika, Monastir, Kosovo: some 95,000 sq. km with a population of 2.4 million. 'Macedonia' in its broadest sense overlapped with 'Albania' as broadly defined. Albania generally meant the region extending from the

2 With over 900,000 inhabitants at the time of the Balkan Wars, Constantinople ranked just below those European cities that topped one million – Moscow, Saint Petersburg, Vienna, Berlin, Paris and – the biggest – London.

southern Adriatic coast to the Dinaric peaks east of the Black Drin river; it could also refer to the wider territory of four vilayets – Scutari (Shkodër/ Skadar), Janina, Kosovo and Monastir.[3]

The control of Macedonia offered a predominant position in the Balkans, but the area was not productive. Chiftliks were falling apart; their increasingly absentee Muslim lords tended to live in Salonika if not in Constantinople, and sold out; their dependent peasants also moved to towns (25 per cent of the population was urban by 1912), emigrated or turned to brigandage. Even though there was a great deal of uncultivated land, and more land was passing to peasants, the region could not support its population, but insecurity was the major factor pushing people out.

It is impossible to determine the ethnic composition of the population, where Orthodox Christians slightly outnumbered Muslims. The major problem was to distinguish between Slavs, as armed bands of unemployed and fanatics had overtaken priests and teachers in their efforts to settle who was who. The establishment of IMRO, and the Romanian government's new interest in the Vlachs, recognized as a separate millet in 1902, further complicated the situation.

The powers pressed for reforms. Russia asked Bulgaria to sever its links with armed bands and to accept Serb clerical participation in patriarchal diocesan administration. IMRO and the Bulgarian-based Supreme Committee were not only in competition, but so interpenetrated that it was difficult to say who was doing what. The 'supremists' wanted to attract European attention, and move towards union with Bulgaria. IMRO just craved for a revolutionary situation.

Mixed nationalist, social and political motives led to the massive but badly organized rising that broke out in August 1903 and soon had most of the vilayet of Monastir under its control. The town dwellers scorned it, the Sofia government was not prepared to get involved, the powers did not want to intervene, the rebels split into rival factions, and the movement was drowned in blood. Reprisals by Ottoman troops from Asia and by Albanian auxiliaries were drastic. Large numbers of exarchist priests and teachers were deported to Asia Minor. An estimated 30,000 people emigrated, mostly to Bulgaria.

The brutality of the repression persuaded the Austrian and Russian emperors to meet in October at Mürzsteg in Styria, to initiate a scheme, reluctantly accepted by the Porte, to manage the Macedonian crisis. An internationally staffed gendarmerie would enforce order; administrative boundaries would be redrawn to produce districts with the greatest possible degree of ethnic homogeneity; the whole reform package would be enforced by supervisors from

3 Scutari, Janina, Kosovo, Monastir, Salonika and Adrianople were the six European vilayets. Adrianople corresponded to southern Thrace. Kosovo vilayet, much larger than the post-Second World War Yugoslav province of Kosovo, extended from the border of Bosnia-Herzegovina deep into Macedonia south and west of Skopje. The seat of its administration was Skopje (Üsküb/ Skoplje), and it comprised the six sanjaks of Priština, Peć, Prizren, Skopje, Novi Pazar and Plevlje.

the five European powers. Local nationalists did their best to provide people with ethnic labels. Villages changed allegiance under threat from rival bands.[4] The Porte did not and could not implement its commitments. Humiliation and frustration were particularly strong in the Salonika-based Third Army. Further European moves in March 1908 triggered off minor garrison rebellions; the CUP moved in.

Once again, bad harvests in Anatolia put pressure on the European provinces, as Kosovo was hit by drought. Shortages directed Albanian unrest against towns and Slav peasants. Rumours that the Austrian army was coming coincided with troops being withdrawn to deal with mutinies further south, and caused concentrations of armed Albanians, which the CUP enlisted. The Young Turks argued that a return to the constitution would undermine foreign intervention.

Abdülhamid's policy of courting the Albanians had failed. Large numbers deserted as more of the military in Macedonia expressed sympathy for the demand to restore the constitution. When in July the commander of the Third Army, Mahmut Şevket Pasha (1856–1913), warned that, should the situation continue, foreign intervention would result in the fall of Abdülhamid, the government pressed the sultan to give in. He announced the reactivation of the constitution of 1876. That was the 'Young Turks' Revolution' of 1908. They believed in their mission to create a modern state based on an Ottoman consciousness, just as the rulers of Germany and Russia were using nationalism to enhance their respective empires. They did not feel strong enough to push through the deposition of Abdülhamid, and remained a pressure group based in Salonika.

The revolution effectively put an end to the Mürzsteg programme. The population of the European provinces initially welcomed the new era. Many of the leaders of bands agreed to a cessation of hostilities and came to the towns to hand in their weapons. Although usually little more than perfunctory, such gestures contributed to a lessening of tension, and all groups took advantage of the period of freedom and uncertainty that followed the announcement of general elections.

A parliament had been called to represent all the Ottoman provinces, including Bosnia, Herzegovina and Eastern Roumelia. In October, in order to ward off the reassertion of Ottoman claims, Bulgaria declared independence, and Austria-Hungary formally annexed Bosnia-Herzegovina. The sanjak of Novi Pazar remained Ottoman by the will of the Dual Monarchy, to keep Serbia and Montenegro separated. The 'Annexation Crisis' ended the cooperation on the Balkan status quo that had been maintained by Russia and Austria-Hungary since the Treaty of Berlin.

---

4 The Ottoman authorities estimated that there were 228 such bands operating in 1907 – 110 Bulgarian, 80 Greek, 30 Serbian and eight Vlach for good measure (Dimitrije Djordjević and Stephen Fischer-Galati, *The Balkan Revolutionary Tradition*, New York: Columbia University Press, 1981, 194).

At the December 1908 Ottoman elections, the CUP won most of the seats,[5] but the constitutional régime was short-lived. The Young Turks' Revolution had obviously not settled the question of Bosnia-Herzegovina and of Eastern Roumelia except in so far as it had served to sever even what remained of a tenuous link with these provinces and with the Principality of Bulgaria. It did not settle Macedonia or Albania either, as both questions drained the resources of the Empire.

Many in the CUP considered Abdülhamid a danger to constitutional government and to their own organization. They managed to whittle down his powers, but in so doing caused a backlash. In 1909 the sultan's supporters attempted a countermove in Constantinople, which the CUP put down by once again calling on Şevket. Abdülhamid II was deposed, imprisoned in Salonika and replaced with his brother Mehmet V (1844–1918). The CUP took a firmer grip on government, but Şevket remained an independent and effective challenge to it until his assassination in 1913.

The question was no longer how to reform the Empire, but how to save the state. The gap grew between official Ottoman policy based on constitutional guarantees, and actual CUP practice. Pro-CUP feelings among non-Turkish nationalities in the European provinces turned sour; ruthless authoritarianism gained ascendancy in government.

The period between 1903 and 1908 had been a confused one in the Albanian lands. Both loyalty to Abdülhamid and cooperation with the Young Turks were based on misunderstandings. Demands for the union of four vilayets into one greater Albanian autonomous unit had been voiced since the turn of the century. The Macedonian rising, the war of bands and the threat of foreign intervention had given them fresh impetus. There were vendettas between ethnic groups, jacqueries of Christian peasants against Albanian lords, Albanian raids on Serbian and Montenegrin territory, and on Ottoman garrisons too. The activities of émigrés had become intense.

Albanian schools, literary societies, clubs and journals had mushroomed from Scutari to Constantinople, tolerated for as long as the honeymoon with the CUP lasted. They soon ran into conflict with the new régime. Albanian deputies began to play an important part in parliamentary opposition; some conservative Albanians supported Abdülhamid's attempted counterrevolution; an All-Albanian Congress convened in Monastir decided in favour of the Latin alphabet for the Albanian language.

Centralists were in control of the CUP after 1909, sharing power with the military. The Porte's determination to remove the Latin script from public use, and to introduce universal conscription undermined Albanian support. Scutari was the smallest vilayet, 95 per cent Albanian, but only 57 per cent Muslim. Hereditary chiefs ran the northern highland clans, in return for

---

5 Of the 280-odd deputies, slightly under half were non-Turks (of whom 60 Arabs, 27 Albanians, 26 Greeks, and sundry Armenians, Slavs, Jews . . .). These figures are estimates, as deputies were not registered as such. About 50 members, mainly non-Turks, subsequently joined the opposition Party of Ottoman Liberals, which favoured decentralization and minority rights.

irregular armed service. In the south, other clans were headed by powerful families with extensive lands and small private armies. The Catholic Mirdites were the most powerful of the highland clans; the Toptanis were the most influential of the southern families. Government control outside the provincial capital was minimal.

The vilayet of Kosovo was both considerably larger than Scutari and had a much higher percentage of non-Albanians. About half the population was Albanian, concentrated in the central sanjaks. The majority of the Orthodox were Slavs, who were scattered though mostly around the provincial capital called Üsküb in Turkish, Skopje locally by the Macedonian Slavs and Skoplje by Serbs.[6] It was the centre of Serb activity. The Muslim Albanian mountain robber barons of the Peć and Prizren sanjaks, equally opposed to Austrian as to Serbian influence, had been the privileged supporters of Abdülhamid. There was no government control in large areas and insecurity forced many to emigrate. Caught between the mountain chieftains and their own restless Slav peasants, the mercantile and landed interests tended to look to the CUP even when they supported Albanian demands.

The population of 545,000 of the vilayet of Janina was about half Albanian-speaking, and also over half Orthodox. The latter were in a majority in the southern sanjaks, where ethnic Greeks formed the largest body of Christians.[7] In the vilayet of Monastir just over half of the population of one million was Muslim, with Albanians concentrated in the west. In these two vilayets, there was a large body of Albanian Christians, who were mainly Orthodox (c. 200,000), and with no outside help. Both the patriarchal hierarchy and the Athens government supported the Greek communities, which were strong in the towns, where their schools spread Greek culture among Orthodox Albanians and attracted even Muslims. Muslim Albanians controlled the land and local administration. The situation was at its most complex in the vilayet of Monastir, with Greeks, divided Slavs, Vlachs and Albanians.

Muslim and Orthodox Albanians in the vilayets of Janina and Monastir strove to get Albanian rights recognized by the new government. A number of the wealthiest landowning beys partook of the local hybrid but dynamic Ottoman urban culture. They spoke Greek or Serbian, and even sent their sons to superior Christian schools. They provided statesmen, officials, generals, scholars, religious dignitaries; some participated in 'Albanian' activities while maintaining their 'Ottoman' identity. As southern Albanian landowners turned to nationalism to counter what they saw as the growing Greek and Slav threat of neighbouring states and dependent sharecroppers, there developed a more genuinely Albanian movement.

The immediate consequence of the alliance between Young Turks and Şevket were successive campaigns from 1909 onwards to destroy the power of the Kosovar chieftains. Resistance hardened and extended, and so did the Porte's

6 It was in Skopje that Mother Teresa of Calcutta was born in 1910, of Catholic Albanian parents.
7 All the above figures are taken from Peter Bartl, *Die albanischen Muslime zur Zeit der nationalen Unabhängigkeitsbewegung 1878–1912*, Wiesbaden: Otto Harrassowitz, 1968, 76–86.

determination to use greater force. As the CUP turned against any special treatment for Muslim minorities, Albanian committees led from Bari, Corfu and Cetinje prepared a general insurrection.

In the spring of 1911, bands assembled in all six European vilayets, including Adrianople, the province nearest to Constantinople. Macedonia was in turmoil. Unable to suppress the Kosovar rebellion, and in order to counteract the failure of the CUP's repressive policy, the Porte made an attempt to conciliate the Albanians. The northern chiefs linked up with the southern nationalists to demand the recognition of the existence of Albania, with Albanian officials, language, schools, local military service, an amnesty and the return of confiscated weapons.

The Porte took fright. In the early summer, the sultan visited Kosovo. Concessions were offered, but the Porte did not countenance the union of the four vilayets nor did the highland chiefs want to give up their privileges. Further concessions were envisaged as war broke out with Italy in Libya in September. The CUP exploited the outpouring of patriotism to persuade Mehmet V to dissolve parliament in January 1912 and call new elections. Intimidation and fraud contributed to a resounding victory for the CUP, which was again in an undisputed position of power, though not quite in undisputed control of government. Albanian disturbances resumed.

CUP influence was challenged by unrest in army units and by the desertion of Albanian personnel. Mutinies had prevented the government from despatching enough troops to put down the Kosovo rebellion, and they precipitated the downfall of the government – by now headed by Şevket. Mehmet V turned to another general, who in August obtained the dissolution of the CUP-dominated Chamber, as Albanian insurgents overran much of the European provinces. The Porte had to seek negotiations. They failed; the rising accelerated; Skopje fell to the rebels without bloodshed.

Turkey was burdened with a new revolt in Yemen and still fighting Italy, but the Albanian insurgency was divided. Kosovar chiefs wanted to march on Constantinople and restore Abdülhamid. They were concerned with the privileges they had had before 1908, and controlled most of the armed rebels. The rebels were also a threat to the beys and merchants who were behind the nationalist programme, yet prone to a compromise solution that would trim the power of Kosovar chiefs. The Porte came very close to recognizing Albanian regional autonomy, a number of Albanians were appointed to important positions, but before a final settlement was reached, the First Balkan War had started in October. Albanian activists united to defend 'their lands' against their neighbours' ambitions and the agitation of minorities, but it was an unevenly developed nationalism.

To escape from the Graeco-Serb embrace, Albanian leaders turned to Italy and Austria-Hungary, who had no intention of allowing Serbia and Greece to have a common border on the Adriatic. That provided a chance of outside support for an Albanian state on the Adriatic. The leadership was taken up by Ismail Qemal (1844–1919), a former Ottoman civil servant who had participated in Young Turk activities in Paris, had been elected to parliament with CUP support, and then formed the opposition Party of Liberals. Soon after the 1912 dissolution, he had gone abroad to seek support for insurrection and autonomy.

Austria-Hungary considered it vital to prevent any takeover from Turkey on the Adriatic, and was willing to support an autonomous, even an independent Albania. As it was evident that the status quo could not no longer be maintained, she agreed that predominantly Albanian districts should form part of such an Albania, but that the results of the war should also be taken into account.

Having returned to Albania in November 1912, Qemal established his headquarters in his family base, the southern port of Valona (Vlorë), where an assembly of delegates gathered to set up a provisional government of Albania under his presidency. The Albanian combatants, who had defeated Ottoman forces only a few months earlier, did not put up much of a fight against the Balkan allies – Serbs, Montenegrins and Greeks – who entered Albanian territory as harsh but often unenthusiastic 'liberators'. Conflict with Constantinople was seen as taking place within a traditionalist structure of power, but faced with an attack from the outside, Albanian leaders seemed reluctant to mobilize the peasants and risk losing control.

In the course of the crisis of detachment from the Ottoman Empire, Albania continued to be dominated by privileged groups that had been integrated, even assimilated, into the Ottoman establishment. The contested authority of Qemal's government was limited to a triangle of territory between Vlorë, Berat and Lushnjë; its call for recognition went unacknowledged. The decisions concerning Albania were made at the London Conference that met in December 1912 to put an end to the war.

A 'GOLDEN AGE'? SERBIA UNDER KING PETER, AND MONTENEGRO

By 1903 the régime of Alexander Obrenović had become isolated at home and abroad. Army officers were particularly resentful of the royal couple and of their entourage who had brought shame on their country. In June (23 May according to the old-style Julian calendar), a group of them entered the royal palace at night, and murdered the 27-year-old monarch, his queen, her two brothers and three of his generals. The conspirators had the support of a group of politicians who had also come to believe that Alexander had to be removed. A provisional government was formed which summoned the last regularly elected parliament to settle the institutional issues.

Parliament called to the throne the obvious claimant in succession to the now extinct Obrenović line. He was the 59-year-old Peter Karadjordjević, son of the last reigning prince of that family. Educated in Paris, he had trained and served for a while as a French officer, and since becoming a widower had lived quietly in Geneva with his children. Parliament also adopted an improved version of the 1888 constitution, with broader powers for the National Assembly.

The decade that follows is often considered the 'golden age' of government in Serbia, if not actually in the Balkans, and so it was – relatively. The change met with public approval, and marked a radical shift in more ways than one. The power of the crown was circumscribed; there was a return to parliamentary government. With the low tax threshold that gave 20 per cent of the population the right to vote, Serbia had one of the highest rates of suffrage in Europe, where only France and Switzerland had a higher percentage. Yet even after 1903, she did not yet have full adult male suffrage, and the government based on a parliamentary majority tacitly acknowledged that it did not control the army. Not only did the conspirators continue for a number of years to have the last say on military matters, but they did not consider political parties capable of carrying out the 'national task'.

In 1911 the conspirators formed themselves into a secret society under the slogan 'Unification or Death' – better known by the name given to them by their opponents, the Black Hand. Their aim was to push for Serbia actively to take on the rôle of Piedmont in the unification of all South Slavs. They listed as 'Serb provinces' Bosnia-Herzegovina, Montenegro, Old Serbia (in the Kosovo area), Macedonia, Croatia, Slavonia, Vojvodina and the littoral. Their lobbying and their support of armed bands operating in Ottoman territory increased with the prestige of the army after the Balkan Wars, and so did tensions with the radical leadership.

Parliament was dominated by the radicals, as voters tended to vote for those in government. The appearance of a new Social Democratic Party did not make up for the fact that the older liberals and progressives no longer played an important part. The radicals were practically divided into two parties since the 'independent radical' faction had disapproved in 1901 of the concessions made to King Alexander Obrenović on the constitutional issue. In 1905 it set itself up as a separate party.

Both held the same views on the organization of the state and on foreign policy. They looked to Russia for protection against the hostility of Austria-Hungary, and hoped to get help from France and Great Britain as well. They had emerged about equal from the elections of 1903 when they formed a coalition, alternated in power between 1904 and 1908, and joined again in an all-party coalition at the time of the Annexation Crisis. The radicals then governed alone under Pašić until the First World War.

The 'golden age' was also tarnished by the fact that Europe had been shocked by the brutality with which the Obrenović royal couple had been killed. The change did not immediately improve Serbia's standing in Europe, where King Peter was initially perceived as having ascended a bloody throne under the control of a military clique. These officers were not above arrogantly reminding him of his debt to them; he was not strong enough always to stand up to them.

The festering issue of civil–military relations came up in the spring of 1914, with the gradual implementation of constitutional order in the new territories. It was linked to radical carpetbagging, and to the revolt of Albanians against annexation to Serbia. As Pašić planned to counter Black Hand influence, and the Black Hand to press for Pǎsić's resignation, the king was on the point of giving in to the military before Crown Prince Alexander and the Russian government intervened. New elections were called for August. King Peter, for reasons of poor health, gave up the exercise of the royal prerogative in favour of the crown prince as regent.

Pressed as before between Austria-Hungary and the Ottoman Empire, Serbia had drawn nearer to other Balkan states. This was to try to undermine Turkish rule to the south, and to stand up to Austro-Hungarian pressure by supporting an intensification of South Slav cooperation from Ljubljana to Sofia. As radicals looked to their friends in Russia, and King Peter to France and the west, who were slow to respond, controversies arose with the Dual Monarchy over railway loans, the purchase of military equipment and commercial arrangements.

Serbia's 1905 trade agreement with Bulgaria initiated closer ties. It provoked pressure from Austria-Hungary, who felt it to be detrimental to her own interests, thus leading to the customs war that started in 1906. The 'pig war' was due to Budapest's clamour for protectionist measures as much as to Vienna's anxiety over Serbia's more independent policies. The Austro-Hungarian customs union came up for renewal every ten years, when Hungarian interests made themselves felt because of Austrian dependence on Hungarian food supplies. A veterinary pretext had been used against Serbian pigs in 1896; in 1906, it came up again to close Austria-Hungary to all Serbian livestock.

In fear of economic dominance, Serbia ignored the blockade and managed to find alternative outlets. She gained economically as well as politically. The need to process pork and other exports for more distant markets helped Serbia to develop her industry, and to end the pig war in 1911 largely on her own terms. Nevertheless, Serbia remained predominantly agricultural, as such industry as there was occupied only 7 per cent of her population of 2.9 million. The dispute had by then merged with friction over the annexation of Bosnia-Herzegovina in 1908. Opinion seemed ready for war, expecting a rising in Bosnia, and a National Defence committee was set up to organize volunteers. More pragmatic, the government recognized the annexation in March 1909, and the National Defence was slimmed down to cultural functions.

Serbia's potential for continued expansion of livestock exports had been exhausted by that time, and the total number of cattle declined. Future prospects for expanded sales to the Monarchy had been much reduced. Wheat and corn exports during the dispute were a great help, but did not make up for reduced cattle exports. Most of the wheat went to Germany, Austria-Hungary's closest ally, while corn was bought by Hungary's stock-raisers. Austria-Hungary's inability to maintain a single market even for Serbia's exports, let alone to apply pressure to her allies, set the stage for her failure to win the tariff war. The inability to retain sufficient economic leverage over Serbia would make the Monarchy resort to military force in 1914.

Serbia feared dependence. Budgets all over the Balkans were mortgaged to foreign loan repayments, and loans were repayable only in the gold denominations on which the major European currencies were based by the 1890s. The Balkans aspired to the gold standard, but continued to accept the bimetallic system of silver- and gold-backed denominations that adherence to the Latin Monetary Union had initiated.

Only the Romanian economy had made the transition rapidly because of its long-standing access to European capital markets. The other Balkan economies remained tied to silver-backed notes as the only means of increasing the money supply. Such issues were limited by the premiums over the franc's exchange rate that the market charged for the silver note's conversion to a gold denomination. The dearth of new long-term European loans after 1890 further heightened the demand for gold at the expense of Serbia's silver dinar. The Belgrade government was successful in limiting the National Bank's issue of silver notes, and in freezing it by 1900.

After 1903 the radical régime drew its strength from anti-Austrian sentiments and provincial exporters rather than from the reputedly pro-Austrian Belgrade importers who lost their ability to pay for their purchases directly in silver dinar notes. The tightened accounting of the parliamentary régime virtually eliminated the gold premium on them, and helped the government to meet its obligations to the National Bank.

In 1898 a new semi-official Mortgage Bank had been created from the State Administration of Funds with the aim of expanding lending. Although it soon became the largest bank after the National Bank, it did not place much over half its assets in long-term loans: public buildings and urban residences received preference over industry and agriculture. A network of small provincial savings banks had appeared, but they remained too small and tied to short-term discounting to offer a potential for long-term agricultural credit. In 1910, only half a dozen of them offered agricultural mortgages for a total amount of no more than one million dinars.

Modernization generally continued to be accompanied by resistance, which cast another shadow on the 'golden age'. Serbia had only a tiny educated élite and no really wealthy class of independent means. The apparatus of the developing state absorbed nearly all educated people. The radicals did rhetorically extol peasant virtues and the feeling of a community, but the idea that they were simply antimodernist pro-Russian Slavophiles is a simplistic one. Czech pan-Slavists had been more influential than the Russians; radicals generally condemned romantic Slavophilism; their expanding system of schools was almost as secular as that of the French radicals. By 1903 they had become attuned to the bourgeoisie and to nationalism, and they increasingly turned to the west for inspiration.

Instead of intimidating Serbia, Austria-Hungary's policy had encouraged her to rely more on France and Russia. The ultimatum to accept the annexation and to ban paramilitary activities in Bosnia led the Pašić government to turn to Paris. Loans on that capital market ensured Serbia's financial survival to the end of the pig war, and enabled her to purchase French rather than Austrian military equipment. Serbia's success in breaking away from Austria-Hungary both increased her prestige and deepened the Yugoslav movement, but beyond unofficial support for nationalist agitation, she had to maintain a policy of restraint towards the Monarchy.

Her practical hopes turned yet again to the sea and to Macedonia, where as a result of the two Balkan Wars of 1912–13, she gained northern and central Macedonia, as well as the 'Old Serbia' area of Kosovo. The campaign medal referred to the 1389 battle of 'Kosovo Avenged', but this military success left Serbia with the task of assimilating in her acquisitions a heterogeneous and neglected population, which included a high proportion of Muslim Albanians, as well as many Orthodox Slavs with no clear national consciousness, many of whom still looked to Bulgaria.

Serbia at last had a common frontier with her sister Montenegro, whose politics after 1860 had been dominated by the strong personality of Prince (later King) Nicholas (1841–1921). With the Treaty of Berlin, Ottoman claims to jurisdiction had come to an end. Doubled in size and reaching the sea, Montenegro had had to accept some Austro-Hungarian conditions. Austrian troops were stationed in the sanjak of Novi Pazar which separated her from Serbia until 1913, and Austrian vessels policed her naval waters.

Nicholas had modernized his administration and his army, but in spite of the gains that had brought in more agricultural land, the territory could not support the population of 370,000, who lived in extreme poverty. Livestock raising made up two-thirds of exports, but could not pay for the food and textiles that had to be imported. Once warfare and pillaging had come to an end, only large-scale emigration was left. By 1912, more than a third of men of working age were leaving to take up seasonal jobs, emigrating temporarily, or permanently to America.

Their remittances helped, but Russian government subsidies covered half the budget and Russia sent wheat. Yet Nicholas did not allow himself to be dominated by any one power. He took Austrian loans and encouraged Italian investments. Encouraged by his dynastic prestige,[8] on the occasion of the fiftieth anniversary of his accession, Montenegro was proclaimed a kingdom in 1910. Nicholas's autocratic rule aroused resentment among the younger and mainly Belgrade-educated intelligentsia who clamoured for constitutional government. A constitution was granted in 1905. It was intended to give Montenegro a European outlook and attract foreign loans, but left government in the ruler's hands, in spite of an Assembly partly elected by open voting and partly appointed by him.

Even so the parliament provided a forum for organized opposition and had to be dissolved. Nicholas managed to control the situation, but younger

---

8 Nicholas had married off his daughters to two Russian grand dukes, to the future King Victor Emmanuel III of Italy, to a Battenberg prince who was the brother-in-law of Princess Beatrice of Great Britain, and to the future King Peter of Serbia (but Princess Zorka, the mother of the future King Alexander of Yugoslavia, died in 1890 before Peter Karadjordjević became king).

opponents went underground, which strained relations with Belgrade, for he believed that they received support from Serbia. Tension eased with the Annexation Crisis and the Balkan Wars, as Montenegro's foreign policy followed Belgrade. On the eve of the First World War, the two governments once again considered the possibility of a union of their states.

The idea of Yugoslav unity had revived at the beginning of the twentieth century. Democratic government in Serbia had unleashed energies. A new political generation in Croatia had brought about a coalition of Croat and Serb parties there. Serbia's prestige had been enhanced. A growing feeling of a common South Slav consciousness had advanced fast, at least in certain quarters, but in 1914 no one envisaged the dissolution of Austria-Hungary in the foreseeable future.

In Serbia, there was ambivalence between a Serbian identity expressed in striving for a greater Serbia – on a par with a greater Greece, a greater Bulgaria and a greater Romania – and a hazier Yugoslav identity, with Serbia as the Piedmont of South Slav unification. As a military Piedmont, Serbia had shown its worth in the Balkan Wars of 1912–13: her soldiers had generally fought well for what they saw as a just cause under a popular leadership. She had been preparing for war after 1903, but her foreign policy remained constrained towards Austria-Hungary, and her war plans were defensive as far as the Dual Monarchy was concerned. In 1914 she was envisaging union with Montenegro only and preparing for a general election to resolve the issue of control of the army.

INDEPENDENCE AND MACEDONIA: BULGARIA UNDER KING FERDINAND

If the absorption of Eastern Roumelia had been more difficult than anyone in Bulgaria had imagined, the Macedonian issue impinged on essential political and diplomatic issues. Nationalists assumed that all the Christians of Macedonia were desperately waiting to join the common Bulgarian homeland outlined at San Stefano. However, developments at the end of the nineteenth century had shown that the progress of Serb and Greek action raised questions about such an assumption, that Albanian feelings could no longer be disregarded, and that even those autonomist Slavs unlikely to be drawn to the Serbian cause were no longer so attracted to the Bulgarian state.

The government struggled with financial difficulties. It needed money for modernization; it could not increase customs because of the link with the Ottoman Empire; it had tried to get more out of the land by returning to a tithe in kind at a time when grain prices were moving up again. Peasants were angry: they paid for the administration and the army, they were indebted for the land they had acquired, they suffered from a series of bad harvests. The tithe was given up; the government had recourse to more foreign loans, from France, who insisted on certain revenues being earmarked to service them.

Short-term ministries after Stoilov struggled to find money, and the ensuing crisis produced the Bulgarian Agrarian National Union, the first and eventually the most powerful of peasant parties in the Balkans. It was set up at the end of 1899 as a pressure group to raise the standing of the peasant and improve agriculture, but more immediately to oppose the tithe. The first agrarian deputies were returned in 1901.

Prince and government had tolerated and even encouraged armed bands in Macedonia in order to gain popular support, but the game was dangerous. The Supreme Committee was becoming a major Macedonian lobby in Bulgaria; rivalry increased between it and IMRO.[9] The government could not control the Macedonians, but it was generally assumed that it did. Russia demanded that both Sofia and Belgrade end all connexions with bands in Macedonia. The dissolution of Macedonian organizations in Bulgaria was ordered and leading activists were arrested.

As Macedonia exploded, the summer of 1903 was a tense one in Bulgaria. Ferdinand had never been more unpopular. The peasants had lost all respect for political parties. The army was not pleased at having to keep order at home when Macedonia was crying out for intervention. After the failure of the ill-fated rising there, Sofia sought to halt a further weakening of the Bulgarian element in Macedonia by seeking accommodation with both Turkey and Serbia. With the Porte it agreed in 1904 to prevent anti-Turkish agitation, in exchange for an amnesty to exarchist priests and teachers, and the setting up of Bulgarian agencies in Macedonian towns. Agreements with Serbia in 1904–5 pledged to stop the fighting between sympathizers, to contain outside interference, to provide mutual military aid in case of an attack, and to establish closer links.

The Bulgarian cause, and with it that of an autonomous Macedonia, was the net loser after 1903. The failure of the rising benefited the patriarchate and, indirectly, Serbian influence as well. Not only could Bulgaria no longer afford to back any armed bands, but the rivalry between organizations weakened potential sympathizers. To make matters worse, by the end of 1907 IMRO also split into a more pro-Bulgarian right wing and a purely autonomist left wing, in conflict with each other and with the supremists. Many Christians in Macedonia abandoned the exarchate, becoming patriarchal (Greek or Serbian), or emigrating to Bulgaria, Greece, Serbia and further afield.

It was felt in Bulgaria that the task of redeeming the 'lost territories of San Stefano' could not be left to adventurers. The strategy advocated by the government was to bide its time until the international situation changed, to continue the policy of modernization and to get the army ready for the task. Other issues had appeared in Bulgaria. As a reaction to developments in Macedonia, there was in 1905–6 a wave of anti-Greek violence causing massive Greek emigration. The leader of the Stambolovists (the National Liberal Party) Dimitŭr Petkov (1858–1907) took over as prime minister.

Disaffected elements of the 'new intelligentsia' – rural teachers, journalists, doctors, priests and others not part of the establishment – turned to the

---

9 Albanian and Slav (Bulgarian, Macedonian and Serbian) bands were all called 'chetas'. The Turks called the members of Macedonian/Bulgarian bands 'comitadjis' (men of the Committee).

movements that aimed to enrol the masses in the political process. The Agrarian Union became a real political party in 1906 under Aleksandŭr Stamboliiski (1879–1923), with a programme to spend more on agriculture and education than on the army. The students of Sofia University (set up in 1904), who came from a humbler background than those who went to study abroad, were also restless. Conditions for the urban poor had generally worsened, affecting students and industrial workers. Their discontent was channelled into a socialist and a trades union movement which, however disunited, was the strongest of its kind in the peninsula.

The railwaymen's strike in 1906 caused the government to mobilize those who were of military age, and to use the army to maintain essential services. Industrial and political dissatisfaction fused in a demonstration against the prince when he opened the new National Theatre on Christmas Day (7 January 1907 according to the new-style Gregorian calendar). Insulted by strikers and students, he had university staff suspended; opposition parties called protest meetings. The strike was ended by conciliation, but Petkov was murdered in the centre of Sofia in March 1907.[10]

At the beginning of 1908 Prince Ferdinand appointed as prime minister the leader of the Democratic Party Aleksandŭr Malinov (1867–1938), who went to the polls in June with the usual methods. His party increased its representation from three to 168, a reversal astonishing even for Bulgaria; not a single Stambolovist was elected, but the agrarians obtained twenty-three seats. Peasant opinion had been mobilized by the cooperative movement with which the Agrarian Union was closely associated, by the impact of rural unrest in Russia and in neighbouring Romania, but most of all by the dominant personality of Stamboliiski.

He saw a modicum of private property as essential to a peasant-based society. All deviations from it he held in contempt, and that included urban life, but even more so the non-productive and parasitical institutions of the state. While preferring a republic, he did not openly advocate it; he wanted to achieve a reconstruction of the state through parliamentary representation, and in the first instance reduce if not abolish the army. He advocated a peaceful foreign policy aiming at a Balkan federation of peasant states. In its dislike of the modern state and of its apparatus, but also of industrialization, his movement went much further than anything ever advocated by Serbia's radicals in their early period.

Malinov had promised reforms. His most ambitious was to replace the professional tax with progressive income tax. Introduced at the end of 1910, it caused so much protest that it was not finalized by the time his government fell in 1911. A start was made with the gradual implementation of proportional representation. Malinov relaxed the press laws and reinstated the suspended academics.

10 Both his sons became agrarian leaders, and died tragically. Petko was murdered by Macedonian terrorists in 1924; Nikola was hanged by the communists in 1947.

His most striking achievement was the declaration of independence in October (22 September according to the old-style Julian calendar) 1908. The Young Turks had stirred up disquiet by their reminders of Bulgaria's vassal status. As neither Vienna nor St Petersburg any longer objected, independence as a kingdom was proclaimed the day before Austria-Hungary's annexation of Bosnia-Herzegovina was announced. Ferdinand took, in Bulgarian, the title of *tsar* (translated more discreetly as 'king'). Russia helped with financial arrangements; in 1909 the issue was settled by compensation, which saved Ottoman face. The occasion was not greeted in Bulgaria with universal rejoicing. The government was accused of treachery to the Slav cause by its collusion with Austria-Hungary over Bosnia-Herzegovina. The Macedonian lobby was displeased that full independence had been declared before full unification.

Such criticism was the result of the release of pent-up frustration after the relaxation of Stambolovist controls. Debates centred on the rôle of Ferdinand, who had never known (and, to be fair, never courted) popularity. There were objections to the enhancement of his monarchical rank. Disapproval intensified with attacks on his 'personal régime', especially from the nationals, now headed by Ivan Geshov (1849–1924). He had taken over from Malinov in March 1911, at the head of a coalition ministry of nationals and progressives, and his first task had been to summon a Grand (revising) National Assembly to pass a number of constitutional amendments.

The nationals were committed to constitutionalism and opposed to the king's manner of ruling; the agrarians aired their republican views without restraint. The monarch's new title was formalized as 'king of the Bulgars'.[11] His prerogative to suspend civil rights in emergencies was limited. The length of a parliament was reduced from five to four years; its annual sessions were increased from two to four months.

The Geshov ministry went on to organize elections for a new regular Assembly in september. The turnout was low; the coalition secured an easy victory. Even though King Ferdinand detested him, Geshov was necessary for the sake of Macedonia, which was both a foreign and a domestic issue. The Annexation Crisis had marked the renewal of Russia's involvement in the Balkans; she was anxious to promote a front to contain Austro-Hungarian ambitions. Sides were being formed in Europe. Serbia leaned to France and Russia. Bulgaria could no longer afford to stand alone and inactive. The Russian factor remained an important one in Bulgarian politics; domestic opinion pressed for action to alleviate the sufferings of Christians in Macedonia.

This was linked to concern over the exarchate, now spread over two separate states. The Porte did not want the exarch to take instructions from the

---

11 This followed the model of the 'king of the Hellenes'. The wording could be interpreted as originating in the Belgian and French style of the monarch being head of a nation of citizens rather than ruler of a territory (the Belgian sovereign was 'king of the Belgians', as Louis-Philippe had been 'king of the French' and the Bonapartes 'emperors of the French'). It was, however, also interpreted as including the as yet unredeemed Bulgars, and as such was meant to appease Bulgaria's Macedonians.

Synod in Sofia, so a separate synod of bishops in Ottoman territory was set up in Constantinople, and the two began to squabble. Russia wanted the exarchate to be confined to Bulgaria so as to end the schism within the Orthodox Church in the Ottoman Empire, and some in Bulgaria would have accepted an autocephalous church of Bulgaria. The exarch, however, remained the chief vehicle of Bulgarian influence in Macedonia, and most would not allow the dismantling of the only institution that united all ethnic Bulgars, particularly as Serbs had been successful in obtaining appointments to patriarchal dioceses in Macedonia.

Geshov was ready for cooperation. He first tried the Porte, in the belief that agreement with the rulers of Macedonia offered the best chance for Bulgars there, but the Young Turks would not favour any one nationality. He then turned to Serbia, but in doing so had to accept the eventual partitioning of Macedonia. That cleared the way for secret military alliances with Belgrade and Athens in the spring of 1912.

The agrarian movement was unable to dent popular enthusiasm for a military solution to the Macedonian question.[12] In the First Balkan War, the eager military overreached themselves in trying to break through to Constantinople. Fearing that Bulgaria would lose out after the fragile Treaty of London, urban opinion, spearheaded by Macedonian exiles, pressed for renewed action against the erstwhile allies Serbia and Greece. So did the army command, concerned with the morale of tired troops awaiting demobilization to be able to get on with the harvest. King Ferdinand aligned himself with the war party, Geshov resigned in despair, the military got their way, and the Second Balkan War ended in disaster for Bulgaria. A cabinet of liberal factions under Vasil Radoslavov (1854–1929) sued for peace.

Bulgaria was left with the smallest portion of Macedonia, and part of Thrace with the Aegean coastline around Dedeagach (Alexandroupolis). She had to cede southern Dobrudja to Romania. Her relations with her neighbours and with Russia were compromised, and her political establishment discredited. Although the mass of the peasantry turned to the parties that had opposed the war, the final settlement of the Treaty of Bucharest created a revanchist mentality in a large body of opinion. The territories aspired to were no longer under the single and enfeebled authority of the Ottoman Empire, but belonged to states as nationalist as Bulgaria. The only exarchists allowed outside Bulgaria were in what remained of Turkey-in-Europe.

The territorial changes were disadvantageous. The strip of Dobrudja ceded to Romania was a productive agricultural area. Varna, which had been developed as the main port with a rail link to the rest of the country, was now deprived of its hinterland. The new territory was backward and sparsely populated, and

12 Textbooks and other history books cast darkness on the Greek world back to Byzantium; Serbs were not too badly presented, even after 1885; the image of Turks was negative. General ignorance of, even more than distorting myths about, Balkan neighbours and their history was such that the noted educationalist (and nationalist) Ivan Shishmanov condemned it when he was minister of education in 1905, complaining that more was known about France and Germany.

money would be needed to repeat for the Aegean coast all that had been done for the Black Sea coast. To finance it and to repay the cost of war, a large loan was needed.

Radoslavov went to the country in November 1913 to secure a reliable Assembly. In the atmosphere of bitter resentment, and with proportional representation, the government parties secured only 97 seats to the opposition's 109. Radoslavov went to the country again in April 1914. The new territories were allowed to take part, although they were not yet integrated into the constitutional system; the opposition was not allowed to campaign there; the Muslims were subjected to pressure. A workable majority was secured.

Bulgaria needed a loan. The French were ready to lend, but in the summer of 1914 they expected a government well disposed to the Entente, and Radoslavov leaned the other way. The loan was raised in Germany, in return for the purchase of military equipment from Austria-Hungary, and the grant of rail and mining contracts to German firms. The debate on the agreement was passionate to say the least; the government had to claim that a show of hands had revealed a majority in favour. The financial pressure of the wars had forced it to raise the loan and to increase indirect taxes, but the economy recovered quickly. 'The most striking feature of Bulgarian history in the forty years after the Liberation is the country's social stability', writes a foremost historian of modern Bulgaria.[13]

Continued Turkish and Muslim emigration released land. Peasants took over public property, encouraged by the convention that working the land for over three years conferred virtual ownership. State land declined by more than 25 per cent between 1897 and 1908; only then were measures taken to curtail the practice. The proportion of people living on the land remained steady at 80 per cent, and so did the distribution of property, as supply kept pace with demand. In 1908, 86 per cent of landowners with less than ten hectares had 53 per cent of the land; another 14 per cent with up to 100 hectares held 43 per cent. A new development was the substantial emigration of Greeks after 1905, and many Bulgars continued to come in from areas outside Bulgaria. Other Muslims, most of them Bulgarian-speaking Pomaks, were incorporated after the Balkan Wars. The percentage of Bulgarian speakers increased from 77.1 per cent in 1900 to 81.2 per cent in 1910.

Peasant proprietors survived relatively well, as urban markets grew and the improvement of communications made them more accessible. Yet the government did little to stimulate agricultural production, in comparison with its efforts to promote industry. The peasant had little extra income or credit to finance the following year's seeding, or to buy extra land without further incurring more debts to keep his inheritance from getting too small.

The cooperatives played an important part in maintaining the relative well-being of the countryside. They flourished in the decade before the First World

13 R.J. Crampton, *Bulgaria 1878–1918: A History*, New York: Columbia University Press, 1983, 511.

War, and it was through them that the agrarians made their principal impact. Most were credit institutions and they brought indebtedness under control, but there were also insurance, production, marketing and other cooperatives. Otherwise the Bulgarian Agricultural Bank, which had taken over from Midhat's savings banks, began to provide mortgage loans to peasants in 1903. It also extended credit to the Agrarian Union's cooperatives, helping them to form their own Cooperative Bank in 1910.

The period brought change to the small manufacturing sector, but this was not sufficiently linked to the agrarian base of the economy. What industrial expansion there was is explained by the rise of the urban population, by the improvement in transport and by guidance from the state. A series of acts from 1894 granted the status of 'encouraged industries' to a whole range of activities, starting with mining, metallurgy, textiles and buildings, and extending by 1912 to practically all factory production.

Bulgaria enjoyed a favourable balance of trade until 1907, but weaponry later upset it. Austria-Hungary remained the chief source of imports, with over a quarter in the period 1908–12, though her primacy was eroded by the advance of Germany and France. While exports (essentially food and drink) to the Ottoman Empire came first with 23 per cent in the same period, Belgium then rose to the first place as she became the major purchaser of Bulgarian grain.

The expansion of the rail network was a considerable achievement, with 2,109 km by 1912 (compared to Serbia's 976 km), passengers increasing from 350,000 in 1895 to 3.4 million in 1911, and freight from 383,000 tonnes to over 2 million tonnes. Such progress was, however, achieved by cutting costs (which meant junctions were not always well sited, that stations were often outside towns, and that there was no bridge over the Danube to link up with Romanian railways). Nevertheless, Bulgaria had acquired the basic infrastructure of a modern state – at the price of dependence on foreign loans and increased taxation. The burden of the 52 per cent tax rise from 1900 to 1912 was inequitable. The urban poor suffered most as a result of reliance on indirect taxation, which was a strong incentive to retain land as a source of untaxable food and fuel. Of the 70 per cent increase in the foreign debt (of over 250 million francs by 1901), less than 18 per cent went on infrastructures, the rest on military expenditure, without which the victories of 1912 would have been impossible.

Such reliance did not greatly constrain Bulgaria's foreign policy before the Balkan Wars, and her debt in 1912 of 149.25 francs per head was less than Turkey's 193.63, Serbia's 235.88 and Greece's 328.88. Significant foreign investments came with the 'encouragement' programme, accounting by the turn of the century for 27 per cent of all capital invested in those industries. By 1911, 69 per cent of foreign capital came from Belgium, British investments ranking second with 21 per cent.

Yet the modernizing impulses did not go far. Social stability also meant social conservatism. Peasants aspired to a reduced rather than to a modernized state. The agrarians captured the mood well by directing their appeal towards cutting down, if not removing, bureaucracy, army, court and even established political parties. The commercial and manufacturing sectors which did have some modernizing aspirations were too weak to impose their ideas; they were rendered even weaker by the removal of the Greek element from political influence.

Bulgaria was in the hands of those with some education, who devised, served and ran the state. More than anywhere else in the Balkans, the state developed into the domain of officials, lawyers, soldiers and professional politicians, the bulk of whom did not come from a commercial or industrial background. Bulgaria's primary and secondary education was unrivalled in the Balkans, but the nation remained peasant and gradually divorced from the state. The policies pursued were determined by the strategic interests of the state, conceived as the only basis to fulfil Bulgaria's destiny in Macedonia and other *irredenta*. The element which saw a stronger and larger territory as a consequence rather than a cause of the movement towards national unity was weaker than in Romania, Greece or Serbia.

By the mid-1890s the contest over the distribution of power was on the whole decided in favour of the executive. The monarch first decided the composition of the government, and controlled diplomacy and defence; the politicians were left free to direct domestic policy as long as they could obtain a parliamentary majority. That was the essence of King Ferdinand's 'personal régime'; his ambition to play a rôle in European affairs called for an enlarged territorial basis. It also led a section of the intelligentsia to turn away from its rôle in propping up such a state, and to renew its links with the peasant nation from which it originated.

CHAPTER 9

The tail end of the nineteenth century, 1900–14 – Part 2

Greece under King George I. Romania under King Charles I. The Balkan Wars and their aftermath. The independence of Albania. National states, peasants and development.

SELF-CONFIDENCE RESTORED: GREECE UNDER KING GEORGE

Nicholas Petrović-Njegoš had, after half a century as ruling prince, promoted himself to be king of Montenegro in 1910; Ferdinand of Saxe-Coburg and Gotha, prince of Bulgaria, had become king of the Bulgars when his country had severed its last ties with the Ottoman Empire in 1908; Peter Karadjordjević had been called to take over as king of Serbia in 1903; Charles of Hohenzollern had been proclaimed king of Romania in 1881 as a consequence of the acknowledgement of the principality's independence in 1878. Christian William Ferdinand Adolphus George of Denmark, King George of the Hellenes since 1863, was the doyen of them all.

As far back as 1875, he had accepted the principle of entrusting the formation of the government to the politician who enjoyed the 'declared' support of a majority. This had been achieved by Trikoupis, who went on to head seven governments that restored Greece's credit-worthiness on international money markets, sought investment capital from abroad and tried to modernize the army. Nevertheless, the turn of the century had been more marked by his rival Deligiannis, in harmony with popular sentiment when he fought the Ottoman Empire over Crete. In spite of a humiliating defeat, he remained popular enough to win the 1902 and 1905 elections, only to be assassinated by a gambler enraged by his drive against gambling.

Crete would not go away; it turned Greek against Greek. In 1905 Prince George, the high commissioner of the self-governing island, clashed with the local liberal leader Eleutherios Venizelos (1864–1936), who had been active in promoting the unionist cause, and was replaced by a former Greek prime minister. The island's constitution was modified and almost completely Hellenized. A Cretan gendarmerie began to take over from the international units, and the last foreign troops were withdrawn in 1909. There was further Turkish emigration.

Union with Greece was declared and prevented once more in 1908 – yet another reaction against the possibility of the Young Turks wanting to reactivate Ottoman rule in territories that had been detached in all but name. In the kingdom, the fumbling response of politicians and the faltering of the economy brought to the surface the widespread malaise which had been building up since 1897. Taxation had increased, so had emigration after the defeat; by 1908 the economic slowdown in the United States had reduced the remittances sent home.

Dissatisfaction was particularly strong in the army, where junior officers were influenced by the actions of their counterparts in Serbia and in Turkey. The Young Turks' promise of equality for all had aroused much enthusiasm in Ottoman lands, even among Greeks, but also fears that a revived Empire would be more difficult to dislodge from Macedonia, whose nerve centre, Salonika, was also that of the Committee for Union and Progress. This was the catalyst for disgruntled officers to combine in a Military League. The original impetus was provided by professional grievances, such as resentment over the blockage of promotions. There was also the feeling that Crown Prince Constantine (1868–1922), who had commanded the army in Thessaly during the war of 1897, favoured his own clique of protégés.

In August 1909, a good proportion of the Athens garrison withdrew to Goudi on the outskirts of the capital, and from there the Military League carried out the 'Goudi coup'. It issued a pronouncement calling for a number of reforms, essentially in military matters, the main ones being that the monarch's sons be removed from the armed forces and that the defence ministries be held by serving officers.

The call was endorsed by huge demonstrations in Athens. Apprentices, shop assistants and students were their backbone, as elsewhere in the Balkans at the time. Following the threat of a military dictatorship, a new government was sworn in to implement a number of the desired measures under the watchful eye of the league. The royal princes relinquished their positions. The officers did not have a candidate of their own to head a reforming government, nor did they have a real political programme. They turned to Venizelos, who had acquired a reputation and popularity in the politics of his native Crete. He was free of association with the discredited political world of the mainland. They invited him to come to Athens in January 1910 to become their political adviser.

Venizelos favoured revising the constitution, but he was concerned about the influence of the military in politics. He came; he persuaded the king to summon a revising constituent Assembly, and the Military League to dissolve. He was appointed prime minister; his supporters won control of the specially elected revising Assembly: 'I steadfastly believe [he stated] that . . . the resources of the Nation are enough, in the hands of committed workers for revival, to re-create a Greece worthy of the demands of present-day civilization, able to inspire the respect of the civilized world, and to assume an honoured place in the family of civilized peoples.' With the king's support and a clear mandate from the electorate, a series of amendments to the constitution were passed, to smooth the way to more efficient legislative work, to reduce the scope for filibustering and to obtain the legal basis for subsequent land reform.

Venizelos's mandate was to modernize and to pursue the Great Idea. To show that he was not a creature of the Gouda officers, he reinstated Crown Prince Constantine to a high position in the army and released the officers imprisoned for trying to oppose the coup. His reforming programme affected the civil service, education and land, and included some social legislation, the legalization of trades unions, and the introduction of progressive income tax (even though this was widely evaded).

By appealing to the peasants and to the incipient working class, he neutralized the development of a more radical movement. By his commitment to an overhaul of the armed forces and by personally taking over the service ministries, he neutralized the military. French and British missions were called to train the army and the navy respectively. He was successful in bringing order into the finances of the state, although Greece had the highest public debt in the Balkans (41 per cent of its budgetary expenditure in 1911 went to servicing it).

Such achievements injected dynamism into public life and forged a new sense of national unity, shown in the elections of March 1912 where Venizelos's liberals were rewarded with a two-thirds majority. The country was placed in a better position to meet the oncoming Balkan crisis. Macedonia was a burning issue in Greece no less than in Bulgaria or in Serbia. Its fate was all the more acute for the emergence of the Albanian movement. The government faced a dilemma. There were ethnic Greeks scattered throughout the Ottoman Empire, in its Asian as well as in its European provinces. With an important concentration in towns, they were vulnerable to Turkish reprisals. Nevertheless, if Greece stood aside, she would lose out on the spoils to the Slavs of the Balkans, eager to exploit Turkey's problems.

Greece linked up with Bulgaria and with Serbia in separate arrangements, and along with her allies went to war against Turkey in October 1912. In November, Greek troops secured the great prize of Salonika; in February 1913 the coveted city of Janina in Epirus was also captured. Greece's newly equipped navy showed its superiority in the Aegean by taking most of the islands – except that early in 1912 Italy had occupied temporarily Rhodes and the Dodecanese, to put pressure on the Turks to withdraw from Libya. After the resentful Bulgars had turned against Greece and Serbia, and the Second Balkan War had been fought between the one-time Balkan allies, Greece emerged in 1913 with sensational territorial gains.

She gained over half the contested Macedonian territory, the union of Crete with Greece was finally recognized, but northern Epirus with a substantial

Greek population was incorporated in an independent Albania. The 'new territories' were a 70 per cent addition to the kingdom, whose population increased from 2.8 million to 4.8 million, yet not all of the new citizens were ethnic Greeks or looked to the Greeks as liberators. Greek sources said that Greeks made up 43 per cent of the acquired population (with 39 per cent Muslims, mostly Turks, 10 per cent Slavs and 8 per cent Jews), but these were denominational statistics that classified the Slavs of the patriarchate as Greeks, and it could be that ethnic Greeks were no more than 25 per cent.

The rich commercial city and great port of Salonika, with its 158,000 inhabitants, ranked second in Greece after the capital Athens. With its peripheral location, it soon became a centre of Greek nationalism, but its largest community was made up of Sephardic Jews – the descendants of those expelled from Spain at the end of the fifteenth century. They still spoke a form of Spanish along with other languages (including the socially distinguishing French they had learnt at the superior French Catholic schools), and viewed the Greeks as competitors for their city's economic life.

Within fifteen years of the traumatic defeat of 1897 at the hands of the Turkish army, Greek self-confidence had been so restored that the realization of the Great Idea, the elusive vision that seemed to have survived only in the dreams of romantic idealists, dawned again as a real possibility. It was at that moment, while on a visit to Salonika, a few months before the fiftieth anniversary of his accession, that King George was assassinated by a lunatic in March 1913. His successor Constantine had gained considerable popularity because of his rôle in the Balkan Wars, when Venizelos had appointed him commander-in-chief. It was widely assumed that since he was named after the last ruler of Byzantium, Constantine XI, he would adopt the style Constantine XII, but although many referred to him as such in Greece, he officially remained plain King Constantine.[1]

The restoration of confidence was actually due more to psychological than to economic causes. By 1910 the government had initiated a reordering of state finances that made revenues more predictable and expenses restrainable. The drachma had returned to par value with the franc. The National Bank obtained agreements from the European Financial Commission that the 1898 ban on new note issue should be lifted. Foreign capital was again interested in Greek treasury loans, even if direct investment in the economy was limited.

Because of the country's commercialized and open economy, Alexandria and other Greek diaspora financiers continued, in alliance with local industrialists, to encourage limited, and even cautiously diversified, industrialization. The government, however, provided little by way of protectionist support. The number of industrial establishments using mechanical power rose from 220 in 1900 to 762 on the eve of the First World War, and the workers employed in

---

1 His cousin Prince Charles of Denmark had taken the name Haakon VII on being elected king of Norway in 1905 after the separation from Sweden. That was to mark the continuity from the Haakons who had reigned over Norway in the middle ages, but it implied no challenge to a neighbouring state.

them from 15,000 to 24,000. The rail network also expanded in the same period, from just over 1,000 to 1,500 km.

The declining share of raisins in exports persisted, as overproduction at the turn of the century left unsold a surplus estimated at half the world demand. Eventually, a series of measures were taken by the government, centred on the establishment in 1906 of a Privileged Bank backed by British and French bankers. The aim was to cut back production, by buying the entire output of vineyards, by controlling the sale on the international market and by subsidizing peasants to destroy the vines. The results were limited as in 1914 vineyards still occupied second place after grain, and accounted for 11 per cent of cultivated land.

Diaspora Greek capital investment from London, Constantinople and the lower Danube improved the steamship-carrying capacity of the merchant fleet from 145,000 tonnes (out of a total tonnage of 391,000) in 1895 to 894,000 tonnes (out of a total tonnage of one million) in 1915 – an acceleration in steam's percentage of the total from 37 per cent to 89 per cent. Great Britain remained Greece's major trading partner, with 24 per cent of both imports and exports in 1911, while Austria-Hungary occupied second place in imports to Greece, and Belgium was second in exports.

Emigration helped to force up wages in struggling factories as well as agricultural labour wages to a limited extent. Its remittances from 1903 cancelled out the import surplus in the balance of payments, but the upward pressure on wages was limited, and the flow of remittances fragile. The US recession of 1908–9, by increasing the number of returnees, thereafter cut net emigration. Nevertheless, by 1912 the gross total approached 10 per cent of the population, the largest proportion of any European state after 1900. Migrant labour within the kingdom mostly came from the new territories after 1913.

TOWARDS ELECTORAL AND AGRARIAN REFORM: ROMANIA UNDER
KING CHARLES

In Romania, too, the period was marked by the long reign and the personality of the monarch – King Charles, who ruled first with the liberals, and then alternated between conservatives and liberals. The basic understanding between the three contributed to the stability of a constitutional system which, however imperfect, functioned without violent swings and with a reasonable appearance.

Through its defensive alliance with Austria-Hungary, the country remained effectively part of the Triple Alliance. It was thus difficult to support the Romanian cause in Transylvania as openly as Serbia, Bulgaria and Greece were pushing their respective aspirations in Macedonia. Ethnic Romanians in Hungary received discreet, essentially cultural, encouragement through the Bucharest-based Cultural League, to which many Transylvanian Romanian intellectuals belonged. Its deeper political character appeared only in 1914 when it changed its name to the League for the Political Unity of all Romanians.

The position of the Romanians in Hungary was increasingly a cause of tension. At the time of the Annexation Crisis there was talk of ending the alliance with the Central powers – Austria-Hungary and Germany. Romanian opinion reacted against Austria-Hungary's anti-Serbian policy; Germany came to realize that, in case of war, public opinion would not allow Romania to side with the Dual Monarchy. Bulgaria's ambitions were also seen as a threat to the Balkan balance of power, the more so since Vienna was eager to win her over as a counterweight to a hostile Serbia. Bucharest had taken an interest in the Vlachs (or Arumanians) of Macedonia in order to play a part there; it secured for them a status from the Porte and gave them support by opening Romanian-language schools. Nevertheless, Romania did not intervene in the First Balkan War.

King Charles was eager to strengthen his country's rôle as local guarantor of the balance of power in the Balkans. He reasoned that the powers, who would have the last word in deciding the fate of Macedonia, would reward Romania as a force of order in the region when peace was restored. In return for her neutrality in 1912 (and in compensation for Bulgaria's declaration of independence in 1908) Romania thought that she could ask for the southern strip of Dobrudja with Silistria that had been left to Bulgaria in 1878. Negotiations were started with Sofia during the peace talks, but came to nothing.

As the division of the Macedonian spoils became more relevant, and under public pressure to intervene against Bulgaria, the Bucharest government agreed to side with Serbia and Greece if they were attacked by their former ally. Romania thus entered the Second Balkan War; her troops met no serious resistance since the Bulgarian army was facing Serbs, Greeks and Turks. Romania emerged with prestige, territory and a feeling of self-confidence from the peace of August 1913, negotiated and signed in Bucharest. Bulgaria had to cede 9,000 sq. km between the Danube and the Black Sea, including Silistria.

Although the Balkan Wars had turned attention away from the deepening conflict between ethnic Romanians and the Hungarian rulers of Transylvania, they had completed Romania's alienation from the Triple Alliance. Relations with Bulgaria were definitely poisoned. The Vlachs of Macedonia, now of little use, were forgotten. Of the 286,000 people acquired with southern Dobrudja, only a small minority was ethnically Romanian. Russia herself made only modest attempts to take advantage of the growing disenchantment with Austria-Hungary, preferring to leave that task to the French, who were slow to reciprocate the Romanians' sentimental attachment. There was not much trade between France and Romania; Germany and Austria-Hungary together provided 60 per cent of Romania's imported goods.

The liberal cabinet of Ion Brătianu junior, better known as Ionel Brătianu (1864–1927), the eldest son of the first Ion Brătianu, signalled the reorientation of Romania's foreign policy in 1913. Although pro-French in feeling, the liberals understood the importance of Austria-Hungary and especially Germany for their country's economic development. They had resisted calls to abandon the Triple Alliance at the time of the Annexation Crisis. Even though the rapprochement with France was well under way by the spring of 1914, Brătianu would not commit his country to the Entente. His foreign policy was to draw closer to it without breaking with the Alliance.

Romania was pushed into that neutral position by Austria-Hungary's ineptness in retaining her as much as by Franco-Russian inducements. Indeed, although opinion leaned towards the Entente on the eve of the First World War, politicians disagreed on the direction to take. Liberals were increasingly of the opinion that Romania should side with the Entente, while the conservatives were divided into at least three factions: those who wanted to honour the alliance with Austria-Hungary, those who advocated a policy of friendly neutrality towards the Central powers, and those who agreed with the liberals. Romania had political leaders with a talent for foreign relations. They usually knew how to make use of inter-power conflicts, but were not so successful in dealing with major domestic issues, perhaps because they felt more in harmony with the Europe they looked up to than with the reality of their own society.

The principal cities had undergone rapid change. The capital not only imitated the public edifices and mansions of Paris to the point where Bucharest was called 'the Paris of the East', it actually developed an indigenous architectural style based on that of its Brâncoveanu prince of the late seventeenth and early eighteenth century, and influenced by that of peasant buildings. By 1904 it had sixty-four motor cars. Debates continued between intellectuals on Romania's identity. Alongside the theoreticians of its Roman origin or of its Dacian continuum, there were also scholars who denounced such obsessions and their use for political ends, and who believed that territorial rights were better based on self-determination of populations than on their origins or continued presence.

As for the merits of European models, the real differences of opinion were on the pace of change, between those who were anxious that progress should not destroy native values, and others who were eager that tradition should not be an obstacle to development. Divisions were not straightforward. The art of the sculptor Constantin Brâncuşi (1876–1957) would not have been possible without the conservative Juminists' reaction against imitative stagnation and political manipulation in literature and the arts. By adopting western constitutionalism and by pushing industrialization, the liberals thought of themselves as guarantors of genuine national development under the motto 'by ourselves'.

All this was beyond the grasp of the 60 per cent of the population that was still illiterate in spite of free and compulsory primary education since 1864. The forms of government were modern, but they were representative of only a small section of the population. The real obstacle to basic minimum participation in politics was not so much the income qualification for the franchise, which was quite low in the third electoral college, but the essential literacy requirement. Although there were demands in the Liberal Party from 1892 for the introduction of universal suffrage, the landowners who still generally called the tune among the conservatives (and even among a share of the liberals) opposed both universal suffrage and land reform until 1914.

Romania was not illiberal. Political debate was free and lively. People from neighbouring states found refuge and opportunity there – not only ethnic Romanians from alien empires, but Bulgars and Serbs as well. Jews had been coming since the 1830s until their numbers in the economic sphere coupled with their lack of integration into the traditional social structure caused the anti-Semitism that turned Romania from a land of Jewish immigration into one of Jewish emigration.

The initiative to modernize came from above. Spearheaded by the broader-minded element of the boier gentry, it remained half-hearted in political and social terms, until popular pressure made it truly radical on the very eve of the First World War. Industry had advanced far more in Romania than anywhere else in the Balkans, even though it had not achieved a takeoff because of the absence of iron, steel and machine building, and accounted for only 17 per cent of the national income by 1914.

Industrial growth was favoured by the capital accumulated by the land-owners, who were the chief exporters of Balkan grain, and the presence of petroleum. Oil and lumber (over 36 per cent of industrial production), and food processing (over 33 per cent) were the dominant industries. The world demand for oil stimulated a spectacular growth in production – from 250,000 tonnes in 1900 to 1.8 million tonnes in 1913 – and drew in more and more foreign capital. By 1914, German capital controlled 35 per cent of refineries, British 25 per cent, Dutch 13 per cent, and French 10 per cent (Romanian capital accounted for only 5.5 per cent). Foreign capital played a crucial rôle more generally in industry. It was predominant in gas and electricity, in sugar and metallurgy, in chemicals and forestry products. It was present in banking, and through loans to the Romanian state for public works programmes.

The accelerated expansion of industry was accompanied by the concentration of capital and production in a relatively small number of enterprises. By 1913, six joint-stock companies held 40 per cent of assets in companies with over 2 million lei of fixed capital. A fully formed banking system satisfied the needs of industry, commerce and the large landowners. It was dominated by nine great banks (four of them foreign-owned), which possessed 70 per cent of the resources of all commercial banks.

The export profits of grain had provided the initial capital, and half the wheat harvest still went for export. The rest was mainly for urban markets, but there was no consistent rise in the production per head of that essentially commercial crop over the last two decades before the First World War. Indeed, the growth rate was zero for grain output between 1901 and 1915, because of rising population (from 6 to 7 million between 1900 and 1910) and prices. The substantial advantage in grain yields per hectare achieved by large estates over small holdings could not push the average above those of Bulgaria and Serbia. Thirty-eight per cent of cultivated land was in units of more than 500 hectares in 1907, but another 40 per cent was in units of ten hectares or less.

The leasing out of estates to management contractors for a fixed rent had become more widespread, and leases were made for shorter periods.

Fifty-seven per cent of all cultivated estate land was thus leased out. The lease-holders made up for their escalating bids for leases with ever-higher terms for the peasants' labour and sharecropping contracts. In Moldavia, leased estate land grew to account for 62 per cent of the total (40 per cent of leaseholders being Jews, and another 13 per cent non-Romanian Christians).

This was the world in which the illiterate peasant masses lived, a world that had little in common with that of the political institutions. The liberal governments did try to help, with schemes to strengthen the position of small-holders without radically altering the tenure structure. They had encouraged the development of popular banks that had begun in the 1890s. Given legal status in 1903, these banks mushroomed from 700 in that year, to 2,900 in 1913, but since loans were too small and too short to pay for land, they were mostly used for living expenses. They did not fulfil their original aim of improving the productivity of smallholders. The liberals also gave legal status to cooperatives in 1904, essentially to enable them to rent land. The conservatives, too, had pushed the sale, on long-term credit, of small plots of state land.

Such measures appealed to the better-off and touched only a small percentage of the peasantry. Twenty-four per cent – some 300,000 – had no land at all, and another 34 per cent – 424,000 – had less than three hectares, or too little to make ends meet. Most peasants were not only voiceless politically, but also defenceless in the face of landowners, leaseholders and moneylenders, as well as natural disasters (such as the droughts of 1899 and 1904) which brought many to the brink of starvation. Of all the peasants of the Balkans, they were the most miserable and they had received least satisfaction. The great uprising of 1907 was their ultimate expression of frustration, and it was the only purely social mass movement in the peninsula.

A disturbance in a village of the district of Botoşani in northern Moldavia quickly turned into a widespread jacquerie. By the end of March, the trouble had spread to western Oltenia, at the other end of the country. If the poorer peasants were the first to rise, they were soon joined by others, priests, teachers and reserve non-commissioned officers eventually providing local leadership. Leaseholders were harassed and even killed, crops burnt, estates occupied, houses and stores destroyed. At one stage, 2,000 peasants occupied the town of Botoşani. In some parts of Moldavia, where Jewish contractors controlled most of the leased properties, the outbreak took on a distinctly anti-Semitic character. (Barred from owning land, Jewish merchants who were immigrants from the Russian or Habsburg empires had taken to such leases as a way to pursue maximum short-term profit.)

The conservative government in power since the elections of 1905 was slow to react. With Bucharest panicking, the opposition clamouring for measures to improve conditions on the land, and the monarch believing that the conservatives were too divided to lead the country out of the crisis, the government resigned. King Charles turned to the elderly liberal leader Dimitrie Sturdza (1833–1914) who became prime minister for the fourth time since

1895. Under pressure from a shocked public opinion which sensed the danger to the existing order, and with a united parliament behind it, the new government undertook to 'solve' the peasant question. It started off by crushing the rising. General Alexandru Averescu (1859–1938), the war minister, mobilized the army and restored order. The number of people killed from the beginning to the end of the rising could be at least 10,000, but losses cannot be accurately tabulated.

Right and left viewed the repression as a tragedy. The government pushed through a series of legislative measures – to regulate and lighten the terms of peasant contracts, and to provide better credit to enable peasants to lease and buy land put on the market by owners. Ionel Brătianu took over as prime minister in 1909, signalling the definitive triumph of the bourgeoisie within the party over its landowner element, but the legislation was insufficient. The reforms reduced the number of contract peasants, and increased that of leasing cooperatives. The land leased by them went up from 73,000 hectares in 1907 to 475,000 in 1914, when there were 459 such cooperatives with 77,000 members, but the amount of land was still no more than a sixth of that leased to manager contractors. The measures had little effect on the majority, because they were badly enforced and once again designed primarily to assist the richer peasants.

Although their left wing pressed for a thorough restructuring of agrarian relations, the liberals in that period of office did not push through any more significant land reform, or for that matter any electoral reform. Ionel Brătianu's principal domestic aim was to go on transforming the economy by promoting industry, although he was ready to make the political reforms necessary to gain acceptance of his vision of Romania's development. As for the conservatives, who came back to office to see the country though the Balkan Wars, they were never united.

A middle-class constituency under Take Ionescu (1858–1922) effectively wanted to modernize the party. While still aspiring to lead a united Conservative Party, he really stood between it and the liberals. He favoured a measure of electoral reform by expanding the franchise and by merging the three colleges into two, as well as a measure of land reform to strengthen middle-sized peasant holdings through the sale of public and even private land. In terms of foreign policy, he also wanted more open support for the aspirations of ethnic Romanians in Hungary, and more open sympathy for France.

Even Petre Carp (1837–1919), the prime minister who succeeded Brătianu, no longer fitted the old conservative stereotype, as he, too, encouraged industry and the purchase of state-owned land by better-off peasants. Yet he still opposed any significant social and political reform, and remained attached to the Central powers, which ran counter to increasing pro-French sentiment. His government initiated no significant reformist legislation, partly because of divergences within the conservatives, but also because of concentration on the Balkan crisis.

After the Second Balkan War, aware that it was not up to dealing with the pressing issues of electoral and agrarian reform, the conservative government resigned in December 1913. The king turned again to Ionel Brătianu. By now following the lead of his left wing, and with the monarch's consent, he issued a liberal programme of reforms which included universal suffrage and the expropriation of privately owned land. The February 1914 elections returned a liberal-dominated parliament which immediately began discussing the reforms. The conservatives were by then resigned to them, feeling the pressure from both the palace and public opinion. A special revising parliament was elected in June, with a large majority in favour of the reforms, to pass the necessary amendments to the constitution; the outbreak of the First World War forced it to postpone them for the duration.

THE BALKAN WARS AND THEIR AFTERMATH

The Balkan states coveted the remaining Ottoman territories in Europe, because expansion would help them economically, and because people there aspired, or were deemed to aspire, to join them in order to escape the sultan's crumbling rule. They feared that Austria-Hungary would try to get a European mandate to occupy Macedonia as she had done for Bosnia-Herzegovina. The collapse of order in the Albanian regions brought the additional danger that one or more of the great powers would want to intervene there as well.

The situation in the European vilayets of Turkey urged on the Balkan governments the need to cooperate on dividing them before the powers became directly involved. Whether it could be done depended above all on relations between Bulgaria and Serbia. They had much improved after 1903, even though Macedonia remained an issue of serious differences. The economic agreement concluded in 1905 signalled their intention to work together. Serbia was the more anxious partner, as Habsburg intervention in the centre of the Balkans or on their southern Adriatic coast and hinterland would have so circumscribed her freedom of action as to bring her independence to an end – at least in practice.

As soon as the Annexation Crisis had passed, talks were resumed between Belgrade and Sofia. The latter wanted autonomy for the whole of Macedonia, the former a division into spheres of action. The war that Italy launched against the Ottoman Empire in September 1911 over Tripoli hastened the resolve to agree. The Bulgarian government acknowledged that 'Old Serbia' (that part of the vilayet of Kosovo which to the Serbs actually was 'Kosovo') should be kept out of the issue, and that Serbia did have interests in Macedonia. The Serbian government approved in principle the idea of autonomy for Macedonia, as long as Serbs and Bulgars had the same rights there, and Macedonia joined their customs union. Eventually two zones of action were agreed, a northern one for Serbia, an eastern one for Bulgaria, and a contested one between them, whose fate would be determined by future negotiation, under the arbitration of the Russian tsar if needed.

On the surface, the treaty concluded in March 1912, after five months of negotiations, was a mutual defence treaty. It was accompanied by a secret annex anticipating war with Turkey and the division of liberated territory, and by a military convention. Negotiations followed with Greece. While agreeing on the coexistence of nationalities under Ottoman rule, Athens resolutely opposed autonomy for Macedonia, and would not even pay lip service to it like Serbia. As time was pressing, the defensive alliance concluded in May, followed by a military convention, postponed the whole territorial issue to the end of a future war. There had also been talks between Serbia and Montenegro, and between Bulgaria and Montenegro.

Italy had extended operations to the Aegean in April and to the Straits in July. Threatened with Ottomanization, with the intervention of the powers, with the unification of the four 'Albanian' vilayets into one autonomous unit, the Balkan governments had managed to triumph over distrust to form a 'Balkan League' that was stronger and more practical than that of the 1860s. The agreements had been communicated to Russia, who had initially encouraged them. The other powers knew about them, although not in detail, and were apprehensive. Austria-Hungary exerted all the pressure she could to thwart the common front. Even Russia feared complications that she could not cope with, and tried to dampen the offensive intentions of the Balkan states. Over the summer, the powers engaged in frenzied diplomacy; in October Austria-Hungary and Russia sent a final warning, but it was too late.

The Balkan states had been encouraged by Russia to counter Austro-Hungarian influence. Heartened by the defeat of the Ottoman army in North Africa and by its inability to overcome the Albanian revolt, they were prompted by the twin dangers of great powers stepping in, and of extremists taking up the initiative. Incidents multiplied until Montenegro invoked a long-standing frontier dispute as an excuse for declaring war in October.[2] Serbia, Greece and Bulgaria followed, accusing the Porte of not having implemented an article of the Treaty of Berlin – to adopt in Macedonia a system similar to the Cretan Statute of 1868.

The Porte had hurried to settle with Italy,[3] and had come close to doing the same with the Albanians. The Ottoman army had been weakened by the war in Libya, by domestic controversies, by financial problems and by desertions. Its forces in Europe were outnumbered by those of the Balkan allies, who, apart from their armies, were able to use the armed bands of Macedonia and northern Albania for guerrilla and sabotage operations behind enemy lines. The Greeks' newly equipped navy controlled the sea.

Within a month the Balkan armies had won spectacular victories on all fronts. They had split Ottoman forces into two, those holding Scutari and

2 The officer in charge of the initial Montenegrin attack was none other than Milovan Djilas's father.
3 By the peace treaty signed in October 1912, Italy kept Libya, in return for paying a large part of the Ottoman debt. The war in the Balkans gave her an excuse to remain in occupation of the Dodecanese.

Janina in the west, and those defending Adrianople in the east. Montenegro and Serbia had played Albanian clans against each other. The Serbs had entered Skopje and joined the Montenegrins in Novi Pazar. The Bulgarians had routed the Turks in eastern Thrace and driven them back to their defensive Çatalca lines 40 km from Constantinople, but the Greeks had beaten them to Salonika. Serbs and Greeks had advanced into controversial Albanian and Macedonian territory. The Turks, who had already appealed for the mediation of the powers, asked for an armistice. The Bulgarians, who had actually thought of going on to Constantinople for the bargaining potential of a temporary occupation of the Ottoman capital,[4] renewed their attack. Their army was showing signs of fatigue after the initial effort, and they failed.

Austria-Hungary threatened Serbia with war if she did not withdraw immediately from the Adriatic. As her intervention would have drawn in Russia, the powers stepped in. In December 1912, they met in London, where they decided to set up an Albanian state, and where they summoned the belligerents to a peace conference at St James's Palace. They accepted that the status quo could not be restored, and that it was up to the parties to settle their future boundaries, with provisos. There would be an Albanian state with borders to be set by the powers, and the privileges of the monastic community of Mount Athos would be retained.

The Ottoman Empire in Europe had been destroyed. Beyond the Çatalca lines, only three besieged towns remained – Adrianople encircled by the Bulgarians, Janina by the Greeks, and Scutari by the Serbs and Montenegrins. The defeat led to the downfall of the Ottoman government. In January 1913, in the course of the peace negotiations, the CUP staged a coup, turning once more to Şevket, who was assassinated later in the year. The new government stopped the negotiations. Hostilities resumed in February: Janina fell to the Greeks, Adrianople to the Bulgars, and finally Scutari to the Montenegrins and the Serbs. The latter eventually had to withdraw from the area, under threat of war from Austria-Hungary, and with a naval demonstration by the powers.

In April, the Peace Conference reassembled in London. The allies had secured victory, but other factors had intruded in the division of the spoils. The insistence on the creation of an Albanian state troubled previous arrangements. It nullified the Serbo-Bulgarian agreement: Serbia would find herself flanked by an Albania under Habsburg protection, and by an unpredictable Bulgaria which could be influenced by Vienna. Albania deprived Serbs and Greeks of anticipated gains on the Adriatic, and so heightened their concentration on Macedonia. They decided to retain occupied territory, which was as yet unassigned and which Bulgaria wanted. As Serbia demanded a revision of the agreement, Austria-Hungary stood by Bulgaria in her determination to hold on to a larger share of Macedonia than she had originally intended to claim.

4 King Ferdinand was said to be thinking of a triumphal entry into Constantinople.

Romania had remained neutral. That had been the powers' advice, which she had readily accepted. Now that all the other Balkan states were questioning such injunctions, and trying to obtain greater concessions from one another, she, too, demanded a reward, which could only be at Bulgaria's expense. That was yet another reason for the Bulgarians to keep hold of as much of Macedonia as possible. The issue was no longer an ethnic one; it was not even one of realizing 'great ideas' at the expense of the Ottoman Empire; it was blatantly about the balance of power between the Balkan states.

The Treaty of London was signed in May 1913 after the parties had been told to sign or leave. It imposed on Turkey the loss of all territory west of a line from Enos (Enez) on the Aegean to Midia (Midye) on the Black Sea. Leaving aside a roughly sketched-out Albania within natural borders of mountainous peaks, and with a coastline from Scutari to Valona, what the Ottoman Empire lost was to be divided among the allies – an impossible task. Bulgaria put forward the principle of proportionality of the acquisitions to the military input. Serbia and Greece countered with the principle of balance – that no state should become too powerful. They had common interests in Macedonia that led them to line up against Bulgaria. Incidents multiplied. Russia tried and failed to arbitrate a tripartite compromise. Bulgarian forces attacked Serbs and Greeks at the end of June.

Romanian, Montenegrin and even Ottoman troops joined in against Bulgaria, and the Second Balkan War ended in disaster for her. The Peace of Bucharest in August brought about a settlement. Serbia generally kept the territories she had obtained in 1912, about a third of Macedonia, northern and central as well as a common frontier with Montenegro in Novi Pazar. Greece secured over half of Macedonia, the southern part of Epirus, an extension into southern Thrace to include Kavalla, and a few more islands. Bulgaria received the smallest part of Macedonia and a section of the Aegean coast, but had to cede southern Dobrudja to Romania. Furthermore, in her peace settlement with the Porte at the Treaty of Constantinople in September, she had to return Adrianople to Turkey, who had retaken it: from Odrin (in Bulgarian) the town again became Edirne (in Turkish).

That was the end of Ottoman rule in the Balkans except for Constantinople and a surrounding strip of Thrace slightly bigger than before the Second Balkan War. That war had cost more lives than the first. It had shattered the Balkan League, which Russia had sponsored as a bulwark against perceived Austro-Hungarian expansion. It had left Bulgaria isolated. Serbia had become more important for Russia, because she stood in the front line against Austria-Hungary with unquestionable credentials, whereas Bulgaria had become suspect, not only regarding the Dual Monarchy, but also for possible aspirations to the Straits.

All participants had behaved in such a way as to show that their aim in Macedonia was not only to acquire territory, but to get rid of rival or antagonistic ethnic groups, at least culturally or statistically. All sides had destroyed villages or quarters, killed civilians, practised extortions and forced assimilation, caused violence and bitterness.[5] When all was said and done, the victors had to face the task of assimilating heterogeneous and neglected populations, including Muslims and many Orthodox Christians with no clear national consciousness, many of whom looked over the border for inspiration and support.

That still left Albania. Austria-Hungary and Italy favoured an Albania that would be in their debt, Russia and France rather supported Serbia's ambitions, so that proposals regarding status and borders varied with the situation on the ground. The London Conference had first come out in favour of an autonomous Albania under Ottoman rule and protection by the great powers. When it became clear that, by losing all of Macedonia, the Ottoman Empire would no longer have any territorial connexion with Albania, the conference opted for independence.

The last Ottoman troops had left in June 1913. Qemal's provisional government was finding it difficult if not impossible to establish its authority in the face of resistance from the great landowners, typified by his rival Esat Pasha Toptani (c.1863–1920) who had commanded Ottoman troops in northern Albania. In July the Conference decided that Albania would be a sovereign, hereditary and neutral principality under the guarantee of the great powers. Rather than recognize the Qemal government, it set up an International Control Commission to elaborate an organic statute, organize an international gendarmerie, and fix the borders on the basis of the indications of the Treaty of London. In December the powers agreed on a prince – William of Wied (1876–1945), an officer in the German army and nephew of Queen Elizabeth of Romania. He hesitated before accepting, was given a guaranteed loan to finance his government, and eventually went out in March 1914 on an Austro-Hungarian warship, escorted by Italian, French and British units. He landed at Durazzo where he set up his capital.[6]

Sent ahead to Valona (Vlorë), the commission had gradually taken over from Qemal, who gave up and left for France. The territory covered some 28,000 sq. km, with some 800,000 inhabitants. Its frontiers, yet to be fixed, left out much of what Albanian nationalists had wanted. The Montenegrins had eventually left the Scutari (Shkodër) area, but Greece still occupied parts of Epirus that were meant for Albania, contesting the borders indicated by the powers.

5 An international commission of enquiry, set up by the young Carnegie Endowment for International Peace, arrived in Macedonia at the end of hostilities. Having enquired for eight weeks, it produced a report that described in detail the treatment meted out by all combatants to their enemies and to the civilian population, usually by irregulars but also by regular army units. Nobody was spared, by the war or by the report: Albanians and Turks mistreated Christians and vice versa, Bulgars mistreated Greeks and Serbs and vice versa (*Report of the International Commission to Inquire into the Causes and Conduct of the Balkan Wars*, printed for the Carnegie Endowment in Aylesbury, Buckinghamshire, 1914; republished in Washington, D.C., in 1993 as *The Other Balkan Wars: A 1913 Carnegie Endowment Inquiry in Retrospect*).
6 In Albanian, he was called *mbret*, from the Latin *imperator*. Thus after Basileus, Caesar, Carolus and Rex, there was also Imperator.

In such conditions, Prince William managed to survive for six months, with an administration of landowning beys and former Ottoman civil servants. His government was dominated by Qemal's one-time rival Esat Toptani, who did his best to make life as difficult as possible for the prince. The Austro-Hungarian and Italian members of the commission were at loggerheads. There was a major peasant uprising in the summer in the central areas. The Muslims listened to Ottoman propaganda that attacked the new régime as being the tool of Christian powers and greedy landowning beys. Economic conditions on the estates were the basic cause of the rising. The Greeks supported their own people in the south. Intriguing with Italy, Toptani stirred up opposition to the government of which he was the most important member, perhaps aiming for the throne himself. He was captured and exiled.

As Austro-Hungarian influence appeared to have come out on top, the prince lost any support he might have had from the Entente powers. The revolt continued, simply a gathering of all those opposed to the new régime, with pro-Austrian and pro-Italian factions fighting each other, the prince and his government losing what little control they had over the countryside. When the First World War started, the commission left. The prince's administration was by then limited in practice to the coastal towns of Durrës and Vlorë. As he had refused to join the war on her side, Austria-Hungary withdrew all support, and he, too, had to leave early in September.

'The last three years of Young Turk rule did more for the development of an Albanian national consciousness than decades of slow cultural endeavours would have achieved.'[7] Yet in spite of the fact that it had saved the Albanian-inhabited regions from total partition as they emerged from the ruins of Ottoman rule, independence opened a period of political anarchy. No sooner was Albania set up as a sovereign principality than it ceased to exist as an independent entity. At the same time, the emergence of an Albanian consciousness had served to undermine the religious basis of the Ottoman Empire. The Albanian movement, culminating in the creation of an independent state, came as a shock to Ottoman statesmen. Albanian nationalism contributed to Turkish nationalism more than the nationalism of Christian communities had done, because it destroyed the unity of the Islamic millet.

The Young Turks' hopes of Ottomanization had perished in the Balkan Wars. Their rule had been unable to halt further decline, yet they held on to government. It was as the Second Balkan War started in June 1913 that the CUP fully took over. The Young Turks brought constitutional government to an end and suppressed other parties, but they never ceased to implement westernizing reforms. The élite who held power had imposed reforms from above in order to safeguard the Empire, but when the defence of an Ottoman Empire encompassing Christian communities was no longer a valid proposition, the alternative was pan-Islamism or a western-style state for the Turkish

7 Stavro Skendi, *The Albanian National Awakening, 1878–1912*, Princeton, NJ: Princeton University Press, 1967, 471–2.

majority. Albania undermined the former. The more extreme Young Turks pushed for westernization to its ultimate end as a necessity for survival, and in so doing accelerated the process of building a Turkish identity.

NATIONAL STATES, PEASANTS AND DEVELOPMENT

Through the setting up of independent states, the revolutionary principle of nationality triumphed over that of empire, at least in the Ottoman Empire, but it also sapped the foundations of the Austro-Hungarian *Ausgleich*, itself in part the consequence of that principle. Although still looking to its western liberal model, the principle of nationality was contaminated by the idea that the continued growth of a nation was dependent on the possession of certain territories. The nations-in-the-making were being tainted by their one-time imperial conquerors.

Whatever the theories, Balkan society was rooted in the village. Liberal and even democratic institutions had gradually been introduced in the new states which had brought most of the peasantry into the workings of their respective polities. In Greece, in Bulgaria, in Serbia, their votes had to be taken into account, if not always by the most honest means. In Romania too, the moment came when all privileged participants in the constitutional process acknowledged the peasants' right to a stake in its workings and in the land itself.

The Balkan states would not have come into being without the revolutionary potential of the peasants. Once set up, they had directed it towards the attainment of national programmes, trying to exploit peasant discontent on the other side of imperial borders. Peasant movements started the Eastern Crisis in 1875, but they were regional, and poorly timed to coincide with the most favourable international climate. The year 1878 marked the end of such attempts.

There continued to be major anti-Ottoman and anti-Habsburg peasant rebellions (and there were rural rebellions in the Balkan states too), but Italy and Germany thereafter set the example that national unification would come as a result of diplomacy and war, not diplomacy and peasant uprising. The Macedonian uprising of 1903 hardly benefited the Balkan states. In 1912 they did not expect a rising behind Ottoman lines, but their peasant conscripts performed better in armies that had been modernized and had money spent on them, than they had in the days when uprisings were assumed.

The contradictions inherent in the relationship between states and peasant masses can be seen in the general momentum of those prewar years. The Balkan smallholder was conservative, yet movements from the outside world continued to reach him from the margins – from the Mediterranean, from transriparian central Europe, and, less directly, from the west. He and his children were less afraid of the outside world than they are today on the eve of the twenty-first century. They took part in an effort, not only militarily but culturally, politically, economically, and more generally in terms of self-confidence. Political parties spoke on behalf of the masses even when they did not specifically express what the peasant majority wanted,[8] and if peasants voted for the party in government, it was because they knew that they could usually get something from it.

The peasant way of life was idealized by part of a new intelligentsia. Others, who had generally studied abroad, worked to precipitate the fall of authoritarian rulers, to adopt representative institutions and limit the monarch's prerogative in the name of an abstract nation. The differences were over the pace of change, and they were within people's minds.

Iorga who, in Romania, emphasized the organic continuity of 'Romanity', also came to stress a common consciousness of Balkan Europe.[9] Romania, who had kept her autonomy, felt pride in pioneering scholarly initiatives for the benefit of all those who had gone through the long period of 'Turkocracy'. Belgrade became the capital of a culture led by a new generation of intellectuals who advocated 'French' ideas of political 'liberty' in opposition to the 'German' notion of historic 'privileges'. Formulated in a French-inspired 'Belgrade style' of brevity and simplicity, they provided a Serbian expression of the Yugoslav idea that was also being aired by some Croat intellectuals in reaction against the historicist tradition of 'state rights'. If Bucharest developed a style of its own, all capitals took to Art Nouveau architecture, which reconciled the requirement of modernization with the assertion of identity through national romanticism. It was their way of showing their independence.

The economic structure that underpinned these developments was changed in the decade before 1914, but, in practice, change was too patchy to accommodate an increasing population in what remained overwhelmingly agrarian societies – growing between 1900 and 1910 at an annual rate ranging from 0.71 per cent in Greece to 1.56 per cent in Serbia. Governments – the principal agents of development – sought to introduce European achievements, but they lacked the economic means to achieve their aims. As decisions had to be made on priorities, the tendency was to emphasize territorial expansion over internal development, yet efforts were made to modernize within existing borders until the Balkan Wars.

Having freed themselves from the chaotic Ottoman monetary orbit, the four states established central banks on European models. The shortage of credit, along with longer-standing patriotic ambition, was the immediate reason. The ordering of state finances, the difficult transition to the gold standard, and

---

8 Only two parties attempted to voice peasant concerns – the radicals of Serbia and the agrarians of Bulgaria. The newly formed social democrats, under the lead of the Bulgarians, who pioneered workers' political associations, organized, and took part in, strikes and demonstrations. They backed the 1903 coup in Serbia and the 1908 coup in Greece. Although influenced by the Balkan revolutionary tradition, they did not yet understand the revolutionary potential of the dissatisfied peasantry. As Austrian socialists favoured ethnic autonomy amounting to a federal Austria, Austro-Marxism was a powerful influence on the South Slav social-democratic parties of the various Habsburg lands. The Serbian social democrats managed to act as a bridge by holding the first Balkan Social Democratic conference in Belgrade in 1910. All social democrats were linked to one class only, that of industrial workers, who were few and far between in the Balkans.
9 *Histoire des Etats balkaniques à l'époque moderne*, first Romanian edition, 1913, with a new edition in French, Bucharest, 1914.

the maintenance of internationally acceptable currencies at par with the French gold franc after 1900, assured them access to further loans. Their success, however, served to bolster their political independence rather than their economic development.

The response of foreign capital otherwise than through bond issues was disappointing. Even Austria-Hungary did not turn to the Balkans for market and investment opportunities. Most bond issues for Balkan states were handled in Paris, the major capital market of pre-1914 Europe. Its banks did seek new investments outside France, but in the form of state loans, at the prompting of the French foreign ministry, for diplomatic advantage. Balkan central banks continued to rely on short-term credit which favoured state and trade rather than industry. Long-term private credit remained the great lack in the otherwise modern financial structures of Balkan states.

The greater availability of foreign loans and the reduction of budget deficits did not lead to a major reallocation of state spending. Although debt repayment and military expenditure were still the main items in every budget, governments, banks and entrepreneurs strove to overcome formidable obstacles – such as the general lack of coal and iron, of adequate markets, capital and labour. Governments did their best when negotiating commercial treaties; they also assisted individual industries in a variety of ways. But since they needed to export their agricultural surplus, they often had to accept tariff conditions that were unfavourable to domestic industrial development. Other moves were undertaken piecemeal in response to the demands of separate sectors.

Few outside European entrepreneurs were attracted to the sort of manufacture growing in the Balkans before 1914. Internal demand was weak, there was no ready access to unskilled peasant labour and no cheap access to skilled labour. Industry was reduced to native entrepreneurs, or at best immigrants from Austria-Hungary with an understanding of local conditions – ethnic Serbs or Romanians, Austro-Germans or Ashkenazi Jews. As the share of the Ottoman market shrank and no advance could be made in the Dual Monarchy, the principal market was provided by the towns – between 14 per cent (in Serbia) and 24 per cent (in Greece) of the population.

Romania enjoyed a clear advantage, with Bucharest, Jassy and the Danubian ports of Brăila and Galaţi concentrating over half of her urban population. The capital itself had approaching 350,000 inhabitants by 1914; it had a higher purchasing power than any of the other capitals, with private residences as lavish as any in pre-1914 Europe. The collection there of over half the country's industrial enterprises was a response to demand. Romania generally made the greatest advances in industry.

The growing industrial sectors in the Balkans were food processing, textiles and construction materials. The refining of home-grown sugar beet in Romania could do no more than hope to capture the essentially urban market from Austro-Hungarian imports. Modern flour mills and breweries remained largely bound to capital cities. Meat packing, if it lacked domestic potential, was the best prospect for export, but took off really only in Serbia, where it spread no further than Belgrade for production and Austria-Hungary for export.

Bulgaria led the region in textile production, with partly mechanized factories since the 1880s. Centred in the upland towns on either side of the Balkan range, that sector had access to the cheap supply of rural labour that largely eluded other manufacturers, but faced serious limits in both demand and supply. The coarseness of Bulgarian wool and the slow spread of cotton cultivation meant that a great part of the raw material had to be imported. Bulgaria's share of the Ottoman market fell drastically after independence, and it faced competition from English and Austrian imports at home.

The manufacture of construction materials was encouraged by the growth of capital cities, but their local production demanded a greater investment in fixed capital and more sophisticated machinery than either food processing or textiles. Once again, the greater size and wealth of Bucharest made it a centre of production. Romanian makers of construction materials had access to accumulated landed wealth and acquired technology,[10] but there were limitations to local demand, and few export possibilities because of bulk and fragility.

Industrial growth in the Balkan states during the last prewar decade was more rapid than that of either exports or revenues, thus laying at least the groundwork for an alternative economic growth. Such stirring was, nevertheless, less impressive than over the border in Habsburg Slovenia, Croatia-Slavonia and Transylvania who, if they had no protection against Czech or Austrian manufactures, did at least attract more industrial investment. During these years, the value-added industrial output of the Balkan states did not amount to 10 per cent of the total gross output of their economies, and no industrial revolution occurred there before 1914.

The agricultural sector provided most of the tax revenue and the bulk of exports. It accounted for over 75 per cent of gross output recorded for Romania, Serbia and Bulgaria. By the last prewar year Romania's export value approached half of the national income, Bulgaria's exceeded one-fifth, and Serbia's fell just short of 15 per cent. In all three, the increase in the export value over the last prewar decade was able to eliminate the large trade deficit that manufactured imports had created before 1900, with only Greece failing to end the import surplus.

Romania provided large amounts of crops (half of her wheat and 40 per cent of her corn) for export, having doubled the area devoted to grain cultivation between 1860 and 1900. The landowning boier class had been able to retain its predominant position, as in the period 1905–8 less than one per cent of landowners possessed almost half of all arable land in estates of over 100 hectares, while over 95 per cent owned 40 per cent in holdings of under ten hectares.

---

10 Cantacuzino and Bibescu princes used family resources to further the study of technology and to introduce modern plants.

Serbia and Bulgaria were at the opposite end of the land structure scale. Units of under ten hectares covered over 53 per cent of the land, held by 86 per cent of owners in Bulgaria. In Serbia, they covered 41 per cent of the land, owned by almost 90 per cent of proprietors. Both countries had an important middle element with another 43–47 per cent in holdings of between ten and one hundred hectares. In Serbia, most managed a surplus which they invested in acquiring more land in so far as it was available. Methods and equipment remained much the same, and there was no turn towards intensive agriculture. Bulgarian smallholders were in a similar situation, except that their future savings were mortgaged to pay for debts incurred in acquiring land from Turkish owners. In both countries, the rapidly rising price of land was a sign of population pressure rather than of increased profitability.

In Greece the problem was the shortage of arable land. In the newer and richer northern territories, the estates which had usually passed to Greek owners, continued by and large to be worked on a sharecropping basis, while in the older southern territories with no more than 20 per cent of arable land, the subdivision of smallholdings limited farming to subsistence at best, especially after the conversion to vineyards. Greece had to import wheat to feed the population that she did not export. Even in Romania and northern Greece, most peasants had some land, but so little that they could not survive without sharecropping.

The principal aid to agriculture was an emphasis on indirect taxation on necessities which peasants either produced themselves or were able to acquire without the knowledge of officialdom. Lampe shows that the tax burden on most Balkan peasants had actually declined substantially by 1910.[11] Approximations of national income per person by the end of the prewar period exceed 200 francs for Bulgaria, and approach 250 francs for Serbia and Romania (averages to be compared with perhaps the equivalent of some 400 francs for Hungary, less than 800 francs for the largely industrialized Czech lands, and nearly 1,000 francs for the leading industrial country of Europe, Germany).

Expanding agricultural exports vied with rising demography, and the land tenure systems did not augur well for the introduction of more modern techniques. The increasing subdivision of smallholdings offered limited prospects. If the large estates offered more, it was at the price of the exploitation of sharecroppers. Increased output for export does not seem to have been seen by the peasants as leading the way to sustained internal development. What they wanted was money to buy more land. In the grain-deficit areas, they migrated in search of seasonal[12] or long-term wage labour. Only in Romania, which had the richest soils and fastest-growing agricultural exports, did peasant discontent turn to widespread revolt, for in addition to the problem of

---

11 John R. Lampe and Marvin R. Jackson, *Balkan Economic History, 1559–1950: From Imperial Borderlands to Developing Nations*, Bloomington: Indiana University Press, 1982, 192.
12 The phenomenon of seasonal migration in search of construction or agricultural labour eludes official data. Poor peasants went to the estates of Wallachia and southern Hungary, to large cities, and into banditry.

access to money, they faced a real land shortage. Sustained agricultural growth on socially tolerable terms was coming to an end.

All in all, the Balkans had perhaps achieved their maximum within the constraints of the old European political order that went back to 1815, and of its evolution as a consequence of the Eastern Question – the power rivalry in the peninsula resulting from the gradual withdrawal of the Ottoman Empire.

CHAPTER 10

The First World War and the Paris peace settlement, 1914–20

'Serbia must die'. The Balkan states between the Central powers and the Entente. Confusion and occupation. The collapse of the Central powers and self-determination. The peace settlements.

It was not obvious that a 'great war' was about to break out in the Balkans in 1914. The peninsula was recovering from a two-year period of warfare, and the European alliance system was intended to maintain the status quo. Relations between states were, however, influenced everywhere by a segment of opinion that had acquired a simplified view of events through patriotism, nationalism or power obsession.

The South Slavs were divided between the two parts of the Dual Monarchy, and the two independent states of Serbia and Montenegro. If the Yugoslav idea received at least tacit support from an increasing section of the public, its vocal proponents formed only a small proportion of educated and semi-educated opinion, and they hardly considered the practical problems of unification. Among its younger adherents were actual and potential revolutionaries, particularly in Bosnia-Herzegovina. The young men of peasant stock attracted to the loose gathering known as Young Bosnia were favourable to some form of Yugoslav unity free from Austria-Hungary. They sought the support or the cover of nationalist organizations in Serbia, such as the National Defence, through which the Black Hand officers also operated.

After the Balkan Wars, some of these officers, like their Greek, Ottoman or Bulgarian counterparts, felt that the politicians were holding back. In the early summer of 1914, Serbia faced a domestic crisis on the question of the government's ability to control the military. It was as a result of civil–military rivalry, in Serbia and in Austro-Hungarian Bosnia, that the twenty-year-old Gavrilo Princip (1894–1918) was able to carry out the bungled yet successful assassination of the heir to the Habsburg crowns on 28 June 1914.[1]

---

1 Its deficiencies notwithstanding, the essential work on the motives of the conspirators, their milieu and their links with organizations in Belgrade, is Vladimir Dedijer, *The Road to Sarajevo*,

FROM SARAJEVO TO SALONIKA

The Austro-Hungarian reaction was one of fear – fear of following the Otto-man Empire on the road to decline, fear of other groups aspiring to the same status as the Austro-German and Magyar establishments. A war party won the day, convinced that a quick military operation against Serbia would solve all problems. She was seen as the fount of South Slav nationalism within the empire: '*Serbien muß sterben*' was its pun slogan ('Serbia must die'). Fear became a 'will to war'.[2]

To the accompaniment of anti-Serbian demonstrations, numerous arrests, some executions, and veritable pogroms of Serbs in Bosnia-Herzegovina, Austria-Hungary delivered an ultimatum to Serbia designed to be rejected. The acceptance of all the demands but one (the participation of Austro-Hungarian officials in the investigations to be carried out in Serbia) was not good enough: the Dual Monarchy declared war on 28 July and attacked. In response, the Serbian government called for the liberation and unification of all Yugoslavs. It had postponed the elections about to be held and removed itself to Niš, along with the outgoing National Assembly. Montenegro immediately expressed her 'Serbian solidarity in defence of the Serbian nation'.

In spite of the clarion call, it was difficult to imagine the disintegration of Austria-Hungary. All over the Habsburg lands, the assassination had pro-voked manifestations of loyalty. Romanian politicians were appalled, for they were inclined to believe that Archduke Francis Ferdinand had been sympath-etic to their cause in Transylvania. Vienna feared the failure of their negotiations with Budapest; Bucharest anticipated with anxiety yet another war that could put in jeopardy the acquisitions of the Second Balkan War. The Romanian National Party of Transylvania went into hibernation.

The majority Croato-Serb Coalition in the Zagreb Sabor was not subvers-ive. Croat and Slovene conservative and clerical parties supported the war against Serbia, with anti-Orthodox tones encouraged by most Catholic bishops. Yet the authorities feared pro-Serbian feelings, and even an uprising in Bosnia-Herzegovina, hence the repression and mob action. Their fears were unfounded, for the mobilization went smoothly everywhere. Some of the divisions that launched the attack on Serbia contained over 50 per cent Croats[3] and 20–25 per cent Serbs.

Serbia was in danger, a small state of 4.5 million inhabitants facing the Dual Monarchy's 52 million. Apart from tiny Montenegro, her allies were far away and concerned with defending themselves from German attacks. The campaigns

---

London: MacGibbon & Key, 1967. His article 'Sarajevo Fifty Years After', in *Foreign Affairs*, 42, New York, 1964, 569–84, says it in a nutshell.
2 To borrow the title of Günther Kronenbitter's study, '"Nur loss lassen": Österreich-Ungarn und der Wille zum Krieg', in Johannes Burckhard, Josef Becker, Stig Förster and Günther Kronenbitter, *Lange und kurze Wege in den Ersten Weltkrieg*, Munich: Ernst Vögel, 1996, 159, 185.
3 Including one Sergeant Josip Broz (the future Marshal Tito), serving with the 10th Company, 25th Croatian Territorial Infantry Regiment, 42nd Division.

in the Balkans would be merely a side show to the main conflicts. For all that, Austria-Hungary's immediate attempt failed. Serbia repelled the invasion, and the battle of Cer was the first victory against the Central powers in the First World War. She went on to counter in Hungary, helped by applause from the French[4] and by the Russian advance into Galicia, but she was soon exhausted. In the space of a fortnight in December, the Serbs lost and regained Belgrade. The Entente had been able to send ammunition through Greece and up the Danube. The front calmed down over the winter and Serbia just about held her own.

The unexpected declaration of war by Austria-Hungary had thrown up the question of unification, now posed publicly to try to ensure the survival of the Serbian state. The government discussed the vision of Yugoslavia (even looking at the possibility of extending it to Bulgaria once again). In December 1914 from its provisional seat in Niš, it proclaimed through the National Assembly that the war was being fought for the liberation and unification of all Serbs, Croats and Slovenes. The Niš Declaration replaced the idea of a Serb nation-state with the new and less clear concept of a wider state of the Yugoslav nation of Serbs, Croats and Slovenes. The government invested energy in propaganda to internationalize the question. It was helped by a number of influential South Slav personalities from Austria-Hungary, mostly Croats and mostly from Dalmatia, who had gone abroad to advocate the union of the Habsburg South Slavs with Serbia and Montenegro. In May 1915, when Italy had entered the war, they formally set up the Yugoslav Committee in London.

By that time, the Young Turks' dictatorship had brought the Ottoman Empire into the war on the side of Germany. It had had to deal with a massive new emigration of Muslims from the territories acquired by Serbia and Greece after the Balkan Wars; it wanted to abolish the Capitulations; it wished to win back lost lands. In Austria-Hungary, most Croat and Slovene politicians assumed the continuity of the Monarchy and wanted to establish a South Slav component within it. The Entente Allies, oblivious of the Yugoslav question, were interested in winning over neutral Italy, who had aspirations to the former Venetian lands of Austria. They succeeded in doing so by the secret Treaty of London of April 1915.

They could use Austrian territory to satisfy Italy, though they were hampered to a certain extent by the knowledge that this was mostly inhabited by South Slavs. However, the needs of the war took precedence. Italy joined in return for promises that included Istria, Trieste and part of Dalmatia. She could keep the Dodecanese and was offered a share of any Ottoman lands to be partitioned.

This was soon balanced out by Bulgaria going over to the Central powers in return for the Serbian part of Macedonia. King Ferdinand and the Radoslavov

---

4 '*Que les Autrichiens aient déjà commencé d'être rossés par les Serbes, c'était prévu*', said a French leader writer on 4 August. Such talk boosted the Serbs' self-confidence, even if their strong resistance had not been anticipated all that much.

government had wanted to keep out of the war for as long as possible. They had declared neutrality and a state of emergency. Popular Russophilia was not extinguished, the government had only just obtained the barest possible electoral majority by the most dubious practices, and an attempt to form an officers' league to sweep away such practices had failed.

Both sides had been eager to secure Bulgaria, who commanded supply routes to Serbia and to Turkey. Austria-Hungary and Germany could invite her to help herself in Macedonia, and offer further acquisitions should Greece and Romania join the Entente. As Bulgaria was gradually pushed in the direction of the Central powers, the opposition parties issued warnings and asked for the recall of parliament, but the government further tightened its control. Over the summer of 1915, Bulgaria's alliance with Germany and Austria-Hungary was settled; in mid-October she joined in the new attack on Serbia.

The move was not popular. The opposition reluctantly gave way, Stamboliiski was gaoled for lèse majesté after a confrontation with the king, mobilization was greeted with sullenness. The new combined offensive overran Serbia. Bulgarian forces cut off her lifeline to Salonika and occupied Skopje. Facing the option of capitulating or risking a mid-winter retreat through the hostile mountains of Albania to the Adriatic coast and Allied shipping, the Serbian government went for the latter.

Albania was in political anarchy. Soon after its newly appointed ruler had left, Esat Pasha had installed himself as president in Durazzo (Durrës) with Italian and Serbian support. Inland, based in Krujë, a movement wanted reincorporation in the Ottoman Empire or the election of an Ottoman prince. The Italians had occupied the southern port of Valona (Vlorë). Qemal had also returned to oppose the Greek troops that had come in the hope of annexing areas with a large Greek minority. In June 1915, Serbian and Montenegrin troops had been successful in what was their fourth attempt since 1912 to get to the sea through northern Albania. They had scattered the Krujë Ottomanists and left Esat in control of central Albania.

During the epic Serbian retreat through Albania of the aged King Peter, officialdom, National Assembly, army and countless refugees, dying of hunger, cold and disease, and pursued by the Austro-Hungarians, the hostile population took its own back. When the decimated Serbs arrived in December 1915 in the northern Albanian ports of Shkodër and Durrës, the French sent their navy to evacuate them, and by the end of February 1916, some 135,000 Serbian soldiers had been taken to the Greek island of Corfu.

Esat Pasha, who had attached himself to the Entente and declared war on Austria-Hungary, also left, taken by a French warship to Salonika, where he set himself up as a head of state in exile. The new star rising in Albania was his nephew Ahmet Zogolli (1895–1961). He had returned from Constantinople in 1911 at the age of sixteen to assume the leadership of the Mati tribe, after his father had gained control of the entire area from the Krujë area to the Mirditë. Careful not to identify himself too closely with one power, he welcomed Austria-Hungary, whose troops were said to have entered Albania only to drive out Serbs and Italians, but it was in Bulgarian-occupied Elbasan in central Albania that he set up a provisional government.

Austria-Hungary, who had turned Durrës into a naval base, soon replaced the Bulgarians in Elbasan. They set up an occupation régime, which offered a limited amount of native participation, the building of roads, bridges and schools, but no political movement in time of war. Zogolli was invited for talks in Vienna, and kept there as a guest for the rest of the war. By the end of 1916, the whole of Albania was under military occupation, the north and the centre under Austro-Hungarians, and the south under French and Italians (preferred by the French to King Constantine's uncertain Greeks).

In January 1916, King Nicholas of Montenegro had left for Serbian-held Shkodër and for Italy, leaving behind a rump government that had capitulated to Austria-Hungary. The Serbian government existed only by courtesy of the Allies on Greek Corfu, where it maintained its symbolic continuity in the most precarious situation. Not only did the unresolved tension with the military resurface with defeat, but the restoration of Serbia after the war became of greater immediate concern than Yugoslav unification. Although he believed in Yugoslavia, Pašić did not understand how different it would have to be from the Serbia he knew. In exile, he acted very cautiously about war claims and aims, intent on keeping what had been attained, on obtaining what he felt was possible, and on controlling the unification process.

Friction developed with the Yugoslav Committee, which did not consider itself as a mere public relations auxiliary, but as a partner. The Serbian government saw unification as a continuation of the struggle for liberation from Turkish rule. It believed that the decisions would be made by the peace treaties; in the meanwhile, it had to convince the Allies of the merits of Yugoslavia. The committee saw the process as resulting more from the right to self-determination than from liberation by Serbia; it was probably influenced by its experience of dualism.

The committee's task was even harder than that of the Serbian government. It was made up of émigrés too, but with no legal status, no mandate to represent the Yugoslavs of Austria-Hungary, no realistic constraints either. With a majority of its members from Dalmatia, it polemized with Italy almost as vigorously as with Austria-Hungary, and was willing to 'give' her less than the Central powers had offered. The friction that developed between the government in exile and the émigré committee did little to convince the Allies that the unification of Yugoslavia was a feasible project.

With its army in occupation of most of Macedonia (in the spring of 1916 the Germans even allowed a push into Greek territory), the Bulgarian government felt confident enough at the end of December 1915 to summon the National Assembly. In January 1916 it defined its war aim, 'to unite the Bulgarian nation within its historic and ethnic borders', a maximalist programme symbolized by King Ferdinand's decision to adopt a new tricolour – black–white–

blue for greater Bulgaria's three sea coasts, the Black Sea, the Aegean and the Adriatic. Various measures were taken to mark the break with the country's pro-Russian past.

All this did not take place without problems. The population at large took exception to some of these measures. There was disagreement over how much territory Bulgaria should take. There was resentment at the exploitation of the country's resources by her allies. There were food shortages in towns, and even more so in the occupied territories where they affected the morale of troops.

Romania's secret alliance with the Central powers had been renewed in 1913; a liberal government under Brătianu, returned to power in 1914, was about to tackle agrarian and electoral reform. King Charles, liberals and conservatives agreed on the need to avoid war, but whereas the monarch favoured the Central powers, to which he felt bound, public opinion was generally hostile to Austria-Hungary. While out of sympathy with Russia, it supported the Entente. Strict neutrality was agreed, on the grounds that the treaty required the signatories to go to war only if one of them had been attacked. Keeping in touch with the Central powers who offered Russian Bessarabia, Brătianu agreed with the Russians on Romania's benevolent neutrality in exchange for a recognition of her aspirations to Transylvania.

When King Charles died in October 1914, neutrality was continued even though his successor Ferdinand was favourably disposed towards the Entente. Romania's economy had already been affected by the disruption of traditional markets and by military preparations. Entente pressure to abandon neutrality intensified in 1916; in August the conditions for Romania's entry into the war were at last settled. Russia and France would provide support against Austria-Hungary and Bulgaria respectively, Romania was given a free hand to acquire Austro-Hungarian territories with a Romanian population, whose rights to self-determination and union with Romania were recognized. The declaration of war on Austria-Hungary was justified by the fact that no satisfaction had been given to Romania's demands in Transylvania.

It was from the Salonika front that the French Armée d'Orient would help Romania. French and British troops had landed there in October 1915, on the territory of neutral Greece, after the failure of the Dardanelles; Entente troops had occupied Corfu the following January to provide a safe haven for the Serbian army and government. Greece's entry into the war was the longest delayed and most controversial of all. It destroyed the remarkable political consensus achieved since 1910, and caused the great cleavage known as the National Schism.

Venizelos was emotionally attached to Great Britain and France. He also enjoyed the support of powerful British-based economic interests. He had received no assurances about future territorial gains, and although he realized that Constantinople had been promised to Russia in the event of victory, he still saw the western powers as those most likely to favour his country's remaining aspirations. King Constantine, who had a greater respect for the military might of the Central powers, wanted Greece to remain neutral.[5]

Anxious not to precipitate the entry of Turkey and Bulgaria into the war, the British had declined Venizelos's offer of help. Even at the beginning of 1915, they were still suggesting that Greece should cede some recently acquired territory to Bulgaria, in return for compensation in northern Epirus and promises of 'important territorial concessions on the coast of Asia Minor'. Seduced by the latter, Venizelos was willing to go along with the proposal. The king wanted more concrete assurances before consenting to give up territory so recently won. Constantine agreed to participate in the Dardanelles landing, but then drew back. Venizelos resigned.

Elections in June 1915 gave him a clear majority, which he regarded as an endorsement of his pro-Entente policy. When Bulgaria attacked Serbia, it was Venizelos who invited Britain and France to send an expeditionary force to Salonika in support of Greece's 1913 partner. King Constantine again drew back, and called on Venizelos to resign. Monarch and prime minister accused each other of unconstitutional action.

When elections were repeated in December, the liberals abstained and the turnout was very low. Venizelos became identified with a policy of intervention in the war to gain more; the king advocated that the country should consolidate its hold over the territories just acquired before embarking on a hazardous future. The 'royalists' represented a large constituency, strongly entrenched in 'old Greece', fearful of the pace of change introduced by Venizelos.

There was mounting discord between the Entente and Athens, which refused to allow Serbian troops to cross by land from Corfu to Salonika to join the Macedonian front. After a Bulgarian–German force had been allowed to make an advance into Greek territory, pro-Venizelos officers mounted an anti-government coup in Salonika in August. Venizelos joined them from Crete, brought in on a French warship. 'New Greece' was committed to him. He formed a provisional (counter-) government, with its own army. The Entente powers gave their blessing, but not formal recognition, for they feared civil war. They actually landed troops in Piraeus in December, to put pressure on the king's government and enforce its neutrality, but had to withdraw. After that, they recognized the Salonika government, helped it to extend its control, and blockaded the territory of the Athens government, causing severe hardship. The 'schism' was complete.

By the end of 1916 all the Balkans were involved in one way or another. The murder in Sarajevo had enabled Austria-Hungary to make war on Serbia, to overrun her territory, to win the support of Turkey and Bulgaria, to occupy

5 Because of his loud and controversial support for the Entente, Venizelos made a greater impact on British and French opinion than either Pašić or Brătianu. He was the inspiration for the Greek prime minister of John Buchan's *The Thirty-Nine Steps*, published at the time of the landing in Salonika. A young Romanian delegate remembers him a few years later at the Paris Peace Conference as a 'political magician, who had such persuasive powers and was so charming that he obtained everything he asked for' (V.V. Tilea, *Envoy Extraordinary: Memoirs of a Romanian Diplomat*, Ileana Tilea ed., London: Haggerston Press, 1998, 39).

Montenegro and most of Albania. Romania had finally sided with the Entente. A bitterly divided Greece had enabled an Allied army, that included a restored Serbian army, to man the Salonika front, to extend into southern Albania and to prepare to attack the Bulgarians.

CONFUSION, DIVISION AND OCCUPATION

Both sets of powers had made promises to attract neutrals to their side, or to prevent them from going to the other side. Bulgaria had fared best from the bidding; the Allied landing in Salonika had failed to deflect her from occupying much of Serbia by the end of 1915, even from taking a number of towns in Greek Thrace the following summer.

Part of the deal to get Romania to wage war on Austria-Hungary had been that the French Salonika-based Armée d'Orient would go into action against Bulgaria. The Romanian army had expanded too rapidly since 1913, with uncertain supplies coming through Russia from the west by way of Archangel and Vladivostok. The objectives assigned to it were huge: to concentrate on Transylvania, but also to defend the Danube frontier and cover a Russian landing in Dobrudja.

General Averescu's troops crossed the Carpathians with enthusiasm. Ethnic antagonism erupted at once and Hungarians fled before the Romanian advance. The French and the Russians were not able to get into action as planned. The Transylvanian offensive was halted to divert troops to the south. All the territory taken was subsequently lost by the end of September 1916. As Averescu withdrew, tens of thousands of ethnic Romanians followed, including officers from the Austro-Hungarian army. The Hungarian government confiscated their property, closed down newspapers, expelled or arrested Orthodox priests. There were mutual accusations of atrocities.

German reinforcements arrived and German generals assumed overall command in the Carpathians and on the Danube. The tide definitely turned in November. The Austro-Germans forced the passes and advanced on Bucharest. King, government and parliament withdrew to Jassy. A Russian intervention in Moldavia helped to stabilize the front, but over half the country was in enemy hands. Austria-Hungary set up a military administration whose main purpose was to requisition food and oil supplies.

Although they had suffered heavy losses, the Romanians held out in Moldavia for as long as they had Russian protection, and a lifeline to their allies through Russian territory. The region was in a critical situation. Jassy was overflowing with refugees, suffering shortages and a typhus epidemic. Brătianu formed a government of national unity (from which only the main conservative group remained aloof) which made agrarian and electoral reform its main domestic aim.

Bulgaria and Romania notwithstanding, the Allied effort in Salonika had not been in vain. The French had rescued the Serbian army and brought it

215

back to life. They had formed an emotional link with soldiers and refugees who looked to them as saviours and friends, and who were eager to free their homeland. The Serbs were placed at the centre of the Allied front, facing Serbian Macedonia. Before the end of 1916, after the great battle of Mount Kajmakčalan, they had retaken a portion of their country with the town of Bitolj (Bitola) that they had had to leave a year before.

The Serbian government faced unsolved domestic issues magnified by exile. To the existing two centres of power constituted by the radical leadership and the Black Hand was added a third being built around the regent with his circle of officers. It was in Salonika in June 1917 that a rigged trial before a Serbian military court had the Black Hand ringleaders executed for an alleged attempt on the life of Prince Alexander. The trial led to the collapse of the wartime coalition. Independent radicals and progressives resigned; Pašić reconstructed a radical-only cabinet.

At the end of 1916, Austria-Hungary was caught between two conflicting developments. On the one hand, after the Russian offensive of that summer, she turned into a military satellite of Germany. On the other, the death of Emperor Francis Joseph in November opened up new possibilities for the Monarchy. The Entente powers wanted to keep it as a counterweight to Germany. They imagined that it could survive the mutilations involved in the promises made to Italy and Romania, even to Serbia, not to mention what Russia coveted.

The following year was a confused one. Russia dropped out of the war, the United States came in, Russia's new leaders and President Wilson talked of the self-determination of nationalities. The Allies, because of their shaky position, and their fear of a vacuum in central Europe, examined the possibility of detaching Austria-Hungary, whose leaders were no less fearful of the consequences of the Russian Revolution.

There were hardly any disorders, however. Most of the emergency measures taken in 1914 were rescinded or relaxed (though not in Bosnia-Herzegovina), opening the door to a flood of demands. The deputies to the Croatian Sabor and the South Slav members of the Austrian parliament met in May as the Yugoslav Parliamentary Group under the chairmanship of the Slovenian clerical leader Anton Korošec (1872–1940). They called for the unification of the lands of the Monarchy where Slovenes, Croats and Serbs lived, into one state under the Habsburg dynasty, based on the principle of nationality and on the rights of the Croatian state.

Neither the Serbian government nor the parliamentary leadership of the Habsburg South Slavs knew what the outcome of the war would be, or what was going to happen to Austria-Hungary. Both played on two fronts, each aiming at ensuring first what could be obtained, and keeping up contacts with the Yugoslav Committee, which advocated a common Yugoslav front towards the Allies. The lines separating 'greater Serbian' and 'greater Croatian' conceptions from open and total 'Yugoslavism' were hazy.

With its formula of partial South Slav unification within a reformed Habsburg Monarchy, at a time when the Allies were exploring the possibility of a separate peace with Austria-Hungary, the 'Yugoslav Group' with its May Declaration appeared as a serious contender for the role of unifier. The exiled Serbian government and the Yugoslav Committee felt it essential to come together and present a concrete programme of complete unification.

The Corfu Declaration that they jointly issued in July 1917 called for one single, united and independent state of all the Serbs, Croats and Slovenes – a constitutional, democratic and parliamentary monarchy under the Karadjordjević dynasty, with toleration of religious and cultural differences. The rest was left to a constituent assembly, elected by universal and secret ballot, that would adopt a constitution by a 'numerically qualified majority'. This and other somewhat vague formulations reflected divisions over differing conceptions of 'Yugoslavia'.

Full unification around Serbia under the Karadjordjević dynasty was thus opposed to partial unification around Croatia under the Habsburgs. Yet both plans were based on the common concerns of self-determination, acceptance of differences and the fear of Italian aspirations. Both were prominently published, and contacts were established in Switzerland.

Austria-Hungary's South Slav parliamentarians continued to be loyal even though they bargained over their loyalty. Her South Slav soldiers still generally put up a good fight, at least on the Italian front, but desertions were increasing. The Serbian government and the Yugoslav Committee had to cooperate on the formation of volunteer units made up from deserters and prisoners of war. Two divisions were eventually organized in Odessa from Austro-Hungarian prisoners, and another on the Macedonian front from various other sources. Most of the recruits were Serbs, as Croats and Slovenes on the whole just wanted to get out of the war and return home. Officers from the Serbian army sent to organize and command acted with little sensitivity to problems. The use of these units in action was not a success, there were many desertions, and tension exploded after the 'February Revolution' (the tsar's abdication on 15 March).

The events in Russia had far greater repercussions in Romania. Supported by both liberals and conservatives, King Ferdinand's proclamation of April 1917, promising land and the vote as soon as peace was restored, had the desired effect of stemming the revolutionary contagion. Amendments to the constitution were pushed through to enable the distribution of land expropriated from foreign and absentee landlords, and to introduce universal male suffrage immediately after the end of the war.

Winter, exhaustion on both sides and the accession of a new monarch in Austria-Hungary had slowed down military operations. A breathing space had been provided. By June, with massive French help, the reorganization of the Romanian army was completed. A Romanian National Committee of émigré personalities from Austria-Hungary recruited ethnic Romanian prisoners of war in Russian camps. Scholars and artists were sent to Paris, London and the United States to promote the Romanian cause.

In July the Romanians attacked again, but the Germans retaliated vigorously and the fighting was fierce. The Romanians held until the 'October Revolution' (the Bolshevik takeover on 7 November) brought Russian support to an end and havoc among Russian units in Moldavia. When the Bolshevik government started negotiations with the Central powers, Romania had to conclude an armistice and begin peace talks in January 1918. Front-line troops were brought back to disarm and expel the anarchic Russian troops, as the new government in Russia broke off relations, accusing Romanian troops of having invaded Russian Bessarabia.

Bessarabia was in turmoil, divided ethnically and politically. In spite of a century of Russification, Romanians were still the largest ethnic group, accounting for over 47 per cent of the population, according to the Russian census of 1897. A series of meetings had demanded autonomy; peasants had begun to take over large estates; the administration was breaking down. Over the summer of 1917, as various organizations strove to gain cohesion and defend their cause against both Bolsheviks and Ukrainian nationalists, army officers took matters into their own hands and summoned a General Council.

Delegates of workers' and peasants' committees, of professional corporations, of local administrations and of military bodies met in December, proclaimed a Moldavian Democratic Republic, and appealed to the Romanian government in Jassy for help in restoring order. They were dispersed by the Bolsheviks, who were in their turn driven out by Romanian troops. In March 1918 the restored General Council voted for union with Romania, setting conditions – to allow Bessarabia to retain its autonomy and implement its own reforms.

The armistice of Brest Litovsk had by then sealed the fate of Romania. The conditions imposed by the Germans for a separate peace were harsh. As neither liberals nor conservatives were eager for the doubtful honour of signing it, King Ferdinand called on the popular war hero, General Averescu, to form a government in February. He signed the preliminaries, but resigned as the liberals opposed final peace. Once the Germans had occupied Ukraine, and thus completely surrounded what was left of free Romania, it was a new prime minister, the pro-German conservative Alexandru Marghiloman[6] (1854–1925), who signed the new Treaty of Bucharest in May. He had remained in Bucharest in the hope that he could soften the terms, but the Central powers wanted to punish Romania.

The Germans assumed control of the economy, and remained in occupation of over 70 per cent of the territory and population. Romania had to demobilize the bulk of her army, hand over equipment and give up Dobrudja and strategic Carpathian passes. In compensation for a German protectorate, she was allowed to increase her unoccupied territory to include the whole of

6 He also left his name to a Romanian culinary speciality, *café Marghiloman*, or Turkish coffee with brandy. One day when he was out shooting, he asked for coffee. There was no water – 'Well, use brandy!' he is alleged to have said.

pre-1812 Moldavia. Marghiloman prepared elections to confer legitimacy on his government. They were held under the old system. The liberals abstained, thus providing him with a majority which ratified the treaty. The king withheld his signature, which had no practical effect, but symbolized the widespread feeling of revulsion and passive resistance, manifested also by the government's refusal to rejoin the war on the side of the Central powers.

The Russian Revolution added to the difficulties caused in Bulgaria by the occupation of Serbian territory, and by exploitation of her economy for the Central powers' war effort. Instant Bulgarianization had been imposed on the occupied territories through schools and conscription, even in areas that had been Serbian since 1878, where people definitely did not feel Bulgarian and were on the edge of starvation.

In 1917, more and more men took to the hills to join the outlaws who had been in hiding since the beginning of the occupation, rather than face fathers and brothers in the Serbian army. Harsh measures of repression by the Bulgarian army affected its morale. There were frequent incidents of fraternization with Serbs and Russians. Pro-Russian feelings revived as the fall of the tsar led to hopes of a separate peace. The opposition parties denounced the extent of territorial occupation. Agrarian propaganda, which called for peace without annexations before it was too late, fed the soldiers' restlessness.

The German emperor came on a state visit in October to reassure Bulgaria, but Radoslavov had to give in to the opposition and recall the Assembly. He survived a stormy debate and a vote of censure by a slender majority, but with a much-diminished authority, through the winter and the worsening food situation, until the Treaty of Bucharest. That was the last straw, for Bulgaria did not even obtain the whole of Dobrudja, as the German military wanted to secure the Constanța–Danube railway. Radoslavov resigned in June.

That month, King Constantine had to go into exile. Allied troops helped Venizelos to assume power in Athens. Under Anglo-French pressure, the king, who did not formally abdicate, left with Crown Prince George, and was succeeded by his second son, Alexander (1893–1920). Now prime minister of a notionally united yet bitterly divided Greece, Venizelos recalled the June 1915 parliament, on the grounds that the following elections had been fraudulent. He proceeded with a wholesale purge of the deposed king's supporters and committed nine divisions to the Macedonian front.

Victorious, defeated, conquered, occupied or divided, all the Balkan states had been affected by Russia's withdrawal from the war, but not yet by the entry of the United States. Beyond resuscitating the Serbian army to advance the Macedonian front to Bitola, and enabling Venizelos to extend his hold over the whole of Greece, the Entente and its troops had not done much in Salonika. Through their direct occupation and military administration of enemy Serbia and Montenegro, as well of the larger part of Albania, through their occupation and economic control of a defeated and reluctantly neutral Romania, and through their exploitation of, and military presence in, an increasingly unwilling allied Bulgaria, the Central powers dominated most of the peninsula.

The First World War ended in the Balkans almost as suddenly as it had started. President Wilson's Fourteen Points at the beginning of 1918, followed by Foch's summer offensive on the western front, coming on top of food shortages, inflation and Bolshevik propaganda, stoked social discontent and nationalist demands in Austria-Hungary, but the first to crack was Bulgaria.

After the resignation of the Radoslavov cabinet, Malinov attempted a broad coalition. He even wanted to bring Stamboliiski out of prison into government, but the king would not accept the agrarian leader's condition of immediate withdrawal from the war. Malinov's somewhat tougher stand towards the Central powers secured the whole of Dobrudja, but could not make up for the weariness of the population. The final collapse was precipitated by the massive attack launched by the Allies from their Macedonian front in mid-September. The Bulgarian army disintegrated. Within a fortnight, the government agreed to an armistice (Salonika, 29 September) as the only way to defend itself from its own troops.

Stamboliiski, finally released, agreed to do all he could to restore order, if the king accepted an immediate peace and the release of all political detainees. Agrarian associates in Radomir, southwest of Sofia, tried to proclaim a republic with Stamboliiski as president; although he claimed not to be associated with the move, he went into hiding. Order had to be restored by German troops before the Allies demanded Ferdinand's abdication as a condition of peace. Realizing that they would both force his abdication and ruthlessly suppress any revolutionary move, he complied on 3 October and left, succeeded by his son, Boris III. All parties were brought together into government, including Stamboliiski.

The collapse of Bulgaria had consequences in Romania and Albania. It brought about Austria-Hungary's withdrawal from Albania; the end of the war found Italy in occupation of the greater part, the French around Korçë in the southeast and Shkodër in the northwest, and the Serbs on the left bank of the river Drin in the northeast. The Marghiloman government resigned in Romania; with the liberals' support, King Ferdinand appointed a cabinet of generals to prepare the army for a resumption of hostilities on the side of the Allies. On 10 November, as French and Serbian troops crossed the Danube, Romania considered herself to be at war with the Central powers, and the Germans began to withdraw. On 1 December the king returned to Bucharest to receive the French.

The Central powers were by then in fact out of the war: Turkey (Moudros, 30 October), Austria-Hungary (Villa Giusti, 3 November) and Germany (Rothondes, 11 November) had all signed armistice terms. Romanian troops nevertheless followed the retreating Germans across the Carpathians, contending with Hungarians for control of Transylvania.

Emperor Charles's Manifesto of 16 October for a reorganized Monarchy had come too late. It had not touched the integrity of the territories of the Hungarian crown, where most Romanians had behaved loyally under severe restrictions. The executive of the Romanian National Party had by then already declared the right of self-determination of the 'Romanian nation of Transylvania', and in Jassy the émigré Romanian National Committee had pronounced itself in favour of union with Romania.

Following the Czech example, national councils of nationalities were appearing all over the Dual Monarchy, as the administrative apparatus collapsed. The Romanian nationals, in agreement with the Romanian social democrats of Transylvania, went on to set up a Romanian National Council, which raised a national guard and gradually assumed control in all the Romanian-inhabited areas of the Hungarian lands. Negotiations with the new Hungarian government having broken down, it convened an ad hoc Grand National Assembly at Alba Julia (Guylafehévár). 852 elected representatives of existing constituencies, and another 376 representatives of churches, of professional, cultural, sports and student organizations, and of the national guard, gathered in late November, with crowds of over 100,000 peasants and workers with red banners.

On 1 December they overwhelmingly endorsed a resolution declaring 'the union of the Romanians living in Transylvania, Banat, Hungary, and their territories, with Romania'. The resolution also expressed the desire that the new united Romania be organized on liberal and democratic lines, with local autonomies, equal rights for all nationalities and religions, and that her final borders be drawn up by the peace conference. It set up a directorate under Maniu to govern until the union had been implemented, and sent Bishop Miron (Cristea, 1868–1939, future patriarch of Romania) to deliver the proposals to King Ferdinand in Bucharest. Ten days later, the Council of Bessarabia removed all its previous conditions for union.

In the meanwhile, the Romanian deputies to the Austrian parliament and to the diet of Bukovina had already met in late October with other prominent individuals, to state their intention to unite with Romania. The National Council which they set up came into conflict with a parallel Ukrainian National Council that had taken control of Ukrainian (Ruthenian)-inhabited districts and of the provincial capital Cernauţi (Czernowitz/Chernovtsy). It appealed to the Romanian government to send troops. They came swiftly, and the Romanian National Council organized a congress which voted for union on 28 November. With the return of Brătianu to office, an extraordinary session of the Romanian parliament in Bucharest endorsed all these motions on 11 January 1919.

At the beginning of 1918, the Allies were still inclined to preserve Austria-Hungary. The Fourteen Points were clear about the restoration of Serbia. They offered her an outlet to the sea, and promised the nationalities of the Dual Monarchy an autonomous development. Most of these had not been insubordinate so far, even when mobilized, with nothing like the French mutinies, let alone the wholesale Russian desertions of 1917. As they awaited the outcome of the Great War, it is difficult to gauge what were the common people's views of the future.

Austria-Hungary's refusal to face the facts and make concessions precipitated events, under the combined effects of Wilsonian and Bolshevik principles.
In February, the naval mutiny at Kotor (Cattaro) indicated a clear change of
heart among South Slav military personnel. More mutinies, anti-Habsburg and
anti-war demonstrations, and massive desertions followed. With the arrival of
prisoners from Russia, unwilling to return to the army, soldiers simply went
off and gathered in armed bands in woods and hills – generally referred to as
the 'green cadre'.

Opposition deputies from the Slovene areas, from Croatia, Dalmatia and
Bosnia-Herzegovina, met in Zagreb in March. They decided in principle to
set up a National Council to regroup all the South Slav parties of the Monarchy.
Yet the main parties of the majority governing coalition were still loath to
break with the formal structures, and there were disagreements over the
extent of unification. It was only when the Allied offensive into Macedonia
started liberating Serbia, when the defeat of Austria-Hungary became evident,
and when the rule of Vienna and Budapest crumbled, that unification presented itself as a fact that could no longer be delayed.

Spurred on by Korošec's Yugoslav Group of Slovenes, Istrians and Dalma-
tians, more vulnerable to Italian claims, the South Slav parliamentary deputies
of the various Habsburg entities gathered again in Zagreb in October. This
time they demanded the unification of all the Yugoslav lands into one independent state. They formally set up the National Council of Slovenes, Croats
and Serbs, under the Slovene Korošec as president, with a Croat and a Serb
vice-president.

Unification was then quickened by the breakdown of authority, Italy's insistence on redeeming the territories promised to her, and the equivocal attitude
of the Allies. Mandated by the National Council to go and see Emperor
Charles about a possible assumption of power, the ban of Croatia was told –
'Do as you wish'. On his return from Vienna, he summoned the Sabor which,
amid much popular pro-Yugoslav rejoicing, on 28 October broke off all links
with the Monarchy. It proclaimed the union of Croatia-Slavonia with Dalmatia
and all the other South Slav provinces into a sovereign state of the Slovenes,
Croats and Serbs on the whole territory inhabited by their nation, and handed
over power to the National Council, which formed a government.

A majority of the population was probably by then in favour of unification,
but the Yugoslav idea had not penetrated in depth, except perhaps in Dalmatia;
the Muslims, together with a vocal minority of republican Croats were clearly
opposed. The 'Slovene–Croat–Serb state' was in a critical situation. It had no
real frontiers, and it was not recognized except, paradoxically, by the moribund
Monarchy, which handed its fleet over to it. Since it envisaged unification
with Serbia and Montenegro, it established contacts with the Yugoslav Committee and the Serbian government.

The presidents of all three bodies were abroad – the Serbian prime minister
Pašić, Ante Trumbić (1864–1938) of the Yugoslav Committee, and Korošec.
After negotiations in Geneva early in November, Pašić undertook to recognize

the government of the Slovenes, Croats and Serbs of the ex-Monarchy and to support their cause with the Allies. It was agreed to keep both the Serbian National Assembly and the Sabor of Croatia-Slavonia until a Constituent Assembly had been elected, and to form a joint commission in Paris to ensure the transition.

The Geneva agreement represented a compromise, with a transitional dualistic arrangement, each side retaining authority over its territory, and was not implemented because of opposition from both parties. In Zagreb, some feared the weight of the Serbian partner, while others wanted Serbia to send troops to Zagreb. The National Council under its Serb vice-president Svetozar Pribićević (1875–1936) argued that it had given no such mandate to its delegation. With the regent's opposition, and a total lack of understanding for Croatia's historic rights, the Serbian government did not ratify the Geneva agreement. Pašić resigned as prime minister.

As chaos challenged the authority of the new Slovene–Croat–Serb government, unification 'happened' in a way that nobody had anticipated. There was no participation of the great powers, and no 'liberation' by the Serbian army. Territories simply detached themselves. Italy proceeded to implement the territorial provisions of the Treaty of London under cover of the armistice terms. These gave the Allies the right to penetrate into enemy territory to occupy military points and ensure order. The Slovene–Croat–Serb government failed to set up its own armed force, and had to call on the services of Serbian military personnel returning from captivity.

The new local authorities of peripheral lands, for whom unification was urgent, entered into direct negotiations with Belgrade. In Bosnia-Herzegovina, social explosion once again turned to ethnic clashes as Serb peasants took revenge on Muslims who had formed the bulk of the special battalions raised by the Austro-Hungarian authorities. The Sarajevo National Council felt it had no option but to call on Serbian soldiers. Although little more than a symbolic presence, they were a powerful symbol, and they also raced to get to Kotor and Dubrovnik before the Italians. They eventually turned up in parts of Bosnia-Herzegovina, Dalmatia, and southern Hungary, as Serb districts declared unilateral unification with Serbia. Even Zagreb had to ask for a Serbian military appearance.

Various delegations hurried to Belgrade, where the government was reorganizing itself; Pribićevic and the Serbian authorities, notably the military, made use of this situation to bring further pressure to bear on Zagreb. The Montenegrin Committee for National Unification, founded in exile in 1917 after the marginalization of King Nicholas, was virtually considered by the Serbian government as the legitimate representative of Montenegro. It organized elections for a Grand National Assembly to decide on her future status. On 28 November, the assembly, by a majority, deposed the Petrović dynasty and proclaimed unification with Serbia. Generally urban, more educated and young, that majority left the rest to nurse its wounded pride at the way in which Montenegro's rôle had been brushed aside.

On the same day the Zagreb National Council sent a delegation to Belgrade. The address read to the regent of Serbia on 1 December 1918 expressed an unconditional will for unification. It left the form of the united state to be decided by the Constituent Assembly, and made no specification regarding the nature of the majority that would decide. When, in his answer, Prince Alexander, in the presence of the Zagreb delegation and of members of the Serbian government, formally proclaimed the unification of Serbia and Montenegro with the lands of the Slovene–Croat–Serb State in one united Kingdom of the Serbs, Croats and Slovenes, he consecrated a process which had already taken place in a haphazard and messy way over the previous weeks.

In the final analysis, there was no alternative. The ideal expressed in 1914 had been achieved at the end of 1918 with the combination of Serbia's prestige and military contribution to the Allied cause, the political realism of the leaders of the Slovenes, Croats and Serbs within Austria-Hungary, and the Yugoslav idealism of those who had gone abroad to propagate the cause of unity and independence.

In the space of a few weeks, a united Romania and a united Yugoslavia had come into being, as a variety of local ad hoc councils and assemblies, under pressure of events, precipitated the unification of Bukovina, Transylvania and Bessarabia with Romania, and of Slovenia, Croatia-Slavonia, Dalmatia, Bosnia-Herzegovina, Vojvodina and Montenegro with Serbia. That pressure and the resultant haste also meant that the various sections had not had the time to work out clearly how union was to be implemented in practice. There were counterclaims and no fixed frontiers to the territories of these two apparently victorious partners of the Allies. Greece was yet to achieve her territorial aims at the expense of Turkey. Bulgaria, who had briefly managed to achieve all of hers and more on the wrong side, now lay prostrate. Albania was yet to be set up.

THE PEACE SETTLEMENTS

The aim of peace settlements since the Congress of Vienna had been to restore relations between great powers and to control changes to the existing international order. This time, as empires collapsed, as the United States came to Europe and withdrew, as France and Great Britain were left alone to enforce the settlement, it was clear that precedents could no longer be followed. To start with, the defeated states were excluded from deliberations; they were only invited to be presented with draft treaties prepared by the Allied and Associated powers.

The Peace Conference of 1919 did indeed establish a new international order in Europe. Often misnamed the 'Versailles settlement', after the treaty with Germany (28 June 1919) which initiated the series, it was in fact the Paris settlement, with other peace treaties signed in localities around the French capital city. The subsequent treaties were those that affected the Balkans more directly – the treaties of Saint-Germain-en-Laye with Austria (10 September 1919), of Neuilly-sur-Seine with Bulgaria (27 November 1919), of Trianon with Hungary (4 June 1920), and of Sèvres with the Ottoman Empire (10 August 1920).

The underlying principle of the settlement – self-determination – had been introduced by President Wilson. Ideally, it would serve as the basis for a new stability to take the place of the old principle of legitimacy, gradually eroded since 1815. Practically, it seemed the only alternative to force for resolving conflicting claims and promises. Britain and France had come to accept it, more through desperation and pressure than from deeply felt conviction. They too, like the Yugoslavs and Romanians, had made no plans to deal with the problems of dissolving empires and of unification across existing international borders.

Self-determination was not well defined. As a liberal American, whose country had, with France, invented the modern political nation, Wilson linked self-determination and popular sovereignty. He did not understand the way in which, driven by history, religion, language and ethnicity, 'nations' had been imagined before popular sovereignty had been achieved. Britain and France generally decided who should be self-determined and to what extent. In that they were constrained, and tainted, by other considerations. Everything was happening at the same time. Those who most rapidly seized their spoils in the collapsing empires were able to present their claims in terms of self-determination. The new entities had to be viable, and they had to conform to the remaining powers' perceptions of their own security and influence.

As it happened, it was to discuss the situation in the Balkans that the Supreme Allied Council had met in Paris in October 1918, when Germany's appeal to Wilson to negotiate peace on the basis of his Fourteen Points changed the agenda. The Peace Conference formally opened on 18 January 1919, and first drafted the Covenant of the League of Nations to be included in all the peace treaties. Real power was concentrated in the hands of the American president and the British and French prime ministers, to whom their Italian colleague was added out of courtesy.

Germany was invited at the end of April, and on 28 June, the anniversary of the Sarajevo assassination, the Treaty of Versailles was signed. The Four then went their separate ways, as the other defeated states were in turn summoned to receive and eventually sign their respective treaties. The Peace Conference formally ended on 21 January 1920; a conference of ambassadors in Paris and a peripatetic Supreme Allied Council would tie up loose ends.

Austria-Hungary, with whom the armistice had been signed, had in fact already dissolved. The historic Hungarian realm, too, was made to understand that it could not survive with its subject nationalities, as it went through revolution, counter-revolution and occupation in the course of 1919. Eventually signed in June 1920, the Treaty of Trianon left Hungary with a third of her prewar territory – the most bitter of the states that wanted to revise the peace settlements (the 'revisionist' states). The tables had been turned on her.

Whereas Magyars had formed under half of the population of her lands before the war, a third of them now found themselves outside Hungary.

The winner was Romania. In the spring of 1919, her troops had penetrated Hungarian territory proper to secure her claims. As the Hungarian communist dictatorship attacked them in a desperate attempt to save itself, the Romanians were soon in Budapest. Brătianu had arrived in Paris expecting to be accorded Bessarabia in addition to the promises of 1916. He was shocked to find that the western Allies considered themselves relieved of their commitments by Romania's capitulation of 1918. He rejected any compromise, was blamed for having precipitated the Hungarian chaos, left Paris in anger, quarrelled with the Allies over the minorities clauses in the Austrian treaty, and resigned in September. After general elections and with a new government, Romania resumed talks with the Allies, accepted the minorities settlement and evacuated Hungary. Over the autumn and winter, agreement was reached.

The Banat issue was the easiest, as it divided two otherwise friendly neighbours, but it was not until July 1920 that the boundary was drawn there between Romania and Yugoslavia. Trying to respect ethnic configuration as much as possible, it allowed Hungary to retain a northern strip and divided the rest between the two contenders. As the Allies first wanted Romania to sign the peace with Hungary, it was not until October 1920 that they recognized her sovereignty over Bessarabia, with a rider. Russia should adhere when she had a government with which they could do business, and any dispute should come to the League of Nations.

In the end, with the acquisition of Transylvania, the greater part of Banat and other Hungarian territory, of Bukovina, of southern Dobrudja and of Bessarabia, Romania more than doubled her prewar area (to 295,000 sq. km) and population (to over 16 million). Hungary, Bulgaria and Russia did not accept Romania's success as final. The Kingdom of the Serbs, Croats and Slovenes – or Yugoslavia ('South-Slavia') as it was commonly known – was altogether a different creation. Its very name symbolized self-determination. Whatever it was, it certainly was not the 'creation of the Treaty of Versailles' (which only mentioned it as a signatory). It had come into being before the Peace Conference; the French had played no part in its birth.

There had been little international support for the idea of a Yugoslav state. The United States had been the first to encourage it from the summer of 1918; they had been the first to recognize it in February 1919. Unlike Poland and Czechoslovakia, it had not been admitted as such to the conference, where it was formally represented only by Serbia. Italy insisted that the Yugoslavs of the former Dual Monarchy were enemies to be excluded from the conference.[7] When France, reluctantly and just after Great Britain, decided to recognize the

7 Its delegation did, however, call itself '*Délégation du Royaume des Serbes, Croates et Slovènes*' and included a Slovene former Austrian cabinet minister. It was this situation, quite apart from the Allies' ingrained habit, that made the Croat Trumbić, Yugoslavia's first foreign minister, instruct his *chef de cabinet*, a Serbian diplomat, not to insist on what Sir Eyre Crowe, the Foreign Office under-secretary, called 'an elephantine designation'.

new state, more than six months after its creation, it was because the Treaty of Versailles was ready. Since Serbia had been at war with Germany, the signature of the government in Belgrade was needed.

Of all the Balkan states, Yugoslavia presented the most complex set of problems. Its only fixed and undisputed frontier was with Greece, and she was in direct confrontation with one of the Big Four – Italy. The first of the Yugoslav issues to come before the conference had been the Banat in January 1919, and although it was also the easiest, it took almost a year and a half to solve.

The conflicting claims of Italy and Yugoslavia to the eastern Adriatic were examined in February. Negotiations gradually whittled down the area of dispute, but the port of Fiume (Rijeka) with its Italian majority was not tackled until April. The situation was then complicated by its seizure in September by the writer Gabriele D'Annuzio as an exercise in private enterprise. When the conference came to an end, the two parties were directed to settle on their own. This was achieved by the Treaty of Rapallo in November 1920, by which Italy obtained Istria, the port of Zara (Zadar) as an Italian-populated enclave in Yugoslav territory, and some islands. Fiume was to be an independent city-state, linked territorially to Italy, but its Slav suburb of Sušak went to Yugoslavia. Perhaps as many as half a million ethnic Yugoslavs found themselves in Italy, with no stipulated protection, unlike the ethnic Italians in Yugoslavia.

The fate of the mixed Austrian province of Carinthia was the first instance, and the only one in the Balkans, of the use of plebiscite to decide between rival claims. The issue was not seriously considered until the spring of 1919, by which time Yugoslav troops were pushing into the province. With no doubts as to the outcome, Slovene politicians proposed a plebiscite. The Conference approved. It divided the territory into a southern, predominantly Slovene zone, which would vote first, and a northern one, which would vote if the south went Yugoslav. Many inhabitants had mixed feelings. Held in October 1920, the plebiscite in the first zone decided in favour of Austria by a 59 per cent majority. Practical reasons had prevailed. There was no need for a vote in the other zone; Carinthia remained Austrian. After a few minor adjustments to the frontier with Bulgaria for strategic reasons, Yugoslavia emerged with 247,000 sq. km and 12 million inhabitants.

Defeated Bulgaria could only expect to lose territory. After King Ferdinand's abdication, elections in August 1919 returned a coalition led by the agrarians under Stamboliiski, which signed the peace treaty in November. Bulgaria was shorn of her acquisitions since 1912, which meant that she was isolated from the Aegean. Required to limit her armed forces and to pay reparations, she felt deeply resentful of the consolidation of her rivals around her, and did not regard the peace settlement as final.

Greece's aspirations obviously went beyond the Bulgarian portion of Thrace, towards the main ethnic Greek settlements left in the Ottoman Empire. Outside Constantinople, these were in the coastal regions of the Sea of Marmara and of the Aegean, in inland Cappadocia, and on the eastern Black Sea Pontic shore.[8] The Ottoman collapse in 1918 had been as sudden as that of Austria-Hungary. Turkey had been at war since 1911. The CUP and its wartime ambitions were finished. Sultan Mehmet V had died in July, and his successor Mehmet VI (1861–1926) formed a new cabinet to conclude an armistice. The government in Constantinople, in reaction against the Young Turks, saw no alternative but full cooperation with the victors. The Allies were free to operate throughout the country.

Their triumph was complete, yet it was the Turkish treaty that took longest to finalize. British and French occupied territories which they had assigned to themselves. Greeks and Italians claimed territory in Anatolia. Italy had been made specific promises. Venizelos, who only had vague promises, presented in February 1919 a formidable shopping list that included northern Epirus from Albania, western Thrace from Bulgaria, and from Turkey eastern Thrace, islands and territories on the Aegean coast of Asia Minor. His overriding objective was Smyrna (Izmir) and its hinterland. Smyrna had a substantial Greek population, although statistics did not agree on whether Greeks or Turks were the majority. For the sake of Smyrna, Venizelos had committed troops to the Allied intervention in southern Russia (where there were also ethnic Greeks). For it he was prepared to be flexible on other claims.

The relevant commission was divided. Angered over Fiume, the Italian prime minister left Paris at the end of April. Italian troops landed in several points in Turkey on the pretext of keeping order. By attempting to pre-empt the decision of the Peace Conference, Italy had prejudiced her position. Fearful of her ambitions in Asia Minor, the Allies gave their blessing to the Greek occupation of Smyrna in May, ostensibly to protect the local population.

Greeks and Italians soon had to resolve their differences, but the Greek landings were marked by atrocities against Turks. Despite ruthless punishment, the irreparable had been done. The intervention acted as a catalyst for Turkish nationalism. It fuelled resentment against the Greeks, against the Allies and against the government in Constantinople. The Salonika-born war hero, General Mustafa Kemal Pasha, the future Kemal Atatürk (1881–1938), sent to restore order among Ottoman forces, began to organize resistance, and, eventually, a viable nationalist movement beyond the reach of Allies and sultan.

At the turn of the year, Britain and France reached agreement on the shape of the settlement in the Near East. In April they incorporated their decisions into the draft peace treaty with Turkey. The Ottoman Empire was practically dismembered in favour of its Christian and Arab populations, and of the Allied powers. Greece would gain most of Thrace, and the islands of Imbros and Tenedos, and thus increase her territory to 151,833 sq. km with 5.5 million inhabitants – an increase in the Greek population of 2.9 million since 1913. She would occupy and administer the Smyrna region for five years, after which, if requested by a plebiscite under the League of Nations,

8 Great Britain had annexed Cyprus in 1914.

she could formally annex it. Venizelos was confident that immigration of Greeks from other regions of Asia Minor would ensure the vote.

The Allies had agreed to elections for a new Ottoman parliament. It met in January 1920 and voted to uphold the territorial integrity and the independence of the state. The Allies persuaded the sultan's government to dissolve it and arrest nationalist leaders. Having occupied Constantinople, they forced the Porte to sign the treaty. Never ratified, it galvanized Turkish opinion, and eventually enabled Turkey to impose her own conditions of peace on the victorious Allies.

The peacemakers knew that pure self-determination could not be achieved, that clear lines could not be drawn around nationalities short of moving them around and changing the geography, that disappointed nationalism could pose a threat to the new international order. They introduced plebiscite as a means of measuring popular feeling when no agreement was reached. They strove to provide protection for the individual rights of members of minority communities, in the hope that it would reconcile the population left on the wrong side of the border. This was an extension of the previous practice of the Treaty of Berlin for religious minorities. Treaties on the protection of minorities were included in the peace settlements, and also concluded with newly created or extended states; all those who subsequently wanted to join the League of Nations had to subscribe to similar undertakings. Thus all the Balkan states were covered, even though it was difficult to impose such protection. The revisionist states exploited the discontented; the new states resented the limitations on their sovereignty.

They had all fought for a long time, and the war had changed everything. They had all suffered much. They were divided between losers and winners. The winners had to cope with success, the losers with bitterness. Both would be exploited. And yet, there were three times as many people freed from alien rule as were now subjected to it,[9] and none of the Balkan states from that time on went to war against another until the great powers once again took advantage of their fragility for their own purposes, as they had done in 1914. For a peace settlement, and one essentially based on the new principle of self-determination, this, on balance, was a positive result.

9 Joseph Rothschild, *Return to Diversity: A Political History of East-Central Europe since World War II*, New York and Oxford: Oxford University Press, 1990, 3.

CHAPTER 11

The 1920s – Part 1: The losers

Exhausted losers and winners face the challenges of new territories, populations and electors. Albania the newcomer. Greece the loser in victory. Bulgaria the loser in defeat.

Ravaged and looted by enemies and allies, both losers and winners in the Balkans were exhausted by war – most of all the old kingdoms of Serbia and Romania. It was around them that the new kingdoms had united – that of the Serbs, Croats and Slovenes, and that of greater Romania. They were the clear winners, with all their aspirations realized. Greece had also come out of the First World War technically victorious at first, until she disastrously failed to achieve her great extra-Balkan dream. She felt no less bitter than Bulgaria, who, having tried to accomplish her ambitions on the side of the Central powers, had been truly defeated. As for Albania, to the extent that she had emerged independent from the discarded European ruins of the Ottoman Empire, she was a winner, but she was a loser insofar as she did not take in all the territory or population to which she aspired.

The whole Balkan peninsula was at last under native rule, but the settlement after a decade or more of warfare and suffering had caused the dislocation of over two million people. These were generally the uprooted kith and kin of the losers, and they came from different backgrounds. As if that were not enough, there was an influx of Russian refugees from the Revolution, bringing both advantages (cultural, professional and technical expertise) and disadvantages (unemployed civil war veterans). The winners had to integrate lands at different stages of development, with ethnic minorities and disrupted economies. All were obsessed by their identity, and equated number and space with strength and might, so that the winners had greater problems of corroded cohesiveness than the losers.

They faced the tremendous challenge of blending new territories, new populations and new electors. They tried to solve what was called the 'national question' by various methods. Treaties sanctioned compulsory and irreversible exchanges of population. There was also some encouragement of voluntary emigration from minority groups to countries of their choice willing to take them. The division of large estates, and more particularly the appropriation of alien estates, favoured landless peasants, war veterans and refugees from the dominant ethnic group. Along with implementation of agrarian reforms, assimilatory policies included the way in which minority rights were, or were not, enforced. All Balkan states resented these as a hypocritical imposition by powers who did not understand local situations and who were not themselves bound by similar rules.

The French-inspired centralized state was kept, even though the new lands and populations differed from the old and from one another. Both Romania and Yugoslavia pushed through updated versions of prewar constitutions, and relied on existing institutions and practices. The political structures generally survived, even if Greece made a scapegoat of her monarchy.

There were reactions against that western model. Other idealized directions were envisaged for future development – traditionalist, peasantist, communist. Communists successfully expressed discontent in the immediate aftermath of war and peace. They had absolute faith in a bolshevik solution to all the problems of the Balkans. In their fear of a western-dominated international conspiracy, the new leaders in Moscow rejected the order established by the peace treaties. In the Balkans, their calls for revolution, secession, division, a communist federation, re-accession to Russia, were not popular. Communists were weakened by their reliance on Russia and by their refusal to cooperate with other parties. Their attempt to enlist rural support was not very successful, and even their appeal to the small industrial proletariat was limited.

Governments nevertheless adopted anti-subversive legislation, aimed principally at the communists; some thought, but no more, was given to a common anti-communist front in 1924. They sought security first and foremost in a foreign policy framework to guarantee the newly acquired status quo. They all implicitly rejected further territorial change, at least in the short term, either because they were satisfied, or because it had brought them disaster, or because they first wanted to consolidate what had been obtained.

The foreign policy of Romania and Yugoslavia was directed to making secure what they had gained. In that they were dependent on the external guarantors of the treaties – the League of Nations, as their immediate underwriter, and France, as the one power who stood firmly by the status quo for its own reasons. Yet France did not initiate the setting up of the Little Entente. All Balkan governments were, in one way or another, anxious to settle relations with neighbours for the sake of stability, even when this did not endear them to parts of their electorate. The greatest of such achievements was Venizelos's reconciliation with Turkey.

At home, those in office searched for steady parliamentary majorities by changing electoral laws. Agrarian reform and peace facilitated the restoration of stability under moderate parties. Governments managed to govern and coped with problems, until authoritarian monarchs, with substantial support in the political class and in public opinion, thought that they could do better, and the Depression destroyed the precarious recovery and stability of the postwar decade.

THE NEWCOMER: ALBANIA

Although the powers had recognized Albania's independence in 1913, the First World War had enabled Serbian, Montenegrin, Greek, Italian, Austro-Hungarian and French troops to occupy parts of her territory for stretches of time. Italy had declared a protectorate over the whole of Albania in 1917, but backed down in 1920 in order to concentrate on her claims further north on the eastern Adriatic. Albania was then admitted to the League of Nations.

Her territory was still in a state of anarchy. Esat claimed to be president and dreamt of being king. Italy had backed a national congress in Durrës in December 1919, which had produced one provisional government. A group of leaders opposed to Italian patronage held a counter-congress at Lushnjë in January 1920 which set up a four-man Regency Council – one from each of the four religious communities (Bektashi and Sunni Muslims, Orthodox and Catholic Christians) – and produced another government. Its strong man and interior minister was the twenty-six-year-old Zogolli, who had returned to Albania, and whose Mati tribesmen had provided protection for the Lushnjë meeting. That government immediately moved to Tirana, close to Zogolli's tribal territory, and encouraged attacks on Italian troops. Its authority gradually extended as foreign troops left.

The Durrës government dissolved itself. Esat was the only Albanian leader to have caught the attention of the Allied public. He was conveniently gunned down by an Albanian opponent outside the Hôtel Continental in Paris in June.[1] The Italian withdrawal enabled Albanians to congratulate themselves on having defeated a European power, and strengthened Zogolli. International recognition followed. The question of Greek and Yugoslav territorial claims was deferred to the Conference of Ambassadors. In November 1921, the conference generally reaffirmed the boundaries of 1913. It also acknowledged Rome's paramount interest by recommending that Italy be entrusted with defending Albania's integrity and independence should they be violated.

With the immediate foreign threat gone, the next few years saw a confused struggle for power between the landowning beys, the clan leaders and the educated members of a tiny urban middle class. Albanian Ottoman administrators and soldiers who had returned to their native land were the only people with any concept of government, and the number of rifles counted more than the number of votes to get into the parliament set up at Lushnjë.

---

1 He is buried in the Serbian military cemetery at Thiais, south of Paris, and the Yugoslav government thereafter paid a pension to his widow in Istanbul. Exiled in London during the Second World War, it still honoured that commitment with a monthly pension of nineteen pounds and five shillings.

The first elected parliament was convened in April 1921. The rich land-owner Shefqet Vërlaci (1880–1946) led the conservatives. Although they called themselves the Progressive Party, they broadly wanted to keep existing Otto-man legislation and have no land reform. Reformists rallied to Zogolli and Fan Noli (1882–1965). The latter was a Greek-educated Albanian cleric from Thrace, who had worked in Athens and Egypt before going to the USA, where he had set up a separate Albanian Orthodox organization in Boston in 1908. He had come to Albania for the first time in 1920 as delegate of the American Albanians to the Lushnjë congress, and his more western ideas appealed to the southern bourgeoisie. Zogolli was an authoritarian who wanted to set up a more efficient centralized state machinery. He usually managed to be home and/or war minister by siding with and manoeuvring between different groups.

Albania was the only European state with a Muslim majority: 67–70 per cent, with 20–21 per cent Orthodox and 10–12 per cent Catholics is a safe approximation in the absence of reliable statistics. Although there was little serious religious tension, the northern Catholics of the Mirdite tribe remained aloof. In the summer of 1921 they attempted to set up a separate republic, with the help of one-time Esat followers and veterans from General Wrangel's defeated 'white' Russian army, and with Yugoslav support. Zogolli's success-ful dealing with the revolt through a combination of military action, propa-ganda and amnesty, further increased his standing.

He acted through weakened governments dominated by landowners, con-spiring behind the scenes with northern clan chieftains and southern urban 'intellectuals'. He believed that Albania should first establish herself as a state before pursuing irredentist aims. When he moved to launch a selective dis-armament campaign, a coup in February 1922, supported by a force of irredent-ists, left him virtually alone in government in Tirana. He managed not only to survive, but to turn the tables on his opponents, thereby adding to his prestige.

Back in control in December, he obtained the resignation of the discredited regents and the appointment of new ones, who gathered a rump parliament to revise the Lushnjë statute. Taking on the premiership, he changed his sur-name to Zogu (Zogolli being judged too Turkish in form). He had by then parted from his one-time more reformist associates gathered around Noli, and as a token of his alliance with the conservatives become engaged to the daugh-ter of their leader Vërlaci.

For the first time, the government was obeyed almost everywhere. By September 1923 Zogu felt strong enough to dissolve what was left of parlia-ment and organize elections for a Constituent Assembly. He failed to secure a safe enough majority for the sort of state that he wanted to set up. Dissatis-faction at his methods grew. An organized opposition was formed in parlia-ment around Noli; there was an assassination attempt in February 1924. Zogu had to resign as prime minister and to operate under cover of his prospective father-in-law.

The situation deteriorated rapidly, as famine came on top of demands from irredentists and demands for promised land reform. When one of his lieutenants was assassinated in May, Noli withdrew from the Constituent Assembly with his supporters. Revolts flared up, military units defected to the opposition, the government and the regency dissolved in June. Left alone once again, Zogu was unable to repeat his feat of 1922 and was forced to retire across the border to Yugoslavia. Noli entered Tirana to form a new government.

The country was not yet a united one; few saw themselves first and foremost as Albanians. Religious and linguistic divisions were lesser obstacles than geography and underdevelopment. Albania is almost cut off from the rest of the Balkans by mountains. Nearly 80 per cent of the country is above 200 metres, with an average height of 708 metres, and the highest peaks at 2,500 metres. There were highland clans in the north, 'feudal' landowners in the central and southern lowlands, and a more educated and urbanized but unarmed population in the Catholic and Hellenized fringes. Religious and social divisions did not coincide. Catholic and Muslim mountaineers lived in the same tribal structures. Muslim and Orthodox lowlanders worked the old sharecropping system under the landowning families that had run the administration in Ottoman times. Ninety per cent of the population was illiterate.

Zogu's accomplishments thus far had been rather meagre – some attempts at a uniform educational system, dispensing with Ottoman titles (pasha, bey) and disarming part of the population. There were no budgetary resources, finances were a shambles, corruption was massive. Power belonged eventually to whoever could muster the superior force, and it was difficult to convince powers and neighbours that the Albanian state could survive.

Noli had seized power with Italian backing, at the head of a motley coalition formed to destroy Zogu, but his only real support in the country came from the petite bourgeoisie. He announced an ambitious programme – to establish democracy, uproot feudalism, ensure the economic independence of the peasantry, disarm the population, balance the budget, organize education and healthcare, encourage foreign capital. Naïve and inexperienced, he pleaded for an international loan under the auspices of the League of Nations, while accusing the organization of being an instrument of the great powers.

His failure to obtain a loan made the situation worse. He frightened the landowners and disappointed the peasants. He annulled the elections of 1923, did not call new ones and pursued his opponents. Forced to abandon irredentism, he lost the support of nationalists but did not gain international acceptance. Belgrade was not willing to recognize him because of his support for Kosovo irredentism, and because it believed he was a tool of the Italians. Rome was no more willing to recognize his government. Italy had just come to an agreement with Yugoslavia, and Mussolini had yet to entrench his power at home. Noli considered recognizing the Soviet régime. He thus frightened everyone, and was embarrassed when a Soviet delegation actually arrived at the end of 1924. By that time, he had alarmed so many people that he had lost most of his support.

Zogu in exile had acted as self-appointed representative of the last 'legitimate' government. He was welcomed by Belgrade, who hoped to extend its influence in Albania by helping him, at a time when Mussolini was crippled by internal problems. Zogu made promises to the Yugoslavs, to the Italians, and to the Anglo-Persian Oil Company. He recruited an armed force of Albanian supporters and unemployed soldiers from General Wrangel's army, with Yugoslav financial and military assistance. In December 1924, he crossed into Albania. Noli's government fled to Italy; its soldiers deserted. When he entered Tirana, Zogu took all powers under martial law until constitutional government could be restored. The last pre-Noli government then briefly resumed office before a rump regency asked Zogu to become prime minister. He reconvened what was left of the 1923 Constituent Assembly for more changes to the Lushnjë statute.

On 21 January 1925, Albania became a republic, with an indirectly elected bicameral legislature. Zogu was elected president with extensive powers for a seven-year term. Tirana was confirmed as the capital, although with its 14,000 inhabitants it looked and felt far less of a 'capital' than rival 22,000-strong Shkodër. Those of Zogu's opponents who had not fled abroad were hunted down, sent into exile, persecuted or silenced through fear. In order to make use of the conservative landowners' government experience, he allowed them to retain their estates, but made them give up their political ambitions under the threat of agrarian reform. Most of the tribal chieftains were also won back with honours, money, guns and an amnesty.

Zogu believed he now had a political structure he could control and modernize. He realized that Albania, in order to survive economically, had to turn to a foreign power for aid. The Kosovo issue separated Albania from Yugoslavia, who was anyhow not strong enough. Italy was the only power willing to extend aid with little chance of real economic benefit. She had no land frontier with Albania, and had in the past supported her territorial integrity and independence. What foreign trade Albania's totally pre-modern economy had was with Italy, who took 59 per cent of exports (mainly lamb and goat skins) and provided 75 per cent of imports. There was a large Albanian settlement in Italy. Turning to her would be less unpopular than turning to Yugoslavia.

Zogu reassured the Italian government, and used his talks with British financial groups to drive as hard a bargain as possible with Rome. Agreements in May 1925 set up a National Bank of Albania, which came under Italian control as Albania was unable to subscribe her intended share of capital. Substantial Italian loans, guaranteed by the revenues of Albanian customs and state monopolies, were granted for public works, and channelled through a Company for the Economic Development of Albania. And so Albania turned out paradoxically to be the only Balkan state in the 1920s to be able to attract the sort of foreign funding that enabled a government not to worry about large budget deficits and the growing issue of bank notes.

In aiding Zogu, the Yugoslav government had expected to be repaid in influence. In fact, he did no more than finalize the border settlement in July 1925 by ceding a disputed monastery on Lake Ohrid. As his economic agreement with Rome further alienated Belgrade, he felt in need of Italian protection.

In August, a secret exchange of letters linked Albania to Italy in a military alliance in case of war with a Balkan state. The exchange would remain secret until both parties agreed to its publication. Zogu had obtained a guarantee against possible Yugoslav military intervention. He considered that the threat of publication was sufficient to prevent any thought of a partition deal between Italy and Yugoslavia.

Actually both Rome and Belgrade intrigued with Zogu's opponents, thus contributing to continued unrest. Another revolt in 1926 among northern Catholic tribesmen, although quickly crushed, drove Zogu closer to Italy. Mussolini had become more demanding. He wanted Zogu to endorse officially the recommendation of the 1921 Conference of Ambassadors, to entrust Italy with the defence of Albania's independence and integrity. Zogu stalled, tried to secure his position with Belgrade and London, but finding himself diplomatically isolated, was forced to give away more than he had intended.

A five-year Pact of Friendship and Security (the first Pact of Tirana) was signed in November 1926. Any threat to the status quo in Albania would be considered contrary to the joint interests of both parties, who would cooperate in their protection. They bound themselves not to conclude with any third party an agreement that would be contrary to these interests. With this extended formalization of the existing secret agreement, Zogu signed away what diplomatic independence he had. Mussolini had essentially obtained his endorsement of Italy's rights under the 1921 recommendations.

The first pact caused more tension with Yugoslavia, a cabinet crisis in Belgrade, and deteriorating relations between Rome and Belgrade over the summer of 1927. Zogu thus had to move even closer to Italy. Realizing that her foreign policy in the Balkans was now reduced to Albania, Italy adopted a softer approach. Zogu wanted more security against his opponents, more assistance for his increasing military establishment, and his elevation to a higher status. Mussolini wanted an extension of the first pact, increased control of Albania's military, and a naval base.

The second Pact of Tirana in November 1927 turned the first one into a twenty-year defence treaty. Through appended secret letters Italy did away with what remained of Albania's military independence. She then proceeded to finance, equip and instruct the Albanian army, which soon came under effective Italian control. Zogu nevertheless tried to keep the civil service, the police and the gendarmerie within his own prerogative. The gendarmerie, which he had nurtured right from the beginning, was placed under retired British officers paid for by the Albanian government. Italian firms were granted concessions to exploit mineral resources, to modernize agriculture and to build schools, roads, bridges and port facilities.

Zogu postponed interest payments on loans by way of bringing some pressure to bear on Italy, because he needed assurances concerning the activities of émigrés. Refugees scattered around Europe could always rely on financial support from some government. He saw plots everywhere, and turned against his prospective father-in-law Vërlaci, as he withdrew from the arranged marriage. He also wanted support for his elevation to kingship and, if possible, the hand of an Italian royal princess.

The elevation to the throne had been the subject of talks as early as 1926. Mussolini promised he would not support émigrés, and granted a moratorium on interest payments. Once the pacts had been signed, he gave his support for the monarchy, but could not go as far as a princess of the house of Savoy. Zogu then sounded out other governments, who were at best benevolently indifferent to what title he adopted.

He took pains to ensure an elevation that was constitutionally correct. Since parliament was not empowered to initiate changes to the constitution, it passed a law providing for its own dissolution, and the election of a special Constituent Assembly to revise it. The outcome needed expenditure, financed by an Italian loan. More money was spent on demonstrations and petitions to the Constituent asking for Zogu to be made king. In September 1928 he was duly proclaimed 'king of the Albanians' – with another change of name. He was to be King Zog (the indefinite form of the name). In December, a new constitution set up a one-chamber parliament, and gave even greater powers to the monarch.

Albania, the poorest and latest addition to the company of independent states in the Balkans, had escaped the ambitions of her neighbours. She had set herself up under an autocratic would-be modernizing monarch whose ambition was to bring her into Europe. Esat Pasha Toptani had tried and failed in his bid to be such a monarch with Entente support; it was Ahmet Bey Zogolli who successfully managed to set Albania up as a nation-state and to lead her. He kept irredentists at arm's length, so as to concentrate on first setting up a state within recognized borders. He was anxious to maintain a thread of legitimacy, however tenuous, from the congress of Lushnjë. He manoeuvred between power groups within the country, and between foreign powers interested in extending their influence over Albania. By the time that he was 'king of the Albanians', not only did his kingdom not encompass all ethnic Albanians, but it had become a client state. Albania had not really taken part in the First World War, and she was a loser.

THE LOSER IN VICTORY: GREECE

Greece had emerged from the First World War as an Allied power; her Great Idea had almost come true, as Greek troops camped around Constantinople and controlled the coast of Asia Minor. Bulgaria was the only truly defeated state in the Balkans. Both, however, were losers.

For Greece, collapse followed on triumph. With the signature of the Treaty of Sèvres, Venizelos's supporters had hailed the emergence of Greece 'of the two continents and the five seas' (Europe and Asia; Ionian, Aegean, Mediterranean, Marmara and Black Sea). Two months later, King Alexander was bitten by a pet monkey and died of blood poisoning. Elections were due. Venizelos, who had just returned from the Paris Conference, expected a victory. The monarch's unexpected death posed the question of the succession.

Constantine had not abdicated; his eldest son George had not renounced his rights; his third son Paul refused the throne. The election of 1920 turned into a contest between Venizelos and the exiled king: 53 per cent of the votes, and two-thirds of the seats, went to the royalist People's Party. Venizelos resigned and left the country.

War weariness, Anglo-French interference in Greek affairs and the Venizelists' vindictive behaviour had been exploited by royalist propaganda. A dubious plebiscite, organized by the populist government, approved Constantine's restoration by a huge majority. Royalists in their turn took revenge on Venizelists. Meanwhile, with most of the Ottoman parliamentary deputies gathered in Ankara, a National Government had been set up under Kemal which had repudiated the Treaty of Sèvres. The French and Italians, resenting what they increasingly felt to be a British settlement, used King Constantine's return as a pretext to come to terms with the new Turkey.

The royalists forgot that they had criticized the prolongation of the war. When talks in London at the beginning of 1921 failed to reconcile the demands of Greeks and of rival Turks, the Greek army began to widen its sphere of control in Anatolia; the Allies declared their neutrality. Refusing further British mediation, the Greeks mounted an offensive. Dangerously extended 500 km into Anatolia, their advance halted. The French and the Italians withdrew, effectively leaving the British and the Greeks to defend the sultan's government and the Sèvres settlement.

In August 1922, the Turks launched a counteroffensive which routed and drove out the Greek forces. Turkish troops moved into Smyrna (Izmir); tens of thousands of Greeks and Armenians were massacred; the Orthodox archbishop was killed by a mob just like the patriarch in Constantinople a century earlier; fire destroyed the Greek, Armenian and European quarters. The remnants of the Greek army with panic-stricken civilians arrived on the Greek islands and mainland. Having secured Anatolia, the Kemalists continued towards Thrace, until the French brokered the armistice of Mudanya (11 October). The Allies evacuated Constantinople, the sultanate was abolished, and the Turkish republic proclaimed in the new capital, Ankara.

A group of Venizelist officers under Colonel (later General) Nikolaos Plastiras (1883–1953) seized power in Athens and made King Constantine a scapegoat. He formally abdicated in favour of his eldest son, George II (1890–1947). Vengeance was also taken on leading political and military figures deemed responsible for the débâcle. A judicial charade led to six executions.[2]

A new peace conference was convened at Lausanne in November. There seemed to be no alternative to the uprooting or compulsory 'exchange of populations'. The new peace treaty, which replaced Sèvres, was signed in July 1923. The exchange was agreed on the old Ottoman basis of religion. Turkish-speaking Orthodox Christians had to abandon Asia Minor; Muslim Albanians

---

2 Prince Andrew (1882–1944), a brother of Constantine's and father of Prince Philip, the future Duke of Edinburgh, had commanded an army corps. He was stripped of his rank and banished. King Constantine died in Palermo four months after his abdication.

left Greek Epirus and Macedonia; Greek-speaking Muslims left Crete. Paradoxically, whereas there was no longer any cause for the latter's departure, the Turks of Greek Thrace were among the exceptions allowed to stay. The others were the Greeks of Istanbul[3] and of the two small islands of Imbros (Imroz) and Tenedos (Bozcaada) which reverted to Turkey. That left about 100,000 Muslims in Greece and the same number of Orthodox in Turkey.[4] Greece kept what she had obtained in eastern Thrace and a few isles. There were no reparations either way.

At the end of a decade of wars and upheavals, Greek society was subjected to the sudden influx of an enormous mass of refugees. In addition to a million or more from Asia Minor, there were the Greeks of southern Russia fleeing the Revolution, and those of Bulgaria coming under a voluntary exchange – some 1.3 million to be integrated into a pre-1914 population of 4.3 million. Many were widows and orphans. Many could not speak the language – those who knew only Turkish, or dialect, or the purified literary Greek they had been taught in their schools. Many who came from Ottoman cities looked down on the 'provincialism' of Greece. They encountered much prejudice. Most were resettled in rural areas, particularly in Macedonia and Thrace, but some 400,000 stayed in shanties around Athens-Piraeus.

Although technically victorious at the end of the First World War, Greece was gripped by a sensation of defeat which caused deep divisions. The bitterness was compounded by the feeling of having been abandoned in her time of greatest need by her traditional friends. After an abortive counter-coup by the royalist General Ioannis Metaxas (1871–1941), which merely reinforced republican feelings, the government called an assembly to revise the constitution. The elections of December 1923 were boycotted by the populists; 250 liberals were elected and 120 republicans. A Venizelist regent took over from King George, who went abroad 'on leave'; Venizelos became prime minister again. He would have preferred to keep the monarchy; when he realized that the Assembly would vote against it, he resigned and returned to Paris. The deputies overwhelmingly voted to set up a republic, ratified by plebiscite in April 1924 with a two-thirds majority.

Large tracts of territory had been acquired only recently. The massive incorporation of newcomers into what had been a rather closed system posed a great challenge to institutions. The structure of the officer corps had been altered through recruitment to meet war demands, followed by contraction dictated by

---

3 The ecumenical patriarch remained in what was now (except in his title) definitely called Istanbul. It was under the transitional 1922–24 incumbency of Patriarch Meletios III that the Gregorian calendar was adopted in the Greek Church. That was part of his striving for a general *aggiornamento* to take into account the end of the Ottoman Empire and of imperial Russia, as well as the new national states of the Balkans. He attempted to hold a pan-Orthodox Council for a reunification of Eastern Orthodoxy, and more generally ecumenical links with other Christians.
4 To quote from Turgut Özal's interesting plea for 'Turkey in Europe' (*La Turquie en Europe*, 1988), that was the end of the process during which 'the Christians gained the Balkans but lost Anatolia' (revised English edition, *Turkey in Europe and Europe in Turkey*, Nicosia, northern Cyprus: K. Rustem & Brother, 1991, 210).

politics. Political participation was broadened and pluralized. The majority of refugees were Venizelists, who explained the failure of their admired leader's vision by the treachery of reactionaries and the machinations of powers. They blamed the monarchy, and some were attracted by the newly founded Communist Party. The appeal of communism would have been greater but for the stand of the Communist International (Comintern) for a separate Macedonia.

The tension of integrating territory had already contributed significantly to the National Schism. It was exacerbated in the 1920s by the refugees, 700,000–800,000 of whom were settled in Greek Macedonia, whose demography they altered, especially with the departure of some 400,000 Turks, Albanians and Bulgars.

The practical problems were relatively efficiently overseen, but refugees still caused a glut on the labour market, many were left on the fringes of large towns and inspired with radical politics. Greece kept a number of small minorities, Turks, Vlachs, Albanians and Macedonian Slavs.[5] With the closure of Bulgar and Serb schools, and the resettlement of refugees, the Slavophones tended to vote against the liberals. The ethnic composition of the new territories was altered, with Greeks now in a clear majority. The prewar political balance was also upset. A republican constitution had been adopted, but for over a year in 1925–26, the country fell under the dictatorship of General Theodoros Pangalos (1878–1952). It was only after his overthrow, followed by elections with proportional representation and the formation of an all-party government, that the constitution was at last applied. Venizelos returned once again in July 1928; he formed his final administration that would last until 1933.

Prime minister off and on since 1910, he had been a force for modernization. Now at sixty-four, he used his skill in domestic politics to stay in power, by changing yet again the electoral system to the advantage of his own liberal majority, and by acquiring legislative weapons to repress subversion. Internal stability became his principal concern. Elections under a majority system turned a 47 per cent vote into a 71 per cent parliamentary majority. A law against attempts to undermine the social order, aimed at the small number of communists, would be widely used by later governments.

Venizelos's talents as a statesman were turned against nationalism, to settling relations with neighbours. The bombastic Pangalos had threatened renewed war against Turkey; he had occupied an area of southwestern Bulgaria for a few days in October 1925 after a border incident with Bulgarian Macedonian extremists that had cost the lives of two Greek officers. Relations with Italy were not much better. She had reneged on the undertaking to cede the Dodecanese. Mussolini, recently installed, had issued a truculent ultimatum to Greece followed by a bombardment of Corfu in 1923, after an incident on the Greek–Albanian border that had killed an Italian general on an Allied mission.

---

5 Some 82,000 of them, according to the 1928 census. There remained over half a million ethnic Greeks in Turkey, Albania, the Italian Dodecanese and British Cyprus (almost half of them).

Even with Yugoslavia, relations were not ideal. Greece had not come to Serbia's help in 1914, and the Serbian army had been placed on Greek territory with the Armée d'Orient. The settlement of a range of issues, from the final fixing of the border to the use of port facilities on the Aegean, had been constantly put off.

Venizelos tried to solve all these problems through bilateral agreements, as he started on the path that would lead to the Balkan Pact of 1934. The Yugoslav issues were settled by the Pact of Friendship, Conciliation and Arbitration of March 1929, after which his greatest diplomatic achievement was reconciliation with Turkey. This was sealed by the October 1930 Convention of Ankara, during his official visit to Turkey, when he also called on the ecumenical patriarch. As an alternative to the lost Great Idea, he entertained a more realistic but no less ambitious programme of internal reconstruction, and of a leading rôle for Greece in the Balkan area – including Turkey – through economic and intellectual pre-eminence.

Promises of land reform, made during the First World War under pressure from the peasantry of the new territories, were gradually implemented. A slow start with the redistribution to landless peasants of land held by major absentee landlords, was accelerated with the influx of refugees, when all holdings over thirty hectares were taken. The 600,000 hectares eventually redistributed represented over 40 per cent of agricultural land (the highest proportion in the Balkans), four-fifths of which went to refugees. In addition, the state set up in 1928 an Agricultural Bank for better credit to peasants.

Towns already accounted for 24 per cent of the population before the war – the highest percentage in the Balkans. The refugees increased it to 42 per cent by the end of the 1920s (with the Athens-Piraeus conurbation numbering 704,000, and Salonika 237,000). Manufacture was boosted by fresh entrepreneur and labour input from the refugees, and by a move of diaspora capital away from banking. The number of industrial establishments rose from 762 (with 24,300 workers) in 1917 to 4,000 (with 110,000 workers) in 1929.

Aided by state purchases, the real value of textile production tripled between 1923 and 1930. With over 20 per cent of overall industrial output, textiles became the largest single industry. The Refugee Resettlement Commission provided long-term loans, and legislation ended restrictions to joint-stock incorporation. Concentration continued in the Athens-Piraeus area, as most of the new firms incorporated were there, with about half of all large-scale industrial labour. Diaspora capital, also attracted by the area's favourable situation for foreign trade, was responsible for an extraordinary development of Greek merchant shipping. Its steamship carrying capacity, which had been reduced by war losses from 894,000 tonnes in 1915 to 291,000 by 1918, reached 1.3 million in 1928.[6]

---

6 By way of comparison, Yugoslavia's steamship carrying capacity – the second in the Balkans – was 46,000 tonnes.

THE LOSER IN DEFEAT: BULGARIA

As a result of defeat, Bulgaria, like Greece, lost its king, but managed to retain its political system, in spite of much tension, radicalism and violence. Because the régime that had brought about defeat had been so much King Ferdinand's own, it was he and his associates who were held responsible rather than the system. The Tŭrnovo constitution survived, and so did the dynasty, albeit with a new, young and inexperienced monarch.[7]

In the general elections of August 1919, the contenders were the parties of the left, reflecting the discontent of the electorate with the conduct of the war. Bulgaria, with the weakest industrial base, had the oldest and strongest socialist movement in the Balkans, but it was split, and its left-wing faction had just become the Bulgarian Communist Party. The Agrarian Union came up top, with 31 per cent of the vote and 85 seats: Stamboliiski was asked to form a government. The communists (18 per cent), spoiling for a revolution, refused to cooperate. With the social democrats equally unresponsive, Stamboliiski had to incorporate some 'established' elements into his cabinet.

To show that the old régime had been discarded, former ministers and prominent Macedonians were arrested, while a civilian was appointed to the war ministry. Like all Balkan leaders, Stamboliiski had spent much time at the Peace Conference. He was trapped between the fear of displeasing the Allies, who still had troops in the country, and that of bringing back terms that would destroy his coalition. By the Treaty of Neuilly, Bulgaria relinquished the Thracian coastline acquired in the Balkan Wars,[8] but was promised economic access to the Aegean. Her army was reduced, and a great burden of reparations imposed – in kind and in gold francs. As Stamboliiski hoped, the financial terms were eventually relaxed.

For the time being, however, there was great resentment. The Communist Party made the most of accumulated dissatisfaction. It called a general strike with demonstrations in Sofia in December, at the request of Russia's bolshevik leadership, which rejected the 'Versailles settlement' and expected a revolutionary upheaval. Stamboliiski declared martial law and opposed the strike with all the means that he could muster. He made the army run the railways; he organized his own party's Orange Guard of peasants to break up demonstrations. The communists had overestimated the revolutionary potential of the situation; the strike collapsed.

Stamboliiski had the Assembly dissolved, and went to the polls again in March 1920. Although his agrarians increased their share of the vote to 39 per cent, they fell short of an absolute majority in the 229-strong parliament. The communists had also increased their share to over 20 per cent and 51 seats. The social democrats were down to seven seats, and the remainder went

7 Even though Boris III, unlike King Constantine, took up the numerical link with medieval rulers.
8 It is difficult to establish just how many Bulgars were left outside Bulgaria. The figure of one million often mentioned in Bulgarian sources probably includes most, if not all, Macedonian Slavs.

to the old parties. By disqualifying thirteen deputies on technical grounds, Stamboliiski obtained the necessary majority for an agrarian government. He had only been able to do so by mobilizing the peasantry, and by resorting to practices that he had earlier denounced.

Bulgaria had lost the war; she was regarded with mistrust by her neighbours; she faced internal threats. Stamboliiski tried to provide a new sense of purpose by pursuing reforms at home and reconciliation with neighbours. The agrarians were driven by their vision of an egalitarian society, which vested the ownership of means of production in those who worked them, eventually through an all-embracing cooperative movement.

Although not much remained to be done for an equitable distribution of land ownership, legislation created a fund of land confiscated from owners who held more than was 'socially acceptable'. That was a maximum of thirty hectares for those who personally worked it, with an extra allowance for families of more than four. 330,000 hectares were eventually squeezed out (6 per cent of agricultural land – the smallest redistribution in the Balkans), mainly from state, local authority and monastic holdings, for 64,000 indigenous Bulgarians and 28,500 refugees. There were also measures to encourage the consolidation of land strips, to strengthen cooperatives, and to improve credit, welfare and educational facilities in the countryside.

'Socially acceptable' norms were also applied to urban property (two rooms and a kitchen per family, with extra rooms for larger families). The most startling innovation was the compulsory labour service introduced for all young men and unmarried women, run on military lines, to replace military service, to absorb excess labour and impart a social commitment to the young. Steps were taken to reduce the public rôle of disliked categories, such as lawyers and merchants. Education was perhaps the greatest achievement of the agrarians. Placing the emphasis on the rural, the elementary and the practical, they built schools, increased the vocational content of curricula, cleansed them of jingoism, and set up new technical high schools and faculties.

They were nevertheless restricted by the Allies' supervisory rôle, by the chaotic conditions bequeathed by the war, and by political constraints. By 1920, the population was over 83 per cent Bulgarian-speaking and Orthodox. The largest minority (just over 11 per cent) was made up of the remaining 534,000 Turks, who were entitled to their own schools. Turks, Greeks and Romanians continued to leave.[9] Perhaps as many as 250,000 Bulgars had come in from surrounding areas. Most of them were in need of public support, and were sympathizers if not militant members of rival irredentist Macedonian organizations. There were also large numbers of Russian refugees, many of them remains of General Wrangel's army – the largest armed force in the land. The white Russians were not favourably disposed towards Stamboliiski, whom

9 240,000 Turks left for Turkey between 1912 and 1930, and another 100,000 thereafter to 1939. In 1920, only 47,000 of the Greeks were left who had been living in and around Plovdiv and on the Black Sea coast – fewer than the 62,000 Gypsies, and only slightly more than the 43,000 Jews.

they hardly distinguished from the bolsheviks. They had prewar links with Bulgarian personalities and were a dangerous presence.

The monarchy, the parliamentary opposition and its press also acted as constraints. The old parties, blamed for the sufferings and failures of the war, were largely reduced to the Sofia-based educated class and were not united. The two largest liberal factions had each retained 4–6 per cent of the votes, while the democrats, the most consistent critics of prewar governments, had managed about 10 per cent. During 1922, Stamboliiski felt secure enough to lift the emergency measures imposed at the end of 1919, and to tackle the potential threats posed by white Russians and Macedonians. He arrested, expelled and disbanded many of Wrangel's followers. His rapprochement with Yugoslavia drove the Macedonians to fulminate against him and commit outrages. He used the Orange Guard against them, arrested their militants and confined them to camps, but could not reach out to their no-go areas or prevent further acts of terrorism.

Far from abating, opposition had intensified. To start with, the agrarians were indisciplined and corrupt. They had taken over the administration with no trained cadres, and many abused their newly acquired positions. There were agrarian politicians who were more or less radical than Stamboliiski. Civil servants, lawyers, journalists, doctors, academics, all suffered from impoverishment and various forms of discrimination. Clergy and devout Orthodox were repelled by Stamboliiski's godlessness, by the confiscation of monastic property and by the scaling down of religious education.[10] More dangerous were the disgruntled officers, who resented the agrarians' antimilitaristic measures and contempt, coming on top of unemployment, diminishing pensions and demeaning jobs. The formation of the Military League in 1922 was the threatening expression of that discontent.

Stamboliiski went to the polls in April 1923. He had previously replaced proportional representation with single-member constituencies, purged his cabinet and the administration, taken action against communists and Macedonians, and galvanized his own party through meetings, oaths of loyalty and the strengthening of the Orange Guard. These moves were perceived as leading to one-party rule, a personal dictatorship, perhaps even a change of constitution. Driven together by the need to survive, the old parties managed to form a Constitutional Bloc. Stamboliiski did not hesitate to use repressive and irregular measures. The agrarians obtained 54 per cent of the votes, the communists over 19 per cent, the Constitutional Bloc over 18 per cent.

In an atmosphere of deep frustration for all shades of the opposition, a conspiracy was hatched, bringing together elements as diverse as the traditional parties, the Military League, IMRO, even social democrats. They knew that they could count on help from the army, and were convinced that the Communist Party would not contest the coup d'Etat. In the night of 8 June

10 Ever since the exarch's death in 1915, no new primate had been installed so as not to exacerbate the irregular status of the Church of Bulgaria, which was anyhow not high on Stamboliiski's list of priorities.

1923, the conspirators took over Sofia and deposed the agrarian government. King Boris, whose relations with Stamboliiski were strained and who was aware of the impending coup, accepted it. With little regard to constitutional niceties, a new government was formed by Aleksandŭr Tsankov (1879–1959), an economics professor backed by a newly formed Democratic Alliance of old political groups, with the Military League and IMRO.

Stamboliiski was found several days later by IMRO and savagely tortured before being beheaded by his captors. His horrible end was the first spectacularly murderous expression of the pathological hatred felt by embittered right-wing radical nationalist movements for 'traitors' to their sacred cause. It would be emulated by Romanian legionnaires and Croatian ustashas. The new government admitted to 3,000 arrests, but that was not the only reason for the amazingly rapid collapse of the agrarian régime. Stamboliiski had appealed to the peasants and provided his country with a new motivation. But he had treated too many people with contempt; he had cracked down hard on too many opponents. The communists stood aside; the Allies did not lift a finger. The Tsankov government continued with land redistribution, support for cooperatives and welfare. It ended censorship and even released communists.

The Comintern in Moscow did not approve of the passivity shown by the Bulgarian party, and ordered a belated rebellion in September 1923. Badly organized and easily suppressed, it gave Tsankov the excuse to turn against the left. A Defence of the Realm Law against terrorist activities enabled the government to use its influence fully in the elections which it called in November to restore parliament. The Democratic Alliance together with the social democrats won 59 per cent of votes. The agrarians still managed over 12 per cent. Even the Communist Party had eight seats, but it was outlawed in April 1924, its trades unions were disbanded and its deputies expelled.

That seemed to strengthen the hand of those dedicated to violent action, which culminated in an attempt to kill King Boris on 16 April 1925 at a funeral service, when a bomb outrage killed 128 people. The attempt provoked the harshest repression to date, and for a while it eliminated the left. The government still had to contend with the Macedonian right, whose violence kept pace with its own and with that of the communists. IMRO was entrenched in the southwestern corner bordering on Greece and Yugoslavia. The Macedonians who accounted for over one in ten of the population of Sofia provided the extremists with ready access to the capital. They operated as a real mafia, demanding sinecures, levying contributions and terrorizing officials.

They also killed one another, for although the IMRO umbrella now covered them all, they were split between 'federalists', who still favoured a separate Macedonia in a Balkan federation, and 'centralists', who wanted the whole of Macedonia annexed to Bulgaria. Their uncontrollable activities threatened relations with neighbours.

The extent of repression soon drew more disapproval than approval. By September, backed by pressure from abroad, the king was saying that the time had come for more relaxed policies. The government was trying to obtain a loan for the welfare of refugees, who were easy recruits for extremes of right and left. It was made to understand that it would not get it for as long as it was headed by Tsankov. In January 1926, the democrat Andrei Lyapchev (1866–1933) took over. A loan for public works and other measures contributed to easing the refugee problem. Trades unions were allowed again and amnesties granted, but the parties supporting the government were splitting up. By 1926, there were nineteen groups represented in parliament. A new electoral law, inspired by Mussolini's innovation of 1923, tried to remedy the situation by giving an automatic parliamentary majority to the party obtaining the largest number of votes.

The May 1927 elections reduced the Democratic Alliance's share to 38 per cent. The fragmentation of party politics continued. It weakened the government, which was in no position to face the coming economic difficulties. By 1930, Lyapchev was losing control of the Assembly, of his alliance, of his own cabinet even. At the June 1931 elections, the last to be really open and free, the Democratic Alliance's 31 per cent gave way to the 47 per cent of the People's Bloc. This centre-left coalition that included the agrarian factions provided Bulgaria with a possible turning point. Its government held for almost three years, trying to alleviate the worst effects of the Depression, while facing renewed challenges from left and right.

Allowed to reappear as the Workers' Party, he communists had gained thirty-one deputies, and went on in 1932 to secure a majority on the city council of Sofia, with votes from diverse disaffected elements. Tsankov moved on to set up a National Social Movement in imitation of the fascists, while IMRO had started up afresh. Fragmented into twenty-nine groups, squabbling and inquorate, the Assembly was all but irrelevant. The agrarian movement was shattered, it had alienated its supporters, yet the majority of the peasantry was unreconciled to those who had since held power. The old parties lacked substantial popular support. The radical extremes were at each other's throats. A general sense of disillusion had set in. The scene was set for the army and the crown: in May 1934, another military coup put an end to real parliamentary life.

Bulgaria had to provide for refugees and to pay reparations. In the event, her actual reparations burden, once negotiated down by 1930, was hardly more than what victorious Romania and Yugoslavia paid on account of war and relief debts, and as their share of Austro-Hungarian obligations. Reparations amounted to about 18 per cent of Bulgaria's total debt, as compared to the war-related debts which were almost half of Yugoslavia's, and just over half of Romania's total debt. These Allied states, however, were compensated by reparations, while Bulgaria could obtain no foreign capital until 1926.

The consequences of King Ferdinand's policy had enabled Stamboliiski to reject the very notion of expansion, and to turn against all that went with it – standing army, large military budget, conscription, officer caste, power patronage. His long-term ideal was a Balkan union of agrarian states, but he could not do much more towards it than give support to the new 'Green International' set up in Prague to provide a context for exchanges between different peasant parties. He did not neglect Bulgaria's interests; she was the first of the defeated states to be admitted to the League of Nations in 1920. He pressed for full implementation of the peace treaty, including the clause concerning economic access to the Aegean, and for protection of the minority rights of Macedonian Slavs in other countries (even though they were not recognized as such in Bulgaria).

He wanted to cooperate with Balkan neighbours, ideally on the basis of a common peasant ideology, but realistically it was first necessary to improve relations with them – such as they were. The outlet to the Aegean was the major issue with Greece. Bulgaria wanted a corridor and rejected Greek offers of a free zone in a port. It was thus difficult to get anywhere on the issue of Macedonian rights, particularly in view of IMRO incursions. This was even more the case with Yugoslavia. Belgrade insisted on the Serbian character of the population of her share of Macedonia, and would not even consider any concessions until measures had been taken to stop IMRO attacks.

Faced with a choice of sacrificing better neighbourly relations with Yugoslavia to appease the inflamed Macedonian lobby in Bulgaria, or of cracking down on Macedonian extremists to win Yugoslav approval, Stamboliiski's inclination and his interpretation of the country's interests led him to choose the latter. After May 1921, having assured Belgrade that he would take measures to contain Macedonian terrorism, he purged the army and the frontier police of IMRO supporters. He visited Belgrade in November 1922; in March 1923 the Niš Convention was concluded on cooperation between Bulgaria and Yugoslavia to contain terrorism. This was followed by concrete measures against terrorism, with arrests and confinements, which earned Stamboliiski the undying hatred of IMRO.

For the vast majority of the population, the First World War had meant privations suffered in vain, hence the rejection of politicians associated with the war. There had been little fighting on Bulgarian soil, but almost 39 per cent of the population had been mobilized by 1918, resulting in a sharp drop in yields. In terms of war losses, there had been an overall decline of 68,000 in the population in 1916–18, and a decline in the birthrate over the 1920s.

Nevertheless, the long-term social and economic effects of war were not profound. Wartime inflation had practically liquidated peasant debts. Over 75 per cent of the population were small proprietors who survived the impact. The social structure of Bulgaria was not altered. The only noticeable change in agriculture was the decline in wheat, and the advance of tobacco, as an export commodity. Tobacco went up from 26 to 40 per cent of export value between 1921 and 1925.

Effective public promotion in the form of loans helped plant selection, irrigation and fertilizers, but that was not enough for tobacco to play the same dynamic rôle in the economy as prewar grain. International tobacco prices were not stable, and declined overall by one-fifth in the 1920s. The long-term credit needed for investments was harder to find. Even short-term credit remained expensive, because of the need to stabilize the currency. When it returned to the gold standard in 1928, the government was forced to cut back on public expenditure to support an overvalued currency. Nor was there much change in industry. The small manufacturing sector remained overdependent on foreign raw materials. Yet its concentration in the capital city was even more pronounced than elsewhere in the Balkans. By 1926, Sofia firms had issued 62 per cent of Bulgaria's industrial shares, and by the 1930s provided 54 per cent of all industrial employment.

CHAPTER 12

The 1920s – Part 2: The winners

The preoccupations of greater Romania. A completely new state misunderstood by its components: the Kingdom of the Serbs, Croats and Slovenes. Recovery and a precarious stability everywhere.

GREATER ROMANIA

Like Greece, Romania had emerged from the First World War on the Allied side. Unlike Greece, she had accomplished all her aims and become 'greater' Romania by more than doubling the territory and population of the 'old' kingdom. She was allowed to build up as a bastion against right-wing revanchism from the collapsed Habsburg Monarchy and left-wing radicalism from the ruined Russian Empire. If all Romanian-speakers, but for half a million or so (including Vlachs), were gathered within her borders, ethnic minorities amounted to almost a third of the total population, and included 1.4 million Magyars.[1] The new lands differed from the old as well as from one another, and there was tension when Bucharest extended its centralized system.

The old kingdom itself had come out of the war ravaged and looted. The immediate problem was to avert famine, when transport was paralysed by a strike in 1919 which extended to coal and oil, before turning in October 1920 to a general strike called by the socialists. Romania went through a year and a half of instability, as political forces adapted to a new landscape. Transylvanian politicians who had been in the Budapest parliament faced the traditional parties in Bucharest; they all confronted new problems and universal suffrage. The conservatives were virtually eliminated. The liberals had returned to power, but their leader Brătianu, who had quarrelled with the Big Four in Paris, had resigned before the first general elections to be held over the territory of greater Romania in November 1919.

---

1 Magyars amounted to 29 per cent of the population of Transylvania, concentrated not on the new border with Hungary, but in the centre. The Hungarian government challenged the figures of the Romanian census of 1923.

No single party predominated. The liberals retained a strong basis, with 18 per cent of seats, the conservatives had 3 per cent and the new Peasant Party, launched to extend the land reform, 11 per cent. The Romanian National Party of Transylvania came out top with 30 per cent. It formed a coalition with the Peasant Party under the Transylvanian leader Alexandru Vaida (1872–1950).

The Peasant Party head Ion Michalache (1882–1963) became minister of agriculture to push through the land reform. The first measures had been taken by the liberals in December 1918, when 2.25 million hectares were earmarked for expropriation and distribution. Michalache's controversial programme would have included a hundred-hectare limit, progressive income tax, an industrial minimum wage, an eight-hour day and urban rent controls. The combined opposition of the palace, of the old parties and of the popular war hero General Averescu stopped the shaky coalition in its tracks. Faced with social and economic crisis, it lacked the appeal of Averescu who expected to be called in as a saviour.

King Ferdinand turned to him in March 1920, and granted a dissolution of parliament. With electoral pacts, his People's League won 43 per cent of the vote. His government ended the strike with martial law. It also enacted in 1921 its own agrarian reform – a compromise between the liberals' and Michalache's. Its terms varied according to the owners, the beneficiaries and the terrain. Maximum holdings were between one hundred and two hundred hectares; plots of five hectares were distributed in return for payments over twenty years. Averescu had to satisfy the peasants and demonstrate his commitment to order. His People's League was riddled with rivalries. Having come to power with the consent of the liberals, he became increasingly subordinate to them and resigned in December 1921. Brătianu was recalled.

Now well reorganized, the extended National Liberal Party (to give it its full name) wanted to strengthen the unified and unitary state with an updated constitution. Elections were held in 1922 for a Constituent Assembly where the liberals found themselves in a two-thirds majority as a result of administrative pressures and of a fragmented opposition. They were back in control. Pushed through in spite of resistance from the representatives of the new territories, and promulgated in March 1923, their constitution extended and modernized that of 1866. It was completed in 1925 by the division of the whole territory into French-style departments.

United with the dioceses of the new territories, the integrated Orthodox Church of Romania, representing 73 per cent of the population, was established under the constitution and elevated to a patriarchate in 1925. Catholics, Protestants, Armenians, Jews and Muslims were state-supported denominations.[2] Jews by 1930 numbered 750,000 (4 per cent of the total population, and 14 per cent of the urban population – around 50 per cent in some Moldavian towns). The treaties enabled them finally to acquire citizenship. Prejudices

---

2 Catholics represented 15 per cent of the population, divided between the essentially Romanian Uniates of Transylvania and the mostly Magyar 'Latins'. The Protestants were mainly Germans.

notwithstanding, they obtained a predominant position in certain economic sectors and professions.

The liberals implemented what was the most extensive agrarian reform in Europe outside Russia. According to official figures, some 4 million hectares were redistributed to 1.4 million peasants. The Peasant Party wanted more equalization, but it never lived up to its 1921 programme, veering to a 'peasantism' that looked like nationalism under another name. It cooperated with the broadly based National Party, which had retained its strength in the ex-Hungarian territories. The two fused in 1926 in the National Peasant Party, which became the main opposition party under Maniu's leadership.

Real left-wing parties had little voice. Having caused industrial havoc in 1919–20, the newly united Romanian Socialist Party split over affiliation to the Communist International. The Communist Party obtained 75,000 votes at the 1922 elections, but stability and the land reform removed much of its audience. When the Comintern in 1924 condemned the states born of 'Versailles' as imperialist creations, and called for the secession of Romania's oppressed minorities, communist activities were seen as treasonable. Outlawed in 1924, the party vegetated underground or abroad, and only occasionally appeared through front organizations. The remaining socialists once again became the Romanian Social Democratic Party, which occasionally cooperated with other parties, but never gained more than 4 per cent of the vote.

In March 1926, following Bulgaria's example, the liberals introduced a new electoral law. The party obtaining at least 40 per cent of the vote automatically had half the seats. The rest were shared proportionally between all the groups above a 2 per cent threshold. The liberal leaders realized that their influence was waning. There were uncomfortable local election results. King Ferdinand was ailing, and they were worried by his heir. Prince Charles (1893–1953), who accepted neither royal discipline nor liberal guidance,[3] had in 1925 been made to renounce his right of succession. The dynastic crisis had weakened Brătianu, who decided to step down for a while. He warned Ferdinand of the danger of machinations between the National Peasant Party and Charles, and again advised recourse to Averescu who was expected to provide a quiet interlude.

At the May 1926 elections, Averescu's electioneering won his league 53 per cent of the vote. Relations with the liberals soured as he attempted various manoeuvres to assert his independence – including talks with Charles. Brătianu forced his resignation, and returned to organize new elections in July. The liberals duly won with 62 per cent, but their era was coming to an end.

The participation had been 23 per cent. A fortnight after the election, Ferdinand's death deprived the liberals of royal support. He was succeeded by his five-year-old grandson, Charles's son Michael, under a three-man regency. Then in November, Ionel Brătianu's death deprived the party of dynamic

---

3 He had been married once without royal assent, then again more regularly but unhappily to Princess Helen of Greece from whom he had subsequently separated. He lived generally abroad with a Romanian divorcée, Mme Lupescu.

leadership. His successor and brother Vintila (1867–1930) did not have the authority to hold together the liberal factions or to face criticism. He resigned in November 1928. The liberals had striven to create a modern framework, and a bourgeoisie to take the leading rôle in transforming Romania into a European nation-state. They had been concerned with economic advancement, reflecting the commercial, industrial and banking interests that predominated in the party and expected its support. Since, however, their bourgeoisie was not strong enough for the task, the state had to step in with a policy of economic nationalism. This gave a special slant to the liberals' 'liberalism'.

Their determination to avoid dependence on foreign investments meant that industrialization was financed to a large extent by the peasantry. Export duties on agricultural products provided home manufacturers with cheap food and raw materials, but raised their price on world markets. Poor harvests sharpened peasants' complaints of ineffective representation of their interests. Romania had become a country of smallholders, with 95 per cent of all property in holdings of less than ten hectares (83 per cent of holdings being under five hectares), but the distribution of land had not brought about prosperity. Many holdings were not viable economically.

The liberals had counted on industrialization, but they only had limited foreign participation so as to help their native supporters, and these could not provide all the necessary capital. They had not won the confidence of the peasantry and had not put the economy on a solid foundation. The National Peasant Party, which by 1928 had become a formidable adversary, launched a campaign against liberal rule, with peasant rallies and the threat of a Mussolini-like march on Bucharest. When Vintila Brătianu submitted his resignation, the regents turned to Maniu, who formed a government and called an election.

The national peasant programme promised a redress to peasant grievances, decentralization and a more welcoming attitude to foreign capital. Even though Maniu's government took some of the usual pre-election administrative measures, the December 1928 elections are held to have been one of the fairest in Romania. The National Peasant Party (in coalition with the social democrats and the German Party of Transylvania) was swept into power with 78 per cent of the vote.

The Maniu government placed agriculture at the centre of its economic policy, with the aim of establishing a strong class of richer peasants. Realizing that native financial sources were not sufficient, and wanting to strike a blow at the economic power of the liberal oligarchy, it removed most of the restrictions on foreign participation in the economy. The strategy of relying on foreign loans paid for by agricultural exports was, however, quickly shattered by the Depression; the voters' expectations remained largely unfulfilled.

The government was not particularly united. It had resorted to force when dealing with industrial unrest, and the National Peasant Party, too, had set up its armed guard. The final blow came when Prince Charles took advantage of weak links in the government to engineer a dramatic return by air to Bucharest in June 1930. Maniu resigned, and left the arrangements for the accession in other hands. After parliament had proclaimed King Charles II – or Carol, as he is better known, even in English, by his Romanian name –[4] Maniu agreed to return as prime minister, but there were irreconcilable differences between him and the new sovereign, notably over the presence of Charles's companion, Mme Lupescu. He resigned definitely in October.

This dynastic crisis had weakened Maniu as the previous one had weakened Brătianu. The prestige of parliamentary parties suffered. A period of instability followed, as King Charles increasingly exploited the divisions between and within the parties. He surrounded himself with new courtiers, and projected the image of a monarch more in tune with the aspirations of 'new' Romania than with the practices of the prewar state.

The prospects for a consolidation of the parliamentary system had seemed good in the aftermath of the First World War. The Conservative Party had collapsed along with the power of the large landowners. The dominant social element became the upper bourgeoisie under the rejuvenated Liberal Party, whose financial oligarchy intertwined banking, industry and politics. While some of its traditional supporters left it for the new Peasant Party, it made a great effort to attract the business interests of the new provinces. It dominated until the united National Peasant Party partly restored the two-party system.

The crown continued to be a key element and retained considerable powers. King Ferdinand respected constitutional practice but, as before, elections were usually held after he had chosen the prime minister, whose party, once in office, had the advantage of being able to 'conduct' the elections. The majority of the peasantry remained apathetic as well as inexperienced. The two main parties never had much cohesion. Groups and individuals – often opposed to the parliamentary system – appeared outside the regular structures. Averescu's league was a *boulangiste* movement, bringing together those who were fearful of violent change yet recognized the need for reform (under 'strong' guidance).

Fringe nationalist movements were sustained by the feeling that a new élite was necessary to bind together the disparate parts of greater Romania, and resented the slowness of parliamentary efforts. They were eager for a moral force to determine the course of development, at a time when Romania's upper classes had become detached from Orthodoxy, and the liberals were motivated only by material forces. The seeds of a moral, anti-Marxist, anti-liberal, and also anti-Semitic, authoritarian nationalism were taken and developed by Corneliu Zelea-Codreanu (1899–1938) from the university milieu of Jassy, where almost half the students were Jews, many of them refugees from Russia and perceived as communist infiltrators.

A student leader who had been conspicuous for violent rhetoric and action against 'bolsheviks' and Jews, he had set up the Legion of the Archangel Michael in 1927 (after a vision he had had in prison), followed in 1930 by its

4 He used the Romanian version of his name even in French and English, contrary to usage, as a concession to nationalist feeling. King Michael reverted to the position of heir to the throne with the title of grand voevod of Alba Iulia, in deference to Transylvania.

green-shirted paramilitary youth force, the Iron Guard. For a while, he had been allowed to operate in Bessarabia by Vaida, the home minister in Maniu's government.

Codreanu's movement found recruits among those who hankered after a new type of revolution that would place the individual back in the community. It had a ready audience in the educated unemployed, as the Depression cut back on the number of posts available. Advocating a Christian crusade for the preservation of the integrity of greater Romania, threatened by a Judeo–communist–foreign conspiracy, he came to enjoy support in diverse circles. He drew his potential strength from the weakening of parliamentary parties, and in particular from the unfulfilled expectations of the national peasant government. The state of peasant agriculture all too often deviated from the 'peasantist' utopia, extolled as a native third way between western capitalism and Russian bolshevism. Codreanu's influence was greater than that of the revolutionary left.

Once the peace and minorities treaties had been signed and ratified, Romania's diplomacy strove to create a security framework that would guarantee the international status granted to her by the treaties. The first move was made towards what the Hungarian press ridiculed as the 'Little Entente' between Czechoslovakia, Yugoslavia and Romania: the name stuck. The Belgrade Declaration of August 1920 was to uphold the Treaty of Trianon. It was a mutual insurance to neutralize a potential Hungarian threat to the status quo of the main successor states to the Habsburgs. It was also an answer to those who wanted a replacement 'Danubian' confederation of sorts to consolidate the dismantled area of the one-time Monarchy.

It was a modest move at first. The acquisition of Bessarabia did not figure in any of the treaties, merely in a declaration of recognition by the Allies in October 1920. Romanians feared Russian more than Hungarian revisionism. France (alleged to have launched the Little Entente) did not lend her support until later, as she did not want to exacerbate the division of Europe into two camps. It was only in 1921 that Romania joined Czechoslovakia and Yugoslavia in a formal defensive and anti-revisionist alliance to uphold Trianon.

Romania's preoccupation with her Russian frontier led Averescu to conclude an agreement with Poland in 1921, turned in 1926 into a full treaty of mutual defence. That year he also signed a treaty of friendship with France, and another with Italy, who was ready to provide financial help. Even though this network of alliances was seen as French-engineered, France had somewhat disappointed the hopes of Bucharest. She was anxious to handle the new Russia with care; her recognition of Romania's acquisition of Bessarabia did not mean that she would defend it.

Greater Romania was mostly the creation of the leaders of the old kingdom. The products of nineteenth-century liberalism, they would have found it difficult to lead greater Romania into the new century even without the Depression. The integration of new territories, new populations and new electors was a tremendous challenge. Romanians predominated in the new provinces, but not in their cities or in their educated élite, hence a policy to Romanianize secondary and higher education. Rural youths, hailed as the embodiment of the Romanian nation, were surprised to find well-prepared fellow students from the overrepresented ethnic minorities. The liberal administration made great efforts to improve education in many ways, increasing the length of required schooling from four to seven years, introducing adult literacy classes, allocating large sums for study abroad.[5]

Romanians were never fully reconciled to the treaty on minorities; its interpretation varied according to parties and minorities. The principle was established that 'national minorities' were guaranteed equal rights, religious freedom and schools in their mother tongue. Jews who did not claim another 'nationality' were regarded as citizens belonging to the main body of the population.

The liberals' electoral law of 1926 improved the minorities' representation as their support was needed. Maniu's government was more accommodating generally, but the minorities problem remained a serious handicap for Romania. Magyars made the most of the treaty provisions. Their nationalism in Transylvania, arising from a feeling of cultural superiority and lost political pre-eminence, was easily exacerbated. Hungarian landowners felt that they had been victimized by the agrarian reform, and appealed to the League of Nations. Bulgarian peasants in Dobrudja complained of being passed over in favour of Romanian (or Vlach) settlers. Bessarabia was not covered by the treaty; it was the focus of both pro-Russian communist and anti-Semitic right-wing radical propaganda.

The intellectual debate about the direction in which the nation-state should develop sharpened. 'Europeanists' sought to adapt it to the western (essentially French) model, while 'traditionalists' looked to Romania's unique (fundamentally rural) heritage. Their discovery of Eastern Orthodoxy as the bulwark of this idealized heritage was due to a sense of frustration and vulnerability, in part a reaction against the way in which the Church had been reduced to being little more than a government department, more a recourse to a cultural form for the preservation of a specific mode of existence locally conditioned than an ecumenical Christian inspiration.[6]

The population in 1930 was more than 18 million, an increase of 2.5 million over the estimates of 1920. The growth had little to do with population movements.[7] Romania presented a contrast between her rural world and agriculture, on the one hand, and her cities and industry on the other. Around 78 per cent

---

5 By 1930 literacy was still no more than 57 per cent, with strong regional variations (from 72 per cent and 67 per cent in Banat and Transylvania respectively, to 38 per cent in Bessarabia). The number of students in higher education went up from 28,000 in 1926/27 to 39,000 in 1933/34, but law and humanities still attracted two-thirds.
6 'We are Orthodox because we are Romanian, and we are Romanian because we are Orthodox' is a typical statement by the philosopher Nae Ionescu (1888–1940).
7 Some 200,000 Magyars left in the immediate postwar years, along with 42,000 Turks from Dobrudja. Over 67,000 emigrants to the USA in the 1920s (more than half of them Jews) were partly compensated by the arrival of 22,000 Jews from Russia and the return of 20,000 Romanians from the United States to their native Transylvania and Bukovina.

of the population was rural, agriculture remained the foundation of the economy, but the land reform left many peasants dissatisfied.

A third of those entitled to land received nothing, as there was not always enough land available locally. At the other end of the spectrum, there were still in 1930 6,600 landowners holding 28 per cent of the total land area. With demographic growth and property fragmentation, an increasing number of peasants had to rent land again. The reform benefited a top layer of smallholders with over fifty hectares. It hardly improved the standard of living of the majority, did not satisfy their land hunger and did not provide credit. Corn continued to be the basic food. Milk and meat consumption remained low.

Agriculture was in a desperate situation at the end of the war when the reform was being prepared. The recovery, slow and uneven, was cut short by the Depression, which began to affect Romania in 1929, with a steady fall in grain prices. Peasants used their land to respond to market conditions as best they could, but the concentration on grain was unsuited to smallholding. It impeded diversification, which could have led to a more intensive use of labour. As it was, the countryside was overpopulated. Even though Romania between the wars was the fifth-largest agricultural producer in the world, her wheat yield of 95 quintals per hectare at the turn of the decade (1928–32) was the lowest in the Balkans except for Greece.

Industrial production had been almost totally disrupted by the war, but recovery was rapid. It was helped by the support of the liberals in office, and by the addition of the coal and iron of Transylvania to the old kingdom's wood and oil. The production of crude oil, down to 1 million tonnes in 1918 (from 1.8 million in 1913), grew to 5.8 million in 1930. Romania was then the sixth world producer (after the United States, Russia, Venezuela, Mexico and Iran), in spite of the struggle between the liberal government and the main foreign companies. Ninety per cent of Romania's crude oil was refined on the spot around Ploeşti, and most of it was shipped abroad as the main export (some 30 per cent in 1921–25) after cereals (32.8 per cent).

The transfer of German and Austro-Hungarian ownership of the largest prewar oil companies, as part of the peace settlement, opened the way for the liberals' nationalization of 25 per cent of crude oil capacity. By 1925, native capital represented 60 per cent in oil firms. Although the national peasant government did open the door to foreign investment, in practice the liberals' policy was more influential. As a result of their protectionist policy, the import of manufactured goods fell steadily. Industrialization grew at one of the highest rates in Europe – an average annual growth of combined labour and horsepower input of 3.23 per cent for the years 1920–29.

Under liberal sponsorship, the Romanian bourgeoisie was partially successful in freeing itself from the tutelage of foreign capital. By 1929, 36 per cent of all capital in the economy was foreign, but it continued to be essential in oil, coal and sugar, where British, French and Belgian eventually replaced Austrian and German capital.

A dynamic banking system, headed by the liberal Banca Româneasca and the Jewish Banca Marmorosch-Blank, took on a larger entrepreneurial rôle than elsewhere in the Balkans. Industrial growth was, however, determined more by government intervention than by consumer demand, which was slow to expand because of the generally low standard of living. The inability of the domestic market to absorb its products was a major weakness of Romanian industrialization. Although industry came to account for 35 per cent of the net national product by 1930, only 9 per cent of the population worked in that sector. About 20 per cent nevertheless lived in towns. Bucharest grew from 382,000 in 1918 to 631,000 in 1930, concentrating administrative, cultural and economic activities; the population of the second largest city, Chişinău was no more than 117,000.

Romania's debts per head of population rose less than those of other Balkan states. Without war and relief debts, they were in fact 15 per cent less in 1930 than in 1911. The liberals were opposed to the resumption of repeated foreign borrowing as they were hostile to foreign investment. Most European capital markets had been closed off by their reluctance to settle wartime debts. They hoped first to revalue the leu in order to restore the prewar gold value by provisions such as a statutory limit on note issues, which remained in force until 1928. Eventually, they were able to stabilize an overvalued leu with the help of good agricultural exports, but the limit on issue restricted the supply of private credit.

THE KINGDOM OF THE SERBS, CROATS AND SLOVENES

The new state was definitely on the winners' side, by virtue of its assimilation with the old Kingdom of Serbia. Serbo-Croat speakers made up 74 per cent of the population, with Slovene speakers another 8.51 per cent; some 720,000 South Slavs remained outside its borders. In terms of religious affiliations, there were 46.67 per cent Orthodox, 39.20 per cent Catholics and 11.22 per cent Muslims. The Kingdom of the Serbs, Croats and Slovenes was thus more complex than 'greater' Romania. Yet outside the majority of the Serb–Croat–Slovene-speaking majority, the ethnic minorities amounted to some two million, or 16–18 per cent of the population, which was a smaller proportion than Romania's 28 per cent (not to mention Poland or Czechoslovakia with over 30 per cent).[8]

The combined losses for the war period 1912–18 have been assessed at 1.9 million, of which 0.9 million were military, with Serbia and Montenegro

8 Estimates vary as the census registered language and religion; Macedonian Slavs were deemed to be Serbs. Ivo Banac works out the following breakdown of 'Yugoslavs' in 1918: 38.83 per cent Serbs, 23.77 per cent Croats, 8.53 per cent Slovenes, 6.05 per cent Bosnian Slav Muslims and 4.87 per cent Macedonian Slavs (*The National Question in Yugoslavia: Origins, History, Politics*, Ithaca and London: Cornell University Press, 1984, 58).

bearing the brunt.[9] The economy was disrupted; the former Austro-Hungarian provinces bore the added presence of Italian troops intent on considering them as enemy territory.

Rare were the protagonists of unification who understood that Yugoslavia (or South-Slavia, the state of the South Slavs) was indeed a new creation, neither an extended Yugoslav version of prewar Serbia nor an improved Yugoslav version of Austria-Hungary. Serbia had a king, an administration, a battle-hardened army and political parties based on universal suffrage. Because of her rôle in the war, she offered it all as a nucleus around which to build Yugoslavia. She did not realize that, worn out as she was by wars, she was not strong enough for the task that she envisaged.

Croatia expected to join a new and better Austria-Hungary where she would play the rôle of Hungary. Furthermore, Bosnia lay between Croatia and Serbia. Both aspired to that territory, whose framework rested on the separation of communities under a controlling power. There was Slovenia, for whom Yugoslavia was really the chance to come into her own. And there were the new Serbian territories from the Balkan Wars, with their mixed, uncertain and even hostile populations.

Yugoslavia (as the country was more generally called) went through a transitional phase. The Constituent Assembly could not be elected until the state had been accepted as part of the public law of Europe. The regent of Serbia was its head, with a cabinet representing all major political groups and regions. A Provisional National Representation was set up from existing regional bodies, to give backing to the executive and to prepare for the Constituent.

There were immediate problems to be tackled. The Serbian army was the only force able to affirm the sovereignty of the state and to maintain order. It was opened up to Austro-Hungarian officers, but they had fought on the opposite side. Their sympathies, particularly in higher ranks, tended to be pro-Habsburg rather than Yugoslav, let alone pro-Serb. Eventually the 3,500 Serbian officers were joined by around 2,500 from the Austro-Hungarian army and a few hundred Montenegrin officers, but the highest ranking officers remained Serbian.[10]

The most pressing problem was the agrarian reform in the former Ottoman and Austro-Hungarian territories. After 1912, the Serbian government had promised a redistribution of Turkish-owned estates in the new territories. In 1917 it had promised land to South Slav volunteers from the Habsburg Monarchy, and the National Council in Zagreb had also made promises. These had been confirmed in a preliminary decree in February 1919, which cancelled rent payments, and committed the state to abolishing sharecropping obligations and redistributing 'large' estates. Priority would be given to war

---

9 Serbia's military losses were accordingly 2.5 times relatively higher than those of France (Ivo J. Lederer's analysis of neutral estimates in *Yugoslavia at the Paris Peace Conference: A Study in Frontiermaking*, New Haven and London: Yale University Press, 221–5).
10 Initially only three Austro-Hungarian and four Montenegrin officers joined the twenty-three Serbian generals. The 200-strong naval officer corps was obviously all non-Serbian.

veterans and war victims. There would be specific legislation for each area; a special ministry was set up to administer the operation.

Elections for the Constituent Assembly eventually took place in November 1920, when the adult male electorate went to the polls to elect 419 deputies by proportional representation. There were around forty active political groups, most of them regional. The Democratic Party (ninety-two deputies, 20 per cent of the vote) and the Radical Party (ninety-one seats, 17 per cent of the vote) were the largest. The democrats brought together the smaller Serbian opposition groups of the urban educated, the Yugoslav-minded independent radicals, the main party of the Habsburg Serbs, others from the Croato-Serb coalition, and the Slovenian liberal urban intelligentsia. Although predominantly Serb, they were the first to represent votes from all regions. They rejected sectional interests as the basis of political action; they advocated centralized parliamentary government and immediate land reform.

Long in power in Serbia, the Radical Party had become more conservative than radical. Yet the prestige of its leader Pašić and its efficient organization had enabled it to retain its hold over the peasants of Serbia, and to attract many Serbs from the former Habsburg territories. War and dissidence had shorn it of many of its newer cadres. Although Yugoslav in principle, it was joined by the activists of heterogeneous Serb communities outside Serbia whose only common aim had been to join Serbia.

There was enough dissatisfaction to provide opposition parties with support. Both major newcomers, the Croatian Peasant Party (CPP) and the Communist Party were opposed to the shape that the new state was taking. The former won fifty seats in 1920. Its leader Stjepan Radić (1871–1928) had by 1918 made the fight for the recognition of a peasant-based Croatian 'statehood' the main plank of its platform. Eclipsing the old parties, it voiced the aspirations of the newly enfranchised Croat peasantry, sick and tired of fighting for and being governed by rulers in a distant capital. A believer in Serbo-Croat brotherhood, Radić was suspicious of Serbia's state machinery.

The communists were born of the division of the newly unified social democrats over membership of the Comintern. Expecting that Yugoslavia would follow Russia into revolution, they exploited all manner of discontent and organized themselves in all regions. They had followed Moscow's call for protest strikes against Allied intervention in Hungary and Russia, even though Yugoslavia had not participated; they had called for revolution. At the local elections earlier in 1920, they had obtained a majority in many towns, including Belgrade and Zagreb. In the Constituent they had fifty-eight members, representing disparate protest votes. The Yugoslav Muslim Organization had followed on from the Muslim Organization of Bosnia-Herzegovina, the clerical People's Party still dominated the Slovenian countryside, and the new Serb Agrarian Party had made gains among the poor Serb peasants of Bosnia.

At the very moment when legitimism seemed to be dead, an increasing number of Croats were torn between the principle of self-determination and the continued existence of their historical entity, between faith in some form of Yugoslav unity and increasing distrust of the tremendous psychological strength of Serbia. The contest was not so much between centralism and federalism as between unitarism and dualism.

Two series of events affected the opposition parties before the Constituent Assembly even settled down to its task. The radical-democrat-backed government decided that the constitution would be passed by a simple majority of 210 out of the total 419 members, and not by any 'qualified' majority. In protest the CPP boycotted the assembly, thus weakening Croatia's case. The communists threatened to turn a coalminers' strike into a general strike. Fearing a disruption of fuel supplies on the threshold of winter, and the party's generally subversive effect, the government took measures aimed at curbing its seditious activities. Although approved by the Constituent Assembly, doubts were cast on the legality of such measures. Communist deputies and local councillors were not interfered with; communist trades unions were soon allowed again.

Pašić returned to head a new government. The politicians of Serbia mistrusted the very notion of federalism, they had no comprehension of the formalism of the 'rights' question which dominated Croatia's political life, but they were not automatically averse to regional autonomy. It was the leader of the Habsburg Serbs, Svetozar Pribićević (1875–1936), now leader of the new democrats, who insisted on rigid centralism. For Pašić, who underestimated the nature of the Croat opposition, the main thing was to have a constitution as soon as possible.

The government draft, as in Romania, merely updated Serbia's form of government, by introducing religious equality,[11] and social and economic principles inspired by the Weimar constitution. The kingdom would be divided into French-style departments, thus abolishing 'Croatia'. For most Croats, this was the anti-climax to the end of the long association with Hungary. For most Serbs, this was all of no consequence once political and religious freedoms had been guaranteed to all.

As other deputies also left, the government ensured the support of Muslim representatives by negotiating concessions on the implementation of the land reform in Bosnia and in 'southern Serbia'. On 28 June 1921, 223 of the 258 members present voted for the constitution – a majority of thirteen on the full strength of the house. Frustrated communists immediately turned to acts of terrorism. A bomb missed the regent as he returned from taking the oath to the constitution, and a month later the home minister was assassinated. In August, the government enacted the Law for the Protection of Public Security and Order, which outlawed the Communist Party. Unable to resist persecution and fragmentation, it was driven underground or abroad.

---

11 With the assent of the ecumenical patriarchate, the several Orthodox ecclesiastical jurisdictions were merged into a single Serbian Orthodox Church having authority over all the Orthodox under a restored patriarchate. It was one of the major faiths recognized by the state, along with the Roman Catholic, the main reformed churches and the Old Catholic, as well as the Muslim and the Jewish.

Although voted by a clear if small majority, the constitution of 1921 was unacceptable to or disapproved of by many. The government went on to implement it, as the smaller Croatian groups joined the CPP in a boycott to strengthen the case for a federal union. The postwar parliamentary system thus had a rather inauspicious start. The multiplicity and diversity of parties meant government by unstable coalition, with increasing royal influence, as Alexander formally ascended the throne on the death of King Peter in August 1921.

As more and more democrats began to see the need to find a third way between Pašić and Radić, their party parted company with the radicals at the end of 1922. The original proportional representation was altered to reduce the number of political groups, and the elections of March 1923 reinforced the differences. The more scattered democrats were down to fifty-one out of 312 seats. Radicals and CPP won most seats, with 108 and seventy respectively; both looked out for allies. Eventually, Pašić tried to come to an agreement with Radić: the CPP would stay away, the government would not go ahead with the administrative division, talks would continue.

As Pašić did no more than keep a purely radical government in place, Radić publicly denounced dynasty, constitution and government. He went to put his case to London and Paris, where he was told to fight his battle in the Belgrade parliament. Returning no further than Vienna, he instructed his deputies to try to agree with the opposition in parliament against the radicals. Unwilling to consider any compromise, a group of hard-line democrats under Pribićević seceded and joined Pašić in government. Radić then went to Moscow in 1924, as the opposition in Belgrade gathered around Ljubomir Davidović (1863–1940). He had brought the independent radicals of Serbia into the Democratic Party, whose leader he now was.

In July 1924, Pašić gave way. An alternative cabinet under Davidović, ready to meet the Croats halfway, barely survived a hundred days in office. Radić returned, his explosive speeches enabled the king to ask Davidović to make way for a broader administration, but it was Pašić who returned with Pribićević to prepare new elections. They decided to apply the Security and Order Act to the CPP as being linked to the Comintern, but its candidates were allowed to stand. The opposition protested. With a third of the vote, the government parties obtained 164 seats at the elections of February 1925. By going to Moscow, Radić had weakened his potential allies, but by branding him as a crypto-communist, the government had not been able to weaken him. The CPP now acknowledged the constitution, rejected any link with Moscow and formed an alliance with the rest of the opposition.

Radić, under arrest, held parallel negotiations with Pašić. A surprise bargain was announced in July: the CPP would join the radicals in government. Judicial proceedings were dropped, Radić at last came to Belgrade and entered the cabinet. Pribićević and his independent democrats angrily turned against the radicals, but opinion welcomed with relief the alliance between the largest Serb and the largest Croat party. King Alexander went to Zagreb in August for the millennial celebrations of the Croatian realm and was received with enthusiasm.

Team work between the two parties was difficult. Radić was totally unpredictable, Pašić at eighty-one all too predictable. While he bargained for the continued existence of his government, a corruption scandal broke out in which his son was implicated. He resigned at the beginning of 1926 and died before the year was out. Other radicals took over, but the party, too, was growing old, increasingly divided, and bitter with the CPP, which broke off in April 1927. Another radical-led cabinet was formed to hold another election.

This was already the first 'palace government'; the elections of September 1927 were the last ones of parliamentary rule. The radicals had 112 members, but were divided into four groups. The most spectacular somersault then linked Radić with the independent democrats. Pribićević, the arch-centralist, had converted to federalism. Disappointed by Belgrade, he had turned to Zagreb. In spite of a short spell of relief all round, the somersaults performed and the apparently tactical bargains struck had left the public bewildered. They had weakened parliament and strengthened King Alexander's disciplinarian prejudices.

Parliament met in an atmosphere heavy with accusations, insults, fisticuffs and obstructionism. Extremist Croats spoke of the need to break away; Radić invited the king to start again from scratch. In June 1928, as a debate turned to pandemonium and insults were answered with revolver shots, two Croat deputies were killed, others were wounded. Radić was mortally wounded. The king hurried to his bedside. Public opinion was numbed. The deputies of Radić's bloc left parliament for Zagreb. Radić died; his party rejected a state funeral. The government resigned; the king tried various formulas. The uncontroversial Slovene populist leader, the Roman Catholic priest Anton Korošec (1872–1940) managed to rally a majority and held out for five months. The last parliamentary government was thus the only one headed by a non-Serb.

Vladko Maček (1879–1964), Radić's successor, told King Alexander that the Croats wanted a new federal constitution. The plan that he sketched out was deemed tantamount to dualism by radical and democrat leaders, but they were willing to discuss it. Not so the monarch, who had already been meddling in party divisions behind the scenes. On 6 January 1929, he dissolved parliament, assumed the task of organizing institutions that would preserve unity, and appointed a new government. Authoritarian régimes were already in place in half-a-dozen European countries, but his was the first in the Balkans.[12] The most domineering king in the region had set a precedent.

The first confused decade of Yugoslavia's history was over. The parliamentary system had not been able to establish a basic consensus between its diverse interests before the monarch declared his impatience with it. Serb parties had indeed dominated, but they could not have governed without the

12 If one does not count Zog's 'constitutionally correct' assumption of a royal title and a powerful prerogative four months earlier in Albania.

self-interested collaboration of Slovene, Muslim and even Croat politicians, who also joined with Serb parties in opposition coalitions. Electoral participation had been high (65–77 per cent) and the parliamentary governments had governed.

As in Romania, the major foreign policy objective had been to secure the frontiers and obtain support. After the initial difficulty over Banat had been solved, good relations continued with Romania. Treaties between Yugoslavia, Czechoslovakia and Romania in 1920–21 completed the Little Entente. Yugoslavia obtained from Greece in 1925 the lease of a free zone in the port of Salonika. In 1923 she even agreed with the agrarian government of Bulgaria on cooperation against terrorism in border areas. In general, Yugoslavia and her partners tried to make for themselves a place in the new European order. Since France was the one power that stood firm on the territorial settlement, she eventually linked herself to the Little Entente. Her treaty with Yugoslavia in 1927 followed that with Romania.

France wanted to offset Italy's friendship with the revisionist states after Mussolini's accession to power, but also to encourage conciliation between Italy and Yugoslavia. Agreement was reached with Rome in 1924, that Fiume should become Italian and that all pending questions be settled. But Italy remained a threat and provoked a crisis between Belgrade and Tirana in 1927.

Belgrade was not strong enough to counter Italian interference in Albanian affairs, let alone impose its will on Albania's rulers. That border was a sore point, because of the ill-disposed Albanian minority in Yugoslavia which was devoid of specific international protection as it formed part of prewar Serbian territory. The resistance to the reimposition of Serbian/Yugoslav rule had been encouraged by incursions from Albania, even though Zogolli had fallen out with Kosovo irredentists and the handful of ethnic Albanian deputies had generally cooperated with the Belgrade government.[13]

Reconstruction had to go hand in hand with integration. The differences were natural as well as historical, and the two did not always coincide. Food shortages, transport disruption, loss of manpower, separation from previous outlets, ensured a discouraging start. There was mutual resentment over the conversion of Austro-Hungarian crowns into dinars, and the setting up of the new National Bank. All that proved no barrier to a cautious financial policy, which stabilized the currency by 1925 with almost no foreign assistance. Yet the economic achievements of the 1920s remain elusive.

The important issue of land reform was met. It was carried out piecemeal, and was not fully settled until the early 1930s. Generally speaking, where there were real agricultural estates of over 100 hectares, they were subject to redistribution. The owners were compensated in state bonds, which the beneficiaries would repay to the state over thirty years, except veterans who

13 Yugoslav census figures of 441,000 ethnic Albanians in 1921 and 505,000 in 1931 were challenged by Albanian memoranda to the League of Nations claiming a million or more. The Yugoslav figure of 20,000 net emigration of Albanians over the decade was also disputed by Tirana's 140,000.

had served with the Allies. Abandoned and uncultivated land was also parcelled out.

Over one-quarter of the arable land was eventually distributed to over one-quarter of the total number of peasant families. Slavs were advantaged in land redistribution everywhere at the expense of minorities. The increase in generally uneconomical holdings of under five hectares was accelerated. They represented 68 per cent of all holdings by 1930, but covered no more than 28 per cent of agricultural land. As in Romania, there was not always enough land available locally to satisfy the peasants' land hunger.

Only in the southern ex-Ottoman areas was there generally more land available, because of population losses through years of insecurity and war, followed by the exodus of part of the Muslim population. Legislation provided for colonization and an extensive programme of land reclamation. Peasants from the barren mountains of Montenegro and Herzegovina initiated a timid reversal of the old Ottoman policy that had favoured the expansion of Muslim Albanians into the plains of Kosovo and the Morava–Vardar corridor in Macedonia. The numbers involved were hardly sufficient to alter the ethnic balance,[14] but the way in which the reform was carried out in Kosovo broadened the gap between Serbs and Albanians.

By the beginning of the 1930s, when the average holding was 8.5 hectares of cultivated land, prewar levels of crop production per head had been recovered, but the land had to provide a living for too many people, and inheritance worsened fragmentation. Eighty-six per cent of the population was still rural; over half of it was estimated as being not really needed.

The state was the biggest capitalist. It owned and operated telecommunications and railways, many forests, mines, lumber mills, spas, sugar refineries, and the tobacco and salt monopolies. It invested in transport, to integrate the rail network; over the decade rail did increase from 0.34 km to 0.73 km/1,000 inhabitants, starting lower and ending higher than any other Balkan state.

Once the most urgent demands for land reform had been met, economic questions were no longer the major issue of the political class, particularly in the face of the mythical peasant way of life, which continued steadfastly. War debts had been repaid by the end of 1926. Currency stabilization opened the door to foreign investment in industry. Before the Depression, direct investment by foreign, essentially British and French, interests in mining had come to own nearly half the Yugoslav industrial stock, but there was little foreign participation in banking, and few loans. The 1927 tariff legislation was the lowest in the Balkans.

Industry recovered rapidly in Croatia. After the land reform, Zagreb's commercial banks could no longer rely on agricultural land mortgages for

---

14 12,000 families in Kosovo and 10,300 in Macedonia, or a total of some 111,000 persons, according to John R. Lampe (*Yugoslavia as History: Twice there Was a Country*, Cambridge: Cambridge University Press, 1996, 147); just over 13,000 families or 70,000 people in Kosovo alone, of whom many left by 1935, according to Noel Malcolm (*Kosovo: A Short History*, London: Macmillan, 1998, 282).

long-term investment, and went into industry. Zagreb thus became the largest industrial centre in the country, retaining its financial advantage over Belgrade. By the mid-1920s, Croatia and Slovenia had 60 per cent of total industrial horsepower, and 45 per cent of total employment in manufacture.

The failure of sufficient market integration and insufficient domestic demand pushed exports to central Europe. Yugoslavia's main exports in 1921–25 were forest products (17.2 per cent) and cereals (17 per cent), with a relative increase (to 20 per cent) in forest products in the second half of the decade. The dominant partnership was with Austria and Italy, who in 1920 together accounted for 63 per cent of Yugoslavia's foreign trade. With an increase in real exports per head that surpassed all other Balkan countries, Yugoslavia's trade balance was favourable in 1924–26. The development of shipping and tourism benefited the balance of payments considerably.

Belgrade's focus of political power as the capital of the new state was not accompanied by the sort of economic leverage that could have furthered greater economic integration. The capital, however, attracted a rich variety of newcomers from across Yugoslavia, as well as many Russian émigrés. Its population doubled from 112,000 in 1920 to 226,000 in 1929 (9 per cent of the total urban population). Both Belgrade and Zagreb (185,000) had by 1920 joined the over-100,000 class of Balkan towns. In spite of three flourishing if parochial cultures, and great variations in the national illiteracy rate of 51 per cent (ranging from 8.8 per cent in Slovenia to over 80 per cent in Bosnia-Herzegovina and Macedonia), Belgrade not only developed considerable cultural and intellectuals links with Zagreb and Ljubljana, but favoured a budding Yugoslav cultural identity attuned to Europe.

The political leaders' vision of a radical transfer of land achieved a national equalization of property structures, but continued fragmentation made it difficult to increase productivity. Foreign industrial investment did at least contribute to reducing the pressure of rural underemployment before the Depression, while net emigration overseas absorbed no more than 13 per cent of the total increase.

Yugoslavia's estimated income per head of working population in 'international units' (the amount of goods and services that could be purchased for one dollar in the USA) over the period 1925–30 was 330 – well above her Balkan neighbours Romania (243) and Bulgaria (284).[15] Miserable poverty (such as in the poorly endowed Karst region) coexisted with better peasant incomes (in the northern plain regions or in Šumadija). Because of its better agricultural performance, the country's growth index was the only one in the Balkans showing enough improvement to keep the gap between its net product and that of the developed European economies from widening.[16]

15 These figures compare with Czechoslovakia's 445, and Great Britain's 1,069 (L.S. Stavrianos, *The Balkans since 1453*, New York: Holt, Rinehart & Winston, 1958, 601).
16 John R. Lampe and Marvin R. Jackson, *Balkan Economic History 1558–1950*, Bloomington, Ind.: Indiana University Press, 1982, 341.

RECOVERY AND PRECARIOUS STABILITY

Postwar Balkan governments generally tried to manage the consequences of the war with the policies that they had quite successfully pursued before the war. This was especially the case with their monetary strategy. Based on the exchange of their currencies at par with the French gold franc to attract European loans, it had seen them through the Balkan Wars, but the First World War had been a different matter.

All their currencies went into inflation, falling to between 25 per cent (for the dinar) and 3.5 per cent (for the leu) of their prewar exchange value by 1923. Whereas Bulgarian and Greek postwar inflation derived from defeat, that in Yugoslavia and Romania derived from victory. On top of debt obligations, the new states had to absorb the depreciating Austro-Hungarian currency which they found both in the newly united lands and in the old kingdoms that had endured occupation. Thus the Romanian leu, the strongest prewar Balkan currency and the only one to adhere formally to the gold standard, had become the weakest.

The restoration of monetary stability was regarded as a matter of urgency. If they could not afford the prewar gold standard to which they had all aspired, the governments were eventually able to return to a fixed exchange rate, albeit well below the prewar level. De facto stabilization was achieved in the mid-1920s. An improved climate, favourable to a revival of foreign lending, made it possible to achieve de jure stabilization of overvalued currencies by the end of the decade.

Not much help could be expected from external sources. Relief was limited in amount and duration, and went mainly to allay famine. Even wartime allies were left to fend for themselves by the powers. There was no alleviation of prewar loans, to which were added massive debt obligations of war and peace. There was no chance of new loans until it was settled how the annual repayments on old ones would be resumed – in gold value, in depreciated francs, or in local currencies. Governments could only reduce expenditure and money supply, which restricted private credit.

Such financial restraints made the industrial growth recorded in the 1920s all the more striking. A large part of the Balkan bourgeoisie welcomed a resumption of the industrialization initiated in the last prewar decade; governments realized the need for it. They used protection, assistance and intervention. Manufacturing generally performed better than crop production.

This was particularly so in Bulgaria and in Greece, who had been less industrialized to start with, and less disturbed by the war. For all her advance, Romania shared common characteristics with the Balkan countries. If her liberals favoured industry, the Peasant Party placed agriculture at the centre of its economic policy, and relied on foreign loans paid for by agricultural exports. Another general problem was that private investors preferred short-term profit to long-term investment, and even governments placed fiscal purposes above development. Finally, the domestic markets were not strong enough to absorb the products of local industries.

The emphasis was still on land, for essentially political motives. Even Albania promised land reform; all the other states implemented it. Governments redistributed land, to redeem promises made during the war, to achieve social stability, to deprive bolsheviks of effective propaganda, to integrate once-imperial borderlands by taking land from members of the former dominant minority to benefit the masses of the ethnic majority. Thus 40 per cent of agricultural land was reallocated in Greece, 20 per cent in Romania, 17 per cent in Yugoslavia and 6 per cent in Bulgaria.

The whole operation was an enormously complex one, and remains one of the most remarkable successes of Balkan states in the interwar period. Even though holdings of under five hectares were thereafter predominant, a proportion of middle-sized owners farmed more land than they owned, and even larger holdings were not eliminated. The reforms expanded an existing system of landowning more than they altered the size of farming units. Former land renters became new peasant owners, but the resulting changes in farming were marginal. Efficiency did not necessarily go with size. Smallholdings near urban centres or with more marketable crops were far more efficient than large collections of landed units farmed out to sharecroppers had ever been.

Furthermore, the impact of markets for foodstuffs did more than reforms for the recovery of agriculture after the war.[17] The marketable share of agricultural production reached 35–40 per cent for all four countries by the late 1920s. Agricultural products and raw materials accounted for the bulk of exports. Although dependence on cereals had diminished, they remained the largest element. Grain production recovered, but not always its output per head; markets were more favourable for other agricultural products and industrial raw materials, such as tobacco, timber and petrol.

By the time Balkan producers were able to return to world markets, these had been tightened. Western Europe was consuming less cereals and protecting domestic producers; there was increased competition from America and Australia. Balkan countries therefore reorientated their foreign trade towards central Europe. Because of their need to earn secure strong currencies to service their debts, and because their trading structures were mostly competitive, Balkan countries drifted away from one another towards industrial countries. As overall commodity prices in the second half of the 1920s fell more quickly than manufacturing prices, terms of trade shifted against Balkan economies.

By the middle of the decade, reconstruction was nearing completion. More stable economic conditions in the late 1920s opened the way to foreign credit once more. Borrowing from abroad was, however, expensive. Only a small proportion of it went into exchange-earning activities. Most of it went to

17 In constant prices, production grew from index 100 in 1921, to the following in 1930: Yugoslavia 139, Greece 143, Romania 155, Bulgaria 195 (Lampe and Jackson, 359–60).

social infrastructural investments, and the payment of interests and dividends. No sooner had conditions eased than the debt burden became heavy and there was little chance that the agrarian sector could generate the surplus of savings to finance further industrial expansion.

Population growth, due more to a lower death rate and reduced emigration overseas than to a high birthrate, renewed pressure on the arable proportion of the land. A larger proportion of people did come to depend on non-agricultural occupations, and marginal changes towards industry took place. Industry absorbed one-quarter more of the 1910–30 increment in the male labour force than the industrial sector employed in 1910, but there was no revolutionary change, and the countryside remained overpopulated.

Progress was achieved before the Depression. All in all, trade did quite well, though relying heavily on the export of primary products and becoming more indebted to creditors. Some growth in income per head was achieved, but it was held back by population increase. The existing prewar gap between the incomes per person of Europe's more developed countries and those of the Balkans could not be diminished.

The foundations of prosperity were fragile, dependent on favourable and expanding markets for primary products, foreign capital and political stability. The balance was a precarious one. If upset, monarchs were tempted to go beyond their wide constitutional prerogatives to try old-fashioned authoritarian solutions. Worse still, right-wing radical movements would spring from resentment at the slowness of parliamentary efforts and disappointment with old and new parliamentary parties alike.

CHAPTER 13

The 1930s – Part 1

Out of Depression into Großraum. *The royal régimes. Balkan cooperation. Yugoslavia under King Alexander and Prince Paul. The* Sporazum. *Bulgaria under King Boris.*

OUT OF DEPRESSION INTO *GROßRAUM*

The Depression had brought postwar recovery to an end. Heralded by the Wall Street crash of 1929, the failure of the Vienna Creditanstalt and the British departure from the gold standard in 1931 affected the Balkan economies. Exports of primary products fell sharply. The disparity between agricultural and industrial prices made the plight of peasants particularly difficult. By 1932–33 many of them were on the verge of bankruptcy, unable to meet tax payments and loan repayments.

Long-term foreign lending stopped, gold and foreign exchange reserves drained away, short-term liquidity dried up. Faced with dwindling revenues and increased relief demands, governments had to curtail expenditure. Intent on defensive orthodoxy to avoid financial collapse, reluctant to relinquish currency parities, their policies were at first deflationary. They resorted to rigorous exchange controls, protectionist restrictions, limitations on debt repayments, the setting up of state purchasing agencies.

Such measures produced results. The capital outflow was stemmed and trade balances improved, but in the longer term adverse side effects outweighed benefits. Imports and debt servicing were more costly, domestic prices rose, exports became difficult. The recovery in internal trade, increased international tension, the economic influence of Germany and the rise of authoritarian régimes, all prompted a shift to more constructive measures of development.

The later 1930s saw a determined effort to industrialize, greater than ever before, for economic necessity, for the substitution of imports that failing agricultural exports could not afford, and for defence. The financial crisis had provoked the disinvestment of much foreign capital, which was anyhow concentrated in energy resources and heavy industry. The state assumed a greater rôle, taking over enterprises that had been under foreign control, promoting cartels as instruments for controlling markets. Public financial institutions grew stronger at the expense of private commercial banking. By the start of the Second World War, defence accounted for around a third of public spending in most budgets.

Indices of manufacturing show the progress of industrial growth against a very unfavourable international background.[1] Sufficient to cut back deficits in the balance of payments, it was not adequate to bring about a radical transformation of economic structures in the time available. The increase in industrial employment could not absorb much of the agricultural overpopulation, which the International Labour Office estimated at 15–20 million. In 1930, the agricultural population was still between 68 per cent (in Greece) and 80 per cent (in Albania) of the total; in 1939, the farm population per square kilometre of cultivated area was between 90 in Romania and an estimated 267 in Albania. Despite an overall declining birthrate, there were still too many people in the countryside; unskilled labour could no longer be exported easily.

Through protection, relief, concessions and incentives, governments achieved marginal improvements in agricultural practices.[2] Balkan exports declined relatively less than the world average for primary-producing countries in the early 1930s, and from 1934 they actually increased their modest share of the total European market. The decline was more an expression of money values; the volume increased despite demographic growth, but there was little structural change. Agriculture could not provide a source of capital accumulation and a market for industrial goods. The overall improvement in the income per head since 1929 was below the European average, even if the comparison with 1913 shows a better relative performance.[3]

Clearing agreements, or the bilateral balancing of claims between countries with exchange controls, had obvious advantages, but they fostered German penetration. Germany was prepared to buy agrarian products and other commodities at reasonable prices, and supply capital equipment in return. The penetration was not sudden or uniform. Germany's increased trade with the Balkans predated the nazis, but with full control of the economy, their government could offer attractive terms. The Reich gained access to much-needed

1 While the overall value of European manufacture grew by an annual average of 1.1 per cent in 1929–38, Greece's growth rate of 5.7 per cent was the fastest in Europe for the decade, Bulgaria's 4.8 per cent was second (along with Sweden and Finland), Romania's 3.4 per cent equal to that of Denmark, and Yugoslavia's 2.4 per cent accelerated to 10.7 per cent from 1936 (John R. Lampe and Marvin R. Jackson, *Balkan Economic History 1558–1950*, Bloomington, Ind.: Indiana University Press, 1982, 483, tables 484–6).
2 Overemployment in agriculture nevertheless kept performance low: the average Balkan peasant at the time grew food for only 1.5 persons, whereas his western European counterpart grew for 4 (Barbara Jelavich, *History of the Balkans, II: Twentieth century*, Cambridge: Cambridge University Press, 1983, 241).
3 Gross national product per capita levels in 1960-US dollars in 1938: Bulgaria 429, Romania 343, Yugoslavia 330, France 936, Europe 671. Percentage changes 1913–38: Bulgaria 59.7 per cent, Romania 7.2 per cent, Yugoslavia 19.4 per cent, France 34.7 per cent, Europe 25.7 per cent (Derek H. Aldcroft and Steven Morewood, *Economic Change in Eastern Europe since 1918*, Aldershot: Edward Elgar, 1995, 84; P. Bairoch, 'Europe's gross national product: 1800–1975', in *Journal of European Economic History*, 5, 1976, 297).

food and raw materials, through overvalued reichsmarks, which could only be used to purchase German goods. Except for Albania, which was Italy's, the Balkans were more or less included in the Reich's *Großraum* by 1938.

Trade with Germany brought salvation. It raised incomes, facilitated the import of machinery and consumer goods, and allowed states to buy arms, but to become a primary producing area for the Reich would not have solved the problem of rural overpopulation. Ironically, the Balkan governments' efforts to assure their security in a darkening international atmosphere, where they felt unprotected by their alliances against threats of aggression, helped open the way to peacetime German penetration. With no real alternative to trade with Germany, they became vulnerable to her pressures. At the end of the interwar period they were once again in the position of imperial borderlands.

The Depression and the change in the European balance of power weakened the forces of democracy. Fears of all sorts surfaced – of revolution, of subversion, of conspiracies, of propaganda, of differences. They called for the maintenance of order and unity at any cost. Rulers resorted to declaring states of emergency and assuming special powers. The dominant parties had not been able to adapt to new territories, new populations, new electorates and new circumstances. Fragile recoveries and hopes of reintegration into the international economy had been shattered. The failure of the parliamentary régimes to cope with the changes, and to satisfy many dreams and aspirations, left the door open to other ideological influences. Alterations in the balance of power gave impetus to forces that sought to undermine existing territorial, political and social patterns. Communism and fascism offered alternatives.

Communism in the Balkans was the weaker of the two forces. Its failure to initiate bolshevik-type revolutions in the immediate postwar period had led to greater dependence on Soviet Russia, with obedience to a centrally determined Comintern line. Local communist parties, already repressed by governments, were affected by the twists and turns of Soviet policy. They found it difficult to cope with peasants who had just been given what they wanted most – land.

Their strength was concentrated in the least developed areas. In order to make use of their revolutionary potential, the Comintern' revisionist policy to 1935 favoured self-determination to the point of secession of all possible territories. It thus had a greater appeal for those who felt nationally disadvantaged, than for the economic underdogs. Revolution and the break-up of states was then abandoned for the time being in favour of national popular fronts against fascism. Disorientated and demoralized by Stalin's purges, communist parties were generally ineffectual.

That they failed to profit from the Depression made it easier for the extreme right to advance. With no clear doctrine, fascism thrived in the latter half of the 1930s. Many already believed that liberal European institutions did not fit the local situation. Peasants were mistrustful of those in power. Impoverished by the Depression, they saw more than ever that money and power were concentrated in the capital for benefit of the capital.

Starting from positivist and reactionary authoritarianism that sought to instrumentalize religion in the service of a paternalistic monarchy, fascism moved on to irrational and elemental impulses that aspired to change the world through revolution. It attracted pell-mell those who longed for a world that had never existed and those attached to the maintenance of existing authority – bourgeois ready to sacrifice liberty on the altar of order and workers drawn to anti-capitalist rhetoric, individuals who were afraid of falling down the social ladder and others who wanted to fight their way up, many semi-educated and educated young men. Made up of paradoxes and contradictions, fascism fed on fear and hatred – of socialism, of communism, of capitalism, of parliamentarianism, of reason, of 'foreigners' within and without.

Native fascists, however, did not accede to power. Neither the political class nor the peasantry turned to them. The failure of the leading parties gave imperative and impatient kings the chance to rule above or without them. The monarchy survived, because it was the ultimate constitutional factor, because it appeared to safeguard the status quo and because it satisfied the need for leadership.

The strong régimes of the 1930s were a return to the nineteenth century, when leadership was in the hands of the monarch and of his advisers. Balkan rulers or their appointed first ministers employed some of the policies and trappings of fascism. After the last real general elections had been held, they dispensed with parliament. They paid lip service to the old order – by keeping parts of the existing constitution or by granting a new one – and to the new one – by invoking corporatism or by setting up a mass movement. Their task was to keep the ship of state intact and to steer it through the storm.

The postwar territorial order in the Balkans had been entrenched by the Paris peace settlement. Britain, who had never felt comfortable about most of its provisions, was soon ready to give up any postwar rôle as a great Allied power. France was the one upon whom it fell to be the main guarantor of that order. She had endorsed it, but it was not, at least as far as the Balkans were concerned, the product of her policies and interests, as is all too often assumed. With the new, renovated or extended states of eastern Europe she never had more than a 'loose network' of diplomatic links.[4] In the Balkans, this concerned Romania and Yugoslavia.

Between 1925 and 1928, Germany's last constraints under the peace settlement had been removed, as both France and Britain sought to organize the peace through reconciliation with her. French proposals for European integration had been well received in the Balkans. All Balkan states at least considered following France in establishing diplomatic relations with the Soviet Union; most eventually did.

The initiative to set up annual Balkan Conferences to study questions of common interest was taken in Greece in 1929. The final aim was some sort of

4 Martin S. Alexander, *The Republic in Danger: General Maurice Gamelin and the Politics of French Defence, 1933–1940*, Cambridge: Cambridge University Press, 1992, 210.

a regional union. In the meanwhile non-governmental initiatives would press governments to a minimum programme, and pave the way for a settlement of outstanding issues. Governments supported the enterprise. It allowed them to test the ground on a variety of issues without committing themselves, but there were problems. Macedonia was a constant irritant, as Greece feared a Yugoslav–Bulgarian rapprochement, and Bulgaria insisted on Macedonian/ Bulgarian minorities.

Nevertheless, sincere efforts were made to overcome difficulties, by concentrating on what could be integrated in economic, social, cultural and technical matters. Even Albania participated from 1931. A customs union was considered, but there was little inter-Balkan trade, and political rather than economic considerations soon prevailed. With Hitler's accession to power, securing frontiers took precedence over economic cooperation. By the time of the fourth annual conference in November 1933, Greece, Romania and Yugoslavia had moved to turn the conferences into a permanent regional organization.

Romania's foreign minister Nicolae Titulescu (1883–1941) had envisaged that all the Balkan states would be members. Greece and Turkey had made up their differences, but Bulgaria and Albania did not join, in spite of Yugoslavia's efforts. The pact signed in Athens in February 1934 between Greece, Romania, Turkey and Yugoslavia was an extension into the Balkans of the principle of regional security of the Little Entente (institutionalized by instruments signed in 1929 and 1933). Intended as a regional compact against all forms of territorial revision, and in support of efforts to outlaw war as a means of settling disputes, it failed eventually to create a united front on vital international issues.

As the pact was designed above all to guarantee existing Balkan frontiers, Bulgaria would not sign it. Although a series of diplomatic niceties left the door open to her, her absence seriously undermined the significance of the Balkan Entente. Yugoslavia argued that the Athens pact had crowned the work of the conferences; Bulgaria and Albania maintained that it had brought it to an end. The fifth conference, due to meet in Istanbul later in 1934, was postponed indefinitely. Another inherent flaw was that, as they formed a political alliance to oppose the revisionism which the Reich supported, the Balkan Entente associates were on the way to becoming economically dependent on Germany.

In 1938, the whole Balkan Entente came to an understanding with Bulgaria: her equal rights in armaments were acknowledged, and all renounced the use of force against one another. The Little Entente did the same with Hungary. By that time, most of the partners had already taken to looking after their own interests without consulting each other. Greece had worked closely with Turkey, both determined not to get embroiled with Russia for the sake of Romania, or with Italy for the sake of Yugoslavia.

Yugoslavia had moved closer to Italy and tacitly assented to the duce's increasing shadow over Albania. She had agreed to back Bulgaria's claim to an Aegean outlet in return for Bulgaria not raising claims to Macedonia. Turkey in 1938 started on a policy of 'repatriating' more Turkish Muslims from the Balkans to Anatolia. Yugoslavia envisaged the possibility of encouraging some 'Turkish' emigration from Kosovo and Macedonia. This was to lessen the danger of the instability of her southwestern border which Italy could manipulate, but the talks with Turkey petered out on the question of financial incentives.

Romania and Yugoslavia kept thinking of Hungary's vigil for her lost territories, which was of no interest to Greece and Turkey. In May 1938, the *Anschluss* had joined Austria to the Reich. Six months later, the partial dismemberment of Czechoslovakia exploded the Little Entente. The Balkan Entente survived, but it was tacitly acknowledged that each member would deal separately with the powers. The two regional ententes were once presented in public relations terms by the Romanian ministry of foreign affairs, as having created, 'from Czechoslovakia to the frontier of Persia, a chain of states [with] identical political interests'.[5] More prosaically, they worked well enough for a number of years to keep at bay the revisionism of Hungary and Bulgaria; they were not strong enough against bigger powers.

Whether measured by commercial or by political criteria, a Balkan realignment unfavourable to France had been taking place since 1936. The Depression, the rise of Hitler, Anglo-French flirtation with Mussolini and the invasion of Ethiopia were serious blows to the Little Entente and the Balkan Entente, as frightened and disoriented members tried thereafter individually to save their skins.

Even the most Francophile among the Balkan rulers and ministers had to adjust to the 1936 Rome–Berlin Axis with its assurances of mutual support and spheres of influence, to the Anti-Comintern Pact (between Germany and Japan in 1936, adhered to by Italy in 1937), and finally to the German-Soviet Pact of 1939. Albania remained fearful and Bulgaria bitter. Nevertheless, Bulgaria's bitterness over Macedonia, Dobrudja and the never-implemented access to the Aegean, and Albania's fear of Yugoslav encroachments and Greek claims, did not lead to war. Restraint was exercised on all sides.

YUGOSLAVIA UNDER KING ALEXANDER AND PRINCE PAUL

Royal influence grew everywhere as political parties splintered. Yugoslavia led the way, when King Alexander abrogated the constitution on 6 January 1929. In so doing he did not use the royal 'we', but the singular 'I', as though to assume personal responsibility for an act that had no formal legal backing.[6] His new government, headed initially by a general who was no more than the monarch's representative, contained known party figures with experience of office. They came from all major parliamentary groups, but only the outgoing prime minister Korošec could claim to have joined with the backing of his

---

5 Press release of 10 February 1934, quoted in Eliza Campus, *The Little Entente and the Balkan Alliance*, Bucharest: Bibliotheca Historica Romaniae, 1978, 80.
6 He again used the singular when he granted a new constitution in 1931.

Slovene clerical party. The others were there as individuals, some against their party's wishes, if not as outright dissidents.

Alexander enacted foundations for his personal rule. He transferred legislative power to the crown. A Law on the Defence of the State strengthened existing anti-communist legislation and extended it to all activities against the new régime. Political parties had to be authorized; those based on sectionalism were banned. Maček welcomed the repeal of the constitution, and so did most Croats, as the first step towards meeting their wishes. Most Serbs thought likewise, because they feared for the unity of the state.

The takeover had been announced as temporary, to allow passions to subside, and to direct minds away from differences to common tasks. The programme was to maintain order and step up integration. Before the end of the year, what remained of legal communist activities through the press and trades unions was suppressed, a unified penal code was introduced, all flags gave way to the Yugoslav tricolour, school curricula were streamlined. The name Yugoslavia was officially adopted. The territory was divided into nine geographical regions that broke up the historical pattern, each headed by a ban — in deference to Croatia's tradition.

Public opinion had been willing to give the king a chance, but different sections had different expectations. Croats had not foreseen a crash programme of Yugoslav patriotism, and quickly saw it as a more efficient way of imposing Belgrade-style centralism, not to say Serbian hegemony. At the time of Radić's death, a former member of parliament, Ante Pavelić (1889–1959) had called for an independent Croatia. Having left the country, he was sentenced in absentia under the Law for the Defence of the State, and began to organize the Ustasha (*ustaša*, insurrectionary) Croatian Liberation Movement. An outgrowth of the 'pure' variant of the Croatian Rights Party, it developed abroad on the fascist model and became the symbol of a radical nationalist fringe. It was given shelter and terrorist training facilities in Italy and Hungary, who would use it as a means to bring pressure to bear on Yugoslavia.

On the economic side, the government provided backing to coordinate the cooperative movements. It set up a Chartered Agricultural Bank to give farmers credit on favourable terms. Measures were taken to educate them in better techniques, to encourage the production of intensive and speciality crops and to stimulate and rationalize exports, until the economy generally began to deteriorate in 1931. The government had responded to falling world prices by setting up a grain export monopoly agency to replace middlemen, and by introducing exchange controls.

Although 1930 passed off quietly, the Croat question had not been solved, and Serbia, too, felt it had been made to give up political liberties gained after a long struggle. The first party leader to come out against the dictatorship, and to be interned in May 1929, had been the Serb Pribićevic, whose independent democrats were allied to the Croatian Peasant Party. In December, Maček himself had been tried, and acquitted, for encouraging those who advocated secession.

His party was changing. From a political organization that had voiced the aspirations of peasants through democracy and social reform within a South Slav federation, it was turning into a movement more sensitive to greater urban interest in the rights of the Croat nation. Although the ustashas had but few supporters at home, the dissatisfaction on which they fed was widespread. By 1931 King Alexander felt that his temporary dictatorship had lasted too long, but that he had not accomplished his aims.

In September 1931, he granted a new constitution, which was seen again as a first step to more change. A bicameral parliament was introduced, with a Senate of appointees and of indirectly elected provincial representatives and a National Assembly elected by universal male suffrage.[7] The government was responsible to the monarch alone. 'Guardian of the unity of the nation and of the integrity of the state', his consent was necessary for any amendment; he was given emergency powers to enact provisional measures in exceptional circumstances.

Only countrywide lists were allowed. Voting was public. The list heading the poll obtained two-thirds of the seats, the rest was shared out in proportion to the number of votes – an improvement on Mussolini's electoral law of 1923. There was only one list – the government's, and over one-third of registered voters did not bother to cast their vote. Parliament gave blanket approval to what the government had done since the last legislature. A government party was set up, soon to be called the Yugoslav National Party, made up of one-time right-wing radicals and of dissidents from the whole former parliamentary spectrum. There was an improvement of the political climate, but King Alexander did not want to move too quickly.

The ustashas stepped up their propaganda, with terrorist backing. In September, a group was infiltrated from the Italian enclave of Zara to incite to rebellion the peasants of the poor north Dalmatian hinterland suffering from the Depression. Police repression was followed in December by bombs in Zagreb. In November, Maček had called for a return to 1918 and to popular sovereignty, attracting expressions of sympathy from different party leaderships. Having made public comments that were considered seditious, he was given a three-year prison sentence in April 1933.

The full effect of the economic crisis hit Yugoslavia just at the time of unrest, with the added misfortune of the exceptionally severe winter of 1931/ 32. Peasants faced ruin. In April 1932, their debts were transferred to the Chartered Agricultural Bank. The larger Zagreb banks were hard hit by the collapse of the Creditanstalt, followed by the British decision to go off the gold standard just as the Yugoslavs settled to go on it. A banking crisis developed, agricultural credit dried up, farm prices were at their lowest in 1933–34. Rigorous exchange controls restricted foreign trade and cut off sources of credit. The dinar depreciated by more than 22 per cent in 1932.

---

7 The upper house was a rarity in the Balkans: it existed in Romania, and in Greece under the republic. It had been tried in King Alexander Obrenović's (equally granted) constitution of 1901. Interestingly, in 1931 the possibility of female suffrage was envisaged (but left at that).

Italy was Yugoslavia's major outlet, and together with Austria and Germany took almost 58 per cent of her exports in 1930. War reparations of technical equipment from Germany had been followed up by demands for the supply of renewals, so that imports from Germany were already 16 per cent of total value in 1925–32. After Hitler's emergence in 1933, trade agreements in 1933 and 1934 increased German purchases and introduced clearing.

Although trade and diplomacy did not coincide, King Alexander reinforced the alignment with the victors of the Great War. In 1929 the Little Entente signed a pact of arbitration and conciliation on the model recently adopted by the League of Nations, and in 1933 formally set up permanent institutions. When Britain and France joined Italy and Germany to cooperate on the maintenance of peace, with no reference to the League, the distrust aroused was another incentive to link the Little Entente to other Balkan states.

In 1929 Greece had agreed to enlarge the Yugoslav free zone in the port of Salonika. The Balkan Conferences had laid the basis for much useful cooperation, in which Bulgaria had participated. Meetings between King Boris and King Alexander in 1933 initiated a political rapprochement, but the Yugoslav monarch found Bulgaria reticent to enter an alliance which implied an acceptance of the territorial status quo.

Yugoslavia had become part of a French-supported buffer zone between central Europe and Soviet Russia (not, as Soviet and communist propaganda said, an auxiliary of France in anti-Soviet containment) and she had established close relations with France. However, while the Yugoslav monarch aimed at the creation of a network centred on Yugoslavia to hinder Mussolini's aims, France, more conscious of the rising strength of nazi Germany, wanted to bring her east European allies and Italy together to check Germany. King Alexander was invited to Paris, to display the Franco-Yugoslav alliance and to carry discussions further. Before setting off, he went to Sofia to keep up the Bulgarian link.[8]

His efforts to strengthen Yugoslavia's external security were closely related to the task of consolidating the country internally. He considered his foreign policy to have yielded results, but was conscious of the fact that his rule had not had the desired effect at home. On the eve of his visit to France, among other indications of impeding change, he had let Maček know that he would be released to negotiate a solution to the Croat problem. The ustashas decided to strike at the man who was the font of all authority. In December 1933, a plot to kill him in Zagreb was foiled. On 9 October 1934, just after landing at Marseilles for the start of his state visit to France, he was shot dead with the French foreign minister who had come to greet him. The assassination was the work of the ustashas; the assassin was an IMRO activist.

Contrary to ustasha expectations, the murder had the immediate effect of bringing his subjects together. Serbs had generally respected the king; most

---

8 On these royal visits, the kings delivered banquet speeches, not in French, but each in his own language without translation, to stress the closeness of Bulgarian and of Serbo-Croatian.

Croats had approved his firm policy towards Italy. The constitution survived without a ruling monarch, as Alexander's successor was his eleven-year-old son Peter II (1923–1970). The late monarch had designated a regency council – his cousin Prince Paul (1893–1976), together with two distinguished but little-known figures. Once again, hopes were raised. Bogoljub Jevtić (1886–1960), diplomat and courtier who had been King Alexander's foreign minister, became prime minister. Maček and others were released. Elections were announced for May 1935.

Before the League of Nations, Yugoslavia charged Italy and Hungary with complicity in the assassination. As France and Britain were anxious not to embarrass Mussolini, the charge against Italy was dropped. A compromise was worked out whereby Budapest declared that it had punished some officials for not checking on the ustashas in Hungary. A French court passed life sentences on three conspirators, and death sentences *in absentia* on three others – including Pavelić who was in Italy.

The regency made conciliatory gestures. The conditions for presenting countrywide lists were eased, and an opposition coalition was revived with Maček as its leader. Its aim was to win the election, and to reorganize the state according to a subsequent all-party agreement. The government ran the election as a plebiscite for the dead sovereign. Despite open voting and manipulation, over 73 per cent of the electorate voted; 37 per cent of votes went to the opposition.

Encouraged by the results, the opposition protested against the way in which the elections had been held. It called for a neutral government to introduce a new electoral law and hold free elections. The Jevtić cabinet broke up. The finance minister Milan Stojadinović (1888–1961), an ex-radical who had built up his own following in the government party, had approached fellow radicals, Slovene populists and Muslims, to form a more solidly based party of government supporters and a government that could seek the cooperation of the Croatian Peasant Party. He had British business connexions and references. He put together a government of which he was also foreign minister. Political prisoners were amnestied, censorship was relaxed, parties were tolerated. A Yugoslav Radical Union was formed as planned. Most of the recently elected government deputies switched allegiance.

Prince Paul was looking for a way out within the existing framework. He needed the safeguard of its royal prerogative; formally the constitution could not be amended during a minority. It was quickly obvious that there would be no early overhaul and no return to real parliamentary government. The old radicals, who had so far kept apart from the united opposition, joined it, thus removing the Serb element of Stojadinović's party.

The worst had not happened after Alexander's assassination and the opposition was raising its head. The pre-1929 political parties were tolerated within limits, including the communists. As the Soviet Union now believed that a break-up of Yugoslavia would serve the interests of nazi-fascist régimes rather than its own, the new 'popular-front' line and the Depression helped the Communist Party's growing emphasis on agitation through legal organizations. King Alexander's attempt to force a Yugoslav national identity was tacitly abandoned, but Stojadinović did no more to solve the Croat problem. He had the support of time-serving Serb politicians, as well as of Slovenes and Muslims who safeguarded their sectional interests. His skill in organizing the new party enabled him to stay in power without constitutional concessions.

The CPP was worried by the ustashas' totalitarian, violent, racial and religious nationalism, and by student response to it. To keep its hold, Maček, with the help of his largely Serb allies of the Independent Democratic Party, developed the parastatal and even paramilitary organization of his Croatian Peasant Party in the spirit of the times. The nuclei of Serbian parties that had not given in to the crown continued to cooperate with Maček, who also had talks with Stojadinović. All were agreed that a solution had to be found to the Croat problem, but the government did not want to have to revise the constitution, and the opposition was not united on how to revise it.

The prime minister's policy was to avoid conflict over delicate issues, and let time work for him, in the belief that economic efficiency and diplomatic realism would do the rest. Harvests were good in 1935 and 1936. The government helped agricultural exports by improving transport and by settling debts. In 1936, these were transferred to the Chartered Agricultural Bank, to which they would be repaid over twelve years. The debts of lower-income farmers were drastically reduced. Bank liabilities moved to deposits in public institutions. The government, with its rearmament programme, was the best customer for this new supply of funds, which allowed the foreign share of the public debt to be reduced from 79 per cent in 1932 to 52 in 1941.

It was under Stojadinović that the foundations of Yugoslavia's mining industries were laid. By 1936 they ranked second in value after agricultural industries. Sixty per cent of the country's industrial capital was foreign. State enterprises accounted for 15 per cent, with another 22 per cent under cartels that were subordinated to government control since 1935. However, the rate of industrial development was too slow to relieve markedly the pressure of rural overpopulation. Industry absorbed only 19 per cent of the new labour force that entered the market in 1918–38.

Stojadinović's efforts to reflate the economy required the isolation from international pressure that the German market promised. By 1936, Germany took 23.7 per cent of exports and provided 26.7 per cent of imports, making up for the loss of the Italian market due to League of Nations sanctions after the invasion of Ethiopia. She came up with the seductive offer of preferential rates and quotas for Yugoslavia's harvest, paid for by transfers of manufactures. By 1937 Germany took 36 per cent of exports and provided 32 per cent of imports. The advantages to Yugoslavia were huge. The prices of agricultural commodities rose again, the currency recovered, the government was able to discard inflationary monetary policies.

With Mussolini now wanting a united Yugoslavia as a check to Germany's ambitions, Stojadinović doubted the wisdom of continuing with sanctions.

To support the duce's involvement in Africa kept him out of the Balkans and released Yugoslavia from increasing economic reliance on Germany. In 1936 Stojadinović was attracted by the prospect of security in the Adriatic. After an agreement to restore trade relations, he was given an elaborate reception in Rome. A Treaty of Non-Aggression and Arbitration followed in March 1937. Italy would respect (and not tolerate activities against) the territorial integrity of Yugoslavia, and grant concessions to her Yugoslav minority, in return for Yugoslav recognition of the empire.

In January, Yugoslavia had signed a one-clause bilateral Treaty of Eternal Friendship with Bulgaria which went against the letter and the spirit of the Balkan Entente. Romania and Greece protested. Having assured Paris and London that Yugoslavia had not given up her old friends, but just wanted to be on good terms with as many powers as possible, Stojadinović went to Berlin in January 1938, to tell Hitler that Yugoslavia would not accept any commitments against Germany. He claimed that his neutral policy enhanced his country's security. Real neutrality, however, was difficult, in view of the growing strength and proximity of Germany and Italy, the material benefits of trade with Germany, and the weakness of what remained of the French security system.

The concordat crisis had shown the lack of homogeneity of the Radical Union. Negotiated under King Alexander and signed in 1935, the concordat with the Holy See integrated the different régimes under which the Catholic Church operated. It satisfied the government and the Catholic Church in Yugoslavia, and was hardly different from the old Serbian concordat. When, however, ratification was tabled in July 1937, the Orthodox Church raised an unexpected storm, not about the concordat as such, but about the terms, which it claimed were better for the Catholic minority than for the Orthodox majority. The aim was essentially to discredit Stojadinović. Serb bitterness ensued, because the concordat was seen as a further component of the Italian connexion. With opposition whipped up in Serbia and lack of interest in Croatia, the concordat was shelved.

Stojadinović was turning the Yugoslav Radical Union into his 'leadership' party, with an unpopular aping of fascist trappings. This was the time when communism again gained some respectability as a progressive force,[9] yet the concordat crisis led not to a popular front but a more closely united opposition. In October 1937 a formal agreement between the opposition parties caused a wave of enthusiasm. It called for a transition to a new constituent assembly which would work out a structure to satisfy a majority of Serbs, a majority of Croats and a majority of Slovenes. Never had Serbo-Croat friendship at popular level seemed so close. Huge crowds greeted Maček when he came to Belgrade in August 1938.

---

9 The drawn-out process by which Tito came to be appointed to head the Communist Party of Yugoslavia started in the summer of 1937, but was not finalized until the autumn of 1940.

Parliament was dissolved and elections called for December. Stojadinović thought that the situation justified his policy not to count on western support and not to tamper with the constitution, but he fared worse than Jevtić in 1935. Almost 75 per cent of voters went to the polls, and almost 45 per cent of the votes went to Maček's opposition list. The prime minister's hopes of playing Italy off against Germany had been dashed. His ambitious manner and his leadership style had caused too many adverse reactions, right up to Prince Paul, who now engineered his fall.

The prince-regent had immediately entered into confidential negotiations with Maček on how to solve the Croat question. By February 1939, an alternative team from the Yugoslav Radical Union was ready and Stojadinović had to resign. The new cabinet, under the ex-radical Dragiša Cvetković (1893–1969), was determined to settle with Maček. On the subject of the constitution, it stated that there would be no formal obstacle to revision once King Peter II had come of age in September 1941.

Talks with Maček were held under pressure of foreign events: Hitler ended the Czechoslovak state in March, Mussolini took over Albania in April, and the two signed their Pact of Steel. The Reich had acquired Yugoslavia's most important source of armaments. Mussolini, wanting to keep all his options open, resumed his links with Croats and extended them to Maček, who used them in order to press Belgrade to give way. The Croat leader told his Serb opposition colleagues that they should trust him and the crown to come to an arrangement, as danger was at the gates. Although they refused to be stampeded into half-measures that would separate Serbs from Croats, Maček felt it urgent to counter Pavelić's appeal before war broke out.

Concluded barely a week before Hitler attacked Poland on 1 September 1939, the Cvetković–Maček Agreement set up a self-governing province of Croatia, with its elected Sabor and an executive under a ban appointed by the crown, responsible for everything except defence, state security, foreign affairs and foreign trade. Its territory would extend over Croatia, Slavonia and Dalmatia, with parts of Bosnia and Herzegovina – a third of Yugoslavia, with a third of the total population (4.4 million, including 866,000 Orthodox Serbs and 164,000 Muslims). General elections would be held under a new electoral law. The agreement was endorsed by the Radical Union's Slovene and Muslim components, by the CPP's Independent Democratic partners and by the Serb Agrarian Party, all of whom joined the government with the Croatian Peasant Party.

The agreement was formalized on 26 August. A new government was appointed under Cvetković with Maček as deputy prime minister. Parliament was dissolved. The government was given full powers to modify the electoral law, the law on the press and the law on parties. A process of constitutional revision was certainly started, but it was not called so. It was extraordinary and provisional, introduced by royal ordinances under the crown's reserved emergency powers. As a compromise, the Cvetković–Maček *Sporazum* of

1939 resembled the *Ausgleich* of 1867 and the *Nagodba* of 1868, but it was only a beginning and was based on unsound foundations.

Serbs and Croats were the nearest to each other, culturally and territorially, but Serbs had reacted as a satisfied majority in the combined state, which had not turned out as Croats had imagined. In the difficult decade of the 1930s, the Serbo-Croat problem was removed from public political discussion. It was transferred to contacts between the leaders of technically illegal opposition parties who wanted to combine against the authoritarian régime, or between part of the opposition and the crown who wanted to divide the opposition. Not all Serb trends had necessarily wanted the constitutional framework to be so centralized, though the crown did. Now that the Croatian peasantist leadership had negotiated a compromise with the crown, the rest of the country remained under the old system.

Even when unity was not actually imposed on the country's diversity, it was superimposed through artificial formulas, and not woven out of the similarities of pluralism. The cultural élite who could have done it was too small, it was linked to the state, and anyhow had too little time between the two world wars. It was either completely attuned to Europe, or sought a model in an idealized illiterate or semi-literate self-centred rural population. Yet governments – such as they were – can be credited with the postwar reconstruction, the agrarian reform, a unified free market, gradual industrialization and a foreign policy which protected Yugoslavia's integrity and independence up to the beginning of the Second World War.

BULGARIA UNDER KING BORIS

The 1931 parliamentary elections, for which proportional representation had been reintroduced, were the last to be held under Bulgaria's Tŭrnovo constitution. The centre-left government of the People's Bloc had come to office at the time of the full impact of the Depression. The previous government had just taken initial measures to reduce peasant debts and set up an official purchasing agency. Diversification of crops was encouraged with a view to export, but the countryside responded by reverting to subsistence farming. As the peasants' purchasing power shrank, so did the market and credit for manufactures; industrial wages fell. There were food shortages in cities. Food had to be imported from Yugoslavia at a cost to currency reserves.

The communists benefited by winning an absolute majority on Sofia City Council in 1932. On the right Tsankov echoed National Social calls for a partnership of capital and labour under state control. The bloc itself squabbled over office and influence, after having railed against such behaviour. It had the election of most of the communists' Sofia councillors and of most of their parliamentary deputies invalidated, but dared not tackle IMRO. Macedonian terrorism continued unabated, despite the fact that it isolated Bulgaria and increasingly alienated opinion.

Neither communists nor Tsankov's National Social Movement attracted the peasantry. The 'national cause' as officially preached, and as practised by terrorists, had lost much of its lustre. Some of the 'intelligentsia' turned to *Zveno* (The Link), a pressure group founded in 1927 by a reserve army colonel, Kimon Georgiev (1882–1969), around a newspaper of that name. Its membership was called to place country before party, to provide efficient guidance from above and to push for better relations with Yugoslavia. Its appeal in the summer of 1930, for a competent administration that would get rid of politicians and Macedonians, had received an enthusiastic reception. Zveno adopted a fashionable fascist idea of reorganizing political life on corporatist lines, and was connected with officers of the Military League.

At the turn of 1933/34, a conspiracy of pro-Zveno officers decided to seize the initiative. Tsankov was planning a huge rally to coincide with a private visit of Göring's, and there were rumours that the king might purge the army of zvenists. The conspirators were also prompted by fears of international isolation. The London Convention on terrorism had included in the definition of terrorism the support of, or failure to take measures against, armed subversive groups, and the Balkan Entente seemed to recreate the 1913 alliance against Bulgaria. A carefully planned and well-executed coup, under Colonel Damyan Velchev (1883–1954) of the Military League, took control on 19 May 1934. King Boris accepted a Zveno government backed by the Military League.

With Georgiev as prime minister, the new régime proceeded to implement the Zveno ideology and programme. The constitution was not abrogated, but ceased to function. The Assembly was dissolved and the government legislated by decrees. Parties were dissolved and their papers closed. The bureaucracy was purged. Trades unions were replaced with a single official Bulgarian Workers' Union. The territory was reorganized into seven provinces. Mayors were appointed. New councils and the new parliament, it was announced, would be based on the 'estates' – workers, peasants, craftsmen, merchants, the intelligentsia, the civil service and the free professions. A Directorate for Social Renewal was set up to propagate ideas through education, the press and culture.

The Zveno régime moved swiftly against Macedonians. Although not destroyed, IMRO was never again the power that it had been, and ceased to be a constraint on the conduct of foreign policy. There were no major internal repercussions. It was possible to move to closer links with Yugoslavia, through cultural and technical cooperation, and through royal visits. Better relations were sought with France and Great Britain; diplomatic relations were established with the Soviet Union in 1934.

Disbanding the Assembly and the parties, and the operation against IMRO, had been popular moves. Politicians had lost all prestige and the Macedonian groups were seen as no better than gangsters. Beyond that, however, the Zveno programme did not enjoy wide popular support. Zveno activists and Military League officers did not represent a single view. The major debate was whether a mass organization should be created to sustain the work of the government. The old party leaderships were still around, operating in the shadows. So was the king, whose formal authority underpinned the government, and whose position had not been sufficiently considered. Velchev wanted a new constitution, with a much reduced royal prerogative, but King Boris was the better political intriguer of the two.

In January, the monarch began to move in stages against the régime that he did not control. He first appointed a royalist general as prime minister instead of Georgiev, then in April a civilian government, and in November the diplomat Georgi Kioseivanov (1884–1960), who was entirely the king's prime minister. Without rejecting the Zveno idea of government, in April Boris had issued a manifesto 'to restore orderly and peaceful life'. The Directorate for Social Renewal was dissolved; a new constitution was promised that would enshrine Bulgaria's national and democratic traditions.

The first aim, however, was to remove the military from politics. Velchev, who had returned after leaving the country, was tried for plotting against the sovereign and government, sentenced to death and reprieved by Boris. The Military League was dissolved, a large number of zvenist officers were retired or transferred. Backed by more senior army officers, King Boris wooed the army into submission.

He was now in full control, groping his way towards a personal régime without ever knowing what type of political system would emerge. He hoped to be able to defend himself from the left, from the right and from the army, to give the army a proper rôle by rearming and modernizing it, and to introduce a 'controlled democracy'. He thought of a new constitution, but did not know where opinion stood. Communists remained a force to be reckoned with, as was shown by a spate of industrial unrest in 1936, while Tsankov's movement gained in fascist self-confidence. Boris feared the election of an assembly dominated by extremes that he could not control. The leaders of the old parties feared an assembly under the King's sway, and tried to form a wide-ranging Constitutional Bloc to return to the Tŭrnovo constitution.

Eventually, King Boris postponed the promised elections and opted for mending the constitution through a series of modifications that would set up a 'tidy and disciplined democracy'. He started with new electoral regulations, tested at local level in January 1937. With no party organizations, candidates had to attest that they were not communists. Later, educational qualifications were introduced, voting was made compulsory for men, and unmarried (or widowed) women were given the vote. Large social movements would be allowed to emerged once 'the soul of people had healed'.

In March 1938, these regulations applied to the first general elections since 1931 – the return, in a long-drawn-out procedure, of 160 deputies from single-member constituencies. The government used its influence to secure ninety-five approved deputies. The leaders of the Constitutional Bloc, who had fought a unified campaign, obtained sixty or so. The communists, who tried to form an anti-fascist coalition, found little support from the traditional parties, but did manage to return five deputies for their Bulgarian Workers' Party – who were expelled. Although dominated by the government, the new Assembly was not entirely quiescent.

The immediate aim of Bulgaria's foreign policy since Stamboliisky had been to escape isolation. The alleviation of the peace terms was to be achieved through 'peaceful revisionism' with the help of Italy, who could act as protector in the League of Nations and would turn a blind eye to IMRO.[10] Efforts were also made to improve relations with neighbours. Nevertheless, peaceful revisionism with the help of Italy did not produce much, and the setting up of the Balkan Entente, which Bulgaria could neither join nor destroy, marked a setback in King Boris's Balkan policy.

His new approach was to avoid commitments to great powers, and to try to circumvent the Balkan Entente by concentrating on building bridges with his western neighbour. Yugoslavia was not happy that Bulgaria remained outside the entente, fearing that she could be an easy prey for the Axis. The 1937 treaty was a symbol of changed attitudes. In July 1938, the Balkan Entente and Bulgaria signed a Treaty of Friendship and Non-Aggression. The entente partners recognized Bulgaria's right to disregard (as she had been doing for some time) restrictions imposed on her rearmament, in return for her pledge to submit to arbitration any dispute with her neighbours.

In October, after the Munich Agreements, Yugoslavia and Bulgaria moved yet closer. The Yugoslavs offered a customs union, a miliary alliance and even frontier rectifications, in return for a renunciation of all claims on Yugoslav Macedonia. King Boris would not go as far as that. At the outbreak of the Second World War in September 1939, Bulgaria was still free of commitments to any great power, but the influence of the west had been weak in comparison to Russia and Germany. Russophile feelings were strong, and so was German cultural and economic influence. Boris's was the only Balkan kingdom whose interests were favourably affected by the German-Soviet Pact.

At that time, Kioseivanov dissolved the Assembly, which was not thought to be docile enough. A snap election was held at the turn of 1939/40. With restrictions for non-government candidates, all but twenty seats were easily secured; Kioseivanov was replaced by a Germanophile academic, Bogdan Filov (1883–1945). Bulgaria was now ready for revisionism through a more intimate relationship with Berlin.

Trade links had been close throughout the interwar period. Forged during the First World War, they had been maintained in the 1920s. The Depression had pushed Bulgaria further towards Germany than was the case with other Balkan countries. Clearing, introduced shortly after the advent of the nazis, worked to the benefit of Bulgarian exports. In 1929 Germany already

---

10 The relationship was symbolized by King Boris's wedding in 1930 to a daughter of King Victor Emmanuel III, whereas other Balkan monarchs were appropriately brothers-in-law. Alexander of Yugoslavia had been married to a sister of Charles II of Romania, who was separated from a sister of George II of Greece, himself married (divorced in 1935) to another sister of the Romanian king. Prince Paul of Yugoslavia was also married to a Greek princess.

bought 30 per cent of Bulgaria's exports, and provided almost as much of her imports. Ten years later, the now greater Reich bought almost 68 per cent of exports, and provided 65.5 of imports. Germany was the dominant trading partner and the provider of weapons.

With the influx of refugees, the proportion of Bulgarian speakers in the population had risen to 86.7 per cent of the 6.3 million population by the 1934 census.[11] The change in the social structure was, however, minimal, with 77.5 per cent being rural in 1937. Of the rest, only 12.5 per cent lived in settlements of over 20,000 inhabitants. Sofia grew from 154,000 in 1920 to 335,000 in 1938. A third of the urban population consisted of the 130,000 public officials with their dependents, a total of 650,000. With increasing pressure on the land, holdings of under ten hectares had increased from 81.5 per cent of the total (58.1 per cent of the total agricultural land) in 1926, to 90.2 per cent (66.9 per cent of the total agricultural land) in 1934. Estates of over twenty hectares (under 1 per cent of the total agricultural area) were as rare as landless agricultural labourers (100,000).

Although Bulgaria was at the forefront of Balkan efforts to modernize agriculture through technical improvements and diversification away from cereals, it remained backward. By 1934–39, wheat yields were 31 per cent above prewar levels, still representing 13 per cent of total export earnings. More striking was the increase in acreage of industrial and specialized crops, principally tobacco, which in 1926–30 accounted for over 38 per cent of total export value. The fall in world prices showed that Bulgaria could adapt to new crops, switching to sunflowers and sugar beet, vegetables, fruit and wine.

Agriculture had continuing access to credit during the 1930s. Membership of cooperative credit associations rose from 199,000 in 1928 to 341,000 in 1939. The merger of the Central Cooperative Bank with the State Agricultural Bank in 1934 added greatly to the funds of cooperatives available for loan, leaving private banks and individuals with less than 40 per cent of agricultural loans – compared to some 75 per cent in neighbouring Romania and Yugoslavia. The government did its best to alleviate the debt problem after the Depression, but it was not until the advent of Zveno that measures were adopted to reduce the principal owed, with lowered interest rates.

As early as December 1930, under the impact of falling world farm prices, an official cereals purchasing agency had been created to subsidize exports. By 1934 the last parliamentary government had extended its powers to a monopoly of purchases. Nevertheless, farm incomes remained depressed. Peasants believed they were unfairly penalized to the benefit of industry and rearmament, and that exports were subsidized at the expense of domestic consumption.

The rôle of the state in the small industrial sector declined slightly. By 1939 state-owned enterprises were responsible for no more than 9 per cent of total production. Foreign ownership of joint-stock industrial capital had increased

---

11 That of Greeks had fallen to below 0.4 per cent, and that of Turks to 9.8 per cent. There was also some encouragement after 1934 to emigrate to Turkey, with added pressure to adopt Bulgarian surnames and to use the Bulgarian language.

from 15 per cent in 1929 to 22 per cent in 1939, bringing little change. Bulgaria's industrial production had grown from 5.1 per cent of her gross national product in 1926, to 5.6 per cent in 1938 – the lowest proportion in the Balkans with the exception of Albania. Industry remained overdependent on foreign raw materials, many of which could have been provided from domestic sources. The size of industrial units, like that of land holdings, remained small. In 1934, only 322 of some 88,000 workshops and factories had more than fifty employees.

By contrast, the state increased its participation in finance and trade. The chaos that followed the collapse of the Creditanstalt forced the introduction of foreign currency restrictions and control over foreign trade. That was done despite a good harvest in 1931 and an export surplus, to save the currency needed to service the foreign debt. Much of the authority that the National Bank had lost at the time of the adoption of the gold standard in 1928 under western pressure, was restored, with new powers acquired during the 1930s to control the sale and the purchase of grain and various other crops.

In 1934, eight of the twelve native joint-stock banks were merged into a single state-supported Bulgarian Credit Bank. Since the predominant financial institution was the State Agricultural Bank, by 1936 state financial institutions accounted for two-thirds of all deposits, and three-quarters of all new credit – surpassing the public concentration of financial power in all the other Balkan states.

Peasants could withdraw into frugal self-sufficiency, but hardship had hit the urban population who, by the late 1930s, spent up to 56 per cent of their income on food. It was in towns that the disparities of wealth were palpable in an otherwise rather egalitarian society. With a lack of any exports in great demand from western European countries that still traded freely, and the incentives to favour clearing, German overtures were irresistible. Dependence combined with resentment to make Bulgaria an easy prey to German influence. Voluntary cooperation with the Reich seemed to offer the chance of preserving independence, of soothing a social problem and of furthering revisionist aims.

CHAPTER 14

The 1930s – Part 2

Greece: exit Venizelos, enter Metaxas. Romania: King Charles II's experiments between fear of Russia and fear of Germany. Albania: the first to lose her independence.

GREECE UNDER VENIZELOS AND METAXAS

Greece was the only Balkan country to have entered the 1930s without a king but with a prewar political leader still at the head of government. Venizelos was the last of the great figures that had dominated Balkan parliamentary politics and government for decades. Romania's liberal Brătianu *père* had died as far back as 1891, and Brătianu *fils* in 1926, the same year as Serbia's radical Pašić, while Bulgaria's agrarian Stamboliiski had been murdered in 1923.

Venizelos had influenced Greek political life at the head of his Liberal Party ever since he had been projected from his native Crete onto the national political scene in 1909. Prime minister between 1910 and 1915, and again between 1917 and 1920, the architect of Greek military and diplomatic victories in the Balkan Wars, the diplomat of the Paris Peace Conference, he had since 1924 divided power with the monarchist interests that had survived the Anatolian disaster and the departure of the king. He and his now essentially personal following had been swept back to office in the 1928 elections with the huge parliamentary majority of 223 out of 250 deputies.

Venizelos's great achievement in foreign policy was reconciliation with Turkey. Although he backed the Balkan Conferences, his preference was for bilateral arrangements. He feared the possibility of Greece finding herself on a collision course with any great power that became involved with the Balkans, and he feared a Yugoslav-Bulgarian rapprochement. It was Venizelos who stressed that the aim of the Balkan Entente should be to guarantee the security of its partners against threats from Balkan states only.

His diplomatic feats took place against the background of the massive world economic slump. Greece had suffered bad harvests in 1928–30, but as the only net importer of cereals in the region, she was not affected as soon as the rest of the Balkans, since the value of her agricultural imports dropped more than earnings from tobacco and other exports.

Actually, Greek agriculture performed rather well during the 1930s. In 1931–35 and again in 1936–38, Greek crops returned to prewar levels, with a striking advance in cereal production per head and per hectare, despite the bad harvests. Land reclamation projects in Macedonia led to continued increase in wheat cultivation, so that Greece was able to meet 64 per cent of her wheat requirements for 1933–37, compared to only 40 per cent in 1928. The country had the smallest rural population in the peninsula (60 per cent of the total), the lowest surplus rural population at the beginning of the decade (only 50 per cent) and the lowest illiteracy rate (27 per cent at the end of the 1930s).

Greece also had the best credit structure, and generally the most consolidated financial structure. Eighty per cent of farmers' debts was owed to public institutions – the National Bank and the new Agricultural Bank. The latter, set up by Venizelos for better access to credit for peasants, granted the majority of its loans to cooperatives and favoured those which grew grain.

The two largest banks were the Bank of Greece and the National Bank of Greece. The former was created in 1928 as the new central bank, with exclusive rights of note issue. It went on to acquire in 1931 the licence to deal in foreign exchange, followed by the channelling of clearing arrangements. Greece's departure from the gold standard in 1932 also enlarged its powers; it held the drachmas released to the International Financial Commission, which still oversaw the foreign debt. Having thus doubled its reserves of gold and foreign exchange in 1933, the Bank of Greece could raise its note issue and enable the lifting of the severe exchange controls in 1936. The National Bank, left to pursue its commercial operations with its semi-official character intact, boosted its share of total commercial liabilities for Greek banks to 69 per cent in 1934.

As the Greek economy was more dependent on British credit and held more British pounds, it was particularly hard hit by the British departure from the gold standard. Bad raisin and tobacco harvests in 1929–31 weakened its capacity to ride it out. The state cereals purchasing agency, set up in 1928 ahead of all the other Balkans countries in order to promote greater productivity for the domestic market, was followed in 1931 by a purchasing agency for tobacco. The Venizelos government also decided to leave the gold standard – the only Balkan country to do so formally. To close the balance of payments deficit, and to meet the foreign debt service, the drachma was devalued to some 43 per cent of its previous parity value with gold, and stringent exchange controls were imposed in 1932–36.

The Greek economy depended on 'luxury' agricultural exports such as raisins, tobacco and olive products, on shipping and tourism, and on remittances from migrants, all of which fell drastically. The economic decline disrupted the care and resettlement of refugees. In 1933 Greece once again had to default on part of its substantial foreign loans.

As elsewhere in the Balkans, state intervention in the economy had increased. Although intended to assist the mass of the population, it actually had the effect of boosting that part of the bourgeoisie tied to the state apparatus. The republic and the liberals notwithstanding, the republican constitution of 1927 was less liberal than the 1911 revised version of the monarchical statute. In such a climate the 'national question' reappeared. Venizelos's concentration on maintaining good relations with Turkey, with Great Britain and with Italy disregarded continued popular rancour with Turkey, the Greek Cypriots' request for union with Greece, and the Dodecanese.

With criticism of the liberal government increasing, royalist forces again gained in popularity. After a full-term Chamber of Deputies, the September 1932 parliamentary elections, held with a return to proportional representation, resulted in deadlock. They ushered in a period of instability and polarization that led to the end of parliamentary rule four years later. The Liberal Party had retained only the narrowest of leads over the monarchist People's Party, but it was the latter's Panagis Tsaldaris (1867–1936) who formed a government which lasted until the new year. Venizelos then returned to office once more (and for the last time), to go to the country afresh, to clarify the situation with another change in the electoral system – the introduction of a majority system. At the March 1933 elections, the populists and their allies this time secured a comfortable majority of 135 deputies over the Venizelists' ninety-six. Tsaldaris became prime minister again.

The results came as a shock to the army, whose officer corps had been purged of royalists and restaffed with republicans. Politicians had their client officers, and once in power dismissed their adversaries' military supporters. Even though Tsaldaris and his People's Party had accepted the republican constitution, officers feared a restoration. The ultra-Venizelist and putsch-veteran Plastiras (he had been involved in the Goudi revolt of 1909 and in the overthrow of King Constantine in 1922) unsuccessfully attempted a coup d'État. Venizelos's complicity was suspected by his opponents. There was an attempt on his life in June; his supporters in turn believed the government was implicated.

Republican officers went on growling and plotting. After a second attempt by his military supporters misfired in March 1935, Venizelos had to flee to France. The last of the grand old men of Balkan politics died in exile the following year. The Tsaldaris government had ample excuse to remove his sympathizers. Some 1,500 officers were stripped of their rank or cashiered, and many civil servants were dismissed. Sixty of those implicated in the attempted coup were sentenced to death (including Venizelos and Plastiras). Most had already fled abroad; two were executed.

The Senate, elected for a nine-year term and controlled by Venizelists, was abolished. There were fresh elections in June. Martial law and the Venizelists' abstention in protest enabled a 65 per cent populist victory to be turned into 96 per cent of seats in the Chamber of Deputies by the majority system.[1] Royalist generals, who wanted an immediate restoration, took over from a cautious Tsaldaris. The Chamber of Deputies declared the restoration of the monarchical constitution, which was quickly ratified by 97.8 per cent of voters in a patently manipulated plebiscite.

George II had been living in exile since the end of 1923, first in Bucharest, the home of his wife, then in London after the break-up of his marriage. He returned to Greece in November 1935, to be king for a second time. Shortly before his death, Venizelos had from Paris urged his followers to cooperate; the republican parties had consented to the monarch's return. He appeared bent on reconciliation, anxious to heal divisions, and resolved not to be the tool of those who had brought him back. He had a non-party caretaker government proclaim an amnesty for republican opponents, and make preparations for the conduct of an honest election in January 1936.

As in 1932, this, the last parliamentary election held in Greece before the Second World War, produced a result that reflected the fact that opinion was evenly divided. The People's Party and the smaller allied royalist parties had 143 seats out of 300, the liberals and sundry affiliated republican groups 141. The fifteen communist deputies, representing 6 per cent of the vote, held the balance. While a non-party government continued in office, the party leaders struggled to find a way to form a government, hampered by diehards on both sides, and secretly bargained with the communists. These negotiations leaked out; they caused concern in the army and the concern was voiced to the monarch.

When the caretaker prime minister died in office in April 1936, the king appointed the war minister, General Metaxas, to take over. Metaxas was a marginal ultra-royalist, contemptuous of politicians. He had opposed both Venizelos's plans to commit troops to the Gallipoli campaign in 1915 and the Anatolian entanglement of 1921, and was no stranger to coups. He won a vote of confidence in parliament, which agreed to adjourn for five months, in an atmosphere of crisis exacerbated by labour unrest. The market for tobacco had been badly hit and debt servicing accounted for almost 40 per cent of the budget. Metaxas played on the seeming inability of politicians to resolve their differences, and on the serious labour problem, to predispose the king to accept his proposals for 'strong government'. He moved quickly against trades unions, declared strikes illegal, and prevented a general strike attempted by the communists in Salonika.

A twenty-four-hour general strike was then announced for the whole country for 5 August. Metaxas persuaded the king to reject a last-minute deal between the two main parties, and to acquiesce in the suspension of key articles of the constitution, on the pretext of thwarting a general strike called by the

---

1 Konstantinos Karamanlis (1907–98), prime minister 1955–63 and 1974–80, president of the Republic 1980–85 and 1990–95, entered politics at the 1935 elections. Born in Ottoman Macedonia, he would secure Greece's accession to the European Community.

communists. On 4 August, a state of emergency was proclaimed and parliament dissolved. Metaxas reorganized his government, taking on foreign affairs and the armed forces (to which he later added education).

The régime of 4 August 1936 was part of the trend towards royal dictatorships, as parliamentary government found it difficult to respond to the stresses occasioned by the slump. Coming after the régime of 6 January 1929 in Yugoslavia and that of 19 May 1934 in Bulgaria, it outlawed political parties and controlled the press. It had little difficulty in neutralizing the opposition, even the experienced but factionalized communists.

Metaxas's position rested on the authority of the constitutional head of state. After a wholesale purge of Venizelist officers, the royalist monopoly of the army became the guarantee of the royal-backed dictatorship, although as a dictator Metaxas was a retired general in mufti. The régime of 4 August resembled the Spain of Primo de Rivera and the Portugal of Salazar more than the Balkan authoritarian régimes that had preceded it, let alone Mussolini's Italy. His was a paternalistic dictatorship, overlaid with some fashionable corporatism and other fascist trappings. Although Metaxas called himself 'leader' (*archigos*), he did not have the duce's charisma, or the machinery, technology, organization and ideology (for what it was worth) of the Partito Nazionale Fascista.

Inspired by the nationalistic Hellenism and the folkloristic populism that had reacted against cultural and political cosmopolitanism after the disaster, Metaxas developed the ideology of the 'Third Hellenic Civilization'. It was meant to synthesize classical Antiquity, Byzantium and . . . Metaxas himself; it was made up of the familiar conservative virtues of family, stability, order and religion, mixed with populism. His government championed the demotic form of the Greek language, with its first grammar. It dragooned the youth into a National Youth Organization to bring together classes and perpetuate Metaxas's ideas, but that was all by way of a mass organization.

Otherwise, the régime vented its spite on the political world, and the left in particular. Metaxas was certainly more dictatorial, and inspired definitely more fear, than his contemporaries Kioseivanov and even Stojadinović, prime minister respectively to the tsar of the Bulgars and the prince-regent of Yugoslavia.

In agriculture, Metaxas's régime continued the policy of granting low-interest medium- and long-term credit to grain-growing cooperatives through the Agricultural Bank. It cancelled private peasant debts if the amounts already paid equalled the principal, and it introduced a minimum wage and other social benefits. There was real industrial growth in the 1930s (from the 1920 = 100 index of gross output, to 1938 = 165 for manufacturing and 171 for extraction). The number of industrial workers increased from 110,000 in 1929 to 140,000 in 1938, until by 1940 industry employed 15 per cent of the population and provided 18 per cent of the national income. The merchant marine had also expanded yet further, having regained its prewar 1,000 tonnage in the 1920s, to reach 1,315 tonnes in 1928 and 1,930 tonnes (98 per cent steam, but mostly built abroad) in 1938.

In the later 1930s, German economic penetration had occurred in Greece as elsewhere in the Balkans, but more slowly because of the continuing import surplus. By 1938, Germany purchased 40 per cent of Greece's exports, and provided 30 per cent of her imports. However large, the turn to Germany was less than in other Balkan countries, because of Greece's orientation to the Mediterranean and the British orbit.

Metaxas did not seek to question a certain traditional pro-British direction in foreign policy. He stuck to the Balkan Entente as much as the other partners, and he worked closely with Turkey. In 1938 he actually proposed a formal treaty of alliance to Britain, who did not then respond, fearing new commitments. He, too, attempted a policy of neutrality. It was only when the Italian occupation of Albania in April 1939 considerably worsened Greece's strategic position, that Great Britain and France offered Greece, along with Romania, a guarantee of territorial integrity provided they resisted aggression, and that Metaxas accepted the offer. When, however, war broke out in Europe in September, he tried to keep out of the war and was careful about relations with Germany. At the same time, in spite of the purges, the régime had maintained a high level of military preparedness.

ROMANIA UNDER KING CHARLES II

Caught between revisionisms – Hungarian and Soviet – backed by totalitarian ideologies of right and left, Romania was the only Balkan country to develop a fascist movement able to attract a real following. Yet the general elections of the 1930s were true campaigns, participation was high, non-government parties usually attracted a majority of the votes, and King Charles II did not dispense with parliament until 1938.

Intelligent and flamboyant, he despised parliamentary government and liked to present himself as the symbol of the new generations. He played off the major parties against one another, exploited divisions within them and resorted to palace favourites. The National Peasant Party remained in office on and off until 1933; popular enthusiasm ebbed away from it because of its internal contradictions and of the expectations it had disappointed.

After Maniu had finally resigned, the king tried various combinations until the problems caused by the Depression made him return to the peasantists. He alternated between Vaida and Maniu, respectively nationalist and mainstream rivals within the party. Inspired by its Bulgarian counterpart, it already had its armed guard. In office for most of 1933, Vaida dealt with social unrest by crushing strikes and dissolving subversive left-wing organizations, but his lack of firmness with the extreme right brought his cabinet down.

Codreanu's Iron Guard (as it was commonly known) had won 32,000 votes (mainly in Bessarabia) at the 1931 elections. The paramilitary wing of the Archangel's Legion had become the usual designation for the movement as a whole. Its 'captain' Codreanu followed existing models for uniform, coloured

293

(green) shirt, salute and leadership, to clothe native anti-Semitism, a sup-posedly Orthodox Manichaean struggle of good against evil, and the cult of the peasant as the embodiment of purity. He took up the existing hostil-ity to cosmopolitanism, rationalism and individualism, to which he added a fascination with death. He was convinced that he was the leader chosen by God to regenerate Romania from the powers of darkness, through his anti-parliamentary, anti-communist, anti-Semitic programme. His message cut across social boundaries, but his strongest constituency was young and urban.

In 1933 Charles invited the liberals' new leader Ion Duca (1879–1933) to form a government. He dissolved the Iron Guard before going to the polls in December. Many peasants, disillusioned with 'their' party, moved to the liberals, who won with 51 per cent. The Iron Guard took its revenge and assassinated Duca. Martial law was declared. The Liberal Party was by now split into two factions, and the king called, not yet another Brătianu, Constantin (1866–1953), who led the official ('old') faction, but the 'young' leader Gheorghe Tătărescu (1886–1957).

The Iron Guard gradually reappeared. It was used by the police to fight communists, and allowed to function as a new party under the name of 'All-for-the-Fatherland'. Parliament having run its term, elections were held in December 1937. Assuming the leadership of the opposition, Maniu signed an electoral 'nonaggression pact' with the Fatherland Party – to support free elections and prevent the return of Tătărescu. His intention was to dis-courage the use of strong-arm methods, but he had given respectability to Codreanu. Even Maniu showed how the leaders of parliamentary parties could, in these difficult times, resort to odd stratagems to defend parliament-ary government.

Romania's elections of 1937 were the swan song of parliamentary govern-ment in the Balkans. They were relatively free, the turnout was untypically low, the king's prime minister lost, no party obtained 40 per cent. Tătărescu's liberals came top with less than 36 per cent. The Peasant Party received less than 21 per cent. The Fatherland polled over 15 per cent. Fourth, with over 9 per cent, came the recently formed National Christian Party – a merger of small extreme-right groups under the poet Octavian Goga (1881–1938). Rather more legally minded than the Iron Guard, it had acquired voters from Averescu's populists, as well as anti-oligarchy defectors from the major parties from Moldavia, Bessarabia and Transylvania.[2]

Charles thought that it was the end of the old parties. To show that his will counted for more than the number of votes, he asked the ultra-royalist Goga to form a government. The result was a strange concoction even for such strange times, with national peasant ministers of the interior, justice and foreign

2 The social democrats' share of the vote had declined to below 1 per cent, from 3.4 per cent in 1933. Outlawed in 1924, paralysed by factional fighting and decimated by Stalin's purges, the communists nevertheless became noticeable again with the Depression, gaining 74,000 votes and five seats for their Peasant Worker Bloc at the 1931 election. Failing to form a popular front, they supported Maniu in 1937.

affairs. Goga created a dangerous situation, with quotas of 'ethnic Romanians' in enterprises and talk of more anti-Semitic measures such as the expulsion of Jews who had arrived since 1918. Outrages were tolerated.

He tried to reach an agreement with Codreanu. There was a flight of capital. The collapse of the leu showed that, contrary to what the guardists said, the Jews were important to Romania's financial stability. The liberals came together and negotiated with Maniu to form a constitutional bloc; some of them urged the king to appoint a government of leading personalities that would temporarily suspend constitutional practice. Major bankers and industrialists appealed to the monarch to end the experiment.

On 10 February 1938, Charles suspended the constitution, dissolved parliament and parties, and appointed an 'advisory government' headed by Patriarch Miron. Seven former prime ministers were included. General Ion Antonescu (1882–1946), Goga's defence minister, was kept, and so was the national-peasant Armand Călinescu (1893–1939), the interior minister, now the strong man of the royal cabinet. The king feared that deals with the Iron Guard could prevent a government nominated by him from securing the required 40 per cent share of the vote for a dependable parliament.

He went on to abolish the 1923 constitution and put a new one to a referendum held under martial law. Accepted by 4.3 million votes, it concentrated power in the crown. A parliament selected on corporatist lines would endorse royal decisions. The seventy-five departments were regrouped into ten regions. The king hoped to strengthen the base of his régime by drawing in the historical parties. They demanded a return to parliamentary rule; he accepted Călinescu's idea of a single organization to mobilize mass support.

In December the National Revival Front was set up, headed by Vaida. The royal régime appeared improvised and superficial. The traditional parties were treated with care, as Charles kept trying to unite them with the non-fascist supporters of his dictatorship. German and Hungarian minority parties received similar treatment, so as not to exacerbate revisionist sentiment. Drastic action was taken against the Iron Guard. Codreanu and his lieutenants were arrested in April, tried and imprisoned for the murder of Duca and for high treason. In November, as they were being transferred to another penitentiary, the 'captain' and thirteen others were killed, allegedly shot while trying to escape. Many adherents were interned or kept under surveillance. The severe repression was motivated by the king's perception of guardists as agents of Germany, whom he feared.

To protect the frontiers obtained at the peace settlement, all Romanian governments had championed collective security. They had relied on the League of Nations, on regional blocs and on the western powers. Britain, however, had no political strategy in the Balkans and regarded Romania as being 'French'; France's political interests were only lukewarm, in spite of what Romanians thought. Having followed the French example of establishing diplomatic relations with the USSR in 1934, Bessarabia notwithstanding, Romania even planned a mutual assistance pact with the Soviet Union. The project came to nothing when Titulescu, the liberal foreign minister closely identified with pro-French policy, was removed from office in 1936.

King Charles had stood by the old alliances for as long as he could. Titulescu's departure had been symbolic of a subtle change in policy, driven by the growing power of Germany, the lack of western firmness and fear of the Soviet Union. In November 1938, Charles went to London and Paris, in search of more substantive support against an increasing German economic presence in the Balkans, but came away disappointed. On his way back, he had a brief meeting with Hitler, to try an offer of closer economic relations with the Reich in return for support against Hungarian and Soviet territorial claims. Hitler urged the king to free Codreanu and form a government with him, which did nothing to allay distrust.

On his return Charles ordered the liquidation of leading guardists. He appointed as foreign minister a pro-western national peasant politician and journalist, Grigore Gafencu (1892–1957), to signal that he would not be committing himself. Charles and Gafencu hoped to play off the German and Soviet threats against each other, and maintain neutrality. But when Hitler took over what remained of Czechoslovakia in March 1939, Romania gave in.

She signed trade agreements that practically placed her economy at the disposal of the Reich. The king saw it as a way to placate Germany and gain time. After Mussolini's occupation of Albania, Britain and France offered guarantees, but the German-Soviet pact put an end to any hope of balance. They did not know the secret protocol that gave the Soviets a free hand in a sphere of influence that included Bessarabia, but Charles and his minister realized that a policy based on interlocking alliances supported by France could no longer defend their country's borders.

On Patriarch Miron's death in the spring of 1939, Călinescu took over as prime minister. When Poland was overrun, the Iron Guard reasserted itself and assassinated him. The monarch brought Tătărescu back. He dictated policy, but could get his way only through bargaining with influential politicians and other interests. Maniu and Constantine Brătianu did not act against his government, but refused to give Charles positive support, which the Iron Guard now decided to provide. Having renounced subversion and sought a reconciliation, its leaders were received by the king in April 1940. Gafencu was replaced in June. The fall of France completely destroyed what remained of the morale of Romania's traditionally Francophile establishment. Assassinations had been tactically passed over by royal advisers and guardist leaders alike. Gafencu accepted the position of minister to Moscow to try and work out a rapprochement with the USSR.

Romania had taken a full part in the cultural life of interwar Europe, yet this was done with more than three-quarters of the active population dependent on agriculture, and half of the rural population over seven years of age still illiterate. From such contrasts, the sudden changes after the First World War had brought to the fore people who did not share the relative civility of the old political society. The official determination to create a new élite that would bind the diverse parts together contributed to the rise of a modern generation of nationalists. The strategy of the liberal élite having failed by 1930, many of the new intelligentsia turned to 'Romanianism', in its 'peasant' garb or in its more exclusively assertive version, in reaction to both western liberalism and godless socialism.

The population had grown to almost 20 million by the end of the decade, but only 72 per cent were ethnic Romanians. The 4.1 per cent German minority was not a problem until after the rise of Hitler, when it gradually became the tool of nazi agents. More or less equal in number, Jews had no structured identity of their own. The older established Jews of prewar Romania differed from the more recent settlers of Moldavia, and they all differed from the Hungarian, German, Russian and Yiddish speakers of the new provinces.

Having affirmed themselves as part of Romania's economic and cultural modernization, they formed a substantial proportion of certain professions, from 27 per cent of lawyers to 70 per cent of journalists. They were often associated with capitalism, socialism, modernization, Russian or Soviet influence and other evils of popular prejudice. Anti-Semitism thus served as a rallying cry for frustrated jingoism in Romania, just as unfair peace settlements or national humiliation did in other parts of the Balkans.

The national peasants' policy had failed to correct the fundamental deficiencies of agriculture before the Depression undid all their efforts. They did not go on to expropriate all holdings above 100 hectares, for fear of disorganizing production, nor did they attempt to consolidate strips, because this was unpopular. Grain prices began to fall as early as 1928. By 1932, they had fallen to two-thirds of their 1929 level, and did not reach their lowest point until 1934. To make things worse, there were climatic reverses in 1932, 1934, 1935 and 1937. Romanian smallholding agriculture in the 1930s was very different from its peasantist vision. With a living standard among the lowest in Europe,[3] Romania was burdened with overpopulation and debt more than elsewhere in the Balkans.

The government's first efforts to combat the Depression thus concerned agriculture. Export duties were replaced with subsidies in 1931. Following the Yugoslav and Bulgarian example, a state purchasing agency was established to support prices above world levels, and minimum prices were set in 1935. Having suspended the forced collection of debt on rural property in December 1931, the government undertook a massive programme of debt conversion in the following years, with a 50 per cent reduction on principal.

In the process, the state-sponsored Popular Banks, which had been the peasants' only source of cheap credit, lost much of their capital. They had appeared in the last decade before the First World War, and by 1929 had provided

---

3 The 1938 national income of 94 dollars per head was higher than Greece's 76 and Bulgaria's 81, but lower than Yugoslavia's 106. By comparison, France's was 246. If the life expectancy of 48–50 years in 1940 had improved from 41 on the eve of the First World War, both the birthrate (28.3 per 1,000 in 1939) and the infant mortality rate (19.2 per 1,000 in 1935) were among the highest in Europe.

one-quarter of agricultural borrowing. It was not until the royal dictatorship that credit for agriculture appeared in useful though still insufficient amounts. The government backed a National Institute of Agricultural Credit to favour better-off peasants. The five-year diversification plan adopted in March 1940, with large budget appropriation, was cut short by the political crisis.

There was little more the government could do, in view of its dependence on grain exports and of falling agricultural prices in the west, until Germany began to buy large quantities of Romanian agricultural commodities in the last years of the decade. Although the hopes placed in the restructuring of agrarian relations in 1921 were not realized, Romania eventually doubled its wheat acreage between 1930 and 1937, thus managing to export significant quantities, and to feed its population, however inadequately.

The Depression persuaded national peasant as well as liberal leaders to support a policy of accelerated industrialization. With the accession of Charles II, statism took over in all areas to back his policy of independence. The state was the main client for industry and regulated trade through its orders and tariffs. By 1937, cartels controlled 46 per cent of industrial capital and 23 per cent of output. The rate of industrial growth picked up again, with an average yearly rate of 3.4 per cent between 1928 and 1938 – one of the highest in Europe. Textiles and metallurgy were the largest and fastest-growing sectors, the latter with the help of rearmament after 1936. At 36 per cent of state expenditure in 1938, military costs were the highest in the Balkans. That peak year produced 133,000 tonnes of cast iron and 284,000 of steel, with 70 per cent of the output going to the state.

Oil production peaked in 1936/37 at 8 million tonnes, before falling to 6 million in 1938 with the gradual depletion of known reserves. It became concentrated in about a hundred companies, with crude oil largely refined around Ploeşti. Most of it went abroad, rising to a record 78 per cent in 1937, mainly to supply Germany, which took 27 per cent of Romanian production, followed closely by Italy. Foreign capital, British and French, continued to play an important part in financing industry, even though the decade witnessed a decline in foreign participation, particularly in heavy industry, where the percentage fell from 70 per cent in 1929 to 40.5 per cent in 1938.

Although some political leaders argued that the state should assume the direction of overall industrial production, this was never the case. Industrialization, as in the 1920s, still tended to be carried out at the expense of agriculture. Production of consumer goods grew at much more modest rates than cast iron or steel, because of the limited domestic market. On the eve of the Second World War, industry still provided no more than 30 per cent of the national income. It was relatively modern, but could not absorb the surplus rural population. No more than 290,000 were employed in manufacturing, compared to 340,000 in public service.

The fall of commodity prices, leading to the shrinkage of export earnings, meant the loss of purchasing power. Importing capital added to an enormous foreign debt, the servicing of which required the export of increased quantities of oil and cereals. Budgetary expenditure and internal debt rose more sharply than in other Balkan countries. The bulk went on rearmament. In order to recover the cost, note issue climbed by two-thirds between 1934 and 1938, then doubled again by 1940. By relying on exchange controls, and giving high premiums on foreign exchange over its leu value, the government eventually succeeded in reducing the share of budget expenditure on debt servicing from 35.3 per cent in 1932/33 (the highest in the Balkans) to 11.7 per cent in 1937/38.

Romanian banking never really recovered from the initial shock of the Depression. Several major banks failed right from the start, including the prominent Banca Marmorosch-Blank.[4] Halved by 1931, commercial bank deposits continued to decline. There were too many small banks, and if their number was reduced by half after 1938, it was through liquidations rather than mergers, with the suspicion that increased anti-Semitism was partly responsible.

Only after the closure of Italian markets as a result of sanctions did Romania begin to turn to clearing. Germany craved for her grain and oil, and offered armaments. The French had no such needs, and could not supply arms. The Romanian government's long struggle with western petroleum companies over control of production played into German hands. A new mining law of 1937 discouraged private enterprise; a state agency was set up in 1939 to conduct further exploration and improve production. In the summer of 1938, German military plans placed Romanian oil high on the list of import priorities, and a trade offensive moved ahead. Germany's attractive terms eventually had to be accepted.

By 1939 the Reich had become Romania's best trade partner, taking over 32 per cent of exports and supplying over 39 per cent of imports. The annexation of the Czech lands further meant that all purchases of machinery and armaments from Czechoslovakia now came from the Reich. With the 1939 trade agreements, mixed German-Romanian companies were formed for oil exploration, drilling and refining, in return for assured deliveries of oil. Germany would assist in the expansion of Romanian agricultural production, and Romania would acquire German military equipment. The German share of foreign investments rose from a low 0.4 per cent in 1937 to over 50 per cent of an admittedly reduced total by 1940.

Romania had become an economic satellite of the Reich. Hitler had not objected to Charles's elimination of Codreanu and other guardists. He wanted Romania to be stable.

ALBANIA UNDER KING ZOG

Albania's newly created monarchy in September 1928, its constitutional niceties notwithstanding, was a framework for Zog's dictatorship, established three

---

4 The rival liberal-owned and state-connected Banca Românesca refused to participate in a joint effort to save it. Lampe and Jackson rightly lament the lack of a monograph on the long and influential history of the Banca Marmorosch-Blank (John R. Lampe and Marvin R. Jackson, *Balkan Economic History 1558–1950*, Bloomington, Ind.: Indiana University Press, 1982, 481–2).

months before that of King Alexander in Yugoslavia. A client of Italy, the Kingdom of Albania fell to Mussolini even before the outbreak of the Second World War. Rome had been the first to recognize King Zog, with a chorus of praise, while the most severe criticism came from Ankara, where President Atatürk described the royal elevation as an anachronistic operetta. At home, the landowning beys were not impressed, the change was generally met with indifference, and the only protests came from Albanian émigrés.

Parliamentary elections were indirect. All males over the age of eighteen (younger than the usual twenty-one) chose the members of a college of electors, who then elected deputies from candidates who made a deposit of 100 gold francs. Political parties were not legal. The king had the sole initiative of legislation and the right of dissolution. Propaganda against him and the constitutional order was prohibited. Elections were held in September 1932. The principle of a representative parliament was established by announcing that there would be no approved list of candidates, but turnout may have been as low as 10 per cent, and ministers generally continued to be the same old hands ready to carry out Zog's orders.

After relying mostly on the northern clans and the big landowners, Zog tried to enlist enlightened support. In October 1935, he switched to a more liberal government under Midhat Frashëri (1880–1949, a son of Abdyl, the principal organizer of the League of Prizren in 1878), who gathered a group of well-educated young ministers and remained in office for a year.

With stability and order achieved, Zog felt that he could move on to gradual modernization, for there was little development, industry, trade, foreign investment or literacy, and few statistics were available. The condition of the peasantry and lawlessness in the northern highlands were the two major problems. The festivities on the occasion of Zog's elevation, his uniform, the civil list to maintain his royal family of a mother and sisters, and the new government buildings in Tirana might have been seen as Ruritanian by many. They were part of his carefully cultivated image of a European reformer. When he had sworn to observe the constitution, and to maintain the unity and independence of Albania, he had done so on both the Koran and the Bible.

The Islamic community had organized itself independently of any outside control in 1923. The Orthodox were, however, still under the patriarch of Constantinople, whose jurisdiction was seen as a vehicle for Greek propaganda. There had been intermittent talks about a separate status since 1921, but not until 1937 was Zog able to obtain properly qualified and consecrated Albanian Orthodox bishops with unblemished autocephaly from the ecumenical patriarchate.[5] His religious policy was linked to his campaign to nationalize education, and to create a national history independent of that of Albania's masters. The only effective schools were run by religious organizations and

5 The Yugoslav and Greek governments had helped as go-betweens, but the Serbian Orthodox Church had earlier connived with exiled Russian bishops at the consecration of some unqualified Albanian bishops. The Catholics were organized in the ancient archbishopric of Durrës and in the metropolitan province of Shkodër.

foreigners. These were the well-established and relatively good system operated by the Orthodox Church in the south, a number of schools run by Catholic orders subsidized and managed by Italians in the north, and a few Italian and American technical schools.

Some progress was made with a state system. Elementary schooling was legally obligatory, but could not in fact be so because of the lack of teachers and buildings. By 1930 580 primary schools had been set up, as well as thirteen secondary schools. They were not sufficient, and state education was not up to the level of Orthodox and Catholic schools. In 1933 King Zog decided to place all education under government control. As this affected the rights of the Greek-speaking minority, Greece complained to the League of Nations and some specifically Greek schools had to be reopened. The same argument could not be used by Italy, who reacted with financial pressure.

State education and national propaganda exalted Skanderbeg, the fifteenth-century Albanian hero who has conveniently gone down in history with his Muslim name. His legend fulfilled the function that Byzantium and other medieval glories performed elsewhere in the Balkans. The language was still very much divided into its northern and southern dialects. Only 36 per cent of children of school age received some education by 1938, and no more than 5,700 attended the twenty secondary schools of various types. Although 400-odd students were attending foreign universities in 1936/37, there were only ninety university graduates in Albania in 1938. Nevertheless, there were lively press debates in Tirana and Shkodër, and poets from epic to modern, some of whom fostered the development of a common literary language. All of this affected only a tiny urban society, generally ignorant of the problems of the countryside.

The king introduced codes of law. He started in 1928 with a civil code patterned on the French (complete with civil marriage and divorce, causing considerable opposition, not least from the Catholic Church), followed by penal and commercial codes. Along with them went a reorganization of the gendarmerie under a British inspector general, to tackle brigandage and blood feud. Zog managed to lay the foundations of the state by welding together the various vested interests through a political, administrative and legal structure of sorts, with a modicum of law and a good deal of (often brutally imposed) order.

Land ownership and the state of the peasantry were a major problem, which Zog tackled in 1930 with the help of Italian experts. Legislation was passed to limit individual holdings to forty hectares of arable land, with a bonus of ten of pasture for every dependent – wife and children. Of the rest, up to two-thirds could be kept for another fifteen years if modernized. At least one-third was to be transferred to tenants, who would pay the state ten annual instalments. Former owners received shares in a State Agricultural Bank, which was to handle these transactions and provide loans to peasants on favourable terms. The government kept the option of expropriating surplus land to resettle refugees from Yugoslavia.

The reform was difficult to enforce and much of it remained on paper. A land survey, started in 1927, was not sufficiently advanced. Attempts to meddle with the traditional system, especially in tribal areas, were strongly resisted. The owners had the time to subdivide their land or turn it to pasture. The State Agricultural Bank was not set up until 1937. By 1938 only 4,700 out of over 48,000 hectares of state property had been affected, and little more than 1,000 out of perhaps 103,000 hectares of private land. An important proportion had been given to refugees. In practice, the reform was little more than a sop to liberals, a threat to unruly landowners and a way to obtain a selected clientèle of refugees.

Zog was a reformer, but also a despot unable to delegate authority. His reformist activity was punctuated by overreaction to acts of rebellion. Austria was the centre of Albanian émigrés, united in nothing else but their opposition to Zog. Since Noli had decided to retire from politics and return to the United States in 1930, they no longer even had a standard-bearer. The king had gone to Vienna for medical reasons at the beginning of 1931; in spite of great security precautions, shots were fired at him one evening as he left the opera. The Italians pointed the finger at Yugoslavia, in order to create tension between her and Albania. Zog clumsily followed suit, although there is no evidence that Yugoslavia was involved beyond the fact that some of the émigrés received financial support.

The following year, an alleged plot was uncovered at Vlorë. A fairly innocuous group was brought to trial for conspiring to overthrow Zog with support from the Yugoslav consulate there. On weak evidence, severe sentences were meted out, including twelve capital ones which the king later commuted to life. The Italians were able to say they had intervened to save lives.

In the summer of 1935, the pathetic Fier rebellion led to thousands of indiscriminate arrests, 160 life sentences and many death sentences – all on hearsay evidence. Once again, most of these were commuted. By the mid-1930s there was genuine, if poorly organized, opposition. It stemmed from the feeling that Zog had allowed Italy to turn Albania into a quasi-protectorate, and from resentment among the professional and educated few at the way in which personal allegiance to the king often determined employment, promotion, patronage and election to parliament.

Overreaction was due to Zog's fear of foreign involvement. The association with Italy had brought security against Yugoslavia and Greece, but he had come to depend on Italian loans. They turned out to be a 'monument to Italian philanthropy',[6] as the moratorium on interest payment was extended, while bondholders were paid by the Italian government. The king feared the disappointment that would grow as a result of the cessation of these loans.

Encouraged by Italy, his affront to Yugoslavia in 1931 weakened his power to resist. The Depression had affected Albania in several ways. Remittances

6 Bernd Jürgen Fischer, *King Zog and the Struggle for Stability in Albania*, New York: Columbia University Press, 1984, 162.

from emigrants had dried up, along with foreign currency earnings from exports. Landowners were selling and reinvesting abroad. Mussolini insisted that a new loan be directly from government to government, and made to appear more like a gift, to emphasize the dependence. There was no interest, and no repayment at all of principal until the Albanian budget had reached 50 million gold francs. Zog had resisted going as far as a customs union. The Tirana Pact was due to expire in 1931, and he did not want to renew it as it caused anti-Italian feelings. Landowners, civil servants and army officers all felt threatened by the presence of Italian advisers.

King Zog turned to the Balkans, and sent representatives to the Balkan Conferences from that year. Greece and especially Yugoslavia used the opportunity to improve relations. Yugoslavia increased her imports from Albania after a commercial agreement in December 1933. In May 1934, another agreement allowed peasants on both sides of the border to ply their goods within a 15-kilometre-wide zone. Yugoslavia wanted to draw Albania into the planned Balkan Pact, but Albania would have been a financial burden. Her adoption would have placed considerable responsibility on Belgrade, as the other potential partners were less keen. Albania did not attend the spring 1934 Balkan Conference in Athens which would have coincided with the signing of the pact. Zog did, however, establish diplomatic relations with the USSR in September.

He moved against Italian-financed schools. Legislation made it an offence to send children to foreign primary and secondary schools, and to accept scholarships. Finally, the closure of all foreign schools was ordered, thus throwing the entire educational system into chaos, until the International Court at the Hague ruled in favour of Greece on the question of minority rights. The Italian government stopped all financial assistance and withdrew its personnel.

The defiance of Italy was popular, but it inflicted real damage. Trade virtually ceased, and so did public works. Cultivating the image of a small nation exploited by a powerful neighbour, Zog prepared a slimmed-down budget. He made cuts in the bureaucracy, the army, the gendarmerie and his civil list. Unprotected employees were dismissed, salaries were cut after they had been months in arrears. By the beginning of 1934, no one was being paid at all. In June Mussolini sent a naval squadron on a 'courtesy visit' to Durrës; it did not salute the Albanian flag, rallied opinion around King Zog and brought Italo-Albanian relations to crisis point.

Failed appeals for loans to Britain, France, Belgium and Holland, the Depression, reforms, attempted Balkan cooperation, and the acute financial crisis, caused adverse reactions in different circles – conservatives, Muslims, nationalists, liberals – and the attempted rebellion of August 1935. Frashëri's new ministry called for a closer relationship with Italy while declaring respect for the League of Nations.

Judging that the crisis had mollified the king of Albania, Mussolini approached him through unofficial channels. He offered further moratoriums and loans. In return he asked for bases, the training of the army and gendarmerie, a customs union and control over foreign policy. There was a thaw, but Zog stalled. In October 1935 he decided not to join in sanctions against Italy; Yugoslavia ended the conversations on Albania's adherence to the Balkan Pact. Neither the League of Nations nor Yugoslavia had been of great economic assistance; Zog reasoned that it was better to get close to Italy again at a time when she was in need of friends.

In March 1936 new comprehensive agreements with Rome were announced. The 1931 loan was cancelled. Italy would make good Albania's budget deficit up to the end of the previous fiscal year, and provide other loans and gifts. Albania granted the use of the port of Durrës, to be developed by an Italian company. Italian advisers returned. Schools were reopened, but not all issues with the Catholic Church were sorted out, there was no customs union and no merger of foreign policy. Zog was obviously behind a parliamentary vote of no confidence in the government in November. He no longer wanted Frashëri's liberals, and he reverted to the sort of government that returned a compliant parliament in January 1937.

He continued with his modernization, symbolized by some well-advertised gestures. At the palace New Year's Eve party for 1937, where guests were required to attend in western dress, he gave a speech stressing that 'we must make speedy and strong paces towards western culture and civilization'. Having persuaded religious elders to declare that Islamic law did not require women to be veiled, he enacted legislation in 1937 making it an offence to wear a veil (the practice continued to be tolerated as long as the face was not completely covered). The move was accompanied by public engagements performed by the royal sisters, unveiled, in western dress and short skirts. The State Agricultural Bank was finally set up. By way of reaction, there was in May a weak attempt at a march on Vlorë, but repression was relatively restrained, with only four death sentences.

The most significant step that King Zog took to ensure the stability of his rule was his marriage. Having broken off his engagement to Vërlaci's daughter in 1927, he had, at the age of forty-four and after a series of known liaisons, embarked on an earnest search for a young and attractive queen. His engagement at the beginning of 1938 to the impoverished and beautiful twenty-two-year-old Hungarian Countess Geraldine Apponyi was well received. The wedding in April was a civil ceremony, with the Italian foreign minister, the duce's son-in-law Count Ciano, as best man.

In spite of undeniable progress, the standard of living of Albania's population of one million in the late 1930s was at the bottom of the European scale. It had the highest birthrate in the Balkans, with 32.4 per thousand in 1935–39. Essential traffic went by sea (on Italian, Greek and Yugoslav ships). Corn was the dominant cereal and the basis of food, with tobacco, olives and vines in the south.

In the plains, reform notwithstanding, the traditional sharecropping estates dominated, private- and state-owned, or to religious organizations. The owners, heirs to the Ottoman military-administrative caste, usually lived in towns, and reinvested in urban-based activities or money lending. Tenants whose holdings were below ten hectares gave 30 per cent of their crops to the landlord, on whom they were also dependent for credit. Since cash was rare, the state had kept, and still farmed, the old Ottoman tithe. Although agrarian reform had hardly affected the rural equilibrium, large holdings were breaking up into smaller units.[7] In the mountains, land remained tribally cooperative, which allowed maximum exploitation of limited arable land, with more sheep (1.6 million in 1938) than grain.

The urban population, 15 per cent of the total population in 1940 according to statistics, was in fact no more than 8 per cent in places of more than 20,000 inhabitants. The number of industrial workers had increased to 7,500 in 1938. Concessions for mineral prospecting were all in Italian hands, with only 20 per cent of investments in native hands. There was some petrol in the coastal plain triangle of Durrës–Berat–Vlorë, but much less than had been expected.

The rapprochement between Yugoslavia and Italy in 1937 increased the latter's influence. On his return from the royal wedding, Ciano pushed for a radical solution leading to annexation, to guard against German expansion in the Balkans. Mussolini was not keen on outright annexation, but after Hitler had marched into Prague without informing him, he was convinced of the need to take some drastic action. On 25 March 1939, he submitted what amounted to an ultimatum for union short of annexation. Italian nationals were evacuated, Zog appealed to the democracies and to the Balkan Entente, and rejected the ultimatum.

Early on the morning of Good Friday, 7 April, over 40,000 Italian troops landed, supported by warships and aircraft. Zog, who was not prepared to be reduced to an outright puppet, had made no serious preparations to resist. He sent his wife and new-born son to Greece and broadcast an appeal to resistance which few people heard as there were few receivers. He made a final and futile attempt to negotiate, and followed his family into exile. Only the gendarmerie around Durrës, under Colonel Abas Kupi (1900–77), provided any real resistance.

Most Albanians, from the king downwards, were resigned to the inevitable. The Italians entered Tirana the following day. Ciano came and set up a provisional committee, which gathered an improvised Constituent Assembly of deputies that could be found, augmented by other individuals. They abolished the dynasty and the constitution of 1928, and expressed the wish for a personal union of the crowns of Albania and Italy. Vërlaci, Zog's sometime prospective father-in-law, reappeared to head a government of frustrated individuals who believed that Albania could not survive outside Rome's sphere. A Statute on Italian fascist lines was adopted in June. King Victor Emmanuel III of Italy accepted the crown of Albania and his minister in Tirana became the lieutenant of his new Albanian realm, whose foreign relations were entrusted to Italy.

---

7 The communists in 1944 expropriated only seven large holdings totalling some 14,000 hectares, as well as more than 4,700 other holdings adding up to 100,000 hectares (with an average of some twenty hectares).

Germany lent its full support to the operation. Greece and Yugoslavia were too frightened to oppose it openly. Only Turkey and Egypt refused to acknowledge it, but no one complained to the League of Nations. Yet despite widespread complacency, Zog was the last victim of appeasement; Britain and France, who had already guaranteed Poland's independence, extended a similar offer to Greece and Romania.[8] The Second World War was about to begin. With or without guarantees, on whichever side they landed, the Balkan kingdoms would, one after the other, lose their independence.

8 Zog went on to Turkey, and to Paris where he remained until the German invasion. London then accepted him only in a private capacity, and he spent the remainder of the war at Sunningdale.

CHAPTER 15

The Second World War, 1939–45

From the Ribbentrop–Molotov Pact to the war in the East. The Balkans in the shadow of other fronts. From Stalingrad to the collapse of Italy. The end and the communist takeover.

FROM THE NAZI–SOVIET PACT TO THE NAZI–SOVIET CLASH

When the German Reich and the Soviet Union partitioned Poland in September 1939, the Balkans were frantically adjusting themselves – with the exception of Albania, who had already been adjusted by Mussolini. Governments manoeuvred to keep the war away.

In Yugoslavia, the Cvetković–Maček compromise satisfied the Croatian Peasant Party leadership, even a minority of the Serb opposition. A political relaxation gave dissatisfied elements the chance to increase their activity. Many Croats thought it was too little; Serbs generally felt frustrated. The privileges granted to one part of the country raised problems – for the rest of the state, for the Serbs of Croatia, for the remainder of the opposition, even for Croatia. Maček talked of peasant democracy, Cvetković of the need to study corporatism; nothing was done about elections. The now governing Peasant Party in Croatia gave more leeway to the extreme right, for whom autonomy was but the first step to secession and who frightened the local Serbs. But, to keep ustashas and communists under control, it tightened the Law for the Defence of the State just as it was being relaxed elsewhere.

The war increased dependence on the Reich and created difficulties for the economy. By 1939 over 50 per cent of exports went to, and 50 per cent of imports came from, Germany. Emergency measures caused inflation. The cost of living rose in 1940, when the harvest, inadequate even for the home market, had to go to Germany. The dinar was devalued in relation to the mark. The price of bread soared. There were demonstrations against the government. Those who still placed some hope in the west felt more than helpless when France fell in June 1940. Diplomatic and trade relations were set up with the Soviet Union.

Surrounded by neighbours who, with the exception of Yugoslavia, all had claims against her, Romania was at the mercy of Hitler and Stalin, and turning towards the former. 'Nothing could put Romania on Germany's side, except the conviction that only Germany could keep the Soviets out of Romania,' remarked a Romanian foreign ministry official to the British minister. Charles II had renounced western guarantees, which existed in name only, since (in the words of Maurice Pearton) his country was 'not on the way to anywhere that cannot be reached more easily by other means'.[1] He had appointed a pro-German government that included Horia Sima (1906–93), Codreanu's successor at the head of the Iron Guard who had been in Germany since 1939, but set up an all-embracing 'Party of the Nation' under his own royal leadership.

Stalin now staked his claim on Romania – the return of Bessarabia, and the cession of northern Bukovina, which had never been Russian but had more Ruthenians than Romanians. The talks, which had dragged on during June, were brought to a brutal conclusion by the ultimatum of 26 June. The Germans told King Charles to accept. Two days later, the Soviets were in control of the mouths of the Danube.[2]

Hungary and Bulgaria followed. Hitler was anxious to settle the dispute over Transylvania quickly and personally, because of the oil fields; the Axis imposed an arbitration on 30 August – the Second Vienna Award. Romania was to cede northern Transylvania (less than Hungary had asked for) and keep the petroleum deposits. After that shock, the Dobrudja dispute seemed peripheral; Romania gave in to Bulgaria, who had the support of both Hitler and Stalin. On 7 September she agreed to restore the 1912 frontier. Without war, she had lost over a third of her territory and a third of her population.

By that time, Charles II had already fallen. Public outrage threatened chaos. Directed against the Axis, it quickly turned against the monarch. The Iron Guard attempted to seize power. Charles turned to General Antonescu as the only person who could restore order. An opponent of the Soviet Union, he was on bad terms with the king, but on good terms with practically everybody else, and he was popular. The German legation promised to support his demand for dictatorial powers, if he accepted close cooperation. The party leaders urged the abdication of Charles. Antonescu obtained 'full powers to lead the Romanian state' and the suspension of the constitution. Twenty-four hours later, King Charles abdicated.[3]

On 6 September, Michael ascended the throne for the second time, as a figurehead who had to appoint Antonescu again to the position of prime minister, and to the institutionalized office of *conducator* (leader). The conducator named a cabinet of generals, technicians and guardists, with Sima as deputy

---

1 In Dennis Deletant and Maurice Pearton, *Romania Observed: Studies in Contemporary Romanian History*, Bucharest: Encyclopaedic Publishing House, 1998, 95–6.
2 The Soviets set up a large part of that territory as the Soviet Socialist Republic of Moldavia. The map appended to the ultimatum indicated the new border with a thick red pencil line that must have covered a seven-kilometre band.
3 The Iron Guard tried to kill him as he left the country. He spent the war years in Mexico and Brazil.

premier.[4] Romania was proclaimed a 'National-Legionary State', with the Guard or Legion as the only political movement.

In October, a German military mission arrived, ostensibly to reorganize the Romanian army, but as it was over 20,000 strong, it was in all but name an occupation force for vital installations. Antonescu visited Hitler and realized that the fuehrer intended to attack the USSR. He signed the Tripartite Pact, the new mutual aid treaty between Germany, Italy and Japan concluded in September. Opinion and the party leaders were ready to go to war for Bessarabia. The conducator hoped that Romania would be rewarded with the return of northern Transylvania. He accepted a ten-year economic agreement that geared Romania to the German war effort.

The new régime was meant to be a partnership between Antonescu and Sima, but neither saw the alliance as anything but temporary. The anti-Semitism that had already become official policy on the eve of Charles's abdication was reinforced. Restrictions were imposed on Jews who had not been resident before the First World War, depriving most of them of the right to own property or hold public office. The Iron Guard took over propaganda and ideology. It sought to impress by quasi-religious public ceremonies, recruited its own police from the dregs of society, and endeavoured to infiltrate the regular police and army. It humiliated, abused, raided, murdered Jews and opponents – including the historian and one-time prime minister Iorga.

When Sima moved to storm Bucharest police stations and barracks in January 1941, both he and Antonescu sought German support. With the backing of party leaders, the conducator ordered the army to restore order, which it did enthusiastically. The rebellion had not spread beyond Bucharest. The Germans had let it be known that they would stand by Antonescu. They did, however, save 700 militants (including Sima) who were taken to Germany.

The events of 1940, the loss of territory, the influx of 300,000 refugees, the anarchy inflicted by the Iron Guard, not to mention a disastrously destructive earthquake in November, had brought the economy to the verge of collapse. As he prepared for operations against Russia and Greece, Hitler definitely preferred military dictatorship to wild fascism in Romania. A fresh cabinet of generals and technicians effectively restored order. The Legion was abolished. Thousands were imprisoned or interned. All was then approved by a 99.9 per cent majority in a plebiscite on 25 March.

To no small extent, it was Germany's meddling in her ally's sphere of interest in the Balkans that triggered off Mussolini's attack on Greece. Metaxas also had tried to keep his country out of the war, accepting western guarantees, but retaining close trade ties with Germany. An Italian political campaign against Greece in 1940, accusations of oppression of her Albanian minority and of breaches of neutrality, was followed by the torpedoing, by an 'unknown submarine', of the cruiser stationed off the island of Tinos (with

4 The Iron Guard had five ministers, including interior and foreign affairs. The latter, scion of a princely family, took to appearing on formal occasions with a green shirt, worn smock-like over morning or evening dress.

its miraculous icon of the Mother of God) for the feast of the Dormition (Assumption) on 15 August. Finally came the ultimatum of 28 October, demanding that Italy be allowed to occupy strategic points in Greece. Metaxas echoed the national mood in a dignified rejection.[5]

On a wave of exaltation and national unity, the Greek army repulsed the Italian invasion back into Albania. Metaxas was careful to decline a British offer of troops in order not to provoke Hitler. As the counteroffensive was also a war for northern Epirus, he would have no truck with possible anti-Italian Albanian support. Winter halted operations and Metaxas died in January 1941. Although King George II appointed a new prime minister who was no dictator, there was no return to constitutional rule. A British expeditionary force was accepted, but serious misunderstandings diminished the slender chances of successful resistance, as Hitler decided to go to Mussolini's help. Greece had to be finished off before he turned against the Soviet Union.

Hitler could not afford to see the British get a foothold in the Balkans, and entice Yugoslavia to join Greece against Italy in Albania. Knowing that the Yugoslav government was preoccupied over its Salonika outlet, to the point of contemplating pre-emption, the Germans set out to use the Aegean port as a decoy. Cvetković was invited to sign the Tripartite as the only way for Yugoslavia to satisfy her aspirations: Serbo-Croat peace, protection from Italy, and Salonika.

Yugoslavia's position was weak. She was surrounded by Axis partners on all sides but Greece. The regency governed on the basis of emergency powers and did not command the loyalty of a substantial portion of public opinion. The united opposition had dissolved. Ustashas and communists were waiting in the wings to appear with one or the other of Germany and Russia, whose rivalry once again loomed over the Balkans. Pressure grew, until Hitler made a firm demand for adherence before 25 March 1941. Prince Paul hesitated before giving in, and on the date, as the Romanians ratified by plebiscite Antonescu's dictatorship, the Yugoslav delegates signed in Vienna. No sooner had they returned than a widespread and unopposed officers' conspiracy proclaimed King Peter II of age on 27 March, six months in advance of his eighteenth birthday.

Most Serbs (and not only Serbs) believed that the traditional Allies would win in the end. The vigour of anti-pact demonstrations was impressive. Prince Paul resigned with his fellow regents and left.[6] The party leaders (except the hitherto government Radical Union) were brought together in a representative cabinet under General Dušan Simović (1882–1962). Hitler gave them no time to think about constitutional or other problems. He ordered that Yugoslavia be destroyed at the same time as Greece. The government gave assurances that the changes had been for domestic reasons only, and turned to

5 28 October was declared a public holiday after the war, as *Okhi* (No) Day.
6 He left with his family for Greece and asked to be allowed to retire to a British territory. That was to be Kenya, until they were allowed to move to South Africa in 1943.

the Soviet Union, which showed its interest by signing with Yugoslavia a Treaty of Friendship and Non-Aggression. That was on 6 April, when after a violent propaganda campaign, setting Croats against Serbs and alleging atrocities against the German minority, the Reich attacked Yugoslavia without ultimatum or declaration of war.

In Bulgaria, the influence of the west had never been as strong as in neighbouring countries, in comparison to that of Germany and Russia. The German-Soviet Pact had helped her to accept an ever-closer relationship with Berlin. A Law for the Defence of the Realm was enacted against subversion. Freemasonry was prohibited. A known anti-Semite became home minister; some restrictions were imposed on Jews. A Directorate of Civilian Mobilization was set up to control the economy. A 'Defender' organization was formed to train the young in the service of 'king, fatherland, state and national aspirations'.

Between the partition of Poland and the end of 1940, Boris refused various offers from the Soviet Union, the moribund Balkan Entente and Italy, but not German help and Soviet acquiescence to secure southern Dobrudja. After a flood of 'tourists' and 'businessmen' from the summer of 1940, the presence of German troops and matériel coming from Romania was formalized in February 1941; Bulgaria adhered to the Tripartite in March. The Assembly ratified the treaty without enthusiasm; the USSR protested. Bulgaria would be used against Greece and Yugoslavia.

The Luftwaffe mercilessly bombed Belgrade, put Yugoslav airfields out of action and disrupted communications. Land forces invaded from Austria, Hungary, Romania and Bulgaria. Italian troops followed from Italy and Albania. Losing control, king, government and high command withdrew to Bosnia, to Montenegro, and finally, by air, to Athens. Simović had instructed his chief of staff to seek an armistice; the Germans imposed an unconditional capitulation. Over 200,000 prisoners of war, including 12,000 officers, mostly Serbs, were taken to Germany and Italy. The partition of the Yugoslav state, considered to have been annihilated along with its armed forces, began before the capitulation had even come into force on 18 April.

The Germans wanted to control communication lines and mineral deposits. They also wanted to punish the Serbs, whom Hitler saw as the disturbers of the European order. An anti-Serb Austrian streak going back to before the First World War erupted, stemming from Hitler's own prejudices and running through the high proportion of Austrians in the occupation apparatus. All claims were accepted, all separatisms encouraged, all tensions exacerbated, to destroy for ever the 'Versailles construct' that was Yugoslavia. Slovenes were to be Germanized, Italianized or dispersed. As for Croats, they were to be brought onto the side of the Axis.

Slovenia was shared between the Reich and Italy, who also annexed important strips of the coast and wished to supervise a string of vassal states on the other side of 'her' Adriatic. She obtained control of a restored Montenegro, while Albania gained most of Kosovo and a slice of Macedonia. The greater part of Vojvodina reverted to Hungary, the Germans administered the rest. Bulgaria helped herself to most of Macedonia.

Almost 40 per cent of the former Kingdom of Yugoslavia became the nominally 'Independent State of Croatia', which extended across Bosnia and Herzegovina to the gates of Belgrade. Shorn of most of its littoral, and divided between an Italian and a German occupation zone, it was placed under the rule of the ustashas and their *poglavnik* (another 'leader') Pavelić. Returning from exile, they outdid the Romanian guardists in the savage fury that they soon vented on Serbs and Jews. The 'residue' of inner Serbia was placed under German military rule.

In the chaos of the last days of Greece's resistance to the invasion and on the very day that the Yugoslav capitulation went into effect, Metaxas's successor committed suicide. King George appointed a Cretan of Venizelist convictions: Emmanouil Tsouderos (1882–1956) widened his government, and after three days withdrew with the king to Crete, and eventually to the Middle East.

Athens had fallen on 23 April. General Georgios Tsolakoglou (1888–1948) had already signed an unauthorized armistice. He became prime minister of a collaborationist government to ensure the day-to-day running of the administration. Greece was divided into occupation zones. The Germans took important points – the Athens-Piraeus area, Salonika and its hinterland, a band of territory along the Turkish border, the greater part of Crete, and three islands in the northern Aegean. The Bulgars were permitted to occupy most of Greek Thrace and part of Macedonia. The rest of the country was entrusted to Italy.

Albania had been used as a base for Italy's attacks on Greece and Yugoslavia. Under the puppet Vërlaci government, the presence of so many Italian civil servants, technicians, firms, and even settlers on the coastal plains, caused discontent, well compensated by the mirage of a greater Albania. If Greek southern Epirus was not taken over, the greater part of Yugoslav Kosovo and Albanian-inhabited parts of Macedonia were annexed (although the Germans kept the important mines under their control in Serbia). Irredentist opinion was pleased. Kosovo Albanians welcomed the opportunity to settle old scores, particularly with those Serbs given holdings there between the wars. Many were killed; more left.

Bulgaria's alignment with the Axis brought short-term benefits. The occupation and administration of Greek and Yugoslav territories was eagerly taken up, even if Hitler chose to withhold full ownership, to ensure that alignment. Intoxicated by the idea that they would at last obtain borders approximating those of San Stefano, Bulgarian administrators and soldiers went on to prepare for annexation.

The inhabitants of Yugoslav Macedonia were treated as compatriots, unless they were obviously Serbs, in which case they were pressed to leave. The Church and the education system were taken over. If many were pleased to see the end of Serbianization, and most accepted the relatively meek Bulgarian régime, they were quickly disappointed to find they had exchanged Serbianization for Bulgarianization. As the population of Greek Thrace and

Macedonia had become mostly Greek since 1912, Bulgarian rule there had to be tougher. A ruthless campaign encouraged Greeks to leave; Bulgars were settled in their place. Persecution resulted in a rising in September 1941, brutally repressed. Perhaps as many as 15,000 perished, and 100,000 more were deported.[7] Most of them were refugees of the 1920s, from Anatolia, Russia and even Bulgaria.

Romania had provided support for the German campaign in the Balkans, but Antonescu had not joined in the scramble for Yugoslavia. Germany began in earnest to take over crucial economic sectors in 1941. The régime's only defences were measures to 'Romanianize' and 'militarize' enterprises. These included more restrictions on what Jews could do, in order to propitiate Hitler and to divert from the difficulties of everyday life, but they were applied arbitrarily; Jews were needed and were discouraged from selling to Germans. No organized opposition was possible, but Maniu and Brătianu were free to express their views to Antonescu. This was a safety valve for the retention of formal independence.

THE BALKANS IN THE SHADOW OF OTHER FRONTS

All Balkan governments were part of Hitler's new order in the late spring of 1941: those who, having aligned themselves with the conquerors, were determined to make the best of it; those who had been brought to power by them; and those who had been put in place to restore administration amid the ruins of defeat. They all promoted varieties of an ideological national pastoralism that glorified simple rural life as compared with the cosmopolitanism associated with democracy and communism. They encouraged a return to native roots under German overlordship.

In the void caused by conquest, occupation and partition in Belgrade and Athens, the politicians appointed by the Germans considered it their prime duty to try and stop anything that could cause further suffering to their compatriots. The 'Greek' government of General Tsolakoglou in Athens was meant to administer a territory that was in fact divided between three rival occupation forces which called the tune. Most of it was under no effective authority, and a large part of the prewar establishment remained in confused inertness in the capital. The 'Serbian' government of General Milan Nedić (1877–1946) in Belgrade had only the residue of what was left of Yugoslavia after all the secessions and appropriations. The establishment had been blown apart, gone with the government, taken to captivity, dazed in various areas.

In the defeated lands, the Germans wanted to restore the economy to an exploitable state and to protect their communications. They were short of manpower. To the extent that they did not share or delegate occupation duties, they preferred subdued remains of establishments to fascist zealots. In the Independent State of Croatia, known by its initials *NDH*, they had no

---

7 Bulgarian sources admit 70,000; Greek sources claim 200,000.

choice. Maček had stayed behind, but he and his Croatian Peasant Party withdrew into passivity. The ustashas had spearheaded the secession.

They had not enjoyed widespread support. What independence they had was due to the rivalry between their German and Italian patrons. The NDH contained almost as many 'aliens' (Orthodox Serbs, Muslims, Gypsies, Jews) as 'pure' Croats. Having granted Muslims the status of Croats, the new régime wanted to get rid of all the others. The Serb third of the population was to be converted, expelled or killed. Unable to extend its writ over the mountainous areas of Bosnia and Herzegovina, the regime was from the beginning a mixture of ferocious racialism and farce.

The rising of the Serb peasantry of the NDH in self-defence was just one of the revolts that occurred in partitioned Yugoslavia in the summer of 1941, as the Reich turned east. Montenegro rejected the Italian attempt to set up a client state. An upsurge of rekindled hope turned against the reduced German occupation in Serbia; it was there that two groups emerged with wider designs.

Colonel Dragoljub Mihailović (1893–1946) had rejected the capitulation. He tried with débris of the army to set up a clandestine military organization loyal to the exiled government, who would promote him to general. Pushed by the popular mood and the communists' zeal, he went into premature action. Josip Broz (1892–1980), known as Tito, newly confirmed leader of the Communist Party, remembered Lenin. He and his underground cadres seized the opportunity created by the destruction of the state and the end of the German-Soviet alliance to advance the cause of revolution. They expected the rapid arrival of the Red Army.

Allied London wanted to see in the risings a sequel to the Belgrade coup of 27 March and a sustained resistance to the Axis. It lionized the government of the young King Peter II which was soon paralysed by old issues hideously magnified by events at home. The exiled cabinet failed to provide guidance for those at home who had risen in self-defence or in the belief that powerful outside help was forthcoming.

The strife that quickly developed between the two groups in Serbia enabled the Germans to restore some order with less effort than expected. Yet they retaliated ruthlessly, terrorizing the population into submission with punitive expeditions, internment in concentration camps and the execution of hostages. By the summer of 1942, they boasted that Serbia was 'free of Jews'.[8]

As repression exploded the bubble of optimism in eastern Yugoslavia, the popular mood turned against confronting the occupation forces. Mihailović

---

8 See Walter Manoschek, *'Serbien ist judenfrei'. Militärische Besatzungspolitik und Judenvernichtung in Serbien 1941/42*, Munich: R. Oldenburg, 1993. In one operation alone, carried out in and around the town of Kragujevac in October, the Germans rounded up and executed 2,778 males, including hundreds of schoolboys, for ten German soldiers killed and twenty-six wounded. The figure of 2,778 is the one now agreed on by the German and the Yugoslav sides, rather than the estimated 7,000 previously accepted by historians (including Stevan K. Pavlowitch, *Yugoslavia*, London: Ernest Benn, 1971, 120). Altogether over 90 per cent of Yugoslavia's 70,000 Jews perished (8,000 in German-occupied Serbia, and the largest number, some 27,000, in the NDH) along with those caught in transit to Palestine.

went underground. With the presence in Serbia of 300,000–400,000 refugees and their tales of ustasha horrors, he wanted to avoid useless sacrifices. He would also try and bring together those insurgents outside Serbia who could contribute to his movement in the service of the legitimate government. Tito went away. He and his communist followers saved themselves by their 'long march' to the other end of the partitioned country, to Bosnia, where the Serb peasantry was most affected of all by the traumas of defeat and massacres, and in need of leadership.

Allied interest in the Balkans lessened in 1942. Insurgents in the Yugoslav lands survived by mimicry and mobility, extending their constituencies and fighting each other. They were essentially Serbs, for they alone were treated collectively as vanquished foe. They first called themselves 'chetniks' – from the word *cheta*, used initially by marauding bands in Montenegro, Herzegovina and northern Albania, and eventually by all the armed bands (Albanian, Bulgar, Macedonian, Serb) of the central Balkans at the beginning of the century. They became 'partisans' if and when taken over or organized by communists. Eventually, most adhered to one or the other of the more ambitious movements. Mihailović, once he had been appointed war minister in the exiled government, called his the Yugoslav Home Army to make it a continuation of the regular army. Tito used the broader terms of National (or People's) Liberation Movement (NOP) and National (People's) Liberation Army (NOV) to extend the basis of the communists' appeal.

Possibilities of action were greater in the Italian zone. Hitler had largely left Italy to occupy (and pacify) the rebellious areas of the Balkans, a task made harder by the Germans' own brutal policies. The problems of Rome's implantation in Dalmatia were complicated by the thuggery of local fascists which led to communist-incited acts of terror in 1942.[9] They were also dependent on the chaos in ustasha territory, where the Italian military had to intervene to end the bloodbath and to stop the insurgency from spreading to the coast. They extended their presence to most of their zone, by coming to terms with many Serb rebels, whom they used to increase their influence.

To justify themselves in the eyes of the population, the chetniks there were anxious to acknowledge Mihailović as a nominal authority. He took the risk and lost the gamble. He knew (as did the Italians) that these local captains would never oppose the British, that they kept the communists in check and that they made his Yugoslav Home Army appear more widespread. Yet he had no effective authority over them; they were increasingly dependent on the Italians; they made it difficult for him to find an audience among Croats; the British never landed; communist propaganda turned it all against him. Out of the complexity of 1942, Tito's movement, which had been almost completely destroyed in the eastern territories, emerged in the west like a phoenix from the ashes.

9 In his recollections (*Esilio*, Milan: Arnaldo Mondadori, 1996), the Italian journalist Enzo Bettiza, born in Split of a local Italian family, gives a fascinating insight into fascist–communist Italian-Slav mutations in that urban milieu.

Greek officers and politicians had lost their bearings. Some managed to make their way to the Middle East. Others sided with the collaborationist government, because they had axes to grind, or because they wanted to spare the Greek nation further suffering. Thousands of officers on active duty were retired. Most did very little. In the urban vacuum, marginal communists with experience of clandestine activity would survive and eventually make themselves felt. The mountainous areas were under no effective authority, which created a favourable environment for such activity, but without the urgency that prevailed in the uplands of Bosnia. By the end of 1941, some armed bands had been formed under republicans or communists.

After the invasion of the USSR, communists moved to give cohesion to the resistance through a National Liberation Front (EAM) in September 1941. The old party leaderships stood aloof. A National Liberation Army (ELAS) organization followed. There were smaller non-communist formations, including the National Republican Greek League (EDES) with its power base in northwestern Greece. Nominally headed by General Plastiras, who was still in France, it was effectively led by the versatile Colonel Napoleon Zervas (1891–1957), who eventually, at British behest, expressed support for the exiled king.

As in Serbia, the Germans struck back pitilessly, burning villages, destroying monasteries, executing hostages, while continuing to help themselves to resources. Large-scale requisitions and the end of wheat imports led to famine over the winter of 1941/42. The plight of city dwellers was such that the British government lifted the blockade to allow the Swedish Red Cross to bring in food supplies. Inflation was astronomical and black market and profiteering flourished as the gold sovereign became effective currency.

Over the following spring and summer, armed groups developed in the mountains. The communists had genuine popular support and used terror against their rivals to gain a monopoly of armed activity. While in Greece the unpopularity of the dictatorship had rubbed off on the king, the British regarded his exiled government in London as the symbol of legitimacy. Divided and weakened by continued prewar controversies like its Yugoslav counterpart, unlike it, however, the government in exile never acquired the allegiance of an insurgent force at home except through the intervention of the British military mission.

Albania did not even have a government in exile. Over the winter of 1940/41, deserters had taken to the mountains. Kupi, who had found refuge in Turkey, had been brought back to Yugoslavia by the British in the hope that he could act against the Italians. He returned to Albania in 1941, where he formed a guerrilla band in support of King Zog. Later that year the Yugoslav communists promoted the setting up of a clandestine Albanian Communist Party under the French-educated teacher Enver Hoxha (1908–85). In September 1942, he set up a National Liberation Movement to organize a broad anti-Italian armed movement. Kupi was the only significant non-communist to attend its foundation.

The move spurred other opponents of Italian rule to form, later in 1942, a rival National Front (Balli Kombëtar or BK). Under the former prime minister Midhat Frashëri it gathered pro-western anti-communist figures who were opposed to Yugoslav influence and to the return of King Zog. They responded to the Allies' acknowledgement at the end of 1941 of Albania's right to the restoration of her sovereignty, but they also wanted to keep the frontiers obtained by Italian rule. The Italians had meanwhile tried to broaden support for their regime in Albania with a new and more nationalist government in December 1941. It freed a large number of internees and made statements about the need to accelerate the departure of Serbs from Kosovo.[10]

Hitler's invasion of the Soviet Union meant that Romania turned to active participation in the war to recover lost territory. Expecting a short campaign, Antonescu committed the bulk of the Romanian army. Leaving the government to his new deputy, namesake but not kinsman, the law professor Mihai Antonescu (1904–46), the conducator took command of the invading forces.

Within a month, they were in possession of the territories lost to the Soviet Union. At that point, the old party leaders wanted to stop, but Antonescu decided to go on. Hitler agreed that the area of Ukraine between the Dniester (Nistru) and the Bug, to be known as 'Transnistria', should be under Romanian military occupation and administration. Romanian forces were also given the task of taking the port of Odessa, the remaining Soviet enclave in that territory. The two-month siege took a terrible toll of Romanian lives; although public opinion was numbed, Antonescu promoted himself to marshal for the capture of Odessa. Many Romanians still felt, with Antonescu, that if they did not go on supporting Germany in Russia, they risked losing the whole of Transylvania to Hungary, but that, conversely, if they fought well, they could recover it all.

Policy towards the Jews became more ominous. Ashkenazi and Russian-speaking Jews in Moldavia, Bessarabia and Bukovina were widely regarded as Russian and a stalking horse for the Soviets. A big pogrom took place in Jassy at the time of the invasion. As Soviet planes bombed the town, the rumour spread that Jews were helping the Russians. The official version was that a fifth column of Jewish communists, backed by Soviet paratroopers, had attacked troops in the city. On 28, 29 and 30 June, thousands were killed, and thousands died as they were evacuated by train.[11] No sooner had Cernauţi (Chernovtsy) and Chişinău (Kishinev) been reoccupied than Jews there were rounded up and ghettos set up.

---

10 It was also snubbed by the landowners. Ciano notes that Vërlaci kept repeating that his successor was only the son of a manservant in Esat Pasha's household (*Diario 1937–1943*, ed. by Renzo De Felice, Milan: Rizzoli, 1980, 570).

11 Civilians, as well as German and Romanian troops participated. German troops were accompanied by *Einsatzgruppen* killing squads, and it was not difficult to excite public opinion in Jassy against Jews.

Regular administration was not restored to the redeemed territories, where repressive action was taken against all those suspected of helping, or benefiting from, the Soviet régime. As had happened with other armies elsewhere in the Balkans in earlier wars, the Romanian military had been humiliated when moving out, by those (Ukrainians, Jews) who welcomed incoming (Soviet) troops, and they were now getting their own back. Many Jews had already fled with Soviet troops. Most of those who had not were deported to Transnistria to be held in camps and used for labour services. The majority did not survive.

Marginalized and despoiled, the bulk of the Jews in the old kingdom did survive. An order in September 1940 to wear the yellow star was soon withdrawn at the urging of the Church hierarchy. In July 1941 all Jewish males between the ages of eighteen and fifty were made liable for labour services at the discretion of the military. The following summer Antonescu agreed to deport some of them to camps in Poland. At the insistence of the king and of the Orthodox bishops, and after contacts with the west, the idea was given up. Instead, the government turned to planning with Zionist organizations their emigration to Palestine.

When in December Antonescu failed to comply with an ultimatum to withdraw to the frontier of 1940, Great Britain declared war. Romania went on to declare war on the United States when Pearl Harbour brought them into the conflict. She was a reluctant and inactive partner in Germany's war against the Western Allies, but the continuation of the war against Russia was now also opposed – by Maniu, by King Michael and by some of the most senior generals.

Relations between French-trained generals and their German counterparts were strained. Resignations, court martials and desertions multiplied. Pressure for more and more manpower and raw materials was unrelenting, as the Romanian government desperately but ineffectively tried to limit German penetration. Germany needed cannon fodder, oil and wheat, but was reluctant to provide modern equipment and arms in exchange.

Her other Balkan ally, Bulgaria, greeted with dismay the attack on the USSR, but suffered less than other lands. War was duly declared on Britain and the United States after Pearl Harbour, but not on the Soviet Union. King Boris argued that his conscripts could not fight against the Russians. They would be better employed defending the Balkans against native insurgents and possible foreign intervention. Bulgarian generals lived in dread of a Soviet invasion by sea. They did not want their badly equipped army to go along the path of the Romanians without even a motivation.

It was difficult to entice Bulgaria to make a greater contribution to the war effort once she had practically achieved her territorial ambitions. There was general satisfaction with the German alliance, which had achieved the nationalists' territorial aims and provided the peasants with an increased demand for their produce. German troops in the country behaved generally well, and there was no looting of resources. Vague constitutional forms were maintained. As in Romania, an opposition was tolerated.

The personal rule of King Boris continued, with tightened controls in 1942. Soviet-infiltrated émigrés had failed in an attempted uprising in the summer of 1941. Although most communists were in prison by the beginning of 1942,[12] there were attempts from the summer to moot a loose communist-dominated clandestine Fatherland Front with agrarians, social democrats and zvenists. Fascists were also kept under observation, for fear that they could be used by the nazis, which is why King Boris would not even allow volunteers to fight on the Russian front.

Whereas Bulgarian occupation troops generally relied on the Slavophones of Greek Macedonia, their methods soon purged most Yugoslav Macedonians of their pro-Bulgarian feelings. Although Hitler had reluctantly accepted that he could not use the Bulgarian army in Russia, he would require of it more and more occupation duties in the Balkans. Bulgaria's 50,000 Jews, who had never been an issue, were subjected in 1941 to increased restrictions, until they were practically expelled from public life. Opposition to enforcement mitigated the harshness of anti-Semitic measures in the pre-1941 frontiers, but not in the new areas under occupation where German-organized deportations went unhindered.

FROM STALINGRAD TO THE CAPITULATION OF ITALY

With the Allied victories at Stalingrad and in North Africa at the end of 1942, interest in the Balkans increased and the mood in the peninsula changed. As the assault on 'Fortress Europe' was being prepared, the Axis had to be misled as to the location of a landing. Importance was attached to diversions in the Balkans, where even guerrilla leaders had to expect a landing. The British wanted coordinated support in all the Adriatic hinterland. They were no longer prepared to tolerate arrangements with the Italian military; they reinforced liaison with Mihailović, and established contact with Tito.

Faced with the impending threat of a Balkan front, the Germans feared that the latent insurgency in the NDH could turn into a danger for the whole peninsula. They decided to eliminate all insurgents from the hinterland, but they could only do it with the Italians, who were increasingly reluctant partners. Their generals did not believe in large-scale anti-guerrilla operations; they had tried to control the area by other means; they were anxious to keep contacts which could lead to the Anglo-Americans.

Hitler imposed a cycle of operations from January to May 1943. The insurgents were defeated militarily, but they escaped. All the contenders, in expectation of a British landing, tried to safeguard their interests and jockeyed for position at each other's expense. The entanglement of antagonisms and arrangements between the different sides of occupation and resistance in Yugoslavia became increasingly bloody. Tito and Mihailović fought to eliminate each

---

12 General Zaimov, a veteran of the 1934 coup, who had had connexions with the Soviet government, was executed for treason in 1942. Vulo Radev's 1966 film, *The King and the General*, is a vivid evocation of the drama.

other before the presumed landing, which the one dreaded, and the other hoped for. The double game between chetniks and Italians broke down, while German generals contemplated an arrangement with Tito.

In spite of disastrous losses, both movements survived. Only part of their forces had been engaged in battle and their leaders were still at large. Subtle political solutions by the Italians, heavy-handed military solutions by the Germans, and the offer of large rewards for the capture of the communist leader and of the king's general, had all failed. Over the summer, helped by the demoralization of the ustasha régime, Tito's mobile force of uprooted peasants and Communist Party members were back in western Bosnia. Among non-Serbs, the communists projected an image of Mihailović as the bearer of Serb vengeance, and among Serbs that of an agent of British interests. Soviet propaganda helped Tito. The British were also looking to him.

By the time of the landing in Sicily in June 1943, they were demanding of Mihailović more than he could or would give without adequate support. They turned to Tito as an additional or alternative source of support, to exploit every opportunity of involving the enemy on the other side of the Adriatic and to give the Soviet ally some satisfaction, if they could not yet give him a second front. When Italy collapsed in September, both movements were on the way to recovery, waiting for its spoils. Mihailović was in the east, with a force mainly of local Serb villagers, commanded mostly by regular army officers; Tito in the west, with a force generally provided by the Serb peasantry of Bosnia and Croatia, and officered by communists. Whereas the Yugoslav Home Army had infiltrated the Nedić administration and gendarmerie, the People's Liberation Army had penetrated the NDH structure and army.

After the initial scramble for Italian territory and equipment, the Germans recovered their balance. They moved into Slovenia, the Trieste area and the Dalmatian coast, exploiting Italo-Slav and communist–'nationalist' animosities. These events brought about the weakening of local chetnik formations dependent on the Italian army, and the strengthening of partisans through the capture of Italian military stock.

The most important reason for Tito's success in the western regions was the failure of sectional nationalism, which was associated with the powers that were now losing the war. In the backward and mixed regions which had suffered so much, the new communist order, with its slogan of 'brotherhood and equality' of communities, was especially attractive. It offered a way out to the increasing number of Croats who wanted to leave the sinking boat of the NDH.

Mihailović had failed to establish any significant appeal there, except as a vague and misappropriated symbol for one of the communities. But in the east, it was to him that the population turned when the capitulation of Italy increased optimism. Having engaged in only very limited action against the Germans since the end of 1941, he emerged again to the point where he is estimated to have led the second most effective resistance movement in occupied Europe after Tito's. Time, however, was against him. Attacked by the partisans as he went for the Germans in eastern Bosnia, he had to withdraw into Serbia.

In Albania, the Italians had tried to deal with a deteriorating situation by more changes at the top in the early months of 1943. A popular general was named as the king's lieutenant. A new government was given its own armed force, and latitude to apply a more 'Albanian' and less fascist policy. Ballists (members of Balli Kombëtar) penetrated the administration; army recruits and released internees went underground. Both ballists and communists had territorial aims that made it difficult for the Allies to help them.

The communists were based in the annexed territories, but they were weak even there. They were dependent on Tito and made common cause with him in order to achieve the final union of Kosovo with Albania, but they had to tread carefully. In March 1943, they set up a People's Liberation Army on the Yugoslav model. Their mobile bands started to carry out attacks on Italian installations with little thought for reprisals, and they were keen to eliminate rivals. This helped or hindered them, depending on the circumstances, the milieu and the consequences. Ballists were dependent on territorial support and worried about reprisals.

In Albania as elsewhere, the British wanted to create the impression that an Allied landing was actually being planned in the Balkans, and the Italians were keen to establish contacts with the underground organizations. Immediately after the fall of Mussolini, British agents arranged a meeting between Balli Kombëtar and the People's Liberation Movement. They agreed to set up a joint committee. The ballists, however, would not launch an armed struggle until the Allies were near enough to intervene directly, and the communists, having repudiated the agreement, launched a violent propaganda campaign against Balli Kombëtar.

As Italian authority collapsed, guerrillas temporarily filled the void as they did in Yugoslavia, helping themselves to arms and equipment. German troops moved in from Greece, occupying the coast and the cities, pushing the guerrillas into the mountains. They presented themselves as liberators in order to ensure some popular acceptance. A group of politicians who had opposed Italian rule accepted the offer to set up a new régime.

A provisional executive freed political prisoners and hurriedly convened an assembly, which ended the personal union under the Italian crown and abolished the fascist Statute. It set up a four-man regency council reminiscent of that of 1920, under another respected member of the Frashëri family. The new government declared the neutrality of Albania. Concerned with the defence of the coast and of lines of communications, Germany recognized Albania's independence, and interfered little with her administration, but gave ostentatious support to her acquisition of Kosovo. There was a new wave of expulsion of Serbs over the winter. The German administration of Serbia estimated in February 1944 that 40,000 Serbs had been expelled from Kosovo since 1941.

Greece also had to believe in the invasion. The British had brought a guerrilla delegation out of Greece to Cairo in August 1943 for talks with the exiled government, but there had been no meeting of minds. The guerrillas' demands, that they should exercise sole power in the areas under their control and that the king's return should be determined by a plebiscite, were not accepted. In expectation of the fall of Italy, and determined to gain control before the landing of an Allied force, ELAS moved against domestic opponents, particularly against the more provocative EDES.

Early in 1943, the Germans had rounded up Jews in areas that they occupied, and almost the whole of the Jewish community of Salonika (some 46,000 individuals, or a fifth of the population of the city) were then deported to Auschwitz. In April they allowed the last of the collaborationist prime ministers in Athens to form Security Battalions to ensure the maintenance of law and order. They enticed extremist Venizelist officers fearful of a royalist restoration or of communist predominance, and even more prominent figures such as General Pangalos, the dictator of 1925–26.

Further east, it was Stalingrad that had the greatest effect, as Romanians had been heavily involved in the battle. One of their divisions was among the captured of Paulus's Sixth Army. The rest beat a disastrous retreat, losing some 300,000 dead, wounded or captured. The Romanian contingent in Russia was reduced to six divisions and the Wehrmacht had to take over in Transnistria. King Michael called for peace. Ever more in need of Romanian soldiers, oil and foodstuffs, Hitler had to agree in January 1943 to equip nineteen reconstituted divisions, in return for immediate payment in oil and food.

As fascist Italy broke down, German armies were being steadily pushed back to the Romanian border, while Romanian troops were still engaged in the Crimea. Fear of a vindictive Soviet Union intensified efforts to seek peace with the Western Allies, who had begun bombing the oilfields. Realizing the need to ward off a Soviet occupation, and fearing a German-initiated revival of the Iron Guard, Antonescu had himself authorized contacts with the west. He kept in touch with the 'tolerated opposition'. Maniu and Brătianu played an important part in approaching the Allies, enquiring whether Romania could be permitted to surrender to Britain and the United States.

Bulgaria, too, was pressed for a greater contribution. Although King Boris refused even to sever diplomatic relations with the Soviet Union, he did agree to extend occupation duties and to participate in anti-insurgent operations in southern Serbia. He had hoped to be able to lead Bulgaria out of the war with its territory intact, but soundings had indicated that the Allies would accept nothing less than unconditional surrender, the evacuation of non-Bulgarian territories and the occupation of Bulgaria. Jews from occupied Thrace and Macedonia had been deported by the Germans to concentration camps, but those within the old borders were saved. In May 1943, they were ordered out of towns to labour gangs or camps. Society generally conspired to protect them, and they were in fact mostly dispersed in the countryside.

Boris III's death of a heart attack at the age of forty-nine in August 1943 caused a crisis at a most difficult time. As his death came a fortnight after a visit to Hitler, it was believed that he had been poisoned for refusing to comply with demands to get rid of the Jews and to send troops to Russia. Boris had been held in some respect. His son and heir Simeon II was only six. A regency council was set up under Filov, who remained as the real power.

The Communist Party had hitherto kept itself for the future. Bulgaria had been little affected by the war; there was no revolutionary situation. There had been a few acts of urban terrorism, and some bands had been formed in the mountains, with scant sympathy from villagers. Fatherland Front broadcasts from the Soviet Union called for an end to Bulgarian participation in anti-insurgent operations in Serbia, for absolute neutrality and the full restoration of civil liberties. The legal opposition, however, had kept aloof, as it resented partisan activity among pro-agrarian peasants. It hoped that King Boris would be able to change camps. Not until September 1943 did a Fatherland Front committee emerge, to split agrarians and social democrats.

THE END

As the Red Army approached, those who wanted to change everything took courage; those who did not, took fright and turned to the west. By the end of 1943, Antonescu knew that Romania had to change sides. Maniu had become a key figure in contacting the British. An emissary went to Cairo, where he was presented with armistice conditions as the Red Army reached the Prut: a complete change of sides, unrestricted movement of Soviet troops and reparations to the USSR. The restitution of territory lost to Hungary could be expected. The Western Allies bombed Bucharest to underline the message. Antonescu rejected the terms; he feared being caught between a nazi–guardist takeover and a Soviet occupation.

The young king was impatient of the caution of Maniu and Brătianu. Opposition to both the war and the dictatorship led to coordinated action between the old parties and the communists. The Red Army had crossed the old border in May. Communists had been brought back from the USSR, local militants were being discreetly released or transferred to places where they could be talked to. Fed by Soviet propaganda, hopes and opportunism, their most important success was the alliance with Tătărescu's faction of once 'right-wing', now 'left-wing', liberals. By June, with King Michael's approval, the old party leaders had formed a National Democratic Bloc with the communists and their allies – to end the dictatorship and accept the Cairo conditions, but the Russians went on negotiating directly with Antonescu and the Anglo-Americans no longer responded.

A massive Soviet offensive began on 20 August. The German-Romanian front gave way. To pre-empt any Soviet move to take over from Antonescu, the conducator was hurriedly dismissed and arrested by the king on 23 August.[13] Maniu was 71 and in bad health; he had refused to lead the government and pressed for a general. General Constantin Sănătescu (1885–1947), the head of the king's military household, had put down the Iron Guard rebellion in 1941 and enjoyed the respect of the army. He had planned the overthrow and thus became prime minister of a cabinet of generals and royal advisers. The party leaders were appointed ministers of state without portfolio. The constitution of 1923 was restored, albeit without a parliament as yet. The Germans were informed that Romania was no longer their ally. The monarch broadcast the changes to the nation.

German troops were asked to leave peacefully and the Romanians stopped fighting the Russians. The latter promptly seized some 30,000 men, and Hitler ordered the occupation of Bucharest to set up a government under Sima. There was fighting in the capital, which was also bombed by the Germans, as the new government proclaimed war with the Reich. Allied planes bombed German troop concentrations on the outskirts. By the end of the month, the Germans were retreating from the country as the Red Army arrived in the capital.

The Soviets took time over the armistice. Its terms were explicit and harsh. Romania was to pay reparations and the costs of occupation, provide support for the war against Germany, and join with twelve fully equipped divisions. A three-power but Soviet-dominated Allied Control Commission would supervise their fulfilment. The only bright spot was support for the abrogation of the Vienna Award on Transylvania. The terms were signed on 19 September, but Romania was not yet out of the war.

The joint Russo-Romanian offensive began immediately. 385,000 Romanian troops fought on alongside the Red Army in Hungary and Czechoslovakia, suffering huge casualties. The bulk of the army was thus removed from Romania, where the Soviets were propelling the Communist Party to power. The Romanian government found it almost impossible to operate outside Bucharest. Moldavia and eventually northern Transylvania were administered directly by the Red Army. Occupation authorities were engaged everywhere in the wholesale removal of war booty, inflicting revenge on an enemy.

Profiting from the Soviet presence, the communists soon promoted a new National Democratic Front and left the Bloc. They urged the formation of a government under their ally Petru Groza (1884–1958), a fellow-travelling politician who had originally come from Averescu's People Party. General Nicolae Rădescu (1874–1953), who had been interned by Antonescu, took over in November. Although Groza was deputy prime minister, the communists continued their campaign for a National Democratic Front government, welcomed all who would join their party, and accused of fascism all those who opposed their endeavours.

13 Both Antonescus were executed in June 1946, after a show trial.

The struggle for power reached its climax on 25 February 1945. There were demonstrations in Bucharest and unexplained victims. The Soviet deputy foreign minister Vishinsky arrived to oversee the appointment of a Groza cabinet. King Michael gave in to a two-hour ultimatum on 27 February. Groza placed communists in all the important ministries but retained Tătărescu as vice-premier and foreign minister.

As the first heavy air raid on Sofia in November 1943 brought the war closer to Bulgaria, her leaders in their turn thought of defecting. Most Bulgarians, however, including communists, found it difficult to contemplate the surrender of their newly acquired lands. The Romanians did at least have a sympathetic relationship with the west (not that it helped them much).

After secret approaches in the spring of 1944, the USSR gradually stepped up its demands, until the changes in Romania brought the Red Army to the Danube more rapidly than Bulgaria feared. Over the summer, there were attempts to form a broadly based government, but authority crumbled. On 2 September a new pro-western agrarian premier conceded neutrality, freed political prisoners, repealed anti-Jewish legislation, and clung to the hope that he could obtain better terms from the west. On 5 September, it was the Soviets who declared war. As Bulgaria then declared war on Germany, she was for a while in the strange situation of being at war with everyone.

When Soviet troops arrived, the Fatherland Front stepped out and took over Sofia in the night of 8 September. The coup had actually been organized by the Zveno experts Georgiev and Velchev, now allies of the communists. A new regency council under a new, communist-appointed government of the groups represented in the Front – zvenists, agrarians, social democrats and communists. Georgiev was premier and Velchev war minister, but communists held the ministries that controlled the police and judiciary. The armistice was signed on 28 October. An Allied Commission assumed 'control' as in Romania, with a Soviet viceregal chairman. The Bulgarian army was required to join Soviet forces in the war against Germany.

Bulgaria emerged from the war and the patronage of Germany with her old order again in disarray. The Soviet Union provided alternative patronage through the communists. With their core of 10,000–15,000 released detainees, they were in a stronger position than in Romania. They had played a rôle and won votes before the war; they had brought real political groups into the Fatherland Front; they were able to tap genuine pro-Russian and anti-dynastic sentiment.

The agrarians were even more popular, and, however shaken, the forces of the old régime had not been destroyed. The communists immediately started to eliminate opponents, by setting up local committees, a people's militia and people's courts to deal with 'war criminals', 'collaborators' and 'fascists'. By February 1945, the former regents, all government ministers since 1941 and all members of the Assembly had been tried, and most of them executed. The civil service was purged, but the Soviet command had to stop similar wholesale action in the army, which would have impaired its fighting efficiency.

Eventually, regular units went on with the Red Army to Yugoslavia (where they returned as liberators), Hungary and Austria, while politicized and reorganized units were kept at home.

Romania's and Bulgaria's enemy status delayed the process of full implementation of communist rule until after the signature of the peace treaties in 1947. The pre-1940 borders were restored, except that the Soviet Union and Bulgaria kept their Romanian acquisitions. Western control, however remote and futile, having been eliminated, elections were held (women were enfranchised, but many others disenfranchised) in circumstances where coercion and fraud produced an 86 per cent majority in Bulgaria in November 1945, 70 per cent in Romania a year later. People's republics were proclaimed. Other parties dissolved themselves, and their leaders were imprisoned or executed.[14]

The end was rapid in Albania, where the Wehrmacht launched violent anti-insurgent operations at the start of the winter of 1943. Albanians, particularly in Kosovo, were recruited into the SS 'Skanderbeg' Division to commit acts of violence against the Serb population and to round up Jews. By the spring, however, the operations had run out of steam. The Tirana government had no powers beyond the main towns and coastal plains, and the armed bands had survived.

Communist partisans dominated in the south. Royalists held sway in the centre. Kupi had broken away from the communists in November 1943 to set up his own Legality movement for the restoration of King Zog, and had infiltrated the military. In the north, traditional clan chiefs shared power with Balli Kombëtar. Ballists, who wanted to see the back of the Germans, had no real quarrel with the regency and soon stopped provoking the Wehrmacht.

British agents were not successful in their attempt to forge some unity of action against the Germans' line of retreat through Albania. In the confusion of the last stages of the war, the communists had clear advantages. They had a purpose, to liquidate their opponents and take power. They enjoyed the backing of the Yugoslav communists and of the Soviet Union. This marked the beginning of a cruel civil war, fought at first in the south. A larger share of Allied military assistance went to the partisans, who were strong enough to harass the Germans at the same time as they fought their opponents. Kupi, who showed real inclination to fight the Germans, was soon discouraged by the communists' intention to destroy all rivals.

When the German-sponsored régime began to fall apart in the spring of 1944, fighting intensified. The People's Liberation Movement held a congress in May in the southern town of Permet. It set up an Anti-Fascist Council of National Liberation on the Yugoslav model, with an executive committee as a counter-government under Hoxha. Having first defeated their rivals in the

---

14 A plebiscite abolished the monarchy in Bulgaria in September 1946, and sent the nine-year-old King Simeon and his mother into exile. The more popular King Michael of Romania had to abdicate without a plebiscite and leave the country in December 1947. The Bulgarian agrarian leader Nikola Petkov was tried and hanged in September 1947. Romanian national peasant leaders were tried the following month; Maniu died in prison in 1953.

south, the communists turned against their rivals in the north with the British supplies they had obtained for use against Germans. Their sense of urgency was prompted by the fear (shared with their Yugoslav patrons) of an Anglo-American landing. The British evacuated Kupi in September in order to save him, and in October Hoxha set up a government in Berat. Ballists and Legality supporters began to change sides.

The communists were the dominant force by the time the Germans withdrew in November. They took over Tirana and were in control of most of the country by the end of the year. Yugoslav partisans, operating with Albanian communists, secured Kosovo for Yugoslavia. All possible 'war criminals', 'collaborators' and 'enemies of the people' were purged, tried and liquidated. A land reform did away with the landowners (the 'beys') in August 1945, even before the general elections of December.[15]

The end in Albania had really been part of the end in Yugoslavia, from the point of view of the German command and of the Yugoslav Communist leadership too. In November 1943 at Jajce, a small town in western Bosnia, NOP had held a session of its Anti-Fascist Council, set up a National Committee as an alternative government under Tito, and made him marshal. The Western Allies, in order to get more out of him, had accepted his view that his was the only resistance movement, but all resistance was once again drastically reduced.

In the spring of 1944, the Germans made one last major attempt against Tito and Mihailović, to clear their sea and land communications, but they could not spare enough troops and both leaders escaped capture, though only just. Tito had to be evacuated by Soviet plane to Allied-occupied Bari in Italy, then taken by British warship to the British-held island of Vis,[16] from which he 'levanted' (as Churchill indignantly put it) in September, again by Soviet plane, to Russian headquarters in Romania.

Meanwhile, at his request the Allies had been bombing towns in Serbia, as well as Zara on the northern Adriatic coast, allegedly because they were German bases, but in fact because they were seen as centres of Mihailovićist legitimism and of Italian implantation respectively. While the Wehrmacht carried out its evacuation of the Balkans through Serbia that summer, partisans fought their way into Mihailović's home territory, but there was no real upsurge of resistance until the Red Army reached Yugoslavia's eastern borders.

Tito needed Soviet help to take Serbia. Soviet troops enabled the partisans to enter Belgrade on 20 October, and went on to Hungary, leaving the Yugoslavs to liberate the rest of the country by themselves and fight their civil war to an end. Disowned even by King Peter, Mihailović's movement collapsed;[17]

15 The one official list of candidates gathered 93 per cent of the vote, and a constitution on the Yugoslav-Soviet model was adopted for the People's Republic of Albania in January 1946.
16 It had already been held by the British in 1811–14, in the war against Napoleon.
17 Mihailović was not captured until March 1946. His trial – the first and the most dramatic of a long series – led to his execution in July.

the anarchic NDH was rolled up as the ustashas fought with suicidal fury; but the war against the Germans in Yugoslavia continued until 15 May 1945, a full week after the official surrender in Berlin.

The occupation had attempted to impose a brutal peace without the strength to enforce it, which was an ideal situation for the propagation of a revolutionary war. Tito had obtained the support of a significant part of the population. The old élites, divided and demoralized, had been destroyed by the nazis, by their ideological wartime allies, and in the civil war. Yet whole regions resisted the communists.

In order to strengthen its international position, the communist leadership made some transient concessions in March 1945: a regency council of its choice to take over from the exiled King Peter II, a provisional government under Tito that included a few token non-communists, and the enlargement by cooptation of the Anti-Fascist Council into a pre-parliament. It then set up people's courts against 'collaborators' and 'enemies of the people'. An electorate of all males and females above the age of eighteen (plus younger ones who had fought with the partisans, minus various disenfranchised categories) cast over 90 per cent of their votes for the single list of the People's Front. The Constituent Assembly thus elected abolished the monarchy by acclamation and proclaimed the Federal People's Republic of Yugoslavia on 29 November 1945.[18]

In Greece as in other occupied lands, communists sought to ensure they would be the only organized armed force when the Germans left. ELAS attacked EDES with Italian arms. The collaborationist government was able to entice into its service those officers whose fears of communism outweighed their dislike of Germans, while ELAS garnered those with a grudge against the king and the right. Belated efforts to reinforce EDES came to nothing as General Alexandros Papagos (1883–1955)[19] and other high-ranking officers were arrested by the Germans. A difficult truce was patched up, with EDES confined to its power base in Epirus. The Committee of National Liberation which administered the ELAS-controlled uplands was a challenge to the government in exile. It sparked off a mutiny in the Greek force in the Middle East, which brought down the Tsouderos government.

Georgios Papandreou (1888–1968), staunch anti-communist with a Venizelist background, recently escaped from Greece, set about forming a government of national unity under British sponsorship at a conference in Lebanon in May 1944, attended by representatives of resistance and political forces. The

18 A Soviet-style constitution was adopted in January 1946. The revolutionary period purged the country of its ethnic as well as political and class enemies. Of the local Germans who had not gone with the Wehrmacht, 85,000 died (directly, or in the course of deportation to the USSR, or in concentration camps) and more were expelled. They had numbered over half a million before the war; by 1948, they were down to 36,000. The peace treaty with Italy in 1947 granted Yugoslavia 7,760 sq. km of additional territory in the northern Adriatic that the partisans had already occupied. The exodus of the Italians was the result of a revolutionary purge that was at once political, social and ethnic.
19 Commander-in-chief in 1940–41 and again in 1949, prime minister in 1952–55.

communists subscribed to a participation that was immediately repudiated by their leadership at home. It demanded a greater share, but then backed down in August after the arrival of a Soviet mission.

When the Germans withdrew, Papandreou's government returned to Athens on 18 October with a 4,000-strong British contingent, and found as many armed ELAS men in the capital. In the climate of famine and disease, fear and suspicion, talks on the demobilization of armed guerrillas and the formation of a national army broke down at the beginning of December. EAM ministers resigned and called for mass demonstrations. Fighting broke out.

Churchill flew in. All political leaders convinced him, and he persuaded George II, of the need for a regency pending a plebiscite on the monarchy. This was entrusted to the popular primate, Archbishop Damaskinos (1889–1949). Papandreou was replaced by General Plastiras, regarded as being more acceptable to the left and flown back from France by the British. British troops gained the upper hand and a cease-fire was arranged. In February 1945, ELAS undertook to disarm in return for an amnesty, and a plebiscite to be followed by a general election. Although EAM controlled most of the country, it could expect no support from the Soviet Union. Peace and reconstruction called for Allied patronage; a new army soon found its officers.

High social tensions imperilled British efforts to stabilize the political situation under a centre-right administration. Ultra-rightists, incensed by left-wing terror during the occupation, turned to counterterror. The elections of 1946, held before the plebiscite (thus reversing the agreed order), produced a populist-dominated government and the restoration of the monarchy. The 1947 peace treaty with Italy at last brought the Dodecanese islands. The subsequent slide to outright civil war in 1947, like the consolidation of communist rule in the rest of the peninsula, opens up another period.

When Hitler attacked the Soviet Union, the whole Balkan peninsula had been conquered, partitioned, subordinated and 'revisioned'. In spite of rhetoric, there was not much of a system, merely ad hoc types of control with conflicting jurisdictions. The Reich nevertheless managed to draw upon significant resources from the Balkans to service its war machine, at considerable cost to the countries concerned.

Despite all the problems of the interwar period, the extreme left had been unable to make sustained headway. It was only when Axis invaders had destroyed states in 1941 that communists were able to turn a miserable peasantry into an instrument of revolution. Where states survived under the Axis, revolutionary manifestations were all but absent.

As in the First World War, the area remained a sideshow to the decisive campaigns waged elsewhere. The Axis powers shared control of the Balkans with increasing mutual mistrust. Italians blamed Germans for policies which stimulated resistance; Germans blamed Italians for failure to obtain results; yet Germany left Italy to occupy most of the conquered lands. Naïve expectations of a Soviet arrival in 1941, real expectations of the Soviet arrival in 1944, induced expectations of an Anglo-American landing in the meanwhile, aroused resistance and rivalries within it. From the German-Soviet Pact in 1939 to the Yalta Conference in 1945, Stalin sought security by empire, but kept all options open pending the outcome of the war, usually trying to accomplish his aims with rather than against his allies – and with a good dose of Marxist belief that history was on his side.

The Western Allies likewise concentrated almost exclusively on the military struggle. The strategy agreed at the Teheran Conference at the end of 1943, was that the Western Allies should invade the Reich from the west to meet the Red Army invading from the east. Some advance from the south was nevertheless necessary for the preservation of Britain's position in the eastern Mediterranean. The informal 'percentages' in the Balkans between British and Russians in 1944 (from 90–10 in favour of the Soviet Union in Romania, to 90–10 in favour of Great Britain in Greece) were simply an attempt by the weaker of the two Western Allies to pin the Soviets down to some limits in a situation where nothing else could stop them.

Stalin's craving for security always recognized that there were limits beyond which he could not go. For a long time, he allowed the west overtly to help the Yugoslav communists more than he could do, he discouraged Greek communists from civil war against the British-backed government, and stopped the Yugoslavs from seizing parts of Italy and Austria for which he would have been held accountable.

In states conquered by the Axis, as soon as the defeat of the Axis was anticipated, local communists attempted to destroy all forces which could oppose the transformation of the struggle for liberation into one for the establishment of their revolutionary rule. In those states which had sided with the Axis, communist revolutionary rule came more gradually and by stealth, by taking over vital parts of government with direct Soviet support. Yugoslavia, Romania, Bulgaria, Greece and Albania re-emerged at the end of the Second World War in recognizable territorial form, in spite of some adjustments. With the exception of the Greek tip of the peninsula, communist domination came to all of them, and subsequent Greek developments were reactions to that domination.

The scale of the losses was huge, far greater than in the First World War. Millions were killed, wounded or displaced. Jewish minorities everywhere were reduced, if not entirely eliminated, and most of their survivors then chose to leave. Of the local Germans, some of whom had already been moved to colonize new areas under nazi rule, many then fled, were deported to the USSR or were driven out. Many had enlisted in the Waffen SS. The communists confiscated their lands before anybody else's. There was widespread destruction of property and equipment, devastation of land, and disorganization of what had been organized. By the end of the war, economic life had, at best, been drastically diminished, at worst reduced to survival. Yugoslavia had suffered most.

CHAPTER 16

Conclusion

The Balkans defined by geography and history. Why 1804 to 1945? And why a history of the Balkans? Romanticism, disdain, division, mystery. Explanations, apologies and acknowledgements

'Le mystère est nécessaire pour qu'il y ait du réel.'

(René Magritte)

JUST A TOPONYM

With no obvious border between the peninsula and the mainland, there is bound to be disagreement on where the Balkans end.[1] The trouble is that extending or shrinking the Balkans is usually a political rather than a geographical exercise. At present the name is not popular. Some parts of the peninsula are said to be Mediterranean (if not actually north Atlantic), or Latin (hence virtually western European), or central European (and woe to anyone who dares hint at the Balkans there), or Alpine (if not actually Austrian). Even that part which is home to the Balkan range and which once tended to monopolize the name is now part of the Francophone community. That leaves only the dregs who are stuck 'in the Balkans' because they are no longer 'in Europe'.

The geographical appellation has become an imprecise and pejorative designation. The wars recently fought in Croatia and Bosnia were 'Balkan wars' although the rest of the peninsula was at peace. Albanian, Serbian and Yugoslav presidents faced risings or fought elections that were 'a Balkan farce' or had 'a spectacular Balkan dimension'. Vesna Goldsworthy, in her study of the images of the Balkans in British literature, suggests that the area is one where Europe's unconscious often plays out its hidden anxieties.[2] The toponym easily becomes an insult, meaning non-Europe or the dark side of Europe. 'Balkan'

---

1 The origins as well as the ups and down of the term have been dealt with by Maria Todorova, *Imagining the Balkans*, New York and Oxford: Oxford University Press, 1997, chapter 1.
2 Vesna Goldsworthy, *Inventing Ruritania: the Imperialism of the Imagination*, New York and London: Yale University Press, 1998, ix, 13.

is used by self-absorbed journalists and tough-guy diplomats to mean 'divisive', 'explosive', 'backward', 'untruthful'.[3] The Balkans may be a dark Europe, or even an untruthful Europe, but Europe they definitely are (a Europe that itself has variable definitions), especially now that Mark Mazower has dubbed it all 'the dark continent'.[4]

In the humble opinion of one who, as they used to say, has been 'a student of the Balkans' for over forty years and who has taught the history of the Balkans for three decades, the area extends from the eastern Alps to the Aegean and the Black Sea, from the Dniester to the Adriatic – over the lands inhabited by Romanian, South Slav, Albanian and Greek speakers. I believe so undogmatically, with apologies to all those who want to be outside the peninsula.

I accept that choices can be made, that communities, like individuals, are not necessarily trapped by the dictates of their history. Nevertheless, what I deal with in this book is a framework in which I see geography and history combining to link regions one to another – from the Aegean northwards to the lands inhabited by Slovenes and to historic Moldavia, and similarly from Macedonia outwards to the continental and maritime fringes. And I use 'Balkan' as a neutral toponym.

The area is not homogeneous; it fades into something else at the edges; but then even the Italian and Iberian peninsulas do so. Its structure has discouraged integration from within. Integration through conquest, culture and even cooperation has come from the outside. The area has never had one great urban centre. In spite of local capitals, all upstart and regional whatever their antiquity and attraction, the Balkans have had three great eccentric capitals: Constantinople, Vienna and Paris.

Constantinople on the very edge of the Balkans was the seat of the Ottoman Porte; it was the caliphate of Islam; it was the primatial see of Orthodoxy; it was the legacy of Byzantium; it was at the crossroads of Europe and Asia. Vienna was the seat of the imperial Habsburg court; it was the conveyor of Catholicism and Enlightenment; it was the first centre of modern education and the first model of good government; it was where north–south and west–east roads met. Paris was the font of popular sovereignty, of the nation-state, of constitutional government; it was the very mirror of European culture; it was an ideal and a dream. The three capitals radiated across the whole peninsula. The three beacons succeeded one another to a certain extent, but they also overlapped to a large extent.

---

3 *The Times* people on the spot are frequent users, but then so is Richard Holbrooke in *To End a War*, New York: Random House, 1998. The use of the adjective is not unlike that of 'Byzantine', except that the latter has the advantage of no longer bearing any relation to the governance and culture of the Eastern Roman Empire. A quantity of incomprehensible or meaningless sounds adds to the Balkan resonance, as in this gem from *The Times* of 16 March 1998: 'There can be few towns as resonantly Balkan as Prizren, where seven competing communities lie stubbornly blind to their similarities among a jumble of churches, mosques and bazaars'. They are: 1. Albanians, 2. Serbs, 3. Turks, 4. Jews, 5. Bektashis (including 6. several dervishes), 7. Gorani.
4 Mark Mazower, *The Dark Continent: Europe's Twentieth Century*, London: Penguin Press, 1998.

The period 1804–1945 may not be as neat as 1800–2000, but it provides a meaningful framework. The year 1804 is a symbol – the date of a rising that marked the beginning of the struggle of nationalities against empires. It was a rising of Serb peasants, but it was Greek intellectuals who introduced the European concept of nationalism to the Balkans. The First Serbian Rising notwithstanding, it was the Greek War of Independence which brought the Balkans to the attention of Europe. The Greek national movement was seen to be heir to a civilization that was universally revered. Educated Europeans thought that they understood what it was about, whereas few knew or cared about Serbs and other Balkan peoples.

The Balkans were the area where the Ottoman conquest and the Habsburg reconquest overlapped to a large extent. The term 'Balkanization' was coined to refer to the break-up of these two dynastic empires; it has since come to mean the fragmentation of larger political complexes into smaller and mutually antagonistic entities. Yet the Balkans were also unique in that people who belonged to distinct ethnic communities related at the same time to a wider common background: mentality, religion, cultural affinities, everyday life, shared experiences. They were becoming European by shredding imperial legacies and by assuming the form of nation-states. Societies that were marginalized historically tried to catch up. They were latecomers, they moved at different speeds and they faced innumerable problems.

The nations of the Balkans were not 'natural', in the sense that no nation was created by God on the sixth day. They were 'man-made' – invented, constructed, imagined at different times and in different circumstances. They evolved, they were imposed, they were rejected, they were discarded, they were lost, they were revived. As they were difficult to define, they did all they could to become more readily definable. They resorted to accelerated cultural assimilation; they also resettled, expelled and eliminated. They needed roots; they relied on myths; they sought territorial justifications in the past; historical rights clashed with self-determination. In all that, they were not so different from other national groups.

The newly shaped nation-states sought the best model of the modern community of citizens to implant in their concrete historical context. That was Belgium. Only a generation later did Italy become a model. Belgium was the first nation to be recognized against the legitimacy principle of the international order set up in 1815. She had won independence from the Netherlands in 1830, and by 1839 the powers had guaranteed her independence, her territory and her neutrality.

A major component of the idea of 'nation' was the popular representation that derived from the French Revolution through the French constitutional laws of 1791, 1814 and 1830. The importance of the Belgian constitution of 1831 was that it originated in these French constitutions. It was unitarist in its formulation, but it also reflected much of the thinking surrounding the British parliamentary reforms enacted the following years. That was a compromise between monarchical legitimism and popular sovereignty. Even its motto, '*l'union fait la force*', was adopted by one of the Balkan states.

Popular representation was initially an acclamation of status, a badge of belonging to the nation and to its history, rather than a participation in actual government. Citizenship was moral and social before it was political. Politics identified nation and state. Modernization and development called for education and a standardized language. State and culture had to coincide. If some sections of the peasantry and if some of the intelligentsia in the Balkans were reluctant to join the modern world in such a way, this again was not fundamentally different from the reluctance experienced in many other countries.

As territorial expansion came to be considered by political leaders as essential to the economic and political survival of the new nation-states, the state grew at the expense of society and of its various autonomous groups. The bourgeoisie everywhere was linked to the state. The nation-state became the pretext for wars. Whenever there was a fixation on cultural–religious identity, it was the consequence more than the cause of unresolved problems. Balkan conscripts were reluctant fighters against each other. States were encouraged and manipulated by the powers in the hope of gaining influence. Their size, shape, stage of growth and even existence were in the final analysis regulated by power consideration. Even the 1923 Treaty of Lausanne – the greatest operation of 'ethnic cleansing' – was controlled by the powers and considered by them as a success.

When the dynastic empires collapsed at the end of the First World War, the self-determination of nationalities came into its own as the ultimate universal principle, more for the winners than for the losers. There were gaps between models and realities, and it was not easy to adapt to the twentieth century, with new territories and new populations. In economic terms, the Balkan states had to contend with enormous agricultural overemployment. The richer parts of Europe had for centuries promoted their agricultural productivity, laying the groundwork for industrial capitalism through mercantile agrarianism, but it was only in the late nineteenth century that the Balkan countries had sufficient social infrastructures to make a start on that path.[5]

What seemed to be a way out in the late 1930s through clearing trade with Germany was, in fact, inclusion in the Reich's *Großraum*. Stalin's Russia and Hitler's Germany filled the power vacuum. Party leaders looked to Mussolinian practices to save parliamentary government. Parliamentary government collapsed as authoritarian royal régimes attempted to keep their states afloat, until Stalin and Hitler introduced a new international order through their pact of 1939.

That new order relied on violence and the pursuit of power for its own sake; it was reduced to the interests which the two partners considered they had the right to impose. The Balkans along with the rest of eastern Europe

5 John C.H. Fei and Gustav Ranis, 'Economic development in historical perspective', in *American Economic Review*, 59, 1969, 386–400.

Conclusion

were again the subject of bilateral deals between two powerful rivals. Their new partnership went against all that the international community (or the 'Concert') had sought to regulate by legitimizing principles and multilateral compromises, from Vienna in 1815, through Paris in 1856 and Berlin in 1878, to Paris in 1919. It soon led to war between Hitler's Reich and Stalin's USSR. The struggle between nazi Germany and communist Russia then brought the whole edifice (or what was left of it) crashing down in the Balkans – international regulation, monarchical legitimacy, popular representation, citizenship, the nation-state, self-determination.

With some similarities to what had happened five centuries earlier, the peninsula was again under the shadow – if not under the control – of an imperial power with a different ideology. It would largely cut off the region from mainstream developments in western Europe, and generally alter the course of the previous evolution of the Balkans. As before, western influence survived, in the Mediterranean fringe, and through tensions in international relations. The new empire and its ideology would in turn be influenced by these tensions and the strains of extension; it would last for four or five decades rather than four or five centuries.

The year 1945 brings this history to an end, however, with the defeat of the Third Reich and the establishment of communist régimes. The problems posed by communism, the Soviet empire, the Cold War and post-communism are different. A different chronological framework is called for, with a different historiography, different sources, a different approach.

THE HISTORY OF THE BALKANS

While acknowledging that history is inseparable from the present, I have chosen to keep that sixty-year distance from our own time, preferring to fill in the part of our common European history in the nineteenth and the first half of the twentieth century that usually appears only when the region explodes.

Western approaches to the Balkans are not often scholarly. Ever since Byron, literary and semi-literary visitors have written with a mixture of disdain and self-righteous support for a sectional cause. Sometimes their heroes are 'westernized' while their villains remain 'Balkan'. At other times (or with other ideologies) the villains are the corrupt 'Europeanized', and the unspoilt *bons sauvages* are the heroes. In one way or another, for good or for ill, the journey is usually 'through savage Europe'.[6]

The bashi-bozuks (irregulars), the hajduks (freebooters) and the comitadjis (who work for committees) of the pseudo-scholarly world (and even at times the straight academic scholars) are prone to emotional links – with a country, a group, a cause, a woman (or man). At one end, romanticizing thrives, acceptable for Romanian queens, less so for potentates from Ali Pasha of Janina to

6 Cf Harry De Windt, *Through Savage Europe: Being the Narrative of a Journey Undertaken as Special Correspondent of the 'Westminster Gazette' throughout the Balkan States and European Russia*, London: T. Fisher Unwin, 1907.

Marshal Tito of Yugoslavia.[7] At the other end, we are subjected to regular intermezzi of the 'bashing' of this or that group that behaves in a way that we cannot understand.[8]

Then there is the fascination with victims. The massacre of populations is more interesting than their daily lives. Ever since the day when John MacGahan, the American who worked for the London *Daily News*, went to Bulgaria to enquire into the story of massacres (so vehemently denied by Disraeli) committed by Turkish troops during the uprising of 1876, journalists have lived to describe Balkan atrocities. Some of the reporting verges on necrophilia. (One of my undergraduates believed, before embarking on his course of Balkan history, that the 'Bulgarian massacres' had been committed by Bulgars – and he was not thinking of the Muslims killed by the insurgents.)

Not all the victims are equal in massacre; those perceived as bad receive no coverage. It all contributes to the view that the peninsula's inhabitants are chronically violent, as if there have been no mass killings elsewhere, even in modern Europe, when systems collapse (or, for that matter, when systems are built).

To compound it all, newspapers are always disposed to ask some historian willing to earn a quick dollar, pound, mark, franc or ECU with a column of instant history, to show that it is all an endless repetition according to a pre-ordained pattern. And so we reach the 'doomed-to-violence' explanation of the master of the genre, Robert Kaplan, whose *Balkan Ghosts*[9] is said to have impressed President and Mrs Clinton.

It all sounds 'so very Balkan', for in the peninsula itself, predetermination, heroic legends, national martyrology, fantastic statistics and the uncritical trumpeting of the Truth are the daily stuff of popular, media and pseudo-scholarly history. They come in a different context – one of fear of the outside world divided into 'friends' and 'foes'. There are, and have been, in all the Balkan countries, in spite of dictatorships and misfortunes, sound history schools and impeccable scholars who approach documents, oral history, artefacts and figures with a critical and open mind. Yet in the best of cases, historiography has (as it has elsewhere) developed in the first instance to provide a parochial account, with scant interest in what had happened across the border. Most Balkan historians know little of the history of neighbouring areas, states, nationalities. Native historians, followed by western specialist scholars, have tended to study individual national histories. With important exceptions, what Balkan history we have is 'divided history'.

---

7 A two-page advertisement appeared recently in the press for Eurostar First Class featuring the train pulling out of the Gare du Nord. A text by Chris Patten (who was said to have 'enjoyed complimentary champagne, a three course meal and a few chapters from a paperback he'd picked up at Waterloo') started with 'My favourite true adventure story, Fitzroy Maclean's "Eastern Approaches", begins with his train pulling out of the Gare du Nord . . .' One almost feels that Eurostar will take us to Zenda. Perhaps they will sell this book at Waterloo International along with the late Sir Fitzroy Maclean's romantic narratives of Tito's rise to power.
8 Cf Richard Clogg, 'Greek-bashing', in *London Review of Books*, 18 August 1994.
9 Robert D. Kaplan, *Balkan Ghosts: A Journey through History*, New York: St Martin's Press, 1993.

Since many of the problems – political, ideological, economic, social, cultural – are common to the region as a whole, even the best of the so-called national histories is distorted by the division. We need to understand better the realities of the Balkans, to look at the history of the peninsula as a region defined by the interaction of its geography and of its history, even when we want to escape from the negative images we have constructed or accepted of it.

Europe (the whole) misunderstands the Balkans (the part) as much as the Balkans misunderstand Europe, while Europe accepts and the Balkans claim that the peninsula is part of the continent. Our approach to the history of the region is strewn with misapprehensions. The Balkan peninsula extends across a zone of fault lines that is also one of passageways and crossroads. Its nations are not nations in the sense given to that word since the French Revolution. They were never really communities of citizens. Yet they are not a pretence. Not only are they deeply (too deeply) felt, but they are not even much more invented than most other European nations. Ethnic communities have developed there without turning into political communities. Each new so-called nation as it emerged wanted to coincide with a territory, and to blend its populations into a whole so as to constitute a nation-state.

In so doing, the élites looked to the past, to the present and to the future. They looked to Europe as a model to try to follow in order to be able to become part of it once again – a continent seen as a civilization. They also looked to the future in order to try to overcome their difficulties, to manage the differences (the Yugoslav idea, various forms of Balkan cooperation), or to face foreign threats (Balkan leagues and ententes, but also the grass-roots feelings of solidarity shown by all the Balkan volunteers who joined in the Greek War of Independence and in the Serb risings of the Eastern Crisis).

The more I taught and the more I studied the Balkans from empires to communism, the more I felt the need for a new general history of the peninsula to build on the work of its predecessors (Leften Stavrianos, 1958 and Barbara Jelavich, 1983). This was because of the constant stream of new scholarship, but also because of the situation in the area, not so much a return to the Middle Ages, or the Barbarians at the gates, but the return with a vengeance of that all too modern challenge since 1804 (and now indeed very much a post-modern one) – how to manage the differences. It is a challenge for the Balkans, and it is a challenge for Europe as a whole. We are still trying to resolve it with nineteenth-century ideas. (The irony of this book is that I had to stop teaching in order to have the time to write. Now that I have my textbook, I no longer have students, which is just as well, as they might have thought it politic to read nothing else.)

The most objective historians have come to accept that the attainment of objectivity is an illusion. To strive for it is, however, more than ever a duty. Historians must want to exploit (but not manipulate) all possible evidence and to leave no stones unturned (but not rearrange them), however frightened they may be of what they could find under them. In spite of the ever-greater abundance of sources, the historian of the nineteenth and twentieth centuries remains an archaeologist, faced with insufficient, discontinuous and erased traces of past reality. He reconstructs painfully a pattern that is not always rational and that is often opaque, that helps to decypher the present but only as part of an indirect and long-term process.

Does the historian then do no more than deepen the mystery? Is the history of the Balkans a mystery? Or is it that reality is just not simple? That all-too-often irrational pattern will perforce continue to remain incomprehensible because so many people prefer it to be so, rather than venture into the mystery to see the reality. I return to Magritte, who said that he could not help it if people 'preferred to try and go through the walls rather than enter by the door'.

EXPLANATIONS, APOLOGIES, ACKNOWLEDGEMENTS

I have not gone to the archives. I have merely read and reread all that I could find in the few languages that I can use. I hope I have not made too many errors of judgement or fact. I also hope to be able to contribute – as I trust I have done with my teaching – to an understanding of the common problems, of the differences and of the similarities, avoiding generalizations that verge on untruths, and not afraid of questions without answers, even when (in the words of my editor) I 'squeeze so much in that the reader gets squeezed out'. Yet there is still so much that has been left out! In the end, the blend and the balance can only be mine, for good or bad.

That goes for personal and place-names too. Place-names are generally given in their Anglicized forms where they exist, or as they were widely known at the time, even when such forms are no longer universally favoured. Otherwise, I tend to adopt the names used by the states that ruled the places, then or now, with alternatives given when several official versions were used at the time, or when the rulers changed. The possibilities are endless. I cannot satisfy everyone. Personal names are only slightly less tricky. I have stuck to the old convention of Anglicizing names of monarchs (when it could be done; heads of churches have been given similar treatment), otherwise generally using the modern spelling or transliteration used by the descendants of the persons named (not as simple as it appears). I have done my best with convention and feeling for transliterations from non-Latin scripts.

I am indebted to too many people to list them. Furthermore, I am afraid of those readers who categorize the names on such lists according to political and ethnic hues, and come to conclusions from their statistics. There are, however, names I cannot avoid: those of scholars and friends from whom I have learnt, not facts and figures, but new developments, new facets, new lights, new insights, new comparisons, new interpretations based on new evidence: the extraordinary Traian Stoianovich, *patron* of all Balkanists, followed by (in alphabetical order) Richard Clogg, Richard Crampton, Dimitrije Djordjević, Alexandru Duțu, Procopis Papastratis, Maurice Pearton, the late Branko Petranović, and, last but not least, Desimir Tošić (who, although not an academic historian, knows more history than many a historian).

I have also learnt from all the doctoral candidates whom I have had the pleasure of supervising, or more simply of advising informally, in particular: Nicholas Fennell, Konstantin Pavlowitch (filiation notwithstanding), Jeffrey Schneider, Gavin Scrase and Heather Williams, who have enabled me to understand better Russo–Greek rivalry on Mount Athos, the unification of Yugoslavia, the Jewish problem in Romania, the 'percentages' of 1944, and the mysteries of the Special Operations Executive respectively. To all of them, I add my editor, Andrew MacLennan, who immediately understood what I wanted to achieve, who was the first to see the gaps between aims and realizations, and who never tired of pointing them out. He was a hard and encouraging 'supervisor'.

Apart from the usual hoped-for readership of students, diplomats, journalists, soldiers, amateurs, rail travellers, cranks, critics and generally interested individuals, not afraid of being squeezed out, I would like it if this book were to help those of my close non-Balkan friends who have been interested, fascinated, put off and bored by the Balkans (*y compris F., si vous le voulez*), and those of my close Balkan friends who generally trust me even when they do not agree with me.

All of this has been left for the Conclusion so as not to impose it right from the start in the Introduction.

St. K.P.
Nicosia, December 1998

Guide to further reading

The following is not a bibliography of all that the author has read before sitting down to write this book, of all the works that he has pillaged for facts, figures, ideas, and of all those that he has discarded. It lists titles in English only, of works selected for further reading, in alphabetical order. They are divided into sections, covering geographical areas corresponding roughly to the states that emerged at the end of the First World War. The list is deliberately kept short. There are far more scholarly monographs in English devoted to Greece than to Albania – with Yugoslavia, Romania and Bulgaria in between; the selection is thus most selective in the case of Greece. Apart from the works of East and Riker on the unification of the Danubian Principalities, no books published before the Second World War have been included.

GENERAL HISTORIES AND OTHER GENERAL WORKS ON THE BALKANS

Berend, István and Ranki, György, *Economic Development in East-Central Europe in the Nineteenth and Twentieth Centuries*, New York: Columbia University Press, 1974.

Clogg, Richard (ed.), *Balkan Society in the Age of Greek Independence*, London and Basingstoke: Macmillan, 1981.

Crampton, R.J., *Eastern Europe in the Twentieth Century*, London and New York: Routledge, 1994.

Djordjević, Dimitrije and Fischer-Galati, Stephen, *The Balkan Revolutionary Tradition*, New York: Columbia University Press, 1981.

Dutton, David, *Politics of Diplomacy: Britain, France and the Balkans in the First World War*, London: Tauris Academic Studies, 1997.

Jelavich, Barbara, *History of the Balkans*, I: *Eighteenth and Nineteenth Centuries*, II: *Twentieth Century*, Cambridge: Cambridge University Press, 1983.

Jelavich, Barbara, *Russia's Balkan Entanglements 1806–1914*, Cambridge: Cambridge University Press, 1991.

Lampe, John R. and Jackson, Marvin R., *Balkan Economic History 1558–1950*, Bloomington, Ind.: Indiana University Press, 1982.

Macfie, A.L., *The End of the Ottoman Empire*, London and New York: Longman, 1998.

Palairet, Michael, *Balkan Economies 1800–1914: Evolution without Development*, Cambridge: Cambridge University Press, 1997.

Stavrianos, L.S., *The Balkans since 1453*, New York: Holt, Rinehart & Winston, 1958.

Stoianovich, Traian, *Balkan Worlds: The First and Last Europe*, Armonk, N.Y. and London: M.E. Sharpe, 1994.

Sugar, Peter F. and Treadgold, Donald W. (ed.), *A History of East Central Europe*, Seattle, Wash. and London: University of Washington Press (VIII: Jelavich, Charles and Barbara, *The Establishment of the Balkan National States 1804–1920*, 1977; IX: Rothschild, Joseph, *East Central Europe between the Two World Wars*, 1974).

Todorova, Maria, *Imagining the Balkans*, New York: Oxford University Press, 1997.

Valiani, Leo, *The End of Austria-Hungary*, New York: Alfred A. Knopf, 1973.

ALBANIA

Fischer, Bernd Jürgen, *King Zog and the Struggle for Stability in Albania*, New York: Columbia University Press, 1984.

Logoreci, Anton, *The Albanians: Europe's Forgotten Survivors*, London: Victor Gollancz, 1977.

Skendi, Stavro, *The Albanian National Awakening 1878–1912*, Princeton, N.J.: Princeton University Press, 1967.

BULGARIA

Bell, John D., *Peasants into Power: Alexander Stamboliski and the Bulgarian Agrarian National Union 1899–1923*, Princeton, N.J.: Princeton University Press, 1977.

Bell, John D., *The Communist Party of Bulgaria from Blagoev to Zhivkov*, Stanford, Calif.: Stanford University Press, 1986.

Black, C.E., *The Establishment of Constitutional Government in Bulgaria*, Princeton, N.J.: Princeton University Press, 1943.

Chary, Frederick B., *The Bulgarian Jews and the Final Solution 1940–1944*, Pittsburgh, Pa: University of Pittsburgh Press, 1972.

Crampton, R.J., *Bulgaria 1878–1918: A History*, New York: Columbia University Press, 1983.

Crampton, R.J., *A Short History of Modern Bulgaria*, Cambridge: Cambridge University Press, 1987.

Jelavich, Charles, *Russian Policy in Bulgaria and Serbia 1881–1897*, Berkeley: University of California Press, 1950.

Jelavich, Charles, *Tsarist Russia and Balkan Nationalism: Russian Influence in the Internal Affairs of Bulgaria and Serbia 1876–1886*, Berkeley, Calif.: University of California Press, 1958.

Lampe, John R., *The Bulgarian Economy in the Twentieth Century*, London: Croom Helm, 1986.

Meininger, Thomas A., *Ignatiev and the Establishment of the Bulgarian Exarchate 1864–1872: A Study in Personal Diplomacy*, Madison, Wis.: State Historical Society of Wisconsin, 1970.

Miller, Marshall Lee, *Bulgaria during the Second World War*, Stanford, Calif.: Stanford University Press, 1975.

Oren, Nissan, *Bulgarian Communism: The Road to Power 1943–1944*, New York: Columbia University Press, 1971.

Oren, Nissan, *Revolution Administered: Agrarianism and Communism in Bulgaria*, Baltimore, Md: Johns Hopkins University Press, 1973.

Rothschild, Joseph, *The Communist Party of Bulgaria: Origins and Development 1883–1936*, New York: Columbia University Press, 1959.

GREECE

Augustinos, Gerasimos, *Consciousness and History: Nationalist Critics of Greek Society 1897–1914*, New York: Columbia University Press, 1977.

Clogg, Richard, *A Concise History of Greece*, Cambridge: Cambridge University Press, 1992.

Close, David H. (ed.), *The Greek Civil War 1943–1950: Studies of Polarization*, London and New York: Routledge, 1993.

Dakin, Douglas, *The Greek Struggle in Macedonia 1897–1913*, Salonika: Institute for Balkan Studies, 1966.

Dakin, Douglas, *The Unification of Greece 1770–1923*, London: Ernest Benn, 1972.

Dakin, Douglas, *The Greek Struggle for Independence 1821–1833*, London: Batsford, 1973.

Dontas, Domna N., *Greece and the Great Powers 1863–1875*, Salonika: Institute for Balkan Studies, 1966.

Frazee, Charles A., *The Orthodox Church and Independent Greece 1821–1852*, Cambridge: Cambridge University Press, 1969.

Hondros, John, *Occupation and Resistance: The Greek Agony 1941–1944*, New York: Pella, 1983.

Kaltchas, Nicholas S., *Introduction to the Constitutional History of Modern Greece*, New York: Columbia University Press, 1940.

Kofos, Evangelos, *Greece and the Great Powers 1875–1878*, Salonika: Institute for Balkan Studies, 1975.

Koliopoulos, John S., *Brigands with a Cause: Brigandage and Irredentism in Modern Greece 1821–1912*, Oxford: Clarendon Press, 1987.

Koliopoulos, John S., *Greece and the British Connection 1935–1941*, Oxford: Clarendon Press, 1991.

Leon, George B., *Greece and the Great Powers 1914–1917*, Salonika: Institute for Balkan Studies, 1974.

Leon, George B., *The Greek Socialist Movement and the First World War: The Road to Unity*, New York: Columbia University Press, 1976.

Levandis, John A., *The Greek Foreign Debt and the Great Powers 1821–1912*, New York: Columbia University Press, 1944.

McGrew, William W., *Land and Revolution in Modern Greece 1800–1881: The Transition in the Tenure and Exploitation of Land from Ottoman Rule to Independence*, Kent, Ohio: Kent State University Press, 1985.

Mavrogordatos, George, *Stillborn Republic: Social Conditions and Party Strategies in Greece 1922–1936*, Berkeley, Calif.: University of California Press, 1983.

Mazower, Mark, *Greece and the Inter-War Economic Crisis*, Oxford: Clarendon Press, 1991.

Papacosma, S. Victor, *The Military in Greek Politics: The 1909 Coup d'Etat*, Kent, Ohio: Kent State University, 1977.

Papastratis, Procopis, *British Policy towards Greece during the Second World War 1941–1944*, Cambridge: Cambridge University Press, 1984.

Pentzopoulos, Dimitri, *The Balkan Exchange of Minorities and its Impact upon Greece*, The Hague: Mouton, 1962.

Petropulos, John Anthony, *Politics and Statecraft in the Kingdom of Greece 1833–1843*, Princeton, N.J.: Princeton University Press, 1968.

Petsalis-Diomidis, N., *Greece at the Paris Peace Conference 1919*, Salonika: Institute for Balkan Studies, 1978.

Psomiades, Harry J., *The Eastern Question, the Last Phase: A Study in Greek–Turkish Diplomacy*, Salonika: Institute for Balkan Studies, 1968.

StClair, William, *That Greece Might Still be Free: The Philhellenes in the War of Independence*, London: Oxford University Press, 1972.

Tatsios, Theodore George, *The Megali Idea and the Greek–Turkish War of 1897: The Impact of the Cretan Problem on Greek Irredentism 1866–1897*, New York: Columbia University Press, 1984.

Veremis, Thanos, *The Military in Greek Politics*, London: C. Hurst, 1997.

Woodhouse, C.M., *The Greek War of Independence: Its Historical Setting*, London: Hutchinson, 1952.

Woodhouse, C.M., *Capodistrias: The Founder of Greek Independence 1821–1829*, London: Oxford University Press, 1973.

Woodhouse, C.M., *Modern Greece: A Short History*, 4th edn., London: Faber & Faber, 1986.

ROMANIA

Bobango, Gerald, *The Emergence of the Romanian National State*, New York: Columbia University Press, 1979.

Bodea, Cornelia, *The Romanians' Struggle for Unification 1834–1849*, Bucharest: Academy of the Socialist Republic of Romania, 1971.

Chirot, Daniel, *Social Change in a Peripheral Society: The Creation of a Balkan Colony*, New York: Academic Press, 1976.

East, William G., *The Union of Moldavia and Wallachia 1859*, Cambridge: Cambridge University Press, 1929.

Eidelberg, Philip Gabriel, *The Great Rumanian Peasant Revolt of 1907: Origins of a Modern Jacquerie*, Leiden: E.J. Brill, 1974.

Evans, Ifor L., *The Agrarian Revolution in Roumania*, Cambridge, Mass.: Harvard University Press, 1962.

Florescu, Radu R.N., *The Struggle against Russia in the Roumanian Principalities 1821–1854*, Munich: Societas Academica Dacoromana, 1962.

Frucht, Richard C., *Dunârea Noastrâ: Romania, the Great Powers, and the Danube Question 1914–1921*, New York: Columbia University Press, 1982.

Georgescu, Vlad, *Political Ideas and Enlightenment in the Romanian Principalities 1750–1831*, New York: Columbia University Press, 1971.

Georgescu, Vlad, *The Romanians: A History*, London and New York: I.B. Tauris, 1991.

Hitchins, Keith, *The Rumanian National Movement in Transylvania 1780–1849*, Cambridge, Mass.: Harvard University Press, 1969.

Hitchins, Keith, *Orthodoxy and Nationality: Andrei Şaguna and the Rumanians of Transylvania 1846–1873*, Cambridge, Mass.: Harvard University Press, 1977.

Hitchins, Keith, *Rumania 1866–1947*, Oxford: Clarendon Press, 1994.

Hitchins, Keith, *The Romanians 1774–1866*, Oxford: Clarendon Press, 1996.

Jelavich, Barbara, *Russia and the Formation of the Romanian National State 1821–1878*, Cambridge: Cambridge University Press, 1983.

Jowitt, Kenneth (ed.), *Social Change in Romania 1860–1940*, Berkeley, Calif.: Institute of International Studies, 1978.

Lungu, Dov D., *Romania and the Great Powers 1933–1940*, Durham, N.C. and London: Duke University Press, 1989.

Michelson, Paul E., *Conflict and Crisis: Romanian Political Development 1861–1871*, New York and London: Garland Publishing, 1987.

Mitrany, David, *The Land and the Peasant in Rumania: The War and Agrarian Reform 1917–1921*, reprint, Oxford: Oxford University Press, 1981.

Nagy-Talavera, Nicholas M., *The Green Shirts and the Others*, Stanford, Calif.: Hoover Institution Press, 1970.

Oldson, William O., *The Historical and Nationalist Thought of Nicolae Iorga*, New York: Columbia University Press, 1973.

Pearton, Maurice, *Oil and the Roumanian State 1895–1948*, Oxford: Clarendon Press, 1971.

Riker, T.W., *The Making of Roumania: A Study of an International Problem 1856–1866*, Oxford: Oxford University Press, 1931.

Roberts, Henry L., *Rumania: Political Problems of an Agrarian State*, New Haven, Conn.: Yale University Press, 1951.

Spector, Sherman D., *Rumania at the Paris Peace Conference: A Study of the Diplomacy of Ion I.C. Brătianu*, New York: Bookman Associates, 1962.

Turnock, David, *The Romanian Economy in the Twentieth Century*, London: Croom Helm, 1986.

THE YUGOSLAV LANDS

Avakumović, Ivan, *History of the Communist Party of Yugoslavia*, I (to 1941), Aberdeen: Aberdeen University Press, 1964.
Dedijer, Vladimir et al., *History of Yugoslavia*, New York: McGraw-Hill, 1974.
Despalatović, Elinor Murray, *Ljudevit Gaj and the Illyrian Movement*, New York: Columbia University Press, 1975.
Djilas, Aleksa, *The Contested Country: Yugoslav Unity and Communist Revolution 1919–1953*, Cambridge, Mass.: Harvard University Press, 1991.
Djilas, Milovan, *Njegoš: Poet, Prince, Bishop*, New York: Harcourt Brace & World, 1966.
Djordjević, Dimitrije (ed.), *The Creation of Yugoslavia 1914–1918*, Santa Barbara, Calif.: Clio Books, 1980.
Hoptner J.B., *Yugoslavia in Crisis 1934–1941*, New York: Columbia University Press, 1962.
Jelavich, Charles, *Russian Policy in Bulgaria and Serbia 1881–1897*, Berkeley: University of California Press, 1950.
Jelavich, Charles, *Tsarist Russia and Balkan Nationalism: Russian Influence in the Internal Affairs of Bulgaria and Serbia 1876–1886*, Berkeley, Calif.: University of California Press, 1958.
Lampe, John R., *Yugoslavia as History: Twice there was a Country*, Cambridge: Cambridge University Press, 1996.
Lederer, Ivo J., *Yugoslavia at the Paris Peace Conference: A Study in Frontier-Making*, New Haven, Conn.: Yale University Press, 1963.
McClellan, Woodford D., *Svetozar Marković and the Origins of Balkan Socialism*, Princeton, N.J.: Princeton University Press, 1964.
MacKenzie, David, *The Serbs and Russian Panslavism 1875–1878*, Ithaca, N.Y.: Cornell University Press, 1967.
Miller, Nicholas J., *Between Nation and State: Serbian Politics in Croatia before the First World War*, Pittsburgh, Pa: University of Pittsburgh Press, 1997.
Pavlowitch, Stevan K., *Yugoslavia*, London: Ernest Benn, 1971.
Pavlowitch, Stevan K., *The Improbable Survivor: Yugoslavia and its Problems 1918–1988*, London: C. Hurst, 1988.
Pavlowitch, Stevan K., *Yugoslavia's Great Dictator, Tito: A Reassessment*, London: C. Hurst, 1992.
Petrovich, Michael B., *A History of Modern Serbia 1804–1918*, 2 vols, New York: Harcourt Brace Jovanovich, 1976.
Roberts, Walter R., *Tito, Mihailović and the Allies 1941–1945*, 2nd edn., Durham, N.C.: 1987.
Rogel, Carole, *The Slovenes and Yugoslavism 1890–1914*, New York: Columbia University Press, 1977.

Rothenburg, Gunther E., *The Military Border in Croatia 1740–1881*, Chicago, Ill.: University of Chicago Press, 1966.

Stokes, Gale, *Legitimacy through Liberalism: Vladimir Jovanović and the Transformation of Serbian Politics*, Seattle, Wash.: University of Washington Press, 1975.

Sugar, Peter F., *Industrialization of Bosnia-Hercegovina 1878–1918*, Seattle, Wash.: University of Washington Press, 1963.

Tomasevich, Jozo, *Peasants, Politics, and Economic Change in Yugoslavia*, Stanford, Calif.: Stanford University Press, 1955.

Vucinich, Wayne S., *Serbia between East and West: The Events of 1903–1908*, Stanford, Calif.: Stanford University Press, 1954.

Glossary

armatoloi local Christian armed irregulars in Ottoman service, in Greece but also elsewhere

Ausgleich the Austro-Hungarian 'compromise' of 1867 that set up Austria-Hungary

autocephaly (adj. autocephalous) status of a local Orthodox church enjoying administrative independence under 'own head'

Balli Kombëtar Albanian 'National Front (Union)', Second World War

ban crown-appointed head of local executive in Croatia under Hungarian rule, and also in royal Yugoslavia from 1939

boiers landed nobles in the Romanian Principalities

chetniks members of chetas (insurgent armed 'bands') in Macedonia at the beginning of the 20th century, and again in occupied Yugoslavia, Second World War

chiftlik private landed estate in the Ottoman Empire

CPP Croat Peasant Party

CUP Comittee for Union and Progress

devshirme levy of Christian boys for conversion and Ottoman service

EAM Greek 'National Liberation Front', Second World War

EDES 'National Republican Greek League', Second World War

ELAS   Greek 'National People's Liberation Army', Second World War

Etairia (Philiki Etairia)   the revolutionary 'Society of Friends' founded in 1814

hajduks   rebel brigands – the Romanian and Slav version of klephts

IMRO   Internal Macedonian Revolutionary Organization

janissaries   Ottoman 'new corps' infantrymen

jihad   a war waged on behalf of Islam

klephts   rebel brigands – the Greek version of hajduks

Megali Idea   the Greek 'Great Idea'

millet   under the Ottoman system of government, a population group ('nation') constituted on the basis of religious confession

Nagodba   the 'compromise' of 1868 that set up Croatia as an 'adjacent territory' of Hungary with a measure of autonomy

NDH   the Ustasha-ruled 'Independent State of Croatia', Second World War

NOP   Yugoslav 'People's Liberation Movement', Second World War

NOV   Yugoslav 'People's Liberation Army', Second World War

pandours   local militiamen in Wallachia, but also elsewhere in Ottoman times

Phanariots   members of the influential Greek or Hellenized families living originally in the Phanar ('Lighthouse') district of Constantinople

poglavnik   the 'leader' of the Ustasha Movement and of the Independent State of Croatia – Ante Pavelić

Porte   the government of the Ottoman Empire

Sabor   the representative assembly of Croatia

sanjak   an Ottoman district, subdivision of a vilayet

sipahis   originally Ottoman officials who provided a number of cavalrymen in proportion to the size of their holdings ('timars')

Sporazum   the Cvetković–Maček 'agreement' of 1939 that set up the Province of Croatia

Tanzimat   the reformist 'reorganization' era of Ottoman history

timar   Ottoman holding awarded to support military service

Uniates (or Greek Catholics)   Eastern Christians in union with Rome

Ustashas   adherents of the Ustaša ('Insurrectionary') Croatian Liberation Movement

vilayet   a province of the Ottoman Empire

voyvod   a military leader, a local ruler, a duke

Young Turks   the adherents of the Committee for Union and Progress

Zveno ('Link')   Bulgarian pressure group set up in 1927

Maps

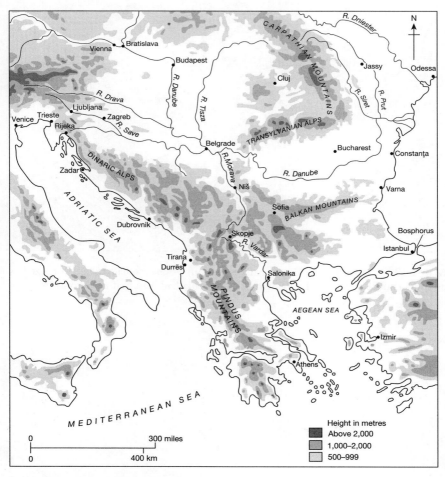

Map 1   Physical map of the Balkans

Map 2   The Balkans in 1833, once the Kingdom of Greece had been recognized as an independent state and the Principality of Serbia had acquired its autonomy

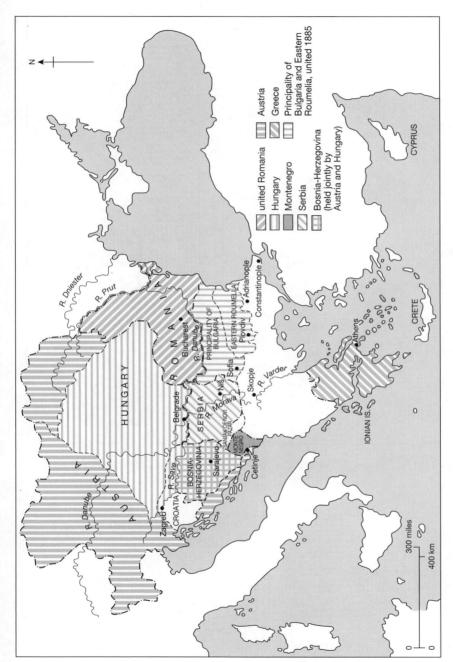

Map 3   The Balkans in 1885, once Eastern Roumelia had united with the Principality of Bulgaria

Map 4   The Balkans in 1913, at the end of the Balkan Wars

Map 5   The Balkans in 1923, after the Treaty of Lausanne

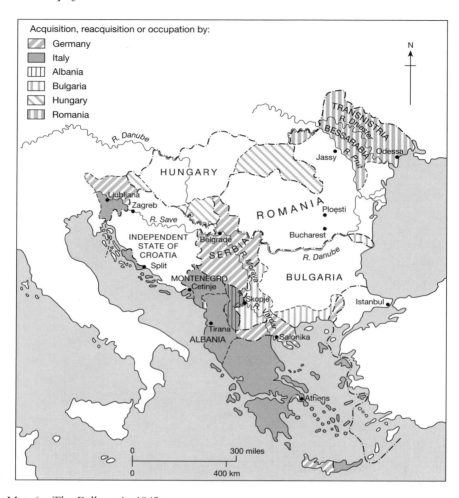

Map 6   The Balkans in 1942

Index